THE SOUL AND SPIRIT OF SCRIPTURE
WITHIN ORIGEN'S EXEGESIS

THE BIBLE IN ANCIENT CHRISTIANITY

VOLUME 3

General Editor
D. JEFFREY BINGHAM

THE SOUL AND SPIRIT OF SCRIPTURE WITHIN ORIGEN'S EXEGESIS

BY

ELIZABETH ANN DIVELY LAURO

Brill Academic Publishers, Inc.
Boston · Leiden
2005

Library of Congress Cataloging-in-Publication Data

Dively Lauro, Elizabeth.
  The soul and spirit of scripture within Origen's exegesis/by Elizabeth Dively
Lauro.
    p. cm.—(Bible in ancient Christianity)
  Includes bibliographical references and index.
  ISBN 0–391–04199–1 (hardcover)
  1. Origen. 2. Bible—Criticism, interpretation, etc.—History—Early church,
ca. 30–600. 3. Christian life—History—Early church, ca. 30–600. I. Title.
II. Series.

BR65.O68D58   2004
220.6'092—dc22   2004005140

BR
65
.O68
D58
2005

ISSN   1542–1295
ISBN   0–391–04199–1

PRINTED IN THE UNITED STATES OF AMERICA

In dedication to
Lino
my partner in the Ascent

CONTENTS

ACKNOWLEDGMENTS

This work began as my doctoral dissertation at the University of Notre Dame. I am indebted first to the wise direction and loyal friendship of John C. Cavadini. I also wish to express my sincere gratitude for the encouragement, feedback, support and friendship of Brian E. Daley, Mary Rose D'Angelo, Robert L. Wilken and Randall C. Zachman. In addition, I am very fortunate to have received generous feedback and perspective as well from a truly great mentor and friend, Rowan A. Greer. I also wish to thank Karen Jo Torjesen for her encouragement and support. Finally, I must also mention my first academic mentor, Carlos Eire, who introduced me to the study of Origen at the University of Virginia in the early 1980s.

On a personal note, I must acknowledge the heroic support and editorial advice of my husband, Lino, to whom I dedicate this work. I also could not have completed this work without the support of my parents, Mona, Robert, Lawrence and Marie, and my brother and sister-in-law, Bob and Kathy. I have a golden list of incredibly supportive friends, and I trust that they know who they are: I thank all of you for your encouragement, faith and prayers.

Finally, I am truly grateful for the support of D. Jeffrey Bingham and the editorial board members for the series The Bible in Ancient Christianity at Brill Academic Publishers. I extend my gratitude to the anonymous readers as well as all the staff at Brill who have helped to bring this work to fruition.

The final stage of revisions on this work coincided with the arrival of Sofia, who is a joy to all and inspires the continual search for wisdom through interaction with great minds such as Origen.

A Note on Translation

Where published English translations of primary sources were not available, I have employed my own translations from the standard critical editions to which I refer. In most cases, however, I have been able to make use of published English translations, in which, at places, I have taken the liberty, in light of the original language

(Greek or Latin), to make minor alterations. These changes include Americanized and/or modernized spellings as well as words that more literally capture the original language. Where my divergence from the modern translator's wording is of significance to my analysis, I offer my explanation in footnote.

ABBREVIATIONS

Primary Works

Comm. Cant.	*Commentary on the Song of Songs*
Comm. Matt.	*Commentary on the Gospel of Matthew*
Comm. Jo.	*Commentary on the Gospel of John*
Comm. Rom.	*Commentary on Paul's Epistle to the Romans*
Dial.	*Dialogue with Heraclides*
Princ.	*De Principiis (Peri archon)*
Hom. Gen.	*Homily on Genesis*
Hom. Ex.	*Homily on Exodus*
Hom. Lev.	*Homily on Leviticus*
Hom. Num.	*Homily on Numbers*
Hom. Josh.	*Homily on Joshua*
Hom. Judic.	*Homily on Judges*
Hom. 1 Sam.	*Homily on 1 Samuel*
Hom. Ps.	*Homily on Psalms*
Hom.Cant.	*Homily on Song of Songs*
Hom. Isaa.	*Homily on Isaiah*
Hom. Jer.	*Homily on Jeremiah*
Hom. Ezech.	*Homily on Ezekiel*
Hom. Luc.	*Homily on the Gospel of Luke*
Hist. Eccl.	Eusebius' *Ecclesiastical History*

Editions, Translations, Series, and Journals

ACW	Ancient Christian Writers Series
ANF	*Ante-Nicene Fathers Series*
ATR	*Anglican Theological Review*
DB	*Dictionnaire de la Bible.* Edited by F. Vigouroux. 5 vols. 1895–1912
FC	The Fathers of the Church Series
GCS	Die griechischen christlichen Schriftsteller
JTS	*Journal of Theological Studies*
LCC	Library of the Christian Classics

LEC	Library of Early Christianity Series
LXX	Septuagint
NA^{27}	Nestle-Aland, *Novum Testamentum Graece*. 27th ed. Stuttgart: Deutsche Bibelgesellschaft, 1898 and 1993.
NS	New Series
PG	Patrologia Graeca, Migne, 1857–1886
PL	Patrologia Latina, Migne, 1844–1864
RSR	Recherches de Science Religieuse
RSV	Revised Standard Version of Bible
SC	Sources Chrétiennes
StPatr	Studia Patristica
SPCK	Society for Promoting Christian Knowledge, London

INTRODUCTION

Contemporary theologians proclaim the enduring significance of Origen's exegesis and theology. Jean Daniélou claims that "Origen and St. Augustine were the two greatest geniuses of the early Church," both foundational to every aspect of Christian thought.[1] Hans Urs von Balthasar places Origen within the whole "history of Christian thought . . . beside Augustine and Thomas."[2] Especially as a Christian exegete, his contribution is superseded by none.[3]

Theologians view Origen's spiritual exegesis as foundational to the development of Christian faith and practice. Henri Crouzel hails him "the great theorist" of spiritual exegesis,[4] which Daniélou defines as a Christian reading of Scripture that leads to a mystical understanding of the soul's ascent to God.[5] Both Daniélou and von Balthasar list the many individuals within Eastern and Western churches who have been influenced by Origen's spiritual exegesis.[6] Also, Rowan A. Greer notes Origen's enduring influence on early monastic movements, stating that "the themes Origen uses in giving definition to the Christian life persist to this day in the classical expositions of Christian spirituality."[7]

---

[1] Jean Daniélou, *Origen* (trans. Walter Mitchell; London and New York: Sheed and Ward, 1955), vii.

[2] Hans Urs von Balthasar, *Origen: Spirit and Fire: A Thematic Anthology of His Writings* (trans. Robert J. Daly; Washington, D.C.: Catholic University of America, 1984), 1; idem, preface to *Origen*, by Rowan A. Greer (The Classics of Western Spirituality; New York: Paulist, 1979), xi.

[3] Daniélou, *Origen*, vii; Henri Crouzel, *Origen* (trans. A. S. Worrall; San Francisco: Harper & Row, 1989), 61; Bertrand de Margerie, *The Greek Fathers* (vol. 1 of *An Introduction to the History of Exegesis*; trans. Leonard Maluf; Petersham, Mass.: Saint Bede's, 1993), 112–113; and Manlio Simonetti, *Biblical Interpretation in the Early Church: An Historical Introduction to Patristic Exegesis* (trans. John A. Hughes; Edinburgh: T&T Clark, 1994), 39.

[4] Crouzel, *Origen*, 61.

[5] Daniélou, *Origen*, vii.

[6] Daniélou lists, among others, the Cappadocians, Eusebius of Caesarea, Jerome, John Cassian and Evagrius Ponticus as well as Hilary of Poitiers and Ambrose of Milan (*Origen*, vii–viii). Additionally, von Balthasar points to the Venerable Bede and others (*Origen: Spirit and Fire*, 1).

[7] Greer, *Origen*, 34.

Other contemporary theologians confirm these commendations of Origen's significance through their in-depth studies of his exegesis and theology.[8] They have contributed to a renaissance of Origen studies that makes both his writings and thought more accessible. Their enthusiasm for his widespread contribution urges continued study of Origen's use of Scripture and its influence on Christian spiritual life and thought.

I. *Statement of the Thesis*

This work continues such studies by exploring *how* Origen interprets biblical passages in order to effect spiritual transformation in his audience. It will reveal that, contrary to the understanding of many contemporary scholars, Origen defines three senses of meaning and offers readings based on these definitions for individual scriptural passages. In order to comprehend fully his definitions of these senses, this book explores, first, his earliest statement of exegetical theory in *Princ.* 4 and, then, his theoretical discussions within later homilies, which continue and expand upon that earlier account. Based on this theoretical evidence, we will see that Origen understands Scripture to contain somatic (or bodily), psychic (or soul's) and pneumatic (or spiritual) meanings. The somatic sense is the literal, straightforward reading of the text that renders either historical information about God's interaction with humankind or morally relevant instruction through precepts or examples that direct growth in specific virtues. The psychic sense is a nonliteral, figurative reading of the text that more generally calls the hearer to shun vice and grow in virtue so that he will become like God. The pneumatic sense is a separate nonliteral sense that enlightens the reader concerning God's plan of salvation through Christ and, more specifically, his Incarnation, the church's emerging role from it, and his culminating power at the Eschaton. Through the instruction and interaction of these three

---

[8] There are quite a few important contemporary Origen scholars, but chapter 1 will concentrate on the views of these following theologians who have focused particularly on the notion of three scriptural senses in Origen's theory and practice: R. P. C. Hanson, Henri de Lubac, Jean Daniélou, Henri Crouzel, Karen Jo Torjesen and Rowan A. Greer.

senses, we will see, Origen understands Scripture to prepare the attentive hearer for salvation.[9]

Considering, next, Origen's exegetical practice, this work will examine texts in which he offers readings of the psychic and pneumatic senses for a biblical passage. Contrary to the contention of many scholars, the use of two distinct, higher senses in his exegesis is identifiable based upon the definitions established in theory. By recognizing them as separate senses, we see how they relate for the hearer's benefit. Here, we will see that the high point of his efforts to facilitate spiritual growth in his audience occurs when he offers the psychic and pneumatic senses together, because the message of each reinforces the beneficial effects of the other's message.[10] We will

---

[9] This work will refer to the first sense as "literal" and the second two senses as "nonliteral." Here, the term "literal" signifies the straightforward reading of the text and "nonliteral" a figurative or metaphorical reading of that same text. Bernard de Margerie, relying on Ferdinand Prat, recognizes that when Origen speaks of the "literal sense" of a biblical passage, he does not mean what students of today's historical-critical method of scriptural interpretation mean (*An Introduction to the History of Exegesis*, 99, citing Ferdinand Prat, *Origène, le théologien et l'exégète* [Paris: Bloud, 1907], xix). Students of the historical-critical method employ "literal" to refer to the human author's intended meaning for the text, rather than as an antonym to "figurative." For such students, what the human author intended is the "proper sense" of the text. If the human author intended a figurative meaning, then that figurative meaning is the proper or literal sense of the text. De Margerie and Prat recognize that, in contrast, Origen did not identify the literal sense with the human author's intended meaning, since he sought only the Holy Spirit's intended meaning in the text. Still, the term "literal" remains problematic, since, more generally, different persons and societies can relate different concepts to the same words. What is a figurative reading of the word for one person may be the literal or "proper" reading of the word for another person. Frances M. Young warns that the term "literal" is confusing since what is important is the author's intended reference, even if the presumed author is divine (*Biblical Exegesis and the Formation of Christian Culture* [Peabody, Mass.: Hendrickson, 2002, 119–213, 285–299]. For example, if the Holy Spirit meant "Bride" to refer to the church in *The Song of Songs*, then "church," according to Young's reasoning, is the proper, literal meaning of "Bride" in the text. However, this work will demonstrate that Origen does not use the term "literal" according to this reasoning. This work's analysis of his *Commentary on the Song of Songs* (in chapter 5) will show that Origen sees it to be a figurative and, thus, nonliteral reading when the Bride refers to anything other than a woman awaiting matrimony. Origen determines what he understands the words of the text to represent straightforwardly rather than figuratively, and he assumes his audience will agree. This work will employ the term "literal" as Origen does—as an antonym for figurative or metaphorical.

[10] According to Origen, not every biblical passage contains a somatic—or literally edifying—meaning, but all passages render psychic and pneumatic meanings for those who, through sufficient study of Scripture, can grasp them. Chapters 2 and 3 will substantiate this understanding of Origen's view.

find that the psychic sense offers a way to pursue temporally the
eternal hope of salvation conveyed by the pneumatic sense as well
as begin now to benefit from its deep truths.[11]

This work's examinations, taken together, will reveal that Origen
understands perfection in virtue and wisdom to constitute the full
imitation of Christ that is necessary for salvation. He understands
Scripture to convey through the three senses God's own virtue and
wisdom. For Origen, Jesus Christ is both the teacher and ultimate
content of Scripture, since Christ is God's own virtue and wisdom.
The human person can achieve perfect imitation of Christ, or God's
virtue and wisdom, if the three human parts within him—body, soul
and spirit—reside in perfect harmony. These parts are rightly ordered
if the soul, the seat of choice, willingly follows the spirit, or divine
imprint, in a life of virtue and thus causes the body to likewise submit to the spirit's guidance. Origen understands that the three senses
of Scripture not only teach this right order of the three human parts
through direct instruction about virtue and wisdom, but their messages interrelate in a way that models this right order: the somatic
and psychic senses gradually lead the hearer to a more complete
understanding of Scripture's pneumatic truths. For Origen, then, his
exegetical method of three senses is drawn from Scripture's own
structure in order to fulfill Scripture's purpose of preparing hearers
for salvation.

To reach these conclusions, this work will proceed according to
the following steps. Chapter 1 will explain how these insights fit with
and build upon the contributions of recent studies of Origen's exegesis. This brief exploration will make it possible to discuss the
significance of this work's findings in greater detail. Chapter 2 will
examine the early exegetical theory in *Princ.* 4 and suggest the most
effective way to recognize Origen's definitions for the three senses
of Scripture within that early work. This analysis will also shed light
on why Origen insists that Scripture has three senses that resemble
his understanding of human nature's three parts. Chapter 3 will consider additional statements of Origen's exegetical theory in his later
homilies. These texts will confirm and fill out the definitions set forth
in *Princ.* 4. Chapter 4 will examine a selection of Origen's homilies

---

[11] We also will see that in relation to the pneumatic sense, the psychic sense is
an intrinsically *Christian* call to virtue, for at its core it is a call to imitate Christ
through intimate engagement with Scripture.

in which he offers full psychic and pneumatic readings for the same biblical passage with explicit language that labels each reading and signals transition from one to the other. These texts will show how such readings, though separately identifiable and edifying, relate so as to effect spiritual growth in the hearer in an ever-increasing way. Chapter 5 will analyze the first book of Origen's *Commentary on the Song of Songs*, in which he offers layered presentations of psychic and pneumatic readings that crescendo into a most powerful unified edification of the hearer. This complex example of the relationship between the two higher senses will underscore the major findings of this work, especially the distinction and relation between the psychic sense's temporal function and the pneumatic sense's eternal focus and function in leading the hearer to salvation.

II. *Primary Texts Under Review*

In order to span the breadth of Origen's theory and practice, this work will take account of *Princ.* 4 as well as his extant and intact homilies and biblical commentaries. For the sake of manageability and relevance, this work will not draw examples of psychic and pneumatic readings within his practice from works that are not primarily or directly exegetical in purpose: namely, the first three books of *De Principiis, Contra Celsum, An Exhortation to Martyrdom, On Prayer, De Pascha, Dialogue with Heraclides*, and the letters to Africanus and Gregory.[12] This work will limit its focus to intact practical works, that is, those that are not substantially fragmentary, because only full texts provide sufficient context for examining Origen's conception and application of the senses and, especially, his understanding of their interrelation. Therefore, this work also will exclude the *Scholia* due to its fragmentary nature. The body of intact, extant exegetical works on which this work will rely and from which it will draw examples for analysis are the following 204 homilies and four commentaries:

---

[12] At places within these excluded works one is likely to find psychic and pneumatic readings of specific biblical texts, such as Origen's commentary-like analysis of the meanings of the Passover in his *De Pascha*. Still, the current work will focus on the most characteristically exegetical texts of the homilies and commentaries. Based on this work's findings, it will be advantageous for the student of Origen to continue research concerning his interplay of the two higher senses by analyzing these additional extant works.

Homilies

   On the Old Testament:
	1. 16 on Genesis	—in Latin (Rufinus)
	2. 13 on Exodus	—in Latin (Rufinus)
	3. 16 on Leviticus	—in Latin (Rufinus)
	4. 28 on Numbers	—in Latin (Rufinus)
	5. 26 on Joshua	—in Latin (Rufinus)
	6. 9 on Judges	—in Latin (Rufinus)
	7. 2 on 1 Samuel	—in Latin (Rufinus), with a Greek excerpt from Eustathius (on 1 Sam. 28:3–25)
	8. 9 on Psalms	—in Latin (Rufinus)
	9. 2 on Cant	—in Latin (Jerome)
	10. 9 on Isaiah	—in Latin (Jerome)
	11. 22 on Jeremiah	—20 in Greek, and 14 (with some overlap) in Latin (Jerome)
	12. 14 on Ezekiel	—in Latin (Jerome)

   On the New Testament:
	39 on Luke	—in Latin (Jerome)

Commentaries

   On the Old Testament:
	on Cant	—in Latin (Rufinus)

   On the New Testament:
	1. on Matthew, 10–17	—in Greek
	2. on John	—in Greek
	3. on Romans	—in Greek (and Rufinus' Latin)

Together, these texts represent the entirety of Origen's extant, directly exegetical exercises, incorporating both genres of homily and commentary as well as covering the variety of genres (legal, historical, sapiential, prophetic, evangelical and epistolary) within the Old and New Testaments.

Chapters 4 and 5, which will examine Origen's psychic and pneumatic readings of biblical passages, will treat only texts in which he offers full readings of each sense and employs explicit and distinct labels to identify each reading. The fullest and most obvious examples have come from homilies concerning historical and legal texts within the Pentateuch as well as the commentary on the sapiential text Song of Songs (or Cant.). They, collectively, will demonstrate that Origen employs a consistent method of interpretation both over time and between homilies and commentaries. They also will equip the student of Origen with the tools necessary to recognize the separate higher senses and their interrelation elsewhere in his works. Of course, these are not the only texts in which Origen offers psychic and pneumatic readings for a biblical passage, and, at appropriate places within chapter 4, this work will alert the reader (in footnote, especially n. 1) to such other texts (though the psychic and pneumatic readings in them are not always fully presented or accompanied by explicit labels). These references will include prophetic texts—namely, homilies on Jeremiah for which the Greek is extant—and texts on New Testament passages, namely, his *Commentary on the Gospel According to John*. These additional examples further substantiate the findings of this work and should encourage continued study of his works for further confirmation of and expansion upon those findings.

The examples treated within this work demonstrate that Origen, across his writing career, was mindful that the height of Scripture's transformative effect occurs through the relationship between full readings of the psychic and pneumatic senses of a biblical passage. However, Origen does not always provide both readings for each passage that he treats. In addition to the fact that he is not a strict systematician but a rich thinker who uses his theology to search for rather than simply convey his understanding of Christian truths, Origen found it prudent to refrain in some cases from full treatments of both higher senses. Logic dictates at least three reasons. First, Origen would take due account of time constraints and/or choose to emphasize certain topics significant to his audience and, thus, deliberately refrain from rendering full readings for both higher senses. Second, he suggests in *Hom. Num.* 27 that he does not yet grasp fully the pneumatic sense of the stages of the Israelites' exodus in Num. 33, even though he is one of the "perfected," who are able to teach others within the church.[13] Third, he may have faced the occasional audience in which he perceived that no member was able as yet to grasp pneumatic truths (perhaps, for example, if the audience consisted wholly of pre-baptismal catechumenates).

III. *Chronology of Origen's Works*

Throughout this work, it will be useful for the reader to keep in mind the general chronology of the examined texts in relation to each other. The timing and order of the works examined will demonstrate consistency, first, between Origen's earlier statement of exegetical

---

[13] See the analysis of *Hom. Num.* 27 at the end of chapter 4.

theory in *Princ.* 4 and later statements of theory in his homilies, and, second, between his theory and actual practice.

Origen likely wrote *De Principiis* during the years 229–230 C.E., at the age of 44 or 45.[14] Though he was already in the second half of his life (with his death falling between 251 and 254 C.E.), he was near the beginning of his writing career. He likely began his first written works around the age of 37 (222 C.E.) with treatises such as *De resurrectione, De naturis, Dialogue with Candidus,* and five books on his *Commentary on the Lamentations,* none of which are known to be extant, as well as 10 books of his *Stromateis,* and 25 books of his *Commentary on the Psalms,* which remain only in fragmentary form. This makes *De Principiis* one of Origen's earliest written works extant in substantial form, and it is the earliest extant work containing a detailed statement of his exegetical theory.

Significantly, Origen wrote the theory in *Princ.* 4 some years before he produced the practical works under review. Origen preached the transcribed homilies[15] (in Caesarea of Palestine) at least ten years after *De Principiis* (written in Alexandria), likely between the years 239 and 242 C.E., or between the ages of 54 and 57.[16] Soon after composing *De Principiis,* he began to write his *Commentary on the Gospel According to John,* which eventually amounted to 32 books after working the rest of his life on it.[17] Except for the first six books of this

---

[14] Though there is no evidence of the exact year of Origen's birth, this work assumes the often accepted year of 185 C.E. For the dates and status of Origen's writings this work will rely generally on the following sources: Pierre Nautin, *Origène: Sa vie et son oeuvre* (Paris: Beauchesne, 1977), 409–412; Crouzel, *Origen,* 1–49; G. W. Butterworth, introduction to *Origen: On First Principles* (trans. G. W. Butterworth; Torchbook Editions; Gloucester, Mass.: Peter Smith, 1973); and Eusebius, *Hist. eccl.* 6.1–39.

[15] For Origen's initial reluctance to have his homilies transcribed, see Butterworth, introduction to *Origen,* xxv, and Eusebius, *Hist. eccl.* 6.36.

[16] Nautin, *Origène,* 409–412. Others more generally surmise that Origen performed the transcribed homilies sometime between 238–244. For example, see Ronald E. Heine, introduction to *Origen: Commentary on the Gospel According to John* (trans. Ronald E. Heine; 2 vols.; FC 80, 89; Washington, D.C.: Catholic University of America, 1989 and 1993) 1:5. Crouzel dates the delivery of most of them, except those on the Gospel of Luke, after 245 (*Origen,* 30). There is general agreement that Origen delivered most if not all of these homilies in Caesarea of Palestine, except for the homily on 1 Sam. 1 (on Samuel's birth), the text of which suggests that Origen performed it in Jerusalem (ibid., 30).

[17] Of the 32 books of the *Commentary on the Gospel According to John* only 9 books remain. These 9 are extant in the Greek: 1, 2, 6, 10, 13, 19 (the beginning and end of book 19 are missing), 20, 28 and 32 (Crouzel, *Origen,* 42). Heine also includes short fragments from books 4 and 5 (FC 80; *Origen: Commentary on the Gospel According to John,* I:158–67). According to Nautin, Origen composed books 1–4 in 231, 5 in

commentary, Origen likely wrote the other extant portions of the intact commentaries either contemporaneously with or sometime after he performed the transcribed homilies.[18]

Of greater importance to this study than the precise dates of these works is the general order of their transcription, upon which scholars generally agree. The general order of his writings falls into three periods: (a) the earlier period (approximately 222–233) during which Origen wrote *De Principiis* and the first five books of his commentary on John; (b) the middle period (approximately 234–242) during which he allowed transcription of his homiletic deliveries and wrote books 6–31 of his John commentary, and (c) the later period (approximately 243–254) during which he composed *Comm. Jo.* 32 and the extant books and portions of his commentaries on the Song of Songs, Matthew, and Romans. The following is a brief time-chart showing the general order of written texts relevant to this work. The years in this chart rely on Nautin's dates and Eusebius' rendition of events.

231–232, 6 beginning in 232 and finishing in 234, and 32 in 248, with 7–31 written some time between 234 and 248 (*Origène*, 410–412). Nautin specifically dates the composition of *Comm. Jo.* 22–31 (and perhaps the beginning of book 32) to 238. Heine argues that Origen wrote books 1–4 in 230–231, 5 in 231–232, 6 beginning in 234, and, in agreement with Nautin, 32 late in life, if not exactly in 248 (introduction to *Origen: Commentary on the Gospel According to John*; 1:4–5).

[18] Origen likely wrote 25 books in total for his *Commentary on the Gospel According to Matthew* of which 10–17 are extant in Greek and cover Matthew 13:36 through 22:33. The first 9 books are lost, except for two short fragments. In the Latin, 145 pieces covering Matthew 22:34 through 27:66 constitute what scholars refer to as the *Commentariorum Series*, likely from the lost parts of Origen's *Commentary on the Gospel of Matthew* (Crouzel, *Origen*, 4–43, esp. 42–43; and John Patrick, introduction to *Commentary on Matthew* [*ANF* 9:411; John Patrick, trans.; 4th Edition; Peabody, Mass.: Hendrickson, 1994]). According to Eusebius (*Hist. eccl.* 6.36), Origen composed this commentary at the time that he wrote his famous apology *Contra Celsum*. Following this timing, Nautin dates the composition of Origen's Matthew commentary to 249, and Patrick dates it to 246–248.

Regarding Origen's *Commentary on the Epistle to the Romans*, 15 books are extant in the Greek and are comprised in 10 books in Rufinus' Latin translation (Crouzel, *Origen*, 43). Nautin gives no date for the composition of the commentary. Peter Gorday places Origen's writing of the Romans commentary late in life, roughly around the time he composed the *Commentary on the Gospel According to Matthew* and *Contra Celsum* (*Principles of Patristic Exegesis: Romans 9–11 in Origen, John Chrysostom, and Augustine* [New York and Toronto: Edwin Mellen, 1983], 46–47). In line, then, with Nautin's other dates, Origen likely wrote his Romans commentary just before or during 249.

Finally, regarding Origen's *Commentary on the Song of Songs*, it originally consisted of 10 books, 5 of which Origen wrote while in Athens and the other 5 later when he was back in Caesarea of Palestine (Eusebius, *Hist. eccl.* 6.32). Nautin places the trip to Athens in 245 and the composition of the second 5 books in Caesarea after this trip during 246–247. R. P. Lawson places the writing of the first 5 books in

Year, C.E.	Origen's Age	Event
185	—	Origen is born in Alexandria
211+	26+	Origen experiences a "spiritual conversion" and sells his secular books and commits to becoming a Christian philosopher
The Earlier Period		
222	37	Origen begins his writing career with the financial support of Ambrose who claimed conversion by Origen
229–230	44–45	Origen writes *De Principiis*
231	46	Origen writes *Comm. Jo.* 1–4
232	47	In Alexandria Origen writes *Comm. Jo.* 5; during Origen's stop at Caesarea of Palestine on a trip to Greece, the Caesarean Bishop Theoctistus (with the backing of Bishop Alexander of Jerusalem) ordains Origen a presbyter, thus giving him official approval to preach from the pulpit in Caesarea (and Jerusalem as well)
The Middle Period		
234	49	From Athens Origen returns to Caesarea, writes *Comm. Jo.* 6 (and perhaps books 7–21 as well), and begins the Caesarean phase of his life, i.e., when he chooses to establish Caesarea, over Alexandria, as his new home since Bishop Demetrius of Alexandria has discredited him
238	53	Origen writes *Comm. Jo.* 22–31 (and perhaps begins book 32).
239–242	54–57	Origen delivers the preaching cycle from which the extant homilies were transcribed
The Later Period		
245–247	60–62	Origen visits Athens during which time he composes the extant books of *Comm. Cant.*
248–249	63–64	Origen finishes *Comm. Jo.* 32, and writes *Comm. Matt.* and *Comm. Rom.* and his apology *Contra Celsum*
251 or 254	66 or 69	Origen dies, after release from confinement and torture under the Decian persecution [Eusebius, *Hist. Eccl.* 6.39]

This order of Origen's writings, when coupled with the analysis of this work, indicates that he held to the same exegetical theory of three senses of meaning throughout his life, maintaining consistent definitions of the senses in the variety of his homilies and commentaries.

---

240 (introduction to *Origen: The Song of Songs Commentary and Homilies* [*ACW* 26:4; New York: Newman, 1957]). Available to us in substantial form from Rufinus' Latin translation are Origen's prologue, *Comm. Cant.* 1–3 and a part of *Comm. Cant.* 4.

Also, although Origen aimed his homilies and commentaries at different audiences, he employed psychic and pneumatic readings in both genres. As chapter 2 will point out, he addressed his early theoretical explanation of the threefold method in *Princ.* 4 to other leaders—teachers and preachers—within the church. As chapter 5 will show, he also addressed the pneumatic and psychic readings in his later composed *Comm. Cant.* to other church leaders. Analysis of these works (as well as portions of his homilies) will reveal that Origen considered himself and other church leaders to be "perfected souls" in the faith, that is, those who are able to grasp at least some pneumatic meanings in Scripture.[19] These perfected souls have the duty to teach others less advanced in faith. Origen considered himself to be a teacher of teachers, with the duty to help other leaders facilitate growth in their congregations as well as aid them in their own continued progress in the faith. Even in many of his homilies, as the examples in chapters 3 and 4 will show, Origen preached to perfected souls as well as the less advanced, by including pneumatic as well as somatic and psychic readings of Scripture. The method that he taught to other teachers in *De Principiis*, he put into practice in both his homilies and commentaries.[20]

---

[19] Throughout this work, I consider Origen's qualified understanding of what he calls the "perfected soul" as one who can grasp all three senses of scriptural meaning but stands to benefit from increased edification from each of them during this life.

[20] Frances Young argues that there is no evidence that different types of exegetical writing were perceived to command different reading strategies, or, therefore, different methods of interpretation (*Biblical Exegesis*, 247). Also, Harry Y. Gamble argues that authors of Origen's day generally assumed that all types of writings would be read aloud and that even commentaries tended to be series of homiletic expositions treating the biblical text with a line-by-line scrutiny (*Books and Readers in the Early Church: A History of Early Christian Texts* [New Haven: Yale University Press, 1995], 204 and 217).

CHAPTER ONE

REHABILITATION OF THE PSYCHIC SENSE

This chapter examines scholars' most recent views concerning Origen's allegorical method of interpreting biblical passages according to three senses of meaning: one literal and two nonliteral senses.[1] Most scholars have referred to the two nonliteral senses as "moral" and "spiritual," even though Origen's own terms for them are, respectively, "psychic" and "pneumatic" (when transliterated from the Greek text of *Princ.* 4). Only for this chapter's discussion of scholars' views does this work principally employ the terms moral and spiritual. The next chapter will explain why psychic and pneumatic are more informative terms.

Much controversy surrounds Origen's conception and use of the middle, moral sense. Some recent scholars observe that he claims a middle sense in his exegetical theory of *Princ.* 4 but does not adequately define it. All agree that he does not implement in his practical works—homilies and commentaries—a middle sense that is separately identifiable from his general spiritualized—in contrast to literal—reading of biblical passages. Karen Jo Torjesen carries this observation of his practice back into his theory and claims that he never intended in *Princ.* 4 to promote three senses of meaning.[2]

Various scholarly opinions about what exegetical method Origen promotes in theory and employs in practice stem from one question: Is Origen's exegetical method arbitrary? By the term "arbitrary," scholars put forward two separate yet related concerns. First, they question whether his method is *subjective*, that is, not adequately focused on the text itself. Second, they question whether it is *inconsistent*, that is, variable within and between his theory and practice.

---

[1] In line with Origen's own usage, this work employs the term "nonliteral" as a synonym for "figurative" or "metaphorical." See the introduction, n. 9, for a fuller explanation of this matter.

[2] Torjesen's views are presented later in this chapter. She offers a formidable reading of Origen's exegesis in response to the concerns of scholars before her. This work relies upon some of her conclusions and diverges from others.

The first concern measures how accurately the method treats Scripture's text, while the latter focuses on the internal coherence of the method and Origen's implementation of it. Both concerns spring forth from the desire for a method that renders truth from Scripture's text. Of course, we can no better *prove* the truth of a text than the right method for extracting it. Still, we can decide whether a particular method is useful and worthy of study.[3]

By suggesting that Origen's method is subjective, some scholars express concern that he employs, either intentionally or unwittingly, an allegorical method so malleable that it results in readings of Scripture not relevant to the text but imposed upon it by his personal interests. They fear that he interpreted Scripture spuriously to support foreign elements from the Platonic philosophy of his day. This led some scholars of the twentieth century to judge Origen's treatment of biblical text against the historical-critical method's goal of unearthing the human author's intended meaning.[4] Because Origen seeks only the auctorial intent of the Holy Spirit and, thus, is willing to read Scripture allegorically without placing value on the human author's intent, some scholars dismiss his exegesis as unworthy of study.[5]

By the middle of the century, however, other scholars began to emerge who would revitalize the study of Origen's exegesis. They stress that Origen's exegesis should be judged according to how well it serves the purpose he perceives in Scripture, not according to a standard foreign to his way of thinking. These proponents establish that he employs the allegorical method to promote his perception of Scripture's spiritual purpose—to bring its hearers to spiritual growth and salvation—not to advance external, Platonic ideals. Thus, these scholars hail his exegesis as worthy of study and its results as relevant to Christian faith today.[6]

---

[3] Torjesen acknowledges the need to redefine the term "method" in relation to Origen, since he does not seek, according to modern, scientific standards, the truth of a text based upon external evidence. As other scholars discussed below, she too argues that it is necessary to judge his method according to his own understanding of how best to measure truth (Torjesen, *Hermeneutical Procedure*, 4f.).

[4] See especially the discussion of de Faye's and Hanson's views below.

[5] See especially the discussion of de Faye's views below.

[6] See the views of de Lubac, Daniélou, Crouzel, Greer, and Torjesen discussed below.

Such scholars recognize that their discovery of his method's aim
to capture Scripture's spiritual purpose does not put to rest the
charges of subjectivity and inconsistency. As for the former, some
praise his personalized readings of Scripture, considering it appropriate to his understanding of the dynamic and transformative nature
of Scripture's communication and necessary to the spiritual director's
task.[7] However, these scholars tend to become critics when turning
to the matter of consistency. While they acknowledge that his allegorical readings of Scripture are useful for directing the Christian's
spiritual life, they often view his theory as unclear or, at least, inconsistent with his practice. Some even claim that this internal inco-
herence exposes a dangerously subjective side to the method—that
results in distortions of Scripture's text[8]—while others argue that,
regardless of the theory, his practice stands on its own as a legitimate contribution to the life of faith.[9]

The question of consistency, then, has not been put to rest, and
its significance remains. If Origen's exegesis is worthy of study and
should be applied to the life of faith, then it is necessary to understand *how* he draws out Scripture's spiritual purpose for his hearer.
What exactly is his exegetical method and how does he implement
it? Without answering these questions, we can be certain neither how
his method has influenced the Christian spiritual life through the
centuries nor how to apply it accurately today.[10]

The details that will emerge from the following review of recent
scholarship will beckon us to seriously reconsider whether Origen
consistently relies upon three senses of scriptural meaning in both
theory and practice. The remainder of this work, then, will build
upon these scholarly views by establishing that Origen clearly defines
three senses in theory and applies them in practice, including a middle, moral sense whose independent function *and* relationship to the
other nonliteral sense constitute the core mechanics of his exegetical effort to spiritually transform Scripture's hearer.

---

[7] See especially the discussion of Daniélou's and Crouzel's views below.

[8] See especially the discussion of Daniélou's views below.

[9] See especially the views of de Lubac, Crouzel and Greer discussed below.

[10] Torjesen offers an explanation of Origen's method (outlined later in this chapter),
which, this work argues, principally describes how he conveys Scripture's meanings
to his audience, not how he determines what those meanings are.

I. *The History of Recent Scholarship*

Eugène de Faye

In his 1926 work, Eugène de Faye dismisses Origen's exegesis as "arbitrary" and thus not worthy of study. He identifies Origen as a philosopher alone, neither a theologian nor an exegete, who stretches Scripture out of shape in order to make it support his own Platonic ideas.[11] For authority, Origen appeals to the Old Testament as an ancient text, but he does not uphold its literal sense, which, as de Faye defines it, reveals the intentions of the human author.[12] According to de Faye, Origen calls this sense the "historical meaning" and either ignores it or declares it "absurd" and untrue, claiming that those who focus on it "worship the letter, ... [and have] not yet advanced beyond the Jewish exegesis."[13] Instead of honoring the literal sense, Origen imposes his allegorical method of interpretation on the text, to stress subjectively his own figurative readings.[14] In this way he is an exegete of invention who

> discovers in the Holy Book *his* own teaching on God and providence, *his* Christological doctrine, *his* doctrine on the origin and end of the Cosmos, on sin and redemption; in short, an entire system of "dogmas" of which the sacred author never dreamt.[15]

Origen, then, is *not* a biblical exegete, but he simply employs the Old Testament nonliterally in order to teach his Hellenistic version of the Christian faith, "tell[ing] us something of his theology, but nothing of the religion of Israel, nothing of the character or function of prophecy."[16] According to de Faye, Origen is also unfaithful to the New Testament texts, applying his allegorical method to the Gospel and Paul's letters as well.[17] While de Faye is unclear as to whether he views Origen to be self-deluded or fully aware of his fanciful interpretations, de Faye is emphatic that Origen's exegetical

---

[11] Eugène de Faye, *Origen and His Work* (trans. Fred Rothwell; London: Allen & Unwin, 1926), 26, 37–52.
[12] Ibid., 49–52.
[13] Ibid., 37–38.
[14] Ibid., 45–46.
[15] Ibid., 37–38, emphasis added.
[16] Ibid., 38.
[17] Ibid., 51.

results are not relevant to biblical studies today—or ever. While
Origen's philosophical views on God and the cosmos are worth study-
ing, it is best to steer clear of his exegetical practice.[18] For de Faye,
Origen's exegesis is self-serving and, thus, dangerously subjective
because it distorts the text.

Henri de Lubac

In contrast, Henri de Lubac, in his 1950 work *Histoire et Esprit*,
defends Origen's exegetical exercises as insightful, profound and
beneficial to the believer by arguing three points:[19] First, Origen's
exegesis and philosophy are mutually supportive and interrelated. He
is a man of the church who does not use Scripture to promote extraneous philosophical arguments. Second, Origen's typological exegesis of Old Testament passages is a legitimate and useful form of
scriptural interpretation for Christian faith today. Third, Origen's
understandings of Scripture stem from both a devotion to Jesus and
a conviction to defend the orthodoxy of the church against exclu-
sionary, Gnostic heresies.

De Lubac concedes to de Faye that Origen is not guided in his
exegesis by "the sense of a certain unity of the world of the Bible,"[20]
that is, Origen does not make it a priority to seek out or rely on
the collective historical circumstances and literary contexts of biblical texts—he does not rely upon the historical-critical method in his
approach to Scripture. Instead, he employs the principle of "pure
faith" to the text and, thus, his method, though maybe "deceptive
for the historian," is a legitimate means of interpreting Scripture for
the spiritual benefit of the Christian believer.[21] In other words, de
Lubac suggests that Origen's works are not dangerously subjective—
they do not unduly distort Scripture's text.

---

[18] Ibid., 42–52.
[19] See generally Henri de Lubac, *Histoire et Esprit: L'intelligence de l'Écriture d'après
Origène* (Paris: Éditions Montaigne, 1950). De Lubac explains that he at first intended
this work as an introduction to the French translations of Origen's homilies on the
Hextateuch which were to appear in volumes of the *Sources Chrétiennes* series, but this
work ultimately turned into a full-blown defense of Origen's exegesis and philosophy.
[20] De Lubac, *Histoire et Esprit*, 314. All English translations of this work are my
own.
[21] Ibid.

In other works (of both 1947 and 1959), though, de Lubac admits inconsistency between Origen's theory and practice. He observes that Origen's theoretical claim in *Princ.* 4 to two nonliteral senses, moral and spiritual, alongside the literal sense, is not evident in the practice of his homilies and commentaries. De Lubac agrees with an earlier scholarly view which contends that Origen most often ignores the middle, moral sense in his exegetical exercises, reducing the threefold theory of *Princ.* 4 to a practical twofold distinction between "the letter and spirit" of the text.[22]

De Lubac also agrees that in certain places within his practice Origen presents both a moral and spiritual meaning but orders them inconsistently: in some passages Origen presents a spiritual meaning and then a moral, in others a moral and then a spiritual.[23] De Lubac explains that these two alternative orderings of moral and spiritual meaning in Origen's practice point to two different categories of moral meaning, neither of which functions as an independent Christian sense. Where Origen offers a "moral or tropological sense" *before* an "allegorical or mystical [or spiritual] sense," he sets forth Philo's moral sense, which focuses on the nature of the human soul,[24] namely, its "faculties" and "virtues."[25] This first category of moral meaning is not uniquely Christian. In other places, and indeed more often,[26] Origen offers the "allegorical or mystical [or spiritual] sense" first, followed by another "spiritual sense" that conveys a moral theme. This second category of moral meaning is intimately related to the one overall (preceding) allegorical, or spiritual sense, emphasizing the theme of the human "soul's . . . interiorization and development in the Christian life" within the context of the spiritual sense's focus on the mystery of Christ.[27]

---

[22] De Lubac, *Medieval Exegesis, The Four Senses of Scripture* (trans. Mark Sebanc; Grand Rapids: Eerdmans, 1998), I:144, [originally Exégèse Médiévale I, Paris: Éditions Montaigne, 1959], citing Ferdinand Prat, "Origène," *DB* 5:1875–1876.

[23] De Lubac, *Medieval Exegesis*, I:144–146; also generally, idem, *Histoire et Esprit*, 139–150.

[24] De Lubac, *Medieval Exegesis*, I:147–50. De Lubac explains that Philo employs a "moral" sense that focuses on the soul's nature and, separately, a "physical" sense that focuses on the nature of the cosmos.

[25] De Lubac, "'Typologie' et 'Allégorisme,'" *RSR* 34 (1947) 180–226, esp. 219–220, n. 152. English translations of this text are my own.

[26] De Lubac, *Medieval Exegesis*, I:144–146.

[27] De Lubac, "'Typologie,'" 219–220, n. 152.

De Lubac explains that the first, Philonic category of moral meaning appears in Origen's exegesis as the "soul" of Scripture, after its
"body" and before its "spirit."[28] It draws "diverse 'moralities'" from
the biblical text that are not innately Christian but can be applied
to Christianity as to any context.[29] It is a "philosophical" and "non-
temporal" look at the soul as a "microcosm" of reality.[30] It does not
facilitate Origen's *Christian* "allegorism"—or reading of the Old
Testament according to the mystery of Christ—but is his more general, *extra*-Christian comment about the soul when meditating on a
biblical passage.[31] Thus, even if it were called a separate "sense," it
is not a *Christian* sense of scriptural meaning.

De Lubac finds more prevalent and significant to Origen's *Christian*
allegory the moral meaning that follows the mystical or allegorical
(spiritual) reading.[32] This meaning is so linked to its predecessor that
it cannot be separated from it, for together they speak of the uniquely
Christian "Mystery."[33] This moral meaning speaks of the soul of the
believer or church in relation to the Christian mysteries set forth by
the preceding allegorical or mystical (spiritual) sense. De Lubac
explains that Origen most often moves from a "brief" retelling of
the "historical sense" to an "interior" sense[34]—the allegorical, mystical,

---

[28] De Lubac, *Medieval Exegesis*, I:146–150, referring to *Princ.* 4.2.4.

[29] Ibid., esp. 147.

[30] Ibid. See the next footnote for an explanation of how this work's findings dis-
agree with de Lubac's observation that this first category of moral meaning is "non-
temporal."

[31] Ibid. For textual examples of this first, more Philonic moral sense, de Lubac
points to texts such as Origen's *Hom. Lev.* 5 (on three sacrificial loaves) and *Hom.
Num.* 9 (on three layers of the almond), as well as others. For the full lists of textual
examples, see *Medieval Exegesis*, I:144–146; and *Histoire et Esprit*, 141–142. Chapter
3 will treat some of these same texts, notably *Hom. Lev.* 5 and *Hom. Num.* 9, as
examples of Origen's continuing exegetical theory. In these homilies, Origen restates
and develops his earlier threefold theory from *Princ.* 4 by reading biblical concepts
metaphorically. This work will suggest that Origen sometimes presents the moral
sense *before* the spiritual sense when explicating exegetical theory.
    Note that de Lubac lists *Hom. Num.* 9 on the almond sprouting forth from Aaron's
rod as an example of this non-Christian moral sense and states that it is "non-
temporal" in character. The analysis of *Hom. Num.* 9 in chapter 3 will demonstrate
that in that homily in particular Origen stresses the *temporal* nature of the literal
(somatic) and moral (psychic) senses in contrast to the *eternal* nature of the third,
spiritual (pneumatic) sense. Origen states there that the first two senses will cease
to edify at the end of time, leaving only the third, pneumatic sense to continue to
edify for eternity.

[32] De Lubac, *Histoire et Esprit*, 147–149.

[33] De Lubac, *Medieval Exegesis*, I:146–147.

[34] De Lubac, *Histoire et Esprit*, 149.

or spiritual sense—that is "christological, ecclesial, and sacramental"[35] in "complexion" and only then may speak of the believer's or church's soul within that interior sense's discussion of "the spiritual life."[36] Hence, de Lubac suggests that this second, Christian category of moral meaning functions as an aspect of the one, multi-focused non-literal sense.[37]

De Lubac concludes that Origen's theoretical claim to a distinct and specifically Christian nonliteral, moral meaning is not essentially substantiated in his practice. Nonetheless, he finds that the moral and other themes of the spiritual meaning together reflect a faith-based approach to Scripture that makes his insights about the text relevant to the Christian life of faith today.

R. P. C. Hanson

R. P. C. Hanson, in his 1959 work, agrees with de Lubac's findings concerning the absence of a separate Christian moral sense in practice. Hanson acknowledges Origen's distinctive definition for the moral sense in *Prin.* 4 as offering the hearer of Scripture "direct

---

[35] De Lubac, *Medieval Exegesis*, I:146–147. Maurice F. Wiles sets forth a similar list of the spiritual sense's themes and suggests that the moral theme is just one among the rest: "There is as good ground for distinguishing a Christological, an ecclesiological, a mystical and an eschatological sense as there is for the distinction between the moral and the spiritual." ("Origen as Biblical Scholar," *The Cambridge History of the Bible*, (eds. P. R. Ackroyd and C. F. Evans; Cambridge: Cambridge University Press, 1970), 1:454–489, quoting 470.

[36] De Lubac, *Medieval Exegesis*, I:146–147.

[37] De Lubac offers the following as textual examples of this second, less distinct, but truly Christian type of "moral" sense: Origen's *Hom. Gen.* 2 (on the three decks in Noah's ark), *Hom. Ex.* 3 (on the three day's journey during the Israelite's exodus), *Comm. Cant.* (on the Bride and Bridegroom as the church and Christ and then as individual soul and Word of God), *Hom. Gen.* 11 (on Isaac's three days at the well of vision), *Hom. Gen.* 12 (on the "two nations" in Rebecca's womb represented by Jacob and Esau), and *Hom. Lev.* 1 (on the notion of "whole burnt offering"). For de Lubac's comments about these and other examples, see *Medieval Exegesis*, I:145–146; and *Histoire et Esprit*, 139–150. This work will examine each of the texts listed here. Chapter 3 will treat *Hom. Gen.* 2 and *Hom. Gen.* 11 as examples of Origen's continuing theory of exegesis. Chapter 4 will examine *Hom. Gen.* 2 again, as well as *Hom. Ex.* 3, *Hom. Gen.* 12 and *Hom. Lev.* 1 as examples of Origen's full presentations of both of the two higher (moral/psychic and spiritual/pneumatic) senses for a single biblical passage, in order to demonstrate the practical application of his theory of two distinct nonliteral senses. Chapter 5 will examine *Comm. Cant.* 1 in order to demonstrate even more fully how these two higher senses are both distinct in Origen's practice and related in such a way as to facilitate the hearer's spiritual growth toward salvation.

edification" by way of moral instruction rather than the "mystical and theological" truths that are the focus of the spiritual sense.[38] However, he finds that this theoretically distinguished moral sense "plays no significant part in Origen's exegesis."[39] He observes that Origen occasionally presents separate moral and spiritual readings in both his homilies and commentaries, but argues that the occasions are too infrequent to carry any significance. Unlike de Lubac but like de Faye, Hanson concludes, that this inconsistency with his threefold theory reveals his intention to read Scripture subjectively, thus, making his exegesis dangerous and not worthy of imitation.

Agreeing with de Lubac's two categories of moral meaning in Origen's practice, Hanson argues that the moral meaning, when contributing to a Christian reading of the text and not simply a borrowing from Philo,[40] is "absorbed" into the spiritual sense.[41] Yet, unlike de Lubac, Hanson believes that this results in a "protean" or overburdened nonliteral sense.[42] All focal "distinctions" to be made at the nonliteral level of interpretation "dissolve" into this one malleable and all-encompassing "'spiritual' sense."[43] In practice, then, Origen either "ignores" the moral sense or "fuses" it with the spiritual so as to make them indistinguishable.[44] Hanson concludes that it is "impossible" for Origen "to maintain the distinction" between the moral and spiritual senses for *Christian* allegorical readings of biblical text.[45]

For Hanson, the malleability of the spiritual sense signals a method that is dangerously subjective. According to Hanson, Origen tries to describe a theory with two nonliteral senses that sounds legitimate, but in practice he applies one sense that is so broad that it cannot serve as any predictable standard of interpretation. He accuses Origen of promoting a pliable threefold theory so as to "rationalize" Scripture

---

[38] R. P. C. Hanson, *Allegory and Event: A Study of the Sources and Significance of Origen's Interpretation of Scripture*, 243 (Richmond, Va: John Knox Press, 1959), referring to *Princ.* 4.2.6 in which Origen offers a definition of the moral, or psychic, sense by analyzing Paul's treatment of Deut 25:4 in 1 Cor. 9:9–12.
[39] Ibid., 243.
[40] Ibid., 242.
[41] Ibid., 243.
[42] Ibid.
[43] Ibid., 257.
[44] Ibid., 236. Wiles similarly argues that Origen's relation of these different concerns results in a "moral" and "spiritual" sense that are not distinct but rather are "confused" in practice ("Origen as Biblical Scholar," 468–469).
[45] Hanson, *Allegory and Event*, 243.

into saying whatever he wants it to say.[46] The absence of a separate, *Christian* moral sense in practice signals an inconsistency between
Origen's theory and practice that, in turn, exposes his intention to
impose his own views upon Scripture. While de Lubac excuses
Origen's theoretical claim to a middle, moral sense and finds relevance and significance in his use of a spiritual exegesis that relies
on a practical twofold distinction between literal and spiritual meanings for fueling the life of faith, Hanson concludes, with de Faye,
that Origen interprets Scripture subjectively, and Hanson emphasizes that Origen does so consciously for self-serving ends.

Jean Daniélou

In his 1973 work, Jean Daniélou defends, with de Lubac, the spiritual nature and relevance of Origen's exegetical intention. However,
like de Faye and Hanson, he argues that through the mechanics of
a fallacious threefold theory Origen effectively imposes his own spiritual experiences upon the biblical text with subjective results that
sometimes distort the text.

Nonetheless, Daniélou is a great contributor to the understanding
and appreciation of Origen's pastoral motivation. He explains that
it blossoms forth from "his own spiritual experience," aiming to bring
his own hard-won wisdom to others.[47] In this way, Origen provides
those who come after him a way to approach and plumb the spiritual mine of Scripture's truths. His distinction in practice between
Scripture's literal and spiritual senses is a legitimate effort to facilitate his audience's progress from carnal to spiritual living.[48] He applies
his spiritual experience to the reading of Scripture through his use
of typologies, all aimed at edifying the "interior life of the individual Christian."[49] Origen, then, comes to the Bible with a clear and
predictable frame of reference: the spiritual journeyer on the road
to salvation. Daniélou points out that Hanson "has failed to grasp
this point, which de Lubac . . . rightly emphasizes, namely that Origen's
spiritual exegesis is for this reason a legitimate aspect of typology."[50]

---

[46] Ibid., 246.
[47] Jean Daniélou, *Gospel Message and Hellenistic Culture* (trans. John Austin Baker;
London: Darton, Longman & Todd; Philadelphia: Westminster, 1973), 278.
[48] Ibid., 274.
[49] Ibid., 278.
[50] Ibid., 279 n. 9, citing Hanson, *Allegory and Event*, and de Lubac, *Histoire et Esprit*,
178–195.

Indeed, for Daniélou, the overall tone of Origen's exegesis is spiritual, not only in his practice but also in the theory of *Princ.* 4,
because it legitimately emphasizes the importance of finding divinely
inspired, spiritual meaning within Scripture. He points out that Origen
considers Scripture's structure ("form") and not just themes ("content") to be divinely inspired.[51] Origen's theory of discerning scriptural meaning "consists in unveiling something originally hidden, not
in discovering something new."[52] Origen seeks to draw out Scripture's
own spiritual aim. Thus, Daniélou joins de Lubac in defending Origen
against the charges, suggested by de Faye and made explicit by
Hanson, that Origen *intended* to use his interpretive approach to
impose extraneous philosophical views onto biblical text.

Still, Daniélou concedes that Origen's specific distinction between
moral and spiritual senses results in a degree of unwanted subjectivity in some of his exegetical results. For Daniélou, the main cul-
prit is Origen's theoretical insistence on a middle, moral meaning.
He agrees with Hanson and de Lubac that Origen does not present
a moral meaning in practice as a separate Christian component of
his allegorical method but does suggest it in theory. Unfortunately,
Daniélou argues, in *Princ.* 4 Origen relies on disparate philosophical
schools to create a fallacious hierarchy of scriptural meanings.[53]
Daniélou examines *Princ.* 4.2.4, in which, as this work will explain
in chapter 2, Origen states that Scripture, as human nature, has a
body, soul and spirit which promote spiritual growth in stages.
Daniélou determines that the tripartite anthropology derives from
the Apologists and the three advancing levels of learning have Stoic
and Philonic roots.[54] He believes that this language in 4.2.4 could
legitimately convey increasing levels of spiritual advancement for the
believer, but they cannot justify three separate senses of scriptural
meaning. Therefore, when Origen claims a corresponding threefold
meaning in Scripture, he sets out a "piece of pure theorizing."[55]

---

[51] Daniélou, *Gospel Message*, 280–281. Daniélou here indicates his opposition to
Hanson's criticisms in this regard, citing specifically Hanson, *Allegory and Event*, 190
(*Gospel Message*, 281, n. 12).
[52] Daniélou, *Gospel Message*, 282. Daniélou also states that "[o]n Origen's interpretation the only advance is in men's knowledge of revealed truth, not in the truth
that is revealed" (282 n. 13, citing as support Marguerite Harl [*Origène et la fonction
révélatrice du Verbe incarné* (Paris: Éditions du Seuil, 1958) 160–163]).
[53] Daniélou, *Gospel Message*, 284, citing in support Hanson, *Allegory and Event*, 237.
[54] Daniélou, *Gospel Message*, 284.
[55] Ibid.

The idea of three scriptural meanings is purely "gratuitous," that is, it places external constructs onto Scripture.[56] Daniélou is glad to observe, however, that this "artificial division" of Scripture into three systematic levels of meaning does not often appear in Origen's other (practical) works.[57]

Daniélou argues that Origen borrowed the notion of a moral sense in his early theory from Paul's rabbinic influence. He focuses on Origen's claim that Paul's interpretation of Deut. 25:4 (on muzzling the ox) in 1 Cor. 9:9–10 figuratively establishes the apostle's right to compensation, thereby showing how Scripture internally promotes the notion of a middle, moral sense. Daniélou argues that while Origen tries to "justify this threefold structure of meaning by appealing to the exegetical method of the biblical writers themselves," he betrays his own understanding of the moral sense as "the kind of interpretation common to all moral allegorism, whether in Palestine or Alexandria, and is extremely rare in the New Testament, being found only in St. Paul, in whom it is a relic of rabbinic education and not a dogmatic principle."[58] According to Daniélou, then, Origen's early theoretical claim to a middle, moral sense, like his practical application of it, is not specific to Christian dogma.[59]

Daniélou contrasts this general moral sense with the distinctively *Christian* spiritual sense that appears in both Origen's theory and practice. This allegorical, spiritual meaning is Christian because it centers on the mystery of Christ. Yet, it is also "Gnostic" in character, for it conveys the "mysteries contained within the letter of

---

[56] Ibid.

[57] Ibid.

[58] Ibid., 285.

[59] Daniélou further clarifies his position by citing (and agreeing with) Hanson's view that the theoretical definition of this moral sense is rabbinic in origin: "Hanson . . . has shown that Paul is making use of an allegorical method which is definitely more rabbinic than Philonian, and which is of extremely questionable exegetical value" (*Gospel Message*, 285, n. 18, citing Hanson, *Allegory and Event*, 28, 78, 273). Elsewhere (*Allegory and Event*, 78–79), Hanson explains that the description of the moral sense in *Princ.* 4.2.6, regarding Paul's interpretation of Deut. 25:4 in 1 Cor. 9:9–12 about muzzling the ox, seems to rely more on rabbinic traditions of interpretation than on Philo's practices. When discussing the appearance of the moral sense in Origen's practice, Hanson agrees with de Lubac that it is Philonic and thus not particularly *Christian* (*Allegory and Event*, 242). Thus, Hanson agrees with de Lubac on the Philonic nature of the moral sense in Origen's practical works, while he agrees with Daniélou that the early theoretical description of the sense, based on Paul's own exegesis, is rabbinic in origin.

Scripture . . . [which] are the secrets of the beginning and end of all
things, and of the heavenly and infernal worlds, in short, a gnosis
in the strict sense."[60] These "hidden things . . . are made clear to
those who are able to extort the meaning," indeed, to "those only
who had been made worthy to . . . understand[] them."[61] Thus,
according to Daniélou, Origen's allegorical, spiritual sense, unfortunately, represents a Christian type of Gnosticism.[62]

Daniélou argues that while Origen's intentions are pastoral, by
using this Gnostic spiritual sense he effectively reads Scripture to
"support [ ] his own speculative ideas."[63] While his spiritual purpose
is praiseworthy and his application of typology appropriate, his theory of three senses, including a rabbinic moral meaning and a Gnostic
spiritual meaning, leads, at times, to subjective readings that distort
Scripture's text. Origen's exegesis is a complex mix of both good
and unfortunate elements. While his typological approach to Scripture
rightly views reality on "the three levels of shadow, image . . . and
reality," the theory of three senses, with its non-Christian influences,
distorts the pattern.[64] Thus, for Daniélou, based on its component
parts, Origen's exegesis, despite its significant and relevant spiritual
aim, breaks down both in theory and practice.

---

[60] Daniélou, *Gospel Message*, 286–287.

[61] Ibid., 286, 287.

[62] Chapter 2 will explain that Origen writes the early theory of *Princ.* 4, at least
in part, to counter Gnosticism and its claim to special knowledge. Also, as stated
above, de Lubac, in *Histoire et Esprit*, argues that Origen makes an intentional move
within *Princ.* 4 to refute and defeat the exclusivity of the Gnostic approach to
Scripture. More generally, chapter 2 will treat Origen's discussion of the relationship between the three senses and the different levels of the hearer's understanding and demonstrate that Origen considers all three senses to apply to *every* human
soul, even though preachers and teachers in the church should expect audiences to
display various stages in spiritual growth and thus different levels of comprehension
of Scripture's truths at any given time.

[63] Daniélou, *Gospel Message*, 288.

[64] Ibid. With a different emphasis, de Margerie agrees that Origen employs the
threefold pattern of shadow, image, and reality in practice rather than three senses
of meaning (de Margerie, *An Introduction to the History of Exegesis*, I:97 citing Daniélou's
view on this point as one to compare with his own, *Gospel Message*, 273–288). He
explains that while Origen's theory posits three senses as the "essential principle of
his method" and that this was "always present in the background of his thought,"
it is not played out in his homilies and commentaries. Instead, in these practical
works, Origen "applies with success . . . a typological theory of three levels (shadow,
image, truth)," and this "constitutes the permanent value of his work." De Margerie
observes that "Origen himself does not seem to have attempted a synthesis of these
two theories," but they both remain important to him.

Henri Crouzel

In more recent decades, three other scholars join de Lubac—and, thus, in part refute Daniélou—in arguing that the spiritual purpose of Origen's exegesis makes its results wholly (rather than only occasionally) beneficial to Christian biblical interpretation today: Henri Crouzel, Karen Jo Torjesen and Rowan A. Greer. Crouzel carries forward Daniélou's observation that Origen seeks the spiritual transformation of his audience by pointing out that he perceives himself to be a "spiritual director" when exegeting Scripture.[65] However, Crouzel emphasizes, this self-perception refutes Daniélou's accusation of Origen's exegesis as distortingly subjective, since the spiritual director's proper aim is not to define Scripture's message as one unified whole but to employ it for the spiritual benefit of each individual:

> The Christian master is an intermediary who helps his disciple to enter into contact with God in prayer. When he is no longer needed, he withdraws. . . . [Origen] does not claim that his interpretation expresses a final and universally valid meaning, but a personal attempt, open to debate but available to others, to reach the profound sense of the passage.[66]

Crouzel suggests here that Origen self-consciously and appropriately drew upon his own views and experiences when interpreting Scripture as a spiritual director. At the same time, however, he was open to other interpretations and meant to offer only a starting point for further exegetical inquiry. According to Crouzel, Origen rightfully viewed Scripture as fluid in meaning and application depending on the individual hearer and, therefore, to some extent inherently—and legitimately—subjective.

Still, Crouzel agrees with his predecessors that Origen does not clearly apply in practice his early theory of three distinct senses from *Princ.* 4.[67] He suggests, as did Daniélou, that Origen conceives of a middle, moral sense for his theory by imposing a tripartite anthropology onto Scripture.[68] As de Lubac, Crouzel finds that in practice Origen sometimes presents this externally imposed moral sense as a "natural morality" that is "independent of the advent of Christ" and

---

[65] Crouzel, *Origen*, 75–76.
[66] Ibid.
[67] Ibid., 79.
[68] Ibid.

thus not strictly Christian.[69] At other times he presents it as a moral focus on the "life of the Christian after that advent."[70] Crouzel observes that it is unclear which category of moral meaning Origen promotes in the theory of *Princ.* 4.

What makes more sense to Crouzel is Origen's practical distinction between a literal reading and either a moral or a mystical (spiritual), nonliteral reading for a biblical passage. Rarely, if ever, does Origen distinguish a moral from a mystical reading in practice, despite what he suggests by his theory of three senses in *Princ.* 4.[71] It is the distinction between literal and nonliteral senses, then, that Origen employs flexibly as the effective tool of his spiritual direction.

Karen Jo Torjesen

Torjesen also commends Origen's exegetical purpose as spiritual, aimed at moving the soul of the hearer toward "perfection" and thus "salvation."[72] She expands upon prior scholars' explanations of his spiritual purpose by explaining how it is centered on Christ: She definitively articulates the now-prevailing view that Origen identifies Scripture with the divine voice of the Logos, or God's own Word made incarnate in Christ. As Torjesen explains, for Origen:

> Scripture is both a mediating activity of the Logos and at the same time has doctrines of the Logos as its content. . . . When [the Logos] reveals the mysteries, the spiritual content of Scripture to his hearers, it is himself that he discloses. The treasures of knowledge when they are opened always contain Christ hidden within. The content of Scripture is nothing other than the Logos incarnate in language. . . .[73]

For Origen, the Incarnate Logos, Christ, is both the teacher and content of Scripture.

Torjesen stresses that for Origen *all* of Scripture's content—that which centers on growth in virtue as well as that which centers on

---

[69] Ibid.

[70] Ibid.

[71] Ibid.

[72] Karen Jo Torjesen, "'Body,' 'Soul,' and 'Spirit' in Origen's Theory of Exegesis," *ATR* 67:1 (1985) 17–30, esp. 20–21; and idem, Karen Jo Torjesen, *Hermeneutical Procedure and Theological Method in Origen's Exegesis* (Berlin: Walter de Gruyter, 1986), esp. 39–43.

[73] Torjesen, *Hermeneutical Procedure*, 119–120.

wisdom and knowledge of God and God's salvific plan—is the pedagogy of the Logos:

> Origen describes the administration of doctrine to the soul as a divine pedagogy of the Logos in two distinct phases, healing from sin and knowledge of mysteries, leading toward perfect union with the Logos. . . . The moral and mystical pedagogy of the Logos are the means by which the soul is returned to its original state of perfection through sanctification and redemption. The moral pedagogy is a preparation for the mystical, and the mystical is a preparation for perfection. . . . This entire hierarchy of doctrines, the moral and the mystical taken together, constitute a way, a path of ascending steps by which the soul in advancing returns to God.[74]

All of Scripture's content is communicated by the Logos: both its moral pedagogy, which calls the human person to virtue, and its mystical pedagogy, which reveals the mysteries of God. Taken with her prior statement, by this description Torjesen suggests that these teachings, for Origen, embody Christ (which is logical if, as later chapters of this work will show, Origen understands Christ to be God's own virtue and wisdom). Through the teachings in Scripture that promote these two aspects of Christ, Christ directs the human person upward toward God. Therefore, following Torjesen's logic, Origen views Scripture's purpose, and, thus, also the purpose of his biblical exegesis, as not merely spiritual but Christ-centered and Christ-directed.[75]

When she turns to *how* Origen interprets Scripture to promote this spiritual, Christ-centered purpose, Torjesen agrees that he does not

---

[74] Ibid., 120–123.

[75] For other scholarly articulations of Origen's understanding that Scripture is to be identified with Christ, see de Margerie, *An Introduction to the History of Exegesis*, 101; and Simonetti, *Biblical Interpretation*, 41–44. John David Dawson also stresses that Origen understands Scripture to be the work of the Divine Logos, and he adds that the Logos, for Origen, is constant throughout human history and his Incarnation makes past events and persons spiritually relevant to hearers in the present and the future (*Christian Figural Reading and the Fashioning of Identity* [Berkeley and Los Angeles: University of California Press, 2002], 127–137). In this way, Dawson helps to defend the relevance of Origen's exegesis to Christian faith against those who have proclaimed it arbitrary (in both senses of subjective and inconsistent) and unworthy of study. Also, concerning Origen's supposed claim to three senses of meaning, Dawson follows Torjesen's position (the explanation of which directly follows; *Figural*, 76, esp. n. 48).

rely on a distinction between moral and spiritual senses of meaning.[76]
Yet, she challenges the view that Origen's theory is inconsistent with
his exegetical practice. Upon her observation, neither in theory nor
in practice does Origen promote "three separate and self-contained
senses of the same text."[77]

According to Torjesen, Origen intends by his discussion of Scripture's
body, soul and spirit in *Princ.* 4.2.4 not three *senses of meaning* but
three *doctrines* or levels of teaching.[78] By explaining these doctrines
in 4.2.4, Origen gives his audience of preachers a set of pedagogical instructions (or his "pedagogical hermeneutic of the soul"), *not*
an exegetical method (or "exegetical hermeneutic of the text").[79] He
explains to them "the movement of edification from the text to the
hearers," *not* "the movement of interpretation from the words of the
text to the spiritual teachings."[80] Thus, according to Torjesen, Origen's
audience of preachers learns from 4.2.4 how to *present* Scripture's
meanings to their own audiences, not how to *interpret* those meanings.

This "threefold . . . ordering of doctrines" in Scripture is pedagogical, because, Torjesen explains, it "corresponds to the progressive steps of the soul's movement toward perfection."[81] Origen uses
the anthropological concepts of body, soul and spirit to outline how
Scripture, when properly exegeted, directs the "three stages of development" ("beginner, intermediate and advanced") in the hearer's
"spiritual ability to understand and receive the teachings" of Scripture.[82]
Thus, Scripture's body, soul and spirit are not only Scripture's doctrines (or teachings), but also, by correlation, they are the human
soul's levels of progress in its ascent to God.

Torjesen reads Origen to suggest that *every* soul ultimately will pass

---

[76] Torjesen, *Hermeneutical Procedure*, 39–43; and idem, "'Body,' 'Soul,' and 'Spirit,'"
19–28.

[77] Torjesen, *Hermeneutical Procedure*, esp. 41.

[78] Ibid., referring especially to *Princ.* 4.2.4. Torjesen's translation of Origen's
description in *Princ.* 4.2.4 reads as follows: "It is therefore necessary to write the
doctrines of the Holy Scriptures three times upon your soul, so that the simple may
be edified by the body of Scripture, for this is what we call the ready-to-hand interpretation, and the one who is somewhat further advanced as it were by the soul
of Scripture, and the perfect . . . by the spiritual law" (*Hermeneutical Procedure*, 39).

[79] Torjesen, "'Body,' 'Soul,' and 'Spirit,'" 22, as well as *Hermeneutical Procedure*,
40–41.

[80] Ibid.

[81] Torjesen, "'Body,' 'Soul,' and 'Spirit,'" 20–21.

[82] Ibid.

through these various levels.[83] This important insight effectively coun-
ters Daniélou's view of Origen's spiritual sense as Gnostic in character, for, as Torjesen explains, Origen views Scripture to direct *every*
human soul ultimately through *all* the levels of progress toward salvation.[84] When preaching, then, the exegete should be mindful to
offer the combination of doctrines that will correspond with his listeners' various levels of progress.[85]

To defend 4.2.4 as a set of doctrines (and, by correlation, levels
of progress), rather than senses, Torjesen points out that Origen
defines a "moral sense," or sense of the "soul" of Scripture, neither
in 4.2.4 nor in subsequent passages of *Princ.* 4.[86] Torjesen identifies
Scripture's "soul" in 4.2.4 as Origen's explanation of an intermediate level of progress for the human soul who has "progress[ed] beyond
the letter" but is "not yet ready for the mysteries" of Scripture's
deepest teachings.[87] Also, when in 4.2.6 Origen offers a passage from
Paul (in 1 Cor. 9:9–12 on the Old Testament law concerning the
muzzle and the ox) as an example of Scripture's soul, Torjesen
explains that Origen simply "shows that Paul when he interprets
Scripture draws out . . . different kinds of *doctrines*."[88] Thus, she argues
that Origen did not intend to provide an exegetical method in *Princ.*
4.2.4.[89]

Rather, Torjesen identifies Origen's *exegetical method* as a multi-step
process—discernible within his practical works—by which he presents each verse or portion of the text to the hearer. In his homily

---

[83] Torjesen, *Hermeneutical Procedure*, 43. She here agrees with M. Harl and dis-
agrees with J. Lebreton: "J. Lebreton, 'Les degrés de la connaissance religieuse
d'après Origène,' *RSR* 12 (1922) pp. 265–296, argues for fixed groups of Christians,
M. Harl, *Origène et la fonction révélatrice du Verbe Incarné* (PatSor 2, 1958), pp. 264–268,
argues for a hierarchy of stages rather than of classes," p. 43.

[84] Torjesen, *Hermeneutical Procedure*, 43.

[85] Ibid.

[86] Ibid., 41.

[87] Ibid.

[88] Torjesen, *Hermeneutical Procedure*, 41, esp. n. 52, emphasis added.

[89] Ibid. In contrast to Torjesen's view, this work will show that while Scripture's
body, soul and spirit (in *Princ.* 4.2.4) are doctrines that correspond to the human
soul's levels of progress toward perfection and salvation, they *also* are, for Origen,
senses of meaning through which Scripture instructs and edifies the human soul.
Logic does not dictate against Scripture's body, soul and spirit being *senses of meaning* which *teach* the human soul how to pass through the various levels of spiritual
progress. Chapter 2 of this work will explain how in *Princ.* 4 (including 4.2.4 and
4.2.6) Origen promotes three separate (bodily, soul's and spiritual) senses of scriptural meaning.

on Psalm 37, for example, she observes four steps: First, Origen
reads the verse aloud. Second, he interprets the verse, trying to capture the attitude conveyed by the words of the Psalmist in the text.
Third, he reads the verse aloud in the first person so that the audience will personalize it. Fourth, he repeats the first step so that the
audience can meditate on the verse again, now laden with personalized meaning.[90] Torjesen proposes that, in this way, Origen makes
the words of Scripture relevant to his audience.[91]

While Torjesen presents the four steps together as comprising
Origen's exegetical method, she acknowledges that the second step
is the locus of his interpretation of the biblical text:

> The decisive step is clearly the second one. In the description of the
> attitude of the one who prays these words, Origen describes both the
> Psalmist and the hearer, through an identity which they have in com-
> mon. . . . The identity which both the Psalmist and the hearers have
> in common, is the identity of the sinner who prays.[92]

Torjesen acknowledges that Origen determines the "attitude, experience and self-understanding" of the Psalmist in the second step,
which he then applies to his audience in the third step.[93] Still, she
considers the whole four-step process to constitute a "system for interpreting" Scripture that is unified by Origen's understanding of the
"literal meaning of the text"[94] as the "journey of the soul."[95] She
considers this multi-step process, which is discernible in his practice—and not the threefold description of Scripture in *Princ.* 4.2.4—

---

[90] Torjesen, *Hermeneutical Procedure*, 27–28; also idem, "Origen's Interpretation of
the Psalms," in *International Conference on Patristic Studies (8th: 1979: Oxford, England)* (5
vols., StPatr 17; ed. Elizabeth A. Livingstone; Oxford: Pergamon, 1982) 2:944–958.

[91] In *Hermeneutical Procedure*, Torjesen demonstrates how this four-step approach is
present also, though sometimes amounting to more or less than four steps, in
Origen's treatment of texts which convey situations or events, e.g., crossing the Red
Sea, and not only for texts that convey self-reflections or prayers, such as the Psalms.
She also shows how the approach is similar in Origen's treatments of all genres of
scriptural text, spanning both the Old and New Testaments. She also analyzes
Origen's *Hom. Cant.* 1 according to this same approach ("'Body,' 'Soul,' and 'Spirit,'"
24–28).

[92] Torjesen, *Hermeneutical Procedure*, 28.

[93] Ibid., 27.

[94] Here, Torjesen seems to mean by "literal meaning" the *proper* meaning of the
text—the meaning intended by its author, who, in Origen's view, is the Holy Spirit.
See footnote 9 at the beginning of the Introduction to this work for an explanation of the term "literal" in the context of Origen's exegesis.

[95] Torjesen, *Hermeneutical Procedure*, 29, 32.

to represent Origen's "exegetical hermeneutic of the text" for extracting Scripture's spiritual, Christ-centered messages.[96]

Rowan A. Greer

With Origen's other proponents, Greer concurs that Origen interprets Scripture according to a Christian, spiritual purpose mainly through the distinction between a literal and a spiritual meaning.[97] Greer explains that Origen's theoretical distinction between Scripture's "soul" and "spirit" in *Princ.* 4.2.4 points not to separate nonliteral meanings, but to separate "dimensions" or aspects of his one "allegorical meaning."[98] In practice, Greer observes, Origen distinguishes between Scripture's "letter" or "body," as the literal, "narrative meaning," and its "spirit," as the figurative, or "allegorical meaning,"[99] the latter of which carries moral and other, spiritual focuses.[100]

Beyond these views, Greer adds insight into Origen's understanding of Scripture's transformative effects:

---

[96] Torjesen, "'Body,' 'Soul,' and 'Spirit,'" 22. The current work's own thesis will suggest that what Torjesen refers to as the "exegetical hermeneutic of the text"—the multi-step process—is actually Origen's "pedagogical hermeneutic" for delivering the meaning of the text to his audience. In contrast, the three senses of scriptural meaning (bodily, soul's and spiritual) constitute the exegetical method that he employs to extract a biblical passage's meanings from the text itself—during what Torjesen refers to as the second step of his process of presentation (in her example of his homily on Psalm 37).

[97] See Greer, "The Christian Bible and Its Interpretation," in *Early Biblical Interpretation* (Rowan A. Greer and James L. Kugel; LEC 3, Philadelphia: Westminster, 1986) 107–208, esp. 180; also idem, *Origen,* 31. For additional articulations of the view that Origen is concerned in practice principally with the twofold distinction between the literal and spiritual levels of scriptural meaning, see Robert M. Grant, *The Bible in the Church: A Short History of Interpretation* (New York: MacMillan, 1948), 69; and Wiles, "Origen as Biblical Scholar," 467–468. In a later work, Grant further states that "as he grew older Origen adhered less closely to his basic [threefold] theory as set forth in the *De Principiis....*" (*The Letter and the Spirit* [London: SPCK, 1957], 104). On the contrary, chapter 3 will consider the later articulations of a threefold theory in Origen's homilies and demonstrate their continuity with the exegetical theory that he set forth earlier in *Princ.* 4.

[98] Greer, *Early Biblical Interpretation,* 180. Thus, we might understand Greer to support, on the one hand, de Lubac's second category for the moral meaning as an aspect of one nonliteral, spiritual Christian sense and, on the other, Torjesen's claim that Origen does not propose separate nonliteral senses in *Princ.* 4.

[99] Ibid.

[100] On the contrary, later chapters, esp. chapters 4 and 5, will demonstrate that Origen relies on the practical distinction between the moral (psychic) and spiritual (pneumatic) senses in order to draw on their mutually informing relationship so as to effect more fully the spiritual transformation of his audience.

Indeed, Origen virtually identifies the spiritual life with the interpretation of Scripture, since to begin to penetrate the deeper meaning of
the sacred text is to participate so far as possible in the ultimate realities that mark the Christian's destiny.[101]

Daniélou observed that Origen "was able to find in the Scriptures
adumbrations of Christian spirituality,"[102] and Torjesen stated that,
for Origen, the "teaching in Scripture . . . refers to an ordering of
doctrines that corresponds to the progressive steps of the soul's movement toward perfection."[103] Yet, here, Greer seems to say more,
stressing that Origen views the believer's interaction with Scripture
not only to lead to the spiritual life but also to be *identical with it*.
Greer arguably suggests that, for Origen, Scripture defines and facilitates the Christian spiritual life, opening this life up to the advancing believer, and, indeed, unfolding into that life itself.

By implication, this insight also suggests that Origen draws his
exegetical purpose and method from Scripture itself.[104] If Origen
identifies the interpretation of Scripture with the spiritual life itself,
then the exegete's task as spiritual director should stem directly from
Scripture's own nature.

Greer arguably touches upon a description of this spiritually transformative nature of Scripture—and, thus, the exegete's method, for
Origen—when he speaks about the "dialectic" between contemplation and moral action.[105] In the course of explaining why Origen
holds to the already Jewish custom of reserving the Song of Songs
for the more mature in faith, that is, those who are better trained
in the interpretation and understanding of Scripture, Greer analyzes
Origen's description of Scripture's education of the soul in the prologue to his *Comm. Cant.*:

Origen's conviction may be related to his understanding of the dialectic between contemplation and action or the life of virtue. Moral
purification is what enables the contemplation of divine truths. The
further Christians have progressed in the virtuous life, the more fully

---

[101] Greer, *Early Biblical Interpretation*, 180.
[102] Daniélou, *Gospel Message*, 278.
[103] Torjesen, "'Body, 'Soul,' and 'Spirit,'" 20–21.
[104] Daniélou does stress that in *Princ.* 4 Origen argued that Scripture is divinely
inspired in content and in form (*Gospel Message*, 280–281; and the discussion of
Daniélou's analysis above).
[105] Greer, *Early Biblical Interpretation*, 191.

they are able to pray and to perceive the mysterious spiritual meaning of Scripture. Interpreting Scripture is a spiritual task. Equally, the mature understanding of Scripture provides solid food for the Christian and enables further moral and spiritual growth. Virtue leads to vision, and vision empowers virtue. A dialectic is established between contemplation and action; and in terms of the function of Scripture, it is virtue that opens its meaning, while it is the apprehension of Scripture's meaning that gives the believer the power to live the Christian life. Origen's view is typical and sets the context in which we may consider the moral and spiritual function of biblical interpretation, that is, the way in which Scripture shapes and guides the Christian life.[106]

Greer explains that Origen, as "typical" of early church fathers, considers that Scripture's purpose, with respect to the advanced hearer, "fully trained in interpreting Scripture," is to transform him by establishing this dialectic between "contemplation" (or the understanding of Scripture's mysterious truths) and "action" (or growth in the life of virtue).[107] Greer observes that it is the growth in virtue that "opens" to the hearer Scripture's spiritual "meaning."

Taken with Greer's first insight about Scripture not only directing but also embodying the person's spiritual life, this second insight could suggest that Scripture also embodies this dialectic between moral action and contemplation by an interaction between figurative moral and spiritual meanings within it. Later chapters of the current work will build upon Greer's important insights by arguing that Origen understands spiritual growth to be effected through the hearer's intimate interaction with Scripture, because it embodies this process of growth through a dialectic between moral and contemplative themes within it. This work will demonstrate that the relationship between two separate moral (psychic) and spiritual (pneumatic) senses embodies this dialectic. Through their practical interrelationship, they lead Scripture's hearers through a transformation toward the spiritual life that signifies salvation. In relation, this work will show that, since Origen views Scripture as the embodiment of the spiritual life, he understands that the exegete finds this guide for spiritual direction (indeed, the right interpretive method) in Scripture itself.

---

[106] Ibid.
[107] Ibid.

II. *The Main Contributions of this Work*

Scholarly debates over the subjectivity of Origen's exegesis have directed the discussion of whether his work is worthy of study and relevant to Christian faith today. Because they perceive that Origen treats Scripture personally in a way that ignores its text and distorts its meaning, de Faye and Hanson dismiss his exegesis as a Platonizing tool. They charge him with intellectual treason, claiming that he uses the authoritative status ascribed by some to Scripture in order to justify views not even relevant to its human authors' intentions.[108]

However, the other scholars under review convincingly urge us to judge Origen's treatment of Scripture according to his own, and not the modern biblical scholar's, understanding of its intended meaning. In *Princ.* 4 Origen clearly states that the Holy Spirit wrote Scripture and structured it to edify the hearer and lead him toward salvation.[109] De Lubac and Daniélou point out that his exegesis strives to fulfill this spiritual purpose.

Origen's other defenders argue that this spiritual aim justifies a subjective approach to Scripture. According to Crouzel, Origen perceives himself to be a spiritual director to his listeners, bringing his own wisdom and personal experience to his readings of Scripture in order to facilitate their spiritually transformative effects on his listeners. Torjesen acknowledges that Origen brings out Scripture's moral and mystical pedagogies, which work together to lead the human soul upward to God. Greer similarly observes that, for Origen, Scripture interacts with the diligent hearer, bringing him into a dialectic between the contemplative (spiritual) and active (moral) lives, so that he can ascend to God.

All of these explanations suggest that Origen understands Scripture to engage dynamically with its hearers. In fact, as Torjesen points out, Origen recognizes Christ, the Incarnate Logos, as the teacher and content of Scripture. Thus, as later chapters will show, for Origen, communication with Scripture is communication with Christ. Because of this, one should come personally to Scripture and expect Scripture to come personally to him. Origen's defenders, then, have

---

[108] As discussed at the beginning of this chapter, these critics judge Origen's exegesis against the standards of the modern historical-critical method of scriptural interpretation.

[109] Chapter 2 will examine thoroughly the theory in *Princ.* 4.

grasped the richness of his exegesis, which stems from his reverence for a living, breathing text.[110]

Still, all the scholars discussed have left it unclear *how* Origen specifically draws out Scripture's transformative meanings for his listeners. It is one thing to declare his exegesis relevant to faith today, but quite another to explain how to apply it. In order to understand his method of interpretation, it is necessary to consider his theoretical claims and how and to what extent he applies them in practice.

Most of Origen's defenders acknowledge that Origen's theory and practice are inconsistent. They agree that he claims a middle, moral sense in the theory of *Princ.* 4 but does not employ it in practice as a separate meaning from his one, spiritual sense. Hanson points to this inconsistency as evidence that Origen intended his allegorical method as a facade for reading Scripture in a self-serving way. De Lubac, however, does not correlate inconsistency with either bad intentions or erroneous results, but he does find that Origen does not offer a separate, Christian moral sense in practice. He finds either a moral meaning that is Philonic and not peculiar to Christian faith or one that is merely part of the larger, spiritual sense. For Hanson, de Lubac's second category of moral meaning signals in Origen's practice one overly broad and, therefore, meaningless spiritual sense that serves as a depository for Origen's extraneous, philosophical views.

However, Daniélou, Crouzel, Torjesen, and Greer join de Lubac's view that Origen legitimately draws spiritual meanings out of Scripture, despite the question of a moral sense in his theory and practice. They stress that Origen seeks to facilitate Scripture's spiritual purpose mainly in the distinction and relationship between a literal and a nonliteral, spiritual sense of meaning.

Torjesen offers an innovative critique of the question surrounding the moral sense, arguing that in his threefold theory in *Princ.* 4.2.4 Origen speaks of *doctrines* in Scripture instead of *senses* of meaning.

---

[110] For another possible approach to defending Origen's allegorical treatment of Scripture against de Faye's and Hanson's charges that he personalized the text to distortion in order to promote Platonic views, see John David Dawson (*Allegorical Readers and Cultural Revision in Ancient Alexandria* [Berkeley and Los Angeles: University of California Press, 1992). He explains how a variety of early Alexandrian allegorists, including Philo and Clement, used Scripture as a framework within which they revised the philosophical and cultural norms of their day, rather than the reverse view that they employed the prevailing norms to revise Scripture.

She locates his exegetical method, instead, in his practice where she finds a multistep process by which he brings Scripture's meanings to his listeners.

Still, Origen's defenders have not clarified *how* Origen interprets the meaning of a biblical passage that he then conveys to his listeners for their spiritual transformation. This work seeks to answer this question by providing a clear explanation of the relationship between Origen's theory and practice. If he posits three categories of doctrine or teaching in *Princ.* 4, why can they not also be senses of meaning? If they are senses of meaning, how does he define them? Once we understand their definitions, can we locate them in his practice? Finally, if the moral and spiritual senses are separate, do they relate in a way that is relevant to how Origen perceives them to transform Scripture's hearer?

In response to these questions this work concludes the following: First, Origen does define three senses of meaning fully and clearly in theory. Second, his practice promotes them as separate senses. Third, the nonliteral, moral sense, and more specifically its practical distinction from and relationship with the other nonliteral, spiritual sense, is the key to his exegetical effort to effect Scripture's spiritual purpose of transforming its hearer in preparation for salvation.

In relation to these three main findings, this work more specifically concludes that the moral sense is not "absorbed" or "fused" into the spiritual sense, as Hanson argues. Rather, in both theory and practice Origen presents a moral (psychic) sense that provides its own message, which, when viewed within the context of its relationship with the spiritual (pneumatic) sense, clearly focuses on Christ. In practice Origen allows each sense to reinforce the spiritual effects of the other's message on his hearer. Their distinction allows their relation, and their relation embodies the dialectic between what Greer calls moral action and contemplation and what Torjesen refers to as Scripture's moral and mystical pedagogies.

CHAPTER TWO

EARLIER EXEGETICAL THEORY

This chapter reviews Origen's earliest extant statement of exegetical theory in *Princ.* 4.[1] As discussed in the prior chapter, recent scholars argue that, even if Origen does claim a middle, nonliteral psychic (sometimes labeled "moral") sense in this work—in addition to the literal somatic (sometimes labeled "historical") sense and a second, nonliteral pneumatic (sometimes labeled "spiritual") sense—he does not clearly define it.[2] These same scholars also find that, in practice, he does not employ a psychic sense that provides a separate Christian meaning from the pneumatic sense. Torjesen goes even further by arguing that he never claimed three senses of scriptural meaning either in theory or practice. This chapter's close analysis of the theory set forth in *Princ.* 4 demonstrates that Origen offers a method of exegesis that relies on three senses or meanings of Scripture, and he defines the distinct focus and function of each sense when applied to a biblical passage.[3]

---

[1] Origen likely wrote *De Principiis* during 229–230 C.E.; see the time chart in the introduction to this work. All translations from *De Principiis*, except for those expressly my own, are from Butterworth, *Origen*. This study employs the following Greek and Latin editions: Henri Crouzel and Manlio Simonetti, trans. and eds., *Origène: Traité des Principes*, 4 vols. (SC 252, 253, 268, 269; Paris: Cerf, 1978, 1980). Butterworth's English translation appears within the text of the paper and the corresponding Greek text or the Latin translation in the footnotes. With regard to the original language, this analysis refers chiefly to the available Greek, since that is the language of Origen's pen. However, because many homilies and biblical commentaries that are treated in later chapters are extant only in Rufinus' or Jerome's Latin translations (especially Rufinus'), this chapter pays due attention to the available, relevant Latin language in *De Principiis* as well.

[2] This chapter explains why the transliterations of Origen's Greek terms for the three senses—somatic, psychic and pneumatic—are more informative than the generally employed terms—literal/historical, moral and spiritual. Also, at appropriate places, this chapter's analysis provides logical conjecture as to why the less descriptive term "moral" was the main referent for the psychic sense in the past.

[3] Origen fills out these definitions in later homiletic explications of his theory, which the next chapter will review. By first establishing that he offers the basic framework for his threefold method in *Princ.* 4 and then observing how he completes it in his extended theory, it will be possible in the final two chapters of this

I. *Origen's Audience and Polemic*

In order to appreciate fully Origen's presentation of a threefold exegetical method in *Princ.* 4, it is useful to begin with a consideration of his perceived audience and what he wishes to convey to them. The following analysis is merely a suggested reading of Origen's purpose in the text. Although it provides a useful context for his discussion and sheds light on its details, this chapter's observation that Origen defines three separate senses of meaning in *Princ.* 4 will stand on its own.

We must consider the fourth book of *De Principiis* within the larger context of the whole work. Butterworth likens the treatise to other texts of Origen's day that deal with questions concerning the origin of the cosmos, human nature, and the like, which were discussed in the various Christian and other philosophical schools of the time.[4] In his preface to the first book, Origen explains that, because "[m]any of those . . . who profess to believe in Christ[ ] hold conflicting opinions" about issues of both great and lesser importance to faith, he finds it "necessary . . . to lay down a definite line and unmistakable rule" for each major issue,[5] including God's nature, creation, human nature, evil, the Incarnation and salvation.[6] By presenting the orthodox view of all such issues—measured by a pious view of God and recognition of God's love for humankind[7]—Origen hopes to enable church leaders to teach believers how to live according to his understanding of true Christian principles.

---

work to recognize that he uses the two separate nonliteral—psychic and pneumatic—senses within his practice as defined by his theory. Only by perceiving their distinction can the student of Origen witness how they relate for the spiritual benefit of Scripture's hearer.

[4] Butterworth, *Origen*, xxxi. Also, Brian E. Daley explains how *De Principiis* compares to similar works by other authors both previous to and contemporary with Origen, stressing its uniquely cohesive Christian and biblically-based character: "[I]t deals with the first principles of a coherent doctrinal system that allows the believing reader to find in the Christian Bible the wisdom that alone gives life" ("Origen's *De Principiis*: A Guide to the Principles of Christian Scriptural Interpretation," in *Nova & Vetera: Patristic Studies in Honor of Thomas Patrick Halton* [ed. John Petruccione; Washington, D.C.: Catholic University of America: 1998], 3–21, quoting 21).

[5] *Princ.* Pref. 1.2 (Butterworth, 1–2); SC 252:78.

[6] *Princ.* Pref. 1 (Butterworth, 1–6); SC 252:76–88.

[7] Rufinus, in the preface to his Latin translation of *De Principiis*, captures Origen's desire to convey orthodoxy by explaining that Origen wishes in this work to turn others to "piety" (τό εὐσέβεια; in Rufinus' Latin, *pietas*) in matters concerning the faith (*Princ.* Ruf. Pref. 3 [Butterworth, lxiii]; SC 252:72). In *Princ.* 3, Origen defines "piety" as "observ[ing] the idea of God, [who is] just and good according to sound

Scripture is integral to this endeavor, because Origen wants to offer "a connected body of doctrine" by using the "illustrations and declarations" found in Scripture.[8] Scripture, for Origen, contains the teachings of Christ himself who "is the truth," and, as the "Word of God," he spoke to Moses and the prophets as well as the apostles.[9] Christ's words are the only "source" of the "knowledge which calls men to lead a good and blessed life,"[10] and the "Holy Spirit [has] inspired their composition" into human language.[11]

Since the Holy Spirit composed Scripture,[12] its deepest meanings are not easy to decipher. It provides not only "obvious" but also "hidden" "meaning,"[13] since "the contents of scripture are the outward forms of certain mysteries and the images of divine things."[14] Origen points out that, even though "the entire Church is unanimous" that the "whole law is spiritual, the inspired meaning is not recognized by all."[15] Rather, only those with "the grace of the Holy Spirit in the word of wisdom and knowledge" grasp its deeper meanings.[16] To this end, after using Scripture to establish for his audience the "manifest proof for our statements" of orthodox faith in the first three books of *De Principiis*, Origen explains in the fourth book "the manner in which [the divine scriptures] are to be read and understood"—"the method" by which they—both the writings of the Old and New Testaments—"ought to be interpreted."[17]

---

doctrine" (*Princ.* 3.1.17, 3.1.9 [my own translation; but see also Butterworth, 193, 171] cf., SC 268:106–108, 52–54).

[8] *Princ.* Pref. 1.10 (Butterworth, 6); SC 252:88. Origen states that he intends the right interpretation of Scripture to be confirmed by logic or reason, but he places primacy on the authority of Scripture.

[9] *Princ.* Pref. 1.1 (quoting John 14:6; Butterworth, 1); SC 252:76.

[10] *Princ.* Pref. 1.1 (Butterworth, 1); SC 252:76.

[11] *Princ.* 4.3.15 (Butterworth, 312); SC 268:398.

[12] Sometimes Origen states that the Holy Spirit inspired the composition of Scripture and at other times that the Holy Spirit composed Scripture. For an occurrence of the latter, see *Princ.* Pref. 1.8 (Butterworth 5); SC 252:84. Origen seems to equate "composition" with "inspiration" when discussing the Holy Spirit's role in relation to Scripture.

[13] *Princ.* Pref. 1.8 (Butterworth, 5); SC 252:84, 86.

[14] *Princ.* Pref. 1.8 (Butterworth, 5); SC 252:86.

[15] *Princ.* Pref. 1.8 (Butterworth, 5); SC 252:86.

[16] *Princ.* Pref. 1.8 (Butterworth, 5); SC 252:86.

[17] *Princ.* 4.1.1, 4.2.1 (Butterworth, 256, 269); SC 268:256, 258; and 268:292. The Greek word for "method" here is τὴν ὁδὸν (ἡ ὁδός), which means way, path or road, as well as method or system. Origen stresses that his method should be applied to the New Testament as well as to the Hebrew Scriptures. *Princ.* 4.2.3 (Butterworth, 274); SC 268:306.

Recent scholars agree that Origen addresses church leaders in *De Principiis*.[18] In his presentation of method, to which we now turn, Origen indicates that he addresses presbyters and elders[19]—that is, those who can comprehend Scripture's deeper meanings and, thus, must, like Origen, judge what teachings are orthodox in accordance with apostolic succession and then convey their saving truths to the rest of the faithful. While the prevailing view is that Origen was not yet ordained a presbyter (one with authority to preach at the pulpit) at the time of writing *De Principiis*,[20] he arguably led the catechetical school in Alexandria at the time and, thus, was an authority on right doctrine. He perceived himself, then, to be a teacher to the church's presbyters.

To persuade this audience of his authority to teach the right method of scriptural interpretation, Origen stresses that his method is a non-negotiable aspect of Christian faith, handed down through apostolic succession:

> Now the reason why all those we have mentioned hold false opinions and make impious or ignorant assertions about God appears to be nothing else but this, that scripture is not understood in its spiritual sense, but is interpreted according to the bare letter. On this account we must explain to those who believe that the sacred books are not the works of men, but that they were composed and have come down to us as a result of the inspiration of the Holy Spirit by the will of the Father of the universe through Jesus Christ, what are the methods of interpretation that appear right to us, who keep to the rule of the heavenly Church of Jesus Christ through the succession from the Apostles.[21]

---

[18] For example, Daley and Torjesen explain that in *Princ.* 4 Origen addresses other leaders in the church, namely preachers and teachers, instructing them on how to present Scripture to their own audiences (Daley, "Origen's *De Principiis*," 15–16; Torjesen, *Hermeneutical Procedure*, 39–40; and idem, "'Body,' 'Soul,' and 'Spirit,'" generally).

[19] In *Princ.* 4.2.4, Origen refers to Hermas' *The Shepherd* as an inspired text that supports his claim to *three* senses of scriptural meaning. While the latter half of this chapter will examine this passage in detail, here it is worth noting that one can understand Origen to suggest (albeit implicitly) that he is Hermas who instructs other teachers within the church how to convey the right interpretation of Scripture to the faithful, and, in particular, is responsible himself for teaching the deepest truths to "presbyters or elders (τοῖς πρεσβυτέροις)" in the church, "to men who have grown grey through wisdom" or the church's top leaders (*Princ.* 4.2.4 [Butterworth, 277]); SC 268:314, 316. On this analysis, Origen intends in *De Principiis* to address the most advanced in the faith who are, by that fact, the top leaders in the church—presbyters and elders.

[20] See the time chart in the introduction.

[21] *Princ.* 4.2.2 (Butterworth, 271–272); Αἰτία δὲ πᾶσι τοῖς προειρημένοις ψευδοδοξιῶν

To his audience Origen explains that the discernment of Scripture's
spiritual nature through employment of the threefold method (which
he is about to set forth) is an integral part of the church's κανών,
"rule, or standard." Origen does not present his threefold method
in *De Principiis* casually or even speculatively but as *the* right, divinely-
ordained way of interpreting Scripture. To remain faithful, Origen's
audience *must* interpret Scripture according to the threefold method
that he will set forth.

Within the presentation of his method, Origen further claims
(indeed, repeatedly) that Scripture itself verifies this method. As we
will consider below, not only does Origen point to Prov. 22:20–21
as announcing a method of three senses, but he even shows that
Paul himself, within New Testament epistles, used nonliteral psychic
and pneumatic readings (in addition to literal readings) of the Hebrew
Scriptures. Origen is convinced—and he impresses upon his audience—that his method was not only handed down from Jesus through
the apostles but is also authorized by the text of Scripture itself.
Thus, he assures his audience that he is working in conformity with
the intent of the Holy Spirit who inspired it.[22]

Origen is aware that many persons both within and outside the
church misapply Scripture for their own impious ends. Building upon
this awareness, he describes three dangerously errant approaches to
Scripture.[23] First, the Jews, by refusing to read the Hebrew Scriptures
figuratively, fail to recognize Jesus as the prophesied Messiah.[24] Second,

καὶ ἀσεβειῶν ἢ ἰδιωτικῶν περὶ θεοῦ λόγων οὐκ ἄλλη τις εἶναι δοκεῖ ἢ ἡ γραφὴ
κατὰ τὰ πνευματικὰ μὴ νενοημένη, ἀλλ᾽ ὡς πρὸς τὸ ψιλὸν γράμμα ἐξειλημμένη.
Διόπερ τοῖς πειθομένοις μὴ ἀνθρώπων εἶναι συγγράμματα τὰς ἱερὰς Βίβλους, ἀλλ᾽
ἐξ ἐπιπνοίας τοῦ ἁγίου πνεύματος βουλήματι τοῦ πατρὸς τῶν ὅλων διὰ Ἰησοῦ
Χριστοῦ ταύτας ἀναγεγράφθαι καὶ εἰς ἡμᾶς ἐληλυθέναι, τὰς φαινομένας ὁδοὺς
ὑποδεικτέον, ἐχομένοις τοῦ κανόνος τῆς Ἰησοῦ Χριστοῦ κατὰ διαδοχὴν τῶν ἀποστόλων
οὐρανίου ἐκκλησίας (SC 268:300). The corresponding Latin text reads: Horum
autem omnium falsae intellegentiae causa his quibus supra diximus non alia extitit,
nisi quod sancta scriptura ab his non secundum spiritalem sensum, sed secundum
litterae sonum intellegitur. Propter quod conabimur pro mediocritate sensus nostri
his, qui credunt scripturas sanctas non per humana uerba aliqua esse conpositas,
sed spiritus sancti inspiratione conscriptas et uoluntate dei patris per unigenitum
filium suum Iesum Christum nobis quoque esse traditas et conmissas, quae nobis
uidetur recta esse uia intellegentiae demonstrare obseruantibus illam regulam disci-
plinamque, quam ab Iesu Christo traditam sibi apostoli per successionem posteris
quoque suis caelestem ecclesiam docentibus tradiderunt.
[22] The analysis below will closely consider Origen's claims to the Holy Spirit's
inspiration and construction of Scripture, but also see *Princ.* 4.1 (Butterworth,
256–268); SC 268:256–292.
[23] *Princ.* 4.2.1 (Butterworth, 269–271); SC 268:292–300.
[24] *Princ.* 4.2.1 (Butterworth, 269–270); SC 268:292, 294, 296.

certain heretical groups, implicitly Marcionites as well as some
Christian Gnostic groups, argue that the Hebrew Scriptures present
a second, angry and destructive god who created the material world
and differs from the God of Jesus. They thereby fail to acknowledge
the *one* true Creator and God.[25] Third, certain believers who are
"simpler"—or less mature in the faith—claim to belong to the church
and acknowledge the one true God, but they make up impious fan-
cies about God.[26] Origen does not elaborate, but perhaps these simpler believers fall into impieties because they read Scripture naively,
not yielding to proper guidance from church leadership.

All three groups relate to Scripture incorrectly. The first group,
the Jews, adhere too closely and exclusively to the letter of the
Hebrew Scripture's text. The third group is irresponsible with the
text, reading it without training or direction. The middle group,
though, is the most troublesome for Origen's audience. They are
Marcionites and Christian Gnostics who read literally the portions
of the Hebrew Scriptures that describe an angry, evil God. This
leads them to manufacture fanciful myths about God, creation, Jesus
and salvation, which they often justified by impious allegorical interpretations of other portions of Scripture.

Origen and his audience would have been concerned to protect
the faithful from Marcionites and Christian Gnostics, since their allegorical readings of Scripture resulted in heretical doctrines. They
either rejected the Creator God of the Hebrew Scriptures (such as
with Marcionites) or made God an impersonal first principle in a
process of creative emanation which, at some point, went awry
through a deviant product of that process (such as with Valentinians).
They tended to view Jesus docetically—as a divine being only appearing to be human—who entered this world to teach the right way
back to the good Divinity. To establish these unorthodox views, they
rejected or relied inappropriately on the Hebrew Scriptures and even
misapplied New Testament texts. For example, Valentinians notably

---

[25] *Princ.* 4.2.1 (Butterworth, 270–271); SC 268:296, 298. Daley also explains that
Origen offers "a way of responding to the alternative readings of Christian Scripture
and tradition offered by Gnostic sects" ("Origen's *De Principiis*," 13). Elizabeth A.
Clark also explains that Origen intends in *De Principiis* to guard the faith against
competing Gnostic and deterministic views of his day (*The Origenist Controversy: The
Cultural Construction of an Early Christian Debate* [Princeton: Princeton University Press,
1992], 7).
[26] *Princ.* 4.2.1 (Butterworth, 271); SC 268:298, 300.

employed the Gospel of John to support their erroneous claims that Jesus came to teach a saving knowledge only to the few ones privileged with sparks of the good Divinity so that they would learn how to escape this inherently evil material realm.[27]

Given these abuses, Origen seems to have anticipated that some members of his audience, while they might accept an allegorical interpretation, may wish to place strong constraints on the use of allegory to teach doctrines about Christ and the salvation process. Such persons would be concerned to avoid any resemblance to Marcionite or Gnostic groups and, thus, want to avoid as undisciplined a use of allegory as they practiced. The way in which Origen presents his method, as explained below, suggests that he expected that these members of his audience considered it necessary to read a biblical passage doctrinally, or pneumatically, only in relation to that passage's literally edifying, or somatic, reading. They would be particularly skeptical of an interpretive approach that allowed the interpreter to claim that a biblical passage is devoid of any literally edifying meaning and then draw from it doctrinally significant pneumatic meaning.[28]

Despite the misgivings of some of his audience members, Origen is committed to a method that does not unduly restrict the discovery of pneumatic meaning in Scripture. As mentioned above, he believes that the two Testaments are, through the inspiration of the Holy Spirit, the living word of Jesus Christ, who is the Incarnate Word of God. Engagement with Scripture is conversation with Christ,[29]

---

[27] For Valentinian views and uses of Scripture, see Bentley Layton, *The Gnostic Scriptures* (Garden City, New York: Doubleday, 1987). Also, see Dawson's analysis of Valentinus' allegorical use of Scripture based on his own personal visions of truth and reality, as well as a helpful summary of core, Gnostic beliefs in the early period of the church (*Allegorical Readers*, 127–182).

[28] We could refer to these skeptical, target members of Origen's audience as strict typologists of the day who claimed that future, spiritual persons or events (relating to the Incarnation or Eschaton) were directly tied to past or present, historically true persons or events, since the salvation history relayed in the Scriptures relied on foreshadowings within the context of human history. Origen was criticized in later generations for his lack of sufficient attention to the historical sense of the text. This conflict over a broader "allegorical" and a stricter "typological" approach (the latter dependent on legitimate literal readings of text) to the Christian Scriptures manifested itself in the well-known rivalries between—respectively—the Alexandrian and Antiochene schools of thought concerning exegesis. As the analysis here will show through examination of the content and order of *Princ.* 4, Origen apparently received criticisms of this kind during his life as well.

[29] For Origen's identity of Scripture with Christ, see the comments just above as

and, he believes, no one should constrain Christ from speaking the truth. He realizes that he must convince his skeptical audience members that it is gravely important to allow Christ to offer pneumatic meanings of the text despite abuses of figurative readings by others.

Origen is committed to offering his audience a middle course between a non-allegorical approach that is incapable of seeing predictions of Jesus in the Hebrew Scriptures and wild (undisciplined or imagined) allegorical readings that say impious things about God and Jesus. Origen's audience of presbyters would expect much of what Origen offers them. They were familiar with figurative readings of documents from the larger, cultural world (Christian and non-Christian) in which they lived. The larger Hellenistic society of the Roman Empire had long applied figurative moral meanings to ancient, classical texts such as those of Homer. Even the Jewish scholar of the first century, Philo, sanctioned the use of allegory when reading the Hebrew Scriptures. Also, before Origen, other church fathers, such as Clement of Alexandria, employed allegory in their readings of Scripture.[30] Origen, therefore, draws upon a common practice of treating authoritative texts allegorically for moral and doctrinal guidance, employing the interpretive tools of his day.[31] Despite concerns about "wild" figurative readings of texts, his audience likely expected that an orthodox method of scriptural interpretation would rely on figurative moral and doctrinally significant mystical readings of text. In other words, his audience was prepared to accept an allegorical method, but the content and limits of this method were open to question.

These concerns explain the emphasis and order of *Princ.* 4.1–3. Origen's presentation of his method falls into three main parts: first, the spiritual purpose of Scripture for which the three meanings function, that is, the reason *why* they are to be conveyed to the hearer of Scripture (in 4.1–4.2.3); second, the process of Scripture's communication (by way of an anthropological analogy to Scripture in 4.2.4), that is, *how* the three senses are to affect the hearer; and,

---

well as the discussion of scholars' views, especially those of Torjesen, in chapter 1. Origen develops this concept further in the practical works treated in chapters 3, 4 and 5.

[30] For in-depth analyses of the allegorical approaches of Philo and Clement, see Dawson, *Allegorical Readers*, generally, esp. 73–126, 183–234.

[31] Young, *Biblical Exegesis*, 76–96, 248–264, and 292–295; also Dawson, *Christian Figural Reading*, generally.

third, the definitions of the three meanings, that is, *what* their respective messages convey to the hearer (in 4.2.5–4.2.6).

By each part, Origen stresses the following for his concerned audience members: First, by establishing that the purpose of Scripture, as the Holy Spirit's construction and Christ's own teaching, is to lead its hearers to salvation, Origen suggests that any undue restriction of its meaning is a restriction of the Holy Spirit as well as Christ, and, in addition, an impediment to leading others to salvation. Second, by explaining that there are three senses and that they are similar to the human person's body, soul and spirit and guide hearers through the various stages of progress toward salvation, he stresses that they work as an integral whole. Each is indispensable to the fulfillment of Scripture's purpose. Third, when the target members finally hear the definitions, they understand that they are to accept them without alteration as constituting the divinely inspired and apostolically ordained method of scriptural interpretation.

Still, recent scholars, as discussed in chapter 1, argue that Origen does not give any real significance to the psychic sense in this early theory, nor does he really define it. Yet, as discussed, he seems to realize that certain presbyters are especially sensitive to unrestrained *pneumatic* readings. In other words, they are worried not about psychic/moral readings, but about limitless pneumatic/doctrinal readings, because of the undisciplined allegorical readings that Christian Gnostics use to support their own errant doctrinal views. Thus, after the three-step presentation, he spends the remainder of 4.2 and all of 4.3 explaining the significance and character of the pneumatic sense and its corresponding validity even where the somatic sense is absent.

Origen stresses (in 4.2.7–4.2.9 and all of 4.3) that the Holy Spirit caused some passages to lack a somatic meaning so that Scripture's students will look for figurative meanings.[32] Then he strives to convince his audience that there is pneumatic meaning in Scripture even where the letter does not carry an edifying—somatic—meaning. He stresses the significance of not restricting the pneumatic sense, because it is the meaning that conveys the invisible and eternal truths about Christ and salvation.[33]

---

[32] Origen assures his audience that even where the somatic sense is absent, the pneumatic and the psychic senses are always present (*Princ.* 4.2.5 [Butterworth, 277–278]; SC 268:316, 318).

[33] Based mainly on Heb. 8–10 (in Origen's view written by Paul), Origen explains

Origen ends his discussion of method by emphasizing that "the beginning or the end of all things could not be comprehended by any except our Lord Jesus Christ and the Holy Spirit."[34] By this he arguably suggests that his audience should trust the voice of Scripture's truths, Christ, and its composer, the Holy Spirit, who together will lead the faithful student into pious readings at the pneumatic level. Even though the method of three senses does not restrict the pneumatic sense to a necessary relationship with historically accurate or logical readings of the text's letter, the one who submits faithfully to Scripture's divine guidance will not fall into the errors of invention that characterize Marcionite and Christian Gnostic systems of thought.

In this presentation as a whole, Origen does give less attention to the psychic sense than the pneumatic sense. However, this does not support the conclusion that he considered it a less important aspect of his method. Rather, his audience members likely did not have problems with drawing psychic meanings from passages independently of their literal readings, since Hellenistic, Jewish and Gnostic groups all exercised this same practice in a manner that sought similar understandings of the moral quest for virtue.[35] Moreover, since, as we will see, the pneumatic sense is doctrinally focused, centering directly on God's plan of salvation through Christ, accurate pneumatic readings of text are integral to safeguarding Christianity's unique and orthodox identity. For these reasons, Origen organized the presentation of his threefold method in *Princ.* 4 so as to address principally his target audience's fears regarding the potentially unbounded nature of a doctrinal, pneumatic sense that had led others into heresy.

Still, by expecting Origen to give equal attention to all the senses, recent scholars have tended to look for their definitions in the language of 4.2.4 where he describes the three senses as Scripture's body, soul and spirit, which bring the hearer in successive stages to salvation. As the analysis below will substantiate, that is not the locus of definitions, but, rather, the definitions follow after this section. As

---

that pneumatic truths contain "the heavenly things" of which earthly things are a shadow (4.3.12). Also, he refers to the "eternal gospel" in Rev. 14:6 (in 4.3.13) as the ultimate reality to which the temporal gospel points. For Origen, the pneumatic truths are about this eternal, invisible reality, and historical and literal (somatic) truths in Scripture are significant only as indicators that point persons toward it.

[34] *Princ.* 4.3.14 (Butterworth, 311); SC 268:394.

[35] Young, *Biblical Exegesis,* esp. 248–264; and Dawson, *Allegorical Readers,* generally.

explained, Origen describes Scripture's process of communication *before* he presents the senses' definitions so that his audience will accept the defined senses as an integral whole, each indispensable to the correct method of interpretation.

Because recent scholars have focused so much attention on the language within 4.2.4, this chapter will analyze each of the three main stages of Origen's presentation in the following order: the spiritual purpose, then the definitions, and only lastly the anthropological analogy in 4.2.4. This revised order will make it possible to focus on the definitions outside the shadow of 4.2.4 as well as explore, with these definitions in mind, the significance of Origen's description of the three senses as Scripture's body, soul and spirit.

II. *The Spiritual Purpose of Scripture's Communication*

Foundational to Origen's presentation of the right exegetical method is his conviction that it promotes Scripture's spiritual purpose to guide human beings to "perfection" and "salvation."[36] Origen explains

---

[36] For the term "perfection," see *Princ.* 4.2.7: "to reach perfection" (Butterworth, 283); τῆς τελειότητος τυχεῖν (SC 268:328). The corresponding Latin text reads: anima ad scientiae perfectionem uenire.

For the term "salvation," see *Princ.* 4.2.4; "for man's salvation" (Butterworth, 276); εἰς ἀνθρώπων σωτηρίαν (SC 268:312). The corresponding Latin text reads: ad hominum salutem.

As Origen will explain by his anthropological analogy to Scripture in 4.2.4, this perfection (τελειότης), or completeness, reflects the harmonious internal order of a human person's three parts: the soul chooses to follow the guidance of the human spirit about how to behave and make decisions during this life, while the body submits to the soul, subduing fleshly tendencies.

Throughout his theory and practice, Origen equates this process of perfection with attaining the virtues, or fruit of the Spirit, and eliminating vices. As I will show in later chapters, at times in his practice Origen refers to Gal. 5 for the identification of these virtues and vices. Specifically, he defines the virtues as the fruit of the Holy Spirit. See Gal. 5:22–23 (virtues), 19–21 (vices). A person strengthens his spirit's ability to guide his soul and body by cultivating fully the fruit of the Holy Spirit. The unqualified leadership of the spirit yields perfection, which is prerequisite to salvation, or eternal union with God. This salvation is the person's telos, or end that brings fulfillment.

The Holy Spirit has designed Scripture both to point the human person toward this end and provide him with the way of arriving there, through achieving an internal, perfect ordering of his three parts. As Origen's practical works will reveal, the right ordering of the three human parts is coordinate with an imitation of Christ. Thus, the content of Scripture is Jesus' own teachings, indeed himself, by which, as prophesied in a hidden way through Moses, or the Law, God has "delivered to men the doctrines of salvation," *Princ.* 4.1.2 (Butterworth, 259); ἐμφαίνει

that the Holy Spirit, who composed Scripture,[37] gave it a "divine character"[38] with a twofold "spiritual aim"[39] designed to effect this end. First, the Spirit aims to offer through the meanings "the rich and wise truth about God" that a soul must grasp in order to "reach perfection":[40]

> [This first] purpose [is] that the man who is capable of being taught might by "searching out" and devoting himself to the "deep things" revealed in the mind of the words become partaker of all the doctrines of the Spirit's counsel.[41]

The "deep things" that constitute the perfecting doctrines include truths about the Trinity, the Incarnation, the saving effects of the Cross, and the reasons for sin and the pervasiveness of evil.[42] By

---

θεὸν ἀληθῶς ἐνανθρωπήσαντα σωτηρίας δόγματα τοῖς ἀνθρώποις παραδεδωκέναι (SC 268:266). The corresponding Latin text reads: manifestissime declaratur deum uere esse, qui homo factus salutaria praecepta hominibus tradidit. For Origen's argument that Jesus' coming into the world made manifest the "spiritual nature of Moses' law" which was hidden before the Incarnation, see *Princ.* 4.1.6 (Butterworth, 264–265); SC 268:280, 282.

[37] While Origen's discussion of Scripture's purpose in this text emphasizes the Holy Spirit's role as composer and architect of Scripture, the discussions regarding Origen's audience (just above) and recent scholarly views (in chapter 1) reveal that Origen effectively considers the Holy Spirit and the Word of God (or Christ) to be interchangeably identified as Scripture's author and architect. At times Origen speaks of the Word of God as the determiner of Scripture's contents (*Princ.* 4.2.9), while at other times he speaks of the Holy Spirit in this capacity (*Princ.* 4.1, 4.2.7–8, 4.3.4, 4.3.15).

[38] Origen refers to it as "the divine character of the scriptures." *Princ.* 4.1.1 (Butterworth, 256); περὶ τῶν γραφῶν ὡς θείων (SC 268:258). The corresponding Latin text reads: quod ipsae scripturae diuinae sint, id est dei spiritu inspiratae.

[39] *Princ.* 4.2.7 (Butterworth, 282); ὁ σκοπὸς . . . πνεύματι (SC 268:326).

[40] *Princ.* 4.2.7 (Butterworth, 283); Εἰς δὲ τὰ περὶ τῶν ψυχῶν, οὐκ ἄλλως δυναμένων τῆς τελειότητος τυχεῖν χωρὶς τῆς πλουσίας καὶ σοφῆς περὶ θεοῦ ἀληθείας (SC 268:328). The corresponding Latin text reads: quia nec aliter potest anima ad scientiae perfectionem uenire, nisi diuinae sapientiae fuerit inspirata ueritate.

[41] *Princ.* 4.2.7 (referring to 1 Cor. 2:10; Butterworth, 282); ἵν᾿ ὁ δυνάμενος διδαχθῆναι ἐρευνήσας καὶ τοῖς βάθεσι τοῦ νοῦ τῶν λέξεων ἑαυτὸν ἐπιδούς, κοινωνὸς τῶν ὅλων τῆς βουλῆς αὐτοῦ γένηται δογμάτων (SC 268, 328). Butterworth employs the phrase "in the spiritual meaning" in place of the more exact translation of τοῦ νοῦ: "in the mind." "Spiritual meaning" suggests that Origen refers here only to the third, pneumatic meaning. I suggest that Origen states here that the soul of Scripture's hearer, in order to reach perfection, must eventually grasp the "mind" of the words of Scripture, referring to all three senses of meanings. The corresponding Latin text reads: ut per haec forte in profundo latentem sensum spiritus dei et sermonis usitata narratione aliorsum prospiciente contectum inuestigare potuisset, atque ita socius scientiae spiritus et diuini consilii particeps fieret.

[42] *Princ.* 4.2.7 (Butterworth, 283–284); SC 268:328, 330.

EARLIER EXEGETICAL THEORY

grasping all such truths, the human soul receives the "mind" of Scripture's own words. To reach Scripture's *whole* mind is to achieve perfection and thus eventually salvation.

The Holy Spirit has a second aim: to provide beginners, those who "were unable to endure the burden of investigating matters of such importance,"[43] with edification at a level more easily grasped than that of Scripture's "deep things." For these persons,

> [the Spirit has] conceal[ed] the doctrine relating to the before-mentioned subjects in words forming a narrative that contained a record dealing with the visible creation . . . and also in other stories that recorded the acts of righteous men and the sins that these same men occasionally committed, seeing they were but human, and the deeds of . . . impious men. . . . [T]he intention was to make even the outer covering of the spiritual truths, I mean the bodily part of the scriptures, in many respects not unprofitable but capable of improving the multitude in so far as they receive it.[44]

The Holy Spirit has placed an ἔνδυμα or *indumentum*, "outer covering"—or "clothing"—over Scripture's deeper, "spiritual truths," so that those who are not ready to grasp them may receive beneficial

---

[43] *Princ.* 4.2.8 (Butterworth, 284); δεύτερος ἦν σκοπὸς διὰ τοὺς μὴ δυναμένους τὸν κάματον ἐνεγκεῖν ὑπὲρ τοῦ τὰ τηλικαῦτα εὑρεῖν (SC 268:332). The fuller corresponding Latin text reads: Cum ergo de his talibus et horum similibus spiritui sancto esset intentio inluminare sanctas animas, quae se ministerio dediderant ueritatis, secundo loco habetur ille prospectus, ut propter eos, qui uel non possent uel nollent huic se labori atque industriae tradere, quo haec tanta ac talia edoceri uel agnoscere mererentur, sicut superius diximus, inuolueret et occultaret sermonibus usitatis sub praetexto historiae cuiusdam et narrationis rerum uisibilium arcana mysteria.

[44] *Princ.* 4.2.8 (Butterworth, 284–285); κρύψαι τὸν περὶ τῶν προειρημένων λόγον ἐν λέξεσιν ἐμφαινούσαις διήγησιν περιέχουσαν ἀπαγγελίαν τὴν περὶ τῶν αἰσθητῶν δημιουργημάτων, . . . καὶ ἄλλαις ἱστορίαις, ἀπαγγελλούσαις δικαίων πράξεις καὶ τῶν αὐτῶν τούτων ποτὲ γενόμενα ἁμαρτήματα ὡς ἀνθρώπων, καὶ ἀνόμων καὶ ἀσεβῶν πονηρίας καὶ ἀκολασίας καὶ πλεονεξίας. . . . Προέκειτο γὰρ καὶ τὸ ἔνδυμα τῶν πνευματικῶν, λέγω δὲ τὸ σωματικὸν τῶν γραφῶν, ἐν πολλοῖς ποιῆσαι οὐκ ἀνωφελὲς δυνάμενόν τε τοὺς πολλούς, ὡς χωροῦσι, βελτιοῦν (SC 268:332, 334). The corresponding Latin text reads: Induciter ergo uisibilis creaturae narratio et primi hominis conditio atque figmentum, tum deinde ex illo per successionem prosecuta progenies, nonnulla quoque rerum gestarum, quae a iustis quibusque gesta sunt, referuntur, interdum autem etiam delicta quaedam ipsorum commemorantur tamquam hominum, tum deinde et impiorum scribuntur aliquanta uel inpudice uel nequiter gesta. . . . [Q]uae singula diuina quadam arte sapientiae uelut indumentum quoddam et uelamen spiritalium sensuum texta sunt; et hoc est quod diximus scripturae sanctae corpus: ut etiam per hoc ipsum quod diximus litterae indumentum, sapientiae arte contextum, possent quam plurimi aedificari et proficere, qui aliter non possent.

instruction from the "bodily part," or literal meaning, and, by implication, become ready for those more difficult truths.[45] Thus, Origen explains that Scripture's design is based on more than one meaning so that it can lead its student to perfection and salvation by edifying him at the various stages of progress throughout his journey to this end.

III. *Scripture's Specific Communications: The Definitions*

A. *The Claim to Three Meanings in Scripture*

The method, then, that Origen perceives is one that helps to extract Scripture's meanings. For Origen, Scripture communicates to the individual human soul according to *three* senses of *meaning*. He focuses directly on this point only briefly in *De Principiis*, leading some to conclude that his early theory does not promote three senses.[46] Nonetheless, when he cites Prov. 22:20–21, he clearly indicates that Scripture has *three meanings*:

> The right way . . . of approaching the scriptures and gathering their meaning, is the following, which is extracted from the writings themselves. We find some such rule as this laid down by Solomon in the Proverbs concerning the divine doctrines written therein: "Do you portray them threefold in counsel and knowledge, that you may answer words of truth to those who question you."[47]

---

[45] I will explain below how elsewhere in *Princ.* 4, namely in the early part of 4.2.4, Origen emphasizes that *every* human soul is meant to receive ultimately *all* three senses of scriptural meaning.

[46] Torjesen, *Hermeneutical Procedure*, 35–43; and idem, " 'Body,' 'Soul,' and 'Spirit,' " and the discussion of her views in chapter 1.

[47] *Princ.* 4.2.4 (quoting Prov. 22:20, 21; Butterworth, 275); Ἡ τοίνυν φαινομένη ἡμῖν ὁδὸς τοῦ πῶς δεῖ ἐντυγχάνειν ταῖς γραφαῖς καὶ τὸν νοῦν αὐτῶν ἐκλαμβάνειν ἐστὶ τοιαύτη, ἀπ᾽ αὐτῶν τῶν λογίων ἐξιχνευομένη. Παρὰ τῷ Σολομῶντι ἐν ταῖς Παροιμίαις εὑρίσκομεν τοιοῦτόν τι προστασσόμενον περὶ τῶν γεγραμμένων θείων δογμάτων· Καὶ σὺ δὲ ἀπόγραψαι αὐτὰ τρισσῶς ἐν βουλῇ καὶ γνώσει, τοῦ ἀποκρίνασθαι λόγους ἀληθείας τοῖς προβαλλομένοις σοι (SC 268:310). My own translation of Origen's rendition of Prov. 22:20–21 is: "And you have written these out in a three-fold way by counsel and by knowledge, having distinguished the truths of the words put forth to you." Note that the LXX contains slightly different wording, indicating that Origen's quotation is a paraphrase of LXX Prov. 22:20–21 or is from another or his own translation from the Hebrew: Καὶ σὺ δὲ ἀπόγραψαι αὐτὰ **σεαυτῷ** τρισσῶς **εἰς βουλὴν** καὶ **γνῶσιν ἐπὶ τὸ πλάτος τῆς καρδίας σου. / διδάσκω οὖν σε** ἀληθῆ λόγον καὶ γνῶσιν ἀγαθὴν ὑπακούειν τοῦ ἀποκρίνεσθαι λόγους ἀληθείας τοῖς

Origen is after a method that extracts the *meaning* of Scripture's truth, or "divine doctrines," and does so in a *"threefold"* way. The Greek word νοῦς, translated here as "meaning," also signifies *mind*. The Greek for "approaching," δεῖ ἐντυγχάνειν, renders the introductory phrase more literally as follows: "The right way of how 'one must meet with, appeal to, obtain an audience with or converse with' the scriptures . . ." The Greek word ἐκλαμβάνω, translated here as "gathering," also means to take or choose out, receive, or hear. Origen offers the right way for a person to meet and converse with, or obtain an audience with Scripture so that he may choose out of, and thus receive from, Scripture its own mind.

In Origen's view, his method gets at the very mind of Scripture, at the understanding that it contains and conveys, and the Holy Spirit relates this understanding "in a threefold way (τρισσῶς)," that is, through *three* meanings. That Origen understands "threefold way" to indicate *three meanings* will be confirmed below by analysis of his distinct definitions for three senses as well as other specific language within *Princ.* 4.[48]

B. *The Elements of the Somatic Meaning*

The three senses that Origen defines in this work he labels (in 4.2.4) as the somatic, psychic and pneumatic senses. He only defines the somatic sense indirectly, probably because he views its message, which arises from a literal—straightforward—reading of the text,[49] to be obvious. Also, likely for the reasons discussed above (namely, that he wishes to convince his audience of presbyters that right pneumatic meaning for a biblical passage need not be tied to an edifying literal reading of that same text), Origen is more preoccupied

---

προβαλλομένοις σοι. (The words and endings in boldface are either omitted from Origen's paraphrase or differ in declination from it). Note also the corresponding Latin text: Verum, ut dicere coeperamus, uiam, quae nobis uidetur recta esse ad intellegendas scripturas et sensum earum requirendum, huiusmodi esse arbitramur, sicut ab ipsa nihilominus scriptura, qualiter de ea sentiri debeat, edocemur. Apud Salomonem in Prouerbiis inuenimus tale aliquid de diuinae scripturae obseruantia praecipi. *Et tu* inquit *describe tibi haec tripliciter in consilio et scientia, et ut respondeas uerba ueritatis his, qui proposuerunt tibi.*

[48] For example, see his treatment of the "two or three firkins" in John 2:6 at *Princ.* 4.2.5, examined later in this chapter.

[49] As explained in the introduction, n. 9, this works understands that for Origen the term "literal" signifies the straightforward, non-figurative reading (as he understands it), as opposed to a metaphorical reading, of the text.

with explaining the somatic sense's absence from some biblical passages than offering a direct description of its edifying message when
it is present. Yet, in the course of arguing its occasional absence, as
well as why and when this absence occurs, he reveals the basic elements of this first sense.

Origen sets the stage for distinguishing the somatic sense from the
two other senses in the following way:

> [S]ince there are certain passages of scripture which . . . have no bod-
> ily sense at all, there are occasions when we must seek only for the
> soul and the spirit . . . of the passage.[50]

For "bodily [or somatic] sense" here Origen employs the Greek word
σωματικόν, the substantive adjective for the noun σῶμα (in Latin,
corpus). In this statement Origen reveals that this "body" is not only
a sense separate from the "soul" and "spirit" of Scripture, but it is
absent from some biblical passages.[51] By logical implication, if the
somatic sense is not always present, it cannot be equivalent to the
"literal" reading, that is, the actual letter or words of the text. Since
all biblical passages necessarily are made up of letters and words,
there is a literal reading for every passage. However, Origen explicitly states that there is *not* a somatic meaning in every biblical passage. Thus, Origen does not consider the terms "somatic" and "literal"
to be synonymous.[52]

If the somatic sense is not equivalent to the literal reading of the
text, then what is it? Two components of the somatic sense are substantiated in Origen's discussion of its absence from some passages.
First, the somatic sense is derived from *a literal* reading of the text,

---

[50] *Princ.* 4.2.5 (Butterworth, 277–278); Ἀλλ᾽ ἐπεί εἰσί τινες γραφαὶ τὸ σωματικὸν
οὐδαμῶς ἔχουσαι, ὡς ἐν τοῖς ἐξῆς δείξομεν, ἔστιν ὅπου οἱονεὶ τὴν ψυχὴν καὶ τὸ
πνεῦμα τῆς γραφῆς μόνα χρὴ ζητεῖν (SC 268:316). The corresponding Latin text
reads: Illud sane non est ignorandum, esse quaedam in scripturis, in quibus hoc
quod diximus corpus, id est consequentia historialis intellegentiae, non semper inuenitur, sicut in consequentibus demonstrabimus; et est ubi ea quam diximus anima
uel spiritus solummodo intellegenda sunt. Note that Rufinus aligns *corpus* with *historialis*, perhaps because he does not think the Latin readers will understand *corpus*
right off to refer to the literal narrative meaning of the text.

[51] In this statement, Origen also implies that the other two senses, those of the
"soul" and "spirit," *are* present for every biblical passage. I will analyze this point
in Origen's exegetical theory later when discussing his definitions for the psychic
and pneumatic senses.

[52] Since Rufinus equated *corpus* and *historialis* here for Latin readers (see n. 51
above), it is possible that the Latin translation has effectively overstated Origen's
intended identity of the somatic sense with the literal reading of the text.

rather than a metaphorical interpretation. Second, it *edifies* the hearer of Scripture, presumably when the literal reading directly aids Scripture's goal of leading the hearer toward perfection and salvation. The somatic sense, then, is the literal reading that spiritually benefits the hearer.

First, when Origen explains why the somatic sense is sometimes absent, he employs terms that emphasize its rendering from a literal reading of text:

> [T]he intention was to make even the outer covering of the spiritual truths, I mean the bodily sense of the scriptures, in many respects not unprofitable but capable of improving the multitude in so far as they receive it. But if the usefulness of the law and the sequence and ease of the narrative were at first sight clearly discernible throughout, we should be unaware that there was anything beyond the obvious meaning for us to understand in the scriptures.[53]

In this passage, Origen speaks of the "bodily sense," σωματικόν, as Scripture's "obvious meaning," the "law" and "narrative" of Scripture, and the "outer covering of the spiritual truths."

The substantive adjective πρόχειρον, translated here as "obvious meaning," also means at hand or handy, readily accessible or external, and ready, easy, convenient, common or ordinary. Butterworth translates Rufinus' corresponding Latin phrase, *quod prima fronte indicabatur*, as "what was indicated at a first glance." The Latin term *frons*, translated here as "glance," means the forepart or front of a thing, as well as the outside, exterior or appearance of a thing. Thus, by πρόχειρον, Origen identifies, and Rufinus understands him to identify, the somatic sense as Scripture's readily accessible exterior or appearance, the common or ordinary meaning that does not require interpretation by way of analogies or implication.

---

[53] *Princ.* 4.2.8–9 (Butterworth, 285); Προέκειτο γὰρ καὶ τὸ ἔνδυμα τῶν πνευματικῶν, λέγω δὲ τὸ σωματικὸν τῶν γραφῶν, ἐν πολλοῖς ποιῆσαι οὐκ ἀνωφελὲς δυνάμενόν τε τοὺς πολλούς, ὡς χωροῦσι, βελτιοῦν. Ἀλλ' ἐπείπερ, εἰ δι' ὅλων σαφῶς τὸ τῆς νομοθεσίας χρήσιμον αὐτόθεν ἐφαίνετο καὶ τὸ τῆς ἱστορίας ἀκόλουθον καὶ γλαφυρόν, ἠπιστήσαμεν ἂν ἄλλο τι παρὰ τὸ πρόχειρον νοεῖσθαι δύνασθαι ἐν ταῖς γραφαῖς (SC 268:334, 336). The corresponding Latin text reads: quae singula diuina quadam arte sapientiae uelut indumentum quoddam et uelamen spiritalium sensuum texta sunt; et hoc est quod diximus scripturae sanctae corpus: ut etiam per hoc ipsum quod diximus litterae indumentum, sapientiae arte contextum, possent quam plurimi aedificari et proficere, qui aliter non possent. Sed quoniam, si in omnibus indumenti huius, id est historiae, legis fuisset consequentia custodita et ordo seruatus, habentes continuatum intellegentiae cursum non utique crederemus esse aliud aliquid in scripturis sanctis intrinsecus praeter hoc, quod prima fronte indicabatur, inclusum.

The Greek and Latin terms for the synonymous phrase "the law and the sequence and ease of the narrative" also suggest the literal reading of the text. The Greek term for the law comes from the noun νομοθεσία, which means "legislation," and the corresponding Latin phrase, *legis consequentia*, means "the consequence or succession of the law." The Greek noun ἱστορία, translated here as "narrative," also means history or historical narrative, as does the corresponding Latin term *historia*. Origen finds, and Rufinus understands him to find, the somatic sense in the literal language of Scripture's law and history, rendering moral instruction from its law as well as historical information from its narrative.

The Greek and Latin terms translated as the "outer covering of the spiritual truths" also indicate the literal reading of biblical texts. The Greek term ἔνδυμα, translated here as "outer covering," means garment, or that which covers over something else. The Latin translation speaks of the *corpus*, or body, of Scripture as the *litterae indumentum*, or outer covering of the letter. As does ἔνδυμα, *indumentum* means garment, clothing, or covering. Both terms can refer to the human body in its capacity of covering over all else that makes up the human person, for instance, his soul and spirit. Scripture's body, then, covers over all of its other meanings that are not obvious or external, namely its soul and spirit. Origen refers to Scripture's πνευματικά or *spiritales sensus*, both plural forms translated here as "spiritual truths." Thus, the somatic sense covers over all spiritual, nonliteral meanings within the biblical text.[54]

Second, in the above quotation, Origen explains that the obvious interpretation of the law and historical narrative, which acts as a cover over Scripture's other senses, must also be "profitable" to and "capable of improving the multitude in so far as they receive it." If the "readily accessible" meaning edifies, it helps the hearer to progress toward his understanding of Scripture's "deeper truths." Yet, the "usefulness" of Scripture's law and historical narratives are not "at first sight clearly discernible throughout" all biblical passages. In other

---

[54] Origen employs the same Greek term (and Rufinus the same Latin term in translation) for "spiritual truths" here that he uses generally in *Princ.* 4 to refer to the third, pneumatic sense. Since "spiritual truths" is plural here, Origen may use it at times to indicate the pneumatic and psychic senses together. However, whether he means here both higher senses or only the third, Origen is stating that the somatic sense clothes Scripture as the human body clothes the human person.

words, the readily accessible reading of some passages does not edify the hearer. As stated above in the discussion of Scripture's purpose, Origen explains that the Spirit designed Scripture so that people will be encouraged to search for edifying figurative readings of the text. To this end, some literal readings do not edify. In these cases, there is no somatic meaning, because only the literal reading *that edifies* renders a somatic sense.

When would a literal reading not be edifying? The literal reading fails to edify when it conveys law that is logically absurd or irrelevant for the hearer to follow,[55] or when it relays history that is untrue and never happened.[56] Origen explains:

> Consequently the Word of God has arranged for certain stumbling-blocks, as it were, and hindrances and impossibilities to be inserted in the midst of the law and the history, in order that we may not be completely drawn away by the sheer attractiveness of the language, and so either reject the true doctrines absolutely, on the ground that we learn from the scriptures nothing worthy of God, or else by never moving away from the letter fail to learn anything of the more divine element.[57]

---

[55] As an example of logical absurdity, Origen argues that certain of the Old Testament dietary laws can no longer be read literally. For this and other examples of commands and precepts not to be taken literally in the Old and New Testaments, see *Princ.* 4.3.2–3 (Butterworth, 290–293); SC 268:346–356. Also, in *Hom. Josh.* 5.5–6, Origen interprets Josh. 5.2 in which God commands Joshua to circumcise the Israelite males "a second time." Origen considers this a physical impossibility, and, thus, he argues that there is no somatic meaning here. Rather, the passage must be read figuratively as indicating that Christ circumcises sins from the believer's soul through "'the baptism of regeneration'" (*Hom. Josh.* 5.6, citing Titus 3:5). This circumcision is necessary even for those who received the "first circumcision through the Law" (*Hom. Josh.* 5.5).

[56] For an example of historical impossibility, Origen states his disbelief in the actual order of events recorded in Genesis for the six days of creation (*Princ.* 4.3.1 [Butterworth, 288]; SC 268:342, 344).

[57] *Princ.* 4.2.9 (Butterworth, 285); ᾠκονόμησέ τινα οἱονεὶ σκάνδαλα καὶ προσκόμματα καὶ ἀδύνατα διὰ μέσου ἐγκαταταχθῆναι τῷ νόμῳ καὶ τῇ ἱστορίᾳ ὁ τοῦ θεοῦ λόγος, ἵνα μὴ πάντη ὑπὸ τῆς λέξεως ἑλκόμενοι τὸ ἀγωγὸν ἄκρατον ἐχούσης, ἤτοι ὡς μηδὲν ἄξιον θεοῦ μανθάνοντες, τέλεον ἀποστῶμεν τῶν δογμάτων, ἢ μὴ κινούμενοι ἀπὸ τοῦ γράμματος, μηδὲν θειότερον μάθωμεν (SC 268:336). The corresponding Latin text reads: ista de causa procurauit diuina sapientia offendicula quaedam uel intercapedines intellegentiae fieri historialis, inpossibilia quaedam et inconuenientia per medium inserendo; ut interruptio ipsa narrationis uelut obicibus quibusdam legenti resistat obiectis, quibus intellegentiae huius uulgaris iter ac transitum neget et exclusos nos ac recussos reuocet ad alterius initium uiae, ut ita celsioris cuiusdam et eminentioris tramitis per angusti callis ingressum inmensam diuinae scientiae latitudinem pandat.

Origen explains that the Word of God has set up "hindrances and impossibilities" in the "law" and "history."[58] Elsewhere, he similarly states that the "literal sense" of the law and history does not edify when it is "absurd and impossible."[59] These "stumbling-blocks" force the attentive and faithful hearer to move from a full reliance on the "attractiveness of the language" to the deeper edifying messages hidden beneath the literal, and sometimes somatic, covering.[60]

Origen does not limit his analysis to the Old Testament, but relates his comments about the somatic sense to the New Testament writings:

> [N]ot only did the Spirit supervise the writings which were previous to the coming of Christ, but because he is the same Spirit and pro-

---

[58] For examples that Origen sets forth from the Old Testament, see esp. *Princ.* 4.3.1–2 (Butterworth, 288–292); SC 268:342–352.

[59] *Princ.* 4.3.4. The fuller English text reads: "[T]he aim of the divine power which bestowed on us the holy scriptures is not that we should accept only what is found in the letter; for occasionally the records taken in a literal sense are not true, but actually absurd and impossible, and even with the history that actually happened and the legislation that is in its literal sense useful there are other matters interwoven" (Butterworth, 293–294). The corresponding Greek texts reads: Ταῦτα δὲ ἡμῖν πάντα εἴρηται ὑπὲρ τοῦ δεῖξαι ὅτι σκοπὸς τῇ δωρουμένῃ ἡμῖν θείᾳ δυνάμει τὰς ἱερὰς γραφάς ἐστιν οὐχὶ τὰ ὑπὸ τῆς λέξεως παριστάμενα μόνα ἐκλαμβάνειν, ἐνίοτε τούτων ὅσον ἐπὶ τῷ ῥητῷ οὐκ ἀληθῶν ἀλλὰ καὶ ἀλόγων καὶ ἀδυνάτων τυγχανόντων, καὶ ὅτι προσύφανταί τινα τῇ γενομένῃ ἱστορίᾳ καὶ τῇ κατὰ τὸ ῥητὸν χρησίμῳ νομοθεσίᾳ (SC 268:356). The corresponding Latin text reads: Haec autem omnia nobis dicta sunt, ut ostendamus quia hic prospectus est spiritus sancti, qui nobis scripturas diuinas donare dignatus est, non ut ex sola littera uel in omnibus ex ea aedificari possimus, quam frequenter inpossibilem nec sufficientem sibi adesse depraehendimus, id est per quam interdum non solum inrationabilia, uerum etiam inpossibilia designantur: sed ut intelligamus contexta esse quaedam huic uisibili historiae, quae interius considerata et intellecta utilem hominibus et deo dignam proferunt legem.

[60] The Greek term, translated here as "language," comes from the noun λέξις, which means speech, word spoken, or the text of an author, as opposed to exegesis. It is the actual letter of the text, or the plain reading. If this explicit language is not edifying, the hearer should be encouraged to "mov[e] away from the letter." The Greek term for "letter" here comes from the noun γράμμα, which means the written character or letter as in the figures of the alphabet. And elsewhere for "literal sense" Origen employs the term ῥητόν (see the previous footnote), meaning the literal contents of a document or the literal, as opposed to the allegorical sense; it is that thing expressly stated, or the word. All these terms, λέξις, γράμμα and ῥητόν, represent the literal reading or letter that may or may not be edifying to the hearer. Origen explains that this letter of Scripture sometimes does not edify so that the hearer will look deeper for the "more divine element" in the text, literally, the "more God-like element" therein, or, as he articulates elsewhere, "the more mystical meanings" hidden beyond the letter—that is, accessible only through figurative readings of the text (*Princ.* 4.2.9 [Butterworth, 285–286]; διὰ τὰ μυστικώτερα (SC 268:338)."

ceeds from the one God he has dealt in a like manner with the gospels
and the writings of the apostles. For the history even of these is not
everywhere pure, events being woven together with the bodily sense
without having actually happened; nor do the law and the commandments contained therein entirely declare what is reasonable.[61]

Origen claims here that the Holy Spirit deals with both the gospels
and the apostolic writings in a manner similar to the Old Testament
texts. Throughout both Testaments, the literal reading may render
a somatic sense or may set forth historical events that did not occur
and laws and commandments unnecessary or unreasonable to follow.[62]
Finally, Origen warns that the somatic sense is usually present:

> We must assert . . . that in regard to some things we are clearly aware
> that the historical fact is true; as that . . . Jerusalem is the chief city of
> Judaea, in which a temple of God was built by Solomon; and thou-
> sands of other facts. For the passages which are historically true are
> far more numerous than those which are composed with purely spir-
> itual meanings.[63]

Origen stresses that literal readings of passages in the Hebrew
Scriptures are historically true and/or morally relevant "far more"

---

[61] *Princ.* 4.2.9 (Butterworth, 287); Οὐ μόνον δὲ περὶ τῶν πρὸ τῆς παρουσίας ταῦτα
τὸ πνεῦμα ᾠκονόμησεν, ἀλλὰ γὰρ ἅτε τὸ αὐτὸ τυγχάνον καὶ ἀπὸ τοῦ ἑνὸς θεοῦ,
τὸ ὅμοιον καὶ ἐπὶ τῶν εὐαγγελίων πεποίηκε καὶ ἐπὶ τῶν ἀποστόλων· οὐδὲ τούτων
πάντη ἄκρατον τὴν ἱστορίαν τῶν προσυφασμένων κατὰ τὸ σωματικὸν ἐχόντων, μὴ
γεγενημένων, οὐδὲ τὴν νομοθεσίαν καὶ τὰς ἐντολὰς πάντως τὸ εὔλογον ἐντεῦθεν
ἐμφαίνοντα (SC 268:340). The corresponding Latin text reads: Non solum autem
de his, quae usque ad aduentum Christi scripta sunt, haec sanctus spiritus procurauit, sed utpote unus atque idem spiritus et ab uno deo procedens, eadem similiter
etiam in euangeliis et apostolis fecit. Nam ne illas quidem narrationes, quas per eos
inspirauit, absque huiuscemodi quam supra exposuimus sapientiae suae arte con-
texuit. Vnde etiam in ipsis non parua permiscuit, quibus historialis narrandi ordo
interpolatus uel intercisus per inpossibilitatem sui reflecteret ac reuocaret intentionem
legentis ad intellegentiae interioris examen.
[62] For examples of New Testament passages (gospels *and* epistles) from which the
somatic sense is absent, see esp. *Princ.* 4.3.1 and 4.3.3 (Butterworth, 289–290 and
292–293); SC 268:344–346 and 352–356.
[63] *Princ.* 4.3.4 (Butterworth, 294–295); λεκτέον ὅτι σαφῶς ἡμῖν παρίσταται περὶ
τινων τὸ τῆς ἱστορίας εἶναι ἀληθές, ὡς ὅτι . . . Ἰερουσαλὴμ μητρόπολίς ἐστι τῆς
Ἰουδαίας, ἐν ᾗ ᾠκοδόμητο ὑπὸ Σολομῶντος ναὸς θεοῦ, καὶ ἄλλα μυρία. Πολλῷ
γὰρ πλείονά ἐστι τὰ κατὰ τὴν ἱστορίαν ἀληθευόμενα τῶν προσυφανθέντων γυμνῶν
πνευματικῶν (SC 268:358). The corresponding Latin text reads: [R]espondendum
ergo est quoniam euidenter a nobis decernitur in quam plurimis seruari et posse
et oportere historiae ueritatem. Quis enim negare potest quod . . . Hierusalem metro-
polis est Iudaeae, in qua constructum est templum dei a Salomone? et alia innu-
merabilia. Multo enim plura sunt, quae secundum historiam constant, quam ea,
quae nudum sensum continent spiritalem.

often than not.[64] He extends this observation to passages in the
gospels and apostolic writings as well.[65]

Thus, in *Princ.* 4 Origen describes the somatic sense as the literal
reading of the text when it edifies the hearer by offering true history or logical and relevant moral instruction.[66] It also acts as a covering or garment over Scripture's other meanings so that the hearer
not yet ready to grasp these other meanings will not be exposed prematurely to them and yet can benefit from the somatic sense's more
obvious meaning. While the Holy Spirit has included somatic meaning in most passages of Scripture, it is absent occasionally as an
incentive for the hearer to seek the deeper meanings.

C. *The Psychic and Pneumatic Meanings as Generally Present*

Even if a biblical passage lacks somatic meaning, it contains psychic
and pneumatic meanings. Origen explains this point by metaphorically reading John 2:6:

> And possibly this is the reason why the waterpots which, as we read
> in the gospel according to John, are said to be set there 'for the puri-
> fying of the Jews,' contain two or three firkins apiece. The language
> alludes to those who are said by the apostle to be Jews 'inwardly,' and
> it means that these are purified through the word of the scriptures,
> which contain in some cases 'two firkins,' that is, so to speak, the *soul*
> meaning and the *spiritual* meaning, and in other cases three, since some
> passages possess, in addition to those before-mentioned, *bodily* sense
> as well, which is capable of edifying the hearers.[67]

---

[64] See esp. *Princ.* 4.3.4 (Butterworth, 294–295); SC 268:358, 360. Here Origen
gives examples of literally true and thus edifying historical fact or events in the
Hebrew Scriptures such as the temple Solomon built for God in Jerusalem and the
burial site of Abraham, Isaac and Jacob. In regard to edifying moral instruction,
he points to the usefulness and necessity of continuing to follow the Decalogue. For
an example of edifying historical fact outside of *Princ.* 4, see *Hom. Jer.* 1.1–3, referring to Jer. 1:1–3, in which Origen explains that the record of when Jeremiah
prophesied is true, and its somatic meaning is significant because it informs us that
God, who is loving and merciful, encouraged the Israelites not to fall into captivity
up to the very last day before it occurred. This teaches Scripture's hearers that
God is patient and persistent in His love for us.
[65] See especially *Princ.* 4.3.4 (Butterworth, 295–296); SC 268:360.
[66] Origen's practice reveals that he understands somatic readings to provide moral
instruction not only by direct command or precept but also by way of example.
See the analysis below of *Hom. Luc.* 38 in which Origen offers both a psychic and
a morally exhortative somatic reading (by way of Jesus' example) of the same text
and yet through them offers distinctive messages to his audience.
[67] *Princ.* 4.2.5 (quoting John 2:6 and referring to Rom. 2:29, emphasis added;

Firkins represent *meanings* of Scripture. The Greek noun λόγος, translated here as "meaning," signifies the word by which the inward thought is expressed, or the inward thought or reason itself.[68] Origen states that these meanings are οἰκοδομῆσαι δυνάμενον, or "capable of edifying or building up" the hearer.

A biblical passage contains either two or three firkins, or senses. Where there are only two firkins, they are the psychic and pneumatic senses. Here, λόγον is modified by ψυχικόν ("soul's" or "psychic") and πνευματικόν ("spiritual" or "pneumatic"), and the substantive adjective σωματικόν ("bodily" or "somatic") also refers back to λόγον. Thus, Origen asserts that a biblical passage either contains psychic and pneumatic meanings or psychic, pneumatic and somatic meanings. Every biblical passage holds edifying meaning, for, even where the literal reading does not edify, the psychic and pneumatic meanings are present to build up the attentive hearer.

It may be tempting to argue that Origen diverges from this early statement of theory wherever in practice he treats only the psychic or the pneumatic sense but not both for a particular text. However, he does not promise in this theory to extract both senses from every passage that he exegetes. He claims only that both *can* be extracted from Scripture's passages. We should expect him to consider the audience and situation of each exegetical exercise and determine whether discussion of one or both of these nonliteral meanings is timely, relevant and merited. Moreover, as I will discuss in chapter 4, he suggests in his interpretation of *Hom. Num.* 27, if not elsewhere

---

Butterworth, 278); Καὶ τάχα διὰ τοῦτο αἱ ἐπὶ καθαρισμῷ τῶν Ἰουδαίων ὑδρίαι κεῖσθαι λεγόμεναι, ὡς ἐν τῷ κατὰ Ἰωάννην εὐαγγελίῳ ἀνέγνωμεν, χωροῦσιν ἀνὰ μετρητὰς δύο ἢ τρεῖς · αἰνισσομένου τοῦ λόγου περὶ τῶν παρὰ τῷ ἀποστόλῳ ἐν κρυπτῷ Ἰουδαίων, ὡς ἄρα οὗτοι καθαρίζονται διὰ τοῦ λόγου τῶν γραφῶν, ὅπου μὲν δύο μετρητάς, τὸν ἵν᾽ οὕτως εἴπω ψυχικὸν καὶ τὸν πνευματικὸν λόγον, χωρούντων, ὅπου δὲ τρεῖς, ἐπεί τινες ἔχουσι πρὸς τοῖς προειρημένοις καὶ τὸ σωματικὸν οἰκοδομῆσαι δυνάμενον (SC 268:316, 318). The corresponding Latin text reads: Quod etiam in euangeliis designari puto, cum dicuntur pro purificatione Iudaeorum sex hydriae positae, capientes metretas binas uel ternas, in quo, ut dixi, hoc uidetur sermo euangelicus indicare de his, qui dicuntur ab apostolo in occulto Iudaeis, quod hi purificuntur per uerbum scripturae, capientes interdum quidem duas metretas, id est animae uel spiritus secundum quod supra diximus intellectum recipientes, interdum autem tres, cum etiam corporalem intellegentiam, quae est historiae, seruare lectio ad aedificationem potest.

[68] This denotation for λόγος corresponds to the meanings of the words νοῦς and νόημα, which Origen uses elsewhere in this theoretical discussion, and, as mentioned above, mean respectively mind and thought, understanding or mind. We may consider that Origen here treats λόγος, νοῦς, and νόημα as synonyms, all conveying the idea of a scriptural passage's "meaning."

as well, that, though he is a legitimate church leader and teacher—
indeed, a "perfected" soul (someone able to grasp all three senses)—
he has not yet achieved the wisdom necessary to offer full readings
of both higher senses (namely, the pneumatic reading) for particularly difficult biblical passages (such as Num. 33).[69] Consistency with
this early theory is dependent upon whether he sometimes extracts
both a psychic and a pneumatic meaning from the same biblical
text, not whether he always does so.[70]

D. *The Elements of the Psychic Meaning*

In *Princ.* 4, Origen sets forth the middle sense's basic components,
which the later theoretical explanations in his homilies will develop
further. The psychic sense is a nonliteral reading of the biblical text
that offers moral direction to the hearer.

Origen gives an example of the psychic reading of Scripture, by
citing Paul's treatment of an Old Testament law in 1 Corinthians:

> But of the kind of explanation which penetrates . . . to the soul an illus-
> tration is found in Paul's first epistle to the Corinthians. "For," he
> says, "it is written; you shall not muzzle the ox that treads out the
> corn". Then in explanation of this law he adds, "Is it for the oxen
> that God cares? Or does he say it altogether for our sake? Yea, for
> our sake it was written, because he that plows ought to plow in hope,
> and he that threshes, to thresh in hope of partaking."[71]

Origen considers Paul's reading of the Old Testament directive about
muzzling an ox to exemplify "the kind of explanation which pene-
trates . . . to the *soul.*" The Greek verb ἀνάγω is the root of the word
translated here as "penetrate," and it means to lead up to or refer
back to something. Origen finds that this Pauline text illustrates the
kind of explanation in Scripture that leads up to or refers back to
Scripture's soul.

---

[69] See the discussion of *Hom. Num.* 27 near the end of chapter 4.
[70] As announced in chapter 1, I will treat in chapters 4 and 5 numerous examples
from his practical works where he explicitly presents both a psychic and pneumatic
sense for a single scriptural passage, each providing separate messages for the hearer.
[71] *Princ.* 4.2.6 (quoting 1 Cor. 9:9–10 which refers to Deut. 25:4; Butterworth,
279); τῆς δὲ ὡς ἂν εἰς ψυχὴν ἀναγομένης διηγήσεως παράδειγμα τὸ παρὰ τῷ Παύλῳ
ἐν τῇ πρώτῃ πρὸς Κορινθίους κείμενον. Γέγραπται γάρ φησιν Οὐ φιμώσεις βοῦν
ἀλοῶντα. Ἔπειτα διηγούμενος τοῦτον τὸν νόμον ἐπιφέρει· Μὴ τῶν βοῶν μέλει τῷ
θεῷ; Ἢ δι' ἡμᾶς πάντως λέγει; Δι' ἡμᾶς γὰρ ἐγράφη, ὅτι ὀφείλει ἐπ' ἐλπίδι ὁ
ἀροτριῶν ἀροτριᾶν καὶ ὁ ἀλοῶν ἐπ' ἐλπίδι τοῦ μετέχειν (SC 268:318, 320).

Both the location of this discussion within the text of *Princ.* 4 and Origen's language underscore that, for him, this example regards *Scripture's* soul, or its middle, psychic sense. This discussion falls directly after Origen's statement that the somatic meaning of a text is obvious[72] and before his description of the "spiritual explanation" (pneumatic sense) of Scripture. This second sense is not obvious, and yet it is different from Scripture's spirit. The Latin version of this text confirms that Rufinus also understands Origen to refer here to *Scripture's* soul:

> But of the kind of explanation which we have spoken of above as the soul, as it were, of Scripture, many illustrations are given us by the apostle Paul, as, for example, first of all in his epistle to the Corinthians.[73]

The Latin text supports our reading of the corresponding Greek text that Origen views this illustration as an exemplary presentation by Paul of the psychic sense, only one of a number of such examples in Paul's exegesis.

---

[72] *Princ.* 4.2.6. The translation from the Greek reads: "That it is possible to derive benefit from the first, and to this extent helpful meaning, is witnessed by the multitudes of sincere and simple believers" (Butterworth, 278). The corresponding Greek text reads: Ἀπὸ μὲν οὖν τῆς πρώτης ἐκδοχῆς καὶ κατὰ τοῦτο ὠφελούσης ὅτι ἔστιν ὄνασθαι, μαρτυρεῖ τὰ πλήθη τῶν γνησίως καὶ ἁπλούστερον πεπιστευκότων (SC 268:318). The translation of the Latin text reads: "How much value there is in this first meaning, which we have called the literal one, is witnessed by the entire multitude of those believers who accept the faith quite trustfully and simply; and this needs no long argument because it is obvious to all." The corresponding Latin text reads: Quanta igitur sit utilitas in hoc primo quem diximus historiali intellectu, testimonio est omnis credentium multitudo, quae et satis fideliter et simpliciter credit; nec multa adsertione indiget quod palam omnibus patet. By this statement, Origen explains that the ways in which the somatic sense is to be identified and benefit the hearer should be obvious, since this sense proceeds from the letter of the text. In the discussion above, we considered his subsequent statements about the somatic sense's absence from some biblical texts, because this discussion shed light on the identifying aspects of the somatic sense that Origen considers to be "obvious" to the many who hear Scripture. However, because the psychic and pneumatic senses are generally found beyond Scripture and are harder to identify, he elaborates on their defining aspects in *Princ.* 4.2.6.

[73] *Princ.* 4.2.6 (quoting 1 Cor. 9:9–10 which refers to Deut. 25:4; Butterworth, 279); SC 268:318, 320. The full Latin text of Origen's illustration here on the muzzle and ox reads: Eius uero intellegentiae, quam velut animam esse scripturae supra diximus, exempla nobis quam plurima dedit apostolus Paulus, sicut est primo in illa epistola ad Corinthios. *Scriptum est enim inquit non infrenabis bouem triturantem.* Tum deinde explanans qualiter praeceptum istud deberet intellegi, addit dicens: *Numquid de bubus cura est deo? Aut propter nos utique dicit? Propter nos enim scriptum est quia debet qui arat in spe arare, et qui triturat sub spe percipiendi.*

By offering this example regarding the muzzle and the ox, Origen claims no less than the authority of Paul for seeking a psychic meaning in Scripture. In the New Testament text, Paul uses a metaphorical, nonliteral reading of an Old Testament passage to argue that he has the moral right to receive material support in exchange for the "spiritual seed" he has "sown" in the Corinthian congregation.[74] Paul offers the Old Testament law as authority for the right of persons to receive material support from those whom they serve. Literally, God commands that the plowman not use the muzzle, even though it prevents the ox from biting or eating and thus consuming the fruits of the plowman's labor. Psychically, according to Paul, the Corinthians, the plowmen, have a moral obligation to provide a portion of their material possessions to Paul, the ox, who directs their spiritual growth. Thus, Paul deserves not to be muzzled but rather to be allowed to receive compensation for his missionary work. This nonliteral reading of the Old Testament text provides a moral precept on how to treat others justly or fairly: the Corinthians should find it their duty to compensate those who provide services to them, such as Paul himself.[75] By this example, Origen portrays the psychic sense as moral instruction found through a nonliteral, or figurative reading of the text.[76]

Directly following this example of a psychic reading and just before his description of the pneumatic sense, Origen makes a qualified comparison between the first, somatic sense and the middle, psychic sense:

---

[74] See specifically 1 Cor. 9:11–12.

[75] After reading this Old Testament law figuratively to establish his right to receive material support from the congregation, Paul announces that he chooses to waive this right so as to "offer [the] gospel free of charge" (1 Cor 9:12b–18, quoting 9:18). Still, Origen offers as evidence of a psychic reading of Scripture Paul's figurative reading of the law as establishing this right.

[76] Daniélou argues that this passage does not constitute a definition for a *Christian* meaning in Scripture, because this is "the kind of interpretation common to all moral allegorism," which Paul has borrowed from his "rabbinic education" (Daniélou, *Gospel Message*, 285; also Hanson, *Allegory and Event*, 28 and 78–79). Still, Origen views Paul's exercises in Scripture to be divinely inspired and directed by the Holy Spirit so that they constitute scriptural authority for the right means of interpretation. Thus, Origen offers this passage as Paul's presentation of the psychic meaning. Further, as I will demonstrate in later chapters on his own practice, Origen applies the psychic reading of biblical passages in a decidedly *Christian* way.

> And most of the interpretations adapted to the multitude which are in circulation and which edify those who cannot understand the higher meanings have something of the same character.[77]

Origen states that "most of the interpretations adapted to the multitude," that is, those reflecting the somatic sense,[78] "have something of the same character" that the Pauline illustration sets forth for the psychic sense. These somatic interpretations differ from the τοὺς ὑψηλοτέρων, or "higher meanings," which in the plural refers to the other two—"higher"—senses, the psychic and pneumatic senses.[79] The similarity refers to the psychic sense's tendency to offer moral instruction. Origen states here that "most" of the somatic interpretations that edify the masses share this moral character. The majority of somatic meanings arise from the literal readings of laws, commands, precepts and living examples in Scripture that are logical and relevant to the Christian hearer and thus offer moral direction, as does the psychic sense.

Because of its moral focus, then, the psychic sense shares a similar character with the somatic sense. By suggesting that it is similar to the somatic sense, Origen informs his reader that the psychic sense is not identical to the pneumatic sense (since it shares a similar thematic focus with the somatic sense) *and* that the psychic sense is not identical to the somatic sense, only *similar*. The psychic and somatic senses share a kindred focus whenever the somatic sense arises from literally edifying moral instruction. Thus, Origen describes the psychic sense as figuratively conveying moral instruction and falling in its specific content somewhere between that of the somatic and pneumatic senses.

Origen does not claim that a morally edifying somatic sense and psychic sense, when both are present in a biblical passage, convey the *same* message to the hearer. He states only that most somatic

---

[77] *Princ.* 4.2.6 (Butterworth, 279). Καὶ πλεῖσται δὲ περιφερόμεναι τοῖς πλήθεσιν ἁρμόζουσαι ἑρμηνεῖαι καὶ οἰκοδομοῦσαι τοὺς ὑψηλοτέρων ἀκούειν μὴ δυναμένους τὸν αὐτόν πως ἔχουσι χαρακτῆρα (SC 268:320).

[78] To see how Origen defines the somatic sense as the interpretation that the "multitudes" can understand, see the text set forth in n. 73 above.

[79] The Greek term τοὺς ὑψηλοτέρων, translated here as "higher meanings," is the genitive plural form of the substantive comparative adjective literally meaning higher things. Origen uses this term to refer to the other two senses, the ones that can be retrieved from beyond the letter, by reading the text figuratively. Thus, the psychic and pneumatic meanings of Scripture are the two "higher" senses.

readings exhibit a moral "character," as does the psychic sense. The
limits of this comparison can be observed in an example from Origen's
practice, *Hom. Luc.* 38,[80] in which he sets forth distinctive moral
meanings, one somatic and the other psychic, for the same scriptural passage.[81]

In *Hom. Luc.* 38, Origen treats Luke 19:41–44, which states that
"Jesus wept" upon approaching and seeing the city of Jerusalem.[82]
Origen explains the somatic reading of Jesus' weeping as follows:

> We must first contemplate his weeping. By his example, Jesus confirms
> all the beatitudes that he speaks in the Gospel. By his own witness,
> he confirms what he teaches. "Blessed are the meek," he says. He says
> something similar to this of himself: "Learn from me, for I am meek."
> "Blessed are the peacemakers." And what other man brought as much
> peace as my Lord Jesus, who "is our peace," who "dissolves enmity,"
> and "destroys it in his own flesh"? "Blessed are they who suffer per-
> secution on account of justice." No one suffered such persecution on
> account of justice as the Lord Jesus did, who was crucified for our
> sins. Thus, the Lord exhibited all the beatitudes in himself. For the
> sake of this likeness, he himself wept, because of what he had said:
> "Blessed are those who weep," to lay the foundations for this beati-
> tude, too.[83]

---

[80] Extant are thirty-nine intact homilies by Origen on the Gospel of Luke, translated into Latin by St. Jerome. All English translations are from Joseph T. Lienhard,
trans., *Origen: Homilies on Luke, Fragments on Luke* (FC 94; Washington, D.C.: Catholic
University of America, 1996), 156–158. I will place the corresponding Latin text
in footnote, employing the Latin edition of Henri Crouzel, Francois Fournier, and
Pierre Périchon, eds. and trans., *Origène: Homélies sur S. Luc* (SC 87; Paris: Cerf,
1962), 442–449.

[81] Analysis of this practical text here for the comparison between the somatic
and psychic senses stands apart from analyses of texts in later chapters which center on the distinction and relation between the psychic and pneumatic senses. Much
more attention to the comparison between the psychic and pneumatic senses is
needed, since their relationship has eluded recent scholarly debates, as outlined in
chapter 1, and, even more importantly, because it will reveal itself to constitute the
height of Origen's intended exegetical effectiveness. It is necessary here to see how
morally edifying somatic and psychic readings can render separate messages for the
same biblical passage.

[82] The scriptural passage reads as follows: "And when he [Jesus] drew near and
saw the city he wept over it, saying, 'Would that even today you knew the things
that make for peace! But now they are hid from your eyes. For the days shall come
upon you, when your enemies will cast up a bank about you and surround you,
and hem you in on every side, and dash you to the ground, you and your children within you, and they will not leave one stone upon another in you; because
you did not know the time of your visitation'" (Luke 19:41–44 RSV).

[83] *Hom. Luc.* 38.1–2 (quoting, in order, Matt. 5:5, 11:29, 5:9; Eph. 2:14–15; Matt.
5:10, 5:4; FC 94:156); Primum ergo de fletu eius videndum. Omnes beatitudines,

Origen's audience has retrospective knowledge of the temple's destruction after Jesus' lifetime in 70 C.E. Origen believes that Jesus wept for the city because of his knowledge concerning this future event. By this weeping, Jesus offers himself as a moral example of the second beatitude listed in Matthew 5, "Blessed are those who mourn, for they will be comforted."[84] As Origen explains, at different times throughout his earthly life, Jesus exemplified each of the beatitudes that he taught in the Sermon on the Mount, and, in so doing, he embodied their virtues. By weeping for Jerusalem, Jesus calls every attentive hearer of Scripture to pattern himself after his model of virtue.[85]

Next, Origen offers a psychic reading of the same event, reading Jerusalem figuratively as the human soul on whom sins and vices wage constant war in this life:

> But I ask whether perhaps that weeping pertains also to this Jerusalem of ours. For, we are the Jerusalem that is wept over . . . because after her sins "enemies have surrounded" her—namely, contrary powers, evil spirits. And they throw up earthworks around her perimeter, and besiege her, "and do not leave a stone upon a stone." This is particularly true if someone is conquered after years of chastity and, enticed by the pleasures of the flesh, loses the will to persevere in purity. If you have fornicated, "they will not leave a stone upon a stone in you." For, in another place Scripture says, "I shall not remember his earlier acts of justice. I shall judge him in his sin, in which he was apprehended." So this Jerusalem is the city that Jesus wept over.[86]

---

quas locutus est in evangelio Iesus, suo firmat exemplo et, quod docuit, proprio testimonio probat. *Beati*, inquit, *mites*. Huic simile de semetipso: *Discite a me*, ait, *quoniam mitis sum. Beati pacifici*. Et quis alius ita pacificus ut Dominus meus Iesus, qui *est pax nostra*, qui *solvit inimicitiam* et *in sua* eam *carne destruxit? Beati, qui persecutionem patiuntur propter iustitiam*. Nemo sic persecutionem passus est propter iustitiam ut Dominus Iesus, qui pro peccatis nostris crucifixus est. Omnes igitur beatitudines in semetipso Dominus ostendit; ad quam similitudinem etiam illud, quod dixerat: *Beati flentes*—ipse flevit, ut huius quoque beatitudinis iaceret fundamenta (SC 87:442).

[84] Matt. 5:4 RSV.

[85] Note that this somatic reading conveys moral instruction by way of example (Jesus' behavior) and not only by direct command (the relevant beatitude). Thus, for Origen, the somatic sense conveys moral instruction either by precept or example.

[86] *Hom. Luc.* 38.3–4 (quoting Ezek. 18:24); FC 94:157; "[S]ed quaero, ne forte et ad hanc nostram Hierusalem fletus iste pertineat. Nos enim sumus Hierusalem, quae defletur . . . quod post peccata *circumdent* eam *inimici*, contrariae videlicet fortitudines, spiritus nequam, et immittant in circuitu eius *vallum* et obsideant eam *et lapidem super lapidem non relinquant*, maxime si post multam continentiam, post aliquot annos castitatis victus quis fuerit et blandimentis carnis illectus patientiam pudicitiae amiserit. Si fueris fornicatus, *lapidem super lapidem non relinquent in te*. Ait enim in

Origen signals a second reading by stating that the "weeping per-
tains *also* [*et*] to this Jerusalem *of ours*." The phrase "this Jerusalem
of ours" refers to the human soul, since the whole passage stresses
the individual human person's ever-present danger of falling prey to
sin and vice throughout this life by succumbing to the "pleasures of
the flesh."[87] Jesus weeps for every soul who has fallen or will fall
prey to sin and its promoters, the "contrary powers" and "evil spir-
its," especially the soul who, after having embraced the faith and
received baptism, falls again into the grip of sin and its promoters.
When Jesus walked on earth, he foresaw that many future souls (in
addition to past and present souls) would so err.

The psychic reading of this passage stresses that the vices will
wage war against the virtues for possession of the soul and will do
so relentlessly throughout this temporal life. The hearer is urged to
be ever on guard against sin and temptation. Thus, this nonliteral,
psychic reading emphasizes the temporal struggle in which the hearer
lives and the moral norm to which he needs to aspire for his own
good.

Both readings in *Hom. Luc.* 38 are morally instructive and point
toward the same end: the pursuit of a virtuous life. However, the
somatic reading gives a literal, historical example of a specific virtue,[88]
that of mourning set forth by the second beatitude and modeled by
Jesus. By a nonliteral, psychic reading of the same account, Origen
impresses upon his hearer more generally the precarious state in
which his soul exists in this life, as the prize that evil forces con-
stantly strive to possess. The hearer is called to fight these evil forces
by achieving a general moral purity, with the assurance that Jesus
is his compassionate advocate in this temporal struggle.

---

alio loco: *non recordabor priorum iustitiarum eius; in peccato suo, in quo deprehensus fuerit, in
ipso iudicabo eum.* Haec est ergo, quae defletur, Hierusalem (SC 87:444).

[87] Note that translator Joseph Lienhard also reads "this Jerusalem of ours" to
refer to the soul, for he states: "Origen identifies Jerusalem with the Christian soul"
(FC 94:157 n. 10). Also, the discussion of Origen's anthropology later in this chapter will show that Origen understands the human soul to be the seat of choice,
called always to choose to live according to virtue or vice.

[88] In *Hom. Luc.* 38 Origen sets forth a somatic reading that offers moral instruction
by way of example. For an example of a moral somatic reading that is based solely
on precept or command, see *Hom. Ex.* 8, in which Origen treats the first two commandments of the Decalogue set forth in Exod. 20:2–5a. In that homily, he treats
these two commandments as literal moral imperatives both for the Israelites leaving
Egypt and for all later hearers of Scripture. Literally, the hearer of Scripture is called
to "have no other gods" and to "not make a graven image, or any likeness...."

The continued exegetical theory (as treated in chapter 3) and the psychic readings in practice (as explored in chapters 4 and 5) will expand upon the definition of the psychic sense, stressing that it broadly focuses on the general temporal plight of the human soul by calling the soul to grow in *all* virtue and flee *all* vice.[89] The message of the moral somatic sense remains distinct by calling the soul only to a specific virtue or set of virtues. Thus, while both the somatic and psychic senses may offer moral instruction, each contains different messages to edify the hearer.

E. *The Labels "Moral" and "Psychic"*

Based on the foregoing, the label "moral" for the middle meaning is inadequate. The somatic sense sometimes offers moral instruction, and the psychic sense offers a broader moral focus than simply urging cultivation of specific virtues (or avoidance of specific vices). Thus, "psychic," the transliteration of Origen's Greek term for the middle sense, is a more apt label for the middle meaning than the potentially misleading term "moral."

Still, it may be useful to consider briefly why scholars have often applied the term "moral" to this middle sense. Since the majority of Origen's extant practical works (especially his homilies) are not available in the original Greek but only in Latin translations by Rufinus or Jerome, we cannot be certain whether Origen ever used ψυχικόν to discuss the psychic sense or signal a psychic reading of text in his homilies and commentaries.[90] When we examine available Latin translations of texts, such as those treated in the next chapters, we learn that Rufinus tended to employ the substantive adjective *moralis* to signal the psychic sense. The few texts that are extant both in Jerome's Latin translation and Greek suggest that Origen used τροπολογία or τροπολογέω—"tropological"—when discussing the psychic sense or announcing a reading of it, with Jerome remaining close to the original by employing its transliteration into Latin—

---

[89] Moreover, from examination of psychic readings in Origen's practice, the psychic sense will emerge as Scripture's call for the hearer to become like Christ and, as part of this process, to pursue ever-deepening understanding of Scripture's pneumatic truths, which essentially are Christ's own wisdom.

[90] For a list of Origen's extant works that indicates which ones are available in Greek and/or Latin translation by Jerome or Rufinus, see the relevant chart in the introduction to this work.

tropologia.[91] The few commentaries and homilies extant in Greek also suggest that Origen avoided the term ψυχικόν when discussing or employing the psychic sense.

It is possible that Origen avoided the term ψυχικόν when presenting the middle sense within his practical works in order to avoid association with Gnostic classifications of humanity. Apart from the exegetical discussion in *Princ.* 4, one finds appearances of ψυχικόν in Origen's intact extant works only in passages where Origen discusses the Gnostic classifications, such as in passages within *Comm. Jo.* where he engages in direct debate with the Gnostic Heracleon.[92]

Surely Origen was aware that certain Gnostics, such as Valentinians (he identifies Heracleon as a likely student of Valentinus),[93] spoke of different types of humanity in their melodrama of creation and salvation with the following terms: the material ones—ὑλικοί, the physical, animal or natural ones—ψυχικοί, and the spiritual ones—πνευματικοί.[94] For Christian Gnostics, the ὑλικοί are empty creatures with no spark of the divine in them, who will experience no redemption or release from this inherently evil material realm. The ψυχικοί enjoy some contact with the divine and will enjoy a partial redemption, yet always reside between shadow and light. The πνευματικοί are the

---

[91] It is useful to consider five occurrences of a form of τροπολογία or τροπολογέω within the homilies on the book of Jeremiah. The following list gives the citations along with the form of the Greek word and Jerome's Latin translation of the term: (1) *Hom. Jer.* 1.7.1; FC 97:8; SC 232:208; PG 13:261–262 (τροπολόγει—*allegorizet*); (2) *Hom. Jer.* 5.13.1; FC 97:54; SC 232:310; PG 13:311–312 (τροπολογιῶν—*Tropologias*); (3 and 4) *Hom. Jer.* 5.14.1; FC 97:57; SC 232:316; PG 13:317–318 (ἐπὶ τὴν τροπολογίαν and τροπολογικῶς—*ad moralem* and *tropologice*); (5) *Hom. Jer.* 7.3.3; FC 97:72; SC 232:348; PG 13:333–334 (κατὰ μίαν τροπολογίαν—*secundum unam tropice*). In three of the five instances Jerome employs the Latin term for "tropological." In the other two instances he employs the Latin terms for "allegorical" and "moral." In all five passages Origen offers a figurative reading of a biblical text that gives moral instruction, and, in most of them, Origen employs a form of the word ψυχή for "soul," thus indicating further his application of a psychic reading in those instances (FC 97; trans. John Smith Clark, *Origen: Homilies on Jeremiah*, Washington, D.C.: Catholic University Press, 1998; SC 232, vol. 1, ed. and trans. Pierre Nautin, *Origène: Homélies sur Jérémie*, Paris, Cerf, 1976.)

[92] See the following passages for Origen's use of ψυχιλός (singular) or ψυχικοί (plural) when discussing Gnostic classifications of humanity with Heracleon: *Comm. Jo.* 2.21.138.3; 10.33.210.3; 10.33.211.7; 10.37.250.3; 13.51.341.4; 13.61.431.1; 13.61.431.6; 13.61.433.6; 20.20.170.3; 20.24.213.4; and 20.33.295.2.

[93] *Comm. Jo.* 2.100.

[94] Heine, *Origen's Commentary on the Gospel According to John*, vol. 2 [FC 89], 141 n. 389.

few who are full of divine light and will enjoy a full redemptive release from this dark material world.

Origen, though, likely employed ψυχικόν sparingly not only because of Gnostic usage but also because of Paul's use of the term. In his New Testament epistles, Paul used this term only once, in 1 Cor. 2:14. In this passage he speaks of the person who is "unspiritual" or "natural" (ψυχικὸς) and, therefore, "does not receive the gifts of the Spirit of God, . . . because they are spiritually (πνευματικῶς) discerned."[95] Paul, then, used the term pejoratively, as an earthly knowledge that cannot comprehend the objects of God's wisdom. Whether Christian Gnostics based their use of the term on Paul's usage or the Gnostics and Paul alike relied on a larger custom usage of the term, Origen surely knew that ψυχικόν was considered by the larger public of his day to represent persons or things opposed to the things of God.

Origen would not need to avoid using the term πνευματικόν for the third, spiritual sense for fear of association with Gnostics or concerns with larger custom usage for two reasons. First, even for Gnostics this term was already associated with the things of God. Second, as his discussion of theory in *Princ.* 4 stresses, Origen considered Scripture to speak to *all* human souls, intending for every one of them to receive eventually the saving truths of all three senses. However, Origen might have been concerned to employ ψυχικόν for fear that readers would understand him to condone fixed classes of persons, some of whom could never grasp all three senses and whom Scripture never intended to lead to full salvation. If Origen wished to avoid association with Christian Gnostic systems of thought, he would not want his readers to assume that he adhered to the most basic, defining notion of Gnostic thought: the idea of an *exclusive* gnosis, or saving knowledge meant only for a few.

---

[95] The full verse reads: "The unspiritual man does not receive the gifts of the Spirit of God, for they are folly to him, and he is not able to understand them because they are spiritually discerned" (1 Cor. 2:14 RSV). The Greek text reads: "ψυχικὸς δὲ ἄνθρωπος οὐ δέχεται τὰ τοῦ πνεύματος τοῦ θεοῦ · μωρία γὰρ αὐτῷ ἐστιν καὶ οὐ δύναται γνῶναι, ὅτι πνευματικῶς ἀνακρίνεται" (NA[27]). The only other occurrence of a form of ψυχικόν within the New Testament texts is found in Jas. 3:15, and it is used in the same way that Paul uses it in 1 Cor. 2:14: "This wisdom is not such as comes down from above, but is earthly, unspiritual (ψυχική), devilish" (RSV).

For this reason, Origen likely avoided the term ψυχικόν wherever possible. Sometimes he needed to employ it when debating with Gnostics, as mentioned above. Also, Origen likely felt free to use ψυχικόν in his presentation of exegetical method to other church leaders in *Princ.* 4, because he considered his audience of presbyters and elders to be experts in the Christian faith and discerning enough to know the difference between his usage of the term and Gnostic usage of it. Moreover, as discussed later in this chapter, he surely found the anthropological term ψυχικόν for Scripture's middle sense to be indispensable to his early discussion of theory, since he wished to explain to his audience of experts how Scripture communicates its three senses in a way that resembles the right order of the human person's three parts. In addition, though he avoided ψυχικόν for reference to the middle sense after *Princ.* 4, in the extended theory in his homilies (for examples, see chapter 3) he continued to use the term ψυχή when referring to this second sense as Scripture's "soul."[96] Thus, it would be wrong to assume that Origen stopped placing importance on the psychic sense in his later, practical works simply because the extant texts do not employ ψυχικόν to describe this sense or announce a reading based upon it.

F. *The Elements of the Pneumatic Meaning*

Origen describes the pneumatic sense according to its three main characteristics: First, it reveals truths about past and future events connected by the saving role of Christ. Second, since these truths reflect God's eternal wisdom, they are mysterious and difficult to grasp. Third, the pneumatic sense is the fulfillment of the whole message that Scripture's other two senses help to convey.

First, Origen explains that the pneumatic sense's main purpose is to clarify the connection between mysterious events that concern human history:

---

[96] See the references to homilies on Jeremiah in n. 92 above. For use of the equivalent Latin term *anima* in his extended theory, see, for example, *Hom. Lev.* 5.5.3; FC 83:100; SC 286:230, and the discussion of *Hom. Lev.* 5 in chapter 3.

[B]ecause the principal aim was to announce the connection that exists among spiritual events, those that have already happened and those that are yet to come to pass, whenever the Word found that things which had happened in history could be harmonized with these mystical events he used them, concealing from the multitude their deeper meaning.[97]

Origen speaks of the mysterious events explained by the pneumatic sense as "spiritual events" (from πνευματικόν) as well as "mystical events" (from μυστικόν). Some of these events "have already happened,"[98] presumably in relation to the time in which Scripture's hearer lives. Yet, other events "are yet to come to pass," with the connotation in the Greek that they "must be done,[99] implying that they have not occurred but are inevitable at some later time. Thus, the pneumatic meaning speaks about spiritual events, some which have occurred already and others which *shall* occur in the future, and informs the hearer of the "connection (εἰρμός)" that exists between them.

Origen explains that the defining connection between these events is Christ. He recalls Paul's description of Christ as πνευματικῆς πέτρας or *spiritali petra*: "[Paul] also gives hints to show what these things were figures of, when he says: 'For they drank of that spiritual rock that followed them, and that rock was Christ.'"[100] Christ is the

---

[97] *Princ.* 4.2.9 (Butterworth, 286). Χρὴ δὲ καὶ τοῦτο εἰδέναι, ὅτι τοῦ προηγουμένου σκοποῦ τυγχάνοντος τὸν ἐν τοῖς πνευματικοῖς εἰρμὸν ἀπαγγεῖλαι γεγενημένοις καὶ πρακτέοις, ὅπου μὲν εὗρε γενόμενα κατὰ τὴν ἱστορίαν ὁ λόγος ἐφαρμόσαι δυνάμενα τοῖς μυστικοῖς τούτοις, ἐχρήσατο ἀποκρύπτων ἀπὸ τῶν πολλῶν τὸν βαθύτερον νοῦν (SC 268:336). The corresponding Latin text reads: Oportet autem etiam illud scire nos quia, cum principaliter prospectus sit spiritui sancto intellegentiae spiritalis consequentiam custodire uel in his, quae geri debent, uel quae iam transacta sunt, sicubi quidem inuenit ea, quae secundum historiam gesta sunt, aptari posse intellegentiae spiritali, utriusque ordinis textum uno narrationis sermone conposuit, altius semper arcanum sensum recondens.

[98] In the Greek this phrase is an accusative plural form of the participle formed from the perfect tense of the deponent verb γίγνομαι, which in relation to events means to occur or happen.

[99] The Greek term for this phrase is the verbal adjective form of the verb πράττω or πράσσω, which means to do, bring about, accomplish or effect. In Greek, the verbal adjective expresses necessity or obligation and, in translation, takes on the idea, expressed passively in the English, that something must be done.

[100] *Princ.* 4.2.6 (quoting 1 Cor. 10:4; Butterworth, 280); Καὶ ἀφορμὰς δίδωσι τοῦ τίνων ἐκεῖνα τύποι ἐτύγχανον, λέγων · Ἔπινον γὰρ ἐκ πνευματικῆς ἀκολουθούσης πέτρας, ἡ δὲ πέτρα ἦν ὁ Χριστός (SC 268:322). The corresponding Latin text reads: [E]t occasionem nobis praestat intellegentiae, ut possimus aduertere quorum figurae erant ista, quae illis accidebant, cum dicit: Bibebant enim de spiritali sequenti petra, petra uero erat Christus.

"pneumatic rock" at the heart of Scripture's pneumatic readings. All things in Scripture are a "figure," or τύπος of Christ. The Greek term τύπος literally means a blow, impression or mark, and metaphorically a type, figure or model. The different events discussed by the pneumatic sense, then, have the very imprint of Christ and are in some way types, figures or models of Christ and his actions.

Origen more specifically describes these events as follows:

> [I]t is a spiritual explanation when one is able to show of what kind of "heavenly things" the Jews "after the flesh" served a copy and a shadow, and of what "good things to come" the law has a "shadow." And, speaking generally, we have, in accordance with the apostolic promise, to seek after "the wisdom in a mystery, even the wisdom that has been hidden, which God foreordained before the worlds unto the glory" of the righteous, "which none of the rulers of this world knew." The same apostle [Paul] also says somewhere, after mentioning certain narratives from Exodus and Numbers, that "these things happened unto them figuratively, and they were written for our sake, upon whom the ends of the ages are come."[101]

Given the fact that Christ, as the pneumatic rock, is the connection between events, the "'good things to come'" for which "the law has a 'shadow,'" and the "narratives from Exodus and Numbers, that . . . 'happened . . . figuratively, . . . written for our sake, upon whom the end of the ages are come,'" implicitly refer to the ways in which the characters, events and law of the Old Testament prefigured the Incarnation and Resurrection of Christ, and by implication the emer-

---

[101] *Princ.* 4.2.6 (referring to Heb. 8:5, Rom. 8:5, Heb. 10:1, and then quoting, in order, 1 Cor. 2:7, 8; 10:11; Butterworth 279–280); Πνευματικὴ δὲ διήγησις τῷ δυναμένῳ ἀποδεῖξαι, ποίων **ἐπουρανίων ὑποδείγματι καὶ σκιᾷ** οἱ κατὰ σάρκα Ἰουδαῖοι ἐλάτρευον, καὶ τίνων **μελλόντων ἀγαθῶν ὁ νόμος ἔχει σκιάν**. Καὶ ἁπαξαπλῶς ἐπὶ πάντων κατὰ τὴν ἀποστολικὴν ἐπαγγελίαν ζητητέον **σοφίαν ἐν μυστηρίῳ** τὴν ἀποκεκρυμμένην, ἣν προώρισεν ὁ θεὸς πρὸ τῶν αἰώνων εἰς δόξαν τῶν δικαίων, ἣν οὐδεὶς τῶν ἀρχόντων τοῦ αἰῶνος τούτου ἔγνωκε. Φησὶ δέ που ὁ αὐτὸς ἀπόστολος, χρησάμενός τισι ῥητοῖς ἀπὸ τῆς Ἐξόδου καὶ τῶν Ἀριθμῶν, ὅτι **Ταῦτα τυπικῶς συνέβαινεν ἐκείνοις, ἐγράφη δὲ δι' ἡμᾶς, εἰς οὓς τὰ τέλη τῶν αἰώνων κατήντησε** (SC 268:320, 322). The corresponding Latin text reads: Spiritalis autem explanatio est talis, si qui potest ostendere quorum *caelestium exemplaribus et umbrae deseruiunt* hi, qui secundum carnem Iudaei sunt, et quorum *futurorum bonorum umbram habet lex*, et si qua huiusmodi in scripturis sanctis inueniuntur; uel cum requiritur quae sit illa sapientia *in mysterio abscondita, quam praedestinauit deus ante saecula in gloriam nostram, quam nemo principum huius saeculi cognouit*; uel illud quod dicit ipse apostolus, cum exemplis quibusdam utitur de Exodo uel Numeris et ait quia *haec in figura contingebant illis, scripta sunt autem propter nos, in quos fines saeculorum deuenerunt*."

gence of the church.[102] Likewise, the "heavenly things" of which "the Jews 'after the flesh' served as a copy and a shadow" implicitly refer to the ways in which the characters, events and law of the Old Testament prefigured the Eschaton and, thus, salvation of the church and its faithful inhabitants.

By stating that the pneumatic truths about these events convey the "wisdom" of God—"'the wisdom in a mystery . . . that . . . God foreordained before the worlds unto the glory' of the righteous, 'which none of the rulers of this world knew'"[103]—Origen stresses the mysterious nature of the pneumatic sense. Ultimately, it speaks of eternal things, relaying mysteries concerning God's past and future relations to humankind, all centering on Christ and conveying truths about the Incarnation, the church and the Eschaton. As the direct communication of God's eternal wisdom, the pneumatic sense cannot be easy for the time-laden person to comprehend fully or even grasp initially.[104]

---

[102] In the later homiletic explications of theory treated in chapter 3, Origen will stress that the church is one of the themes of the pneumatic sense. Also, in the practical examples treated in chapters 4 and 5, Origen will show that pneumatic readings focus on the church as the receiver, protector and earthly dispenser of divine truths as well as the collective beneficiary of God's gift of salvation.

[103] Origen borrows much of the language for this last passage from New Testament passages that he attributes to Paul. In this way, he relies on the authority and precedent of Paul for describing the pneumatic sense, just as he relied on Paul's treatment of the Old Testament text about the muzzle and the ox in order to offer an example of the psychic sense. By these examples and references, Origen claims that his threefold method carries the authority of Scripture and apostolic precedent. In addition to Origen's use of Prov. 22 as instruction for a threefold method, he also understands scriptural authority for this approach to reside in Paul's promotion of it by example and, in the case of the pneumatic sense, by description as well. Throughout *Princ.* 4.2.6, Origen cites passages from Hebrews, Romans, First Corinthians and Galatians, attributing them all to Paul. Although biblical scholars today understand certain of these books to be written by persons other than Paul, what is important here is that Origen cites each text to establish Paul, and thus Scripture itself, as the authority and precedent for seeking pneumatic and psychic meanings in Scripture. For Origen, such passages substantiate his earlier claim that the threefold method is part of the rule of faith (*Princ.* 4.2.2; [Butterworth 271–272]; SC 268:300, and this chapter's earlier discussion of this passage and more generally the discussion of the spiritual purpose of Scripture's communication).

[104] Origen suggests here in *Princ.* 4, and confirms in later theory (for example, *Hom. Num.* 9, treated in chapter 3), that to comprehend pneumatic truths is to engage in the transforming contemplation of divine things (theosis), and in so doing to become like God—indeed, taking on God's own wisdom. The practical examples of chapters 4 and 5 will substantiate this understanding of the pneumatic sense.

Also, in the above passage, Origen refers to this eternally focused sense as the πνευματικὴ διήγησις or "spiritual explanation" in Scripture. The Greek term διήγησις, translated here as "explanation," means narration or statement of the case, and derives from the deponent verb διηγέομαι, which means to describe or narrate *in full*. This term suggests that the pneumatic sense stands apart from the other two senses in its ability to narrate the scriptural passage *in full*. In other words, this third sense somehow completes the story that the three senses together tell for the particular passage. The pneumatic sense is the fulfillment of the passage's whole message, and, indeed, of Scripture's entire narration.[105]

Scripture's story, which the pneumatic sense completes or fulfills, seems ultimately to concern salvation. For from the above explanations of the pneumatic sense, we understand the following (which will be confirmed by Origen's extended theory): The past spiritual events for which Christ is the center relate to the Incarnation, and the inevitable future spiritual events pertain to the Eschaton. Christ connects the events of the Incarnation with those of the Eschaton by offering himself on the Cross for the sins of humankind so that persons might reach salvation. The pneumatic sense, then, brings out of biblical passages types or figures of Christ that inform the hearer of aspects pertaining to the Incarnation and/or the Eschaton, as well as the main events that stem from them: the emergence of the church and its eventual salvation.

Origen confirms this understanding of the pneumatic sense's focus and content by offering a passage from Paul's Letter to the Galatians as an illustration of pneumatic reading:

---

[105] The pneumatic sense also is the telos, or perfection, of the human person. As considered above, for Origen, the Holy Spirit designed Scripture to help the individual soul reach the telos of human nature, eternal salvation. Since the pneumatic sense offers truths directly related to salvation, it is equivalent with that goal. As homiletic passages on exegetical theory will reveal (in chapter 3), the pneumatic sense and eternal salvation are essentially one and the same, for this third sense, according to Origen, will live on after this life even though the somatic and psychic senses will fade away at the final resurrection. This pneumatic sense is eternal, because it is the wisdom of God. In the early theory of *Princ.* 4, Origen only sets the stage for developing a fuller understanding of the pneumatic sense by stressing that it directly conveys God's wisdom to those prepared to receive it, and, as they understand divine wisdom with increasing intimacy, they more nearly approach the activity of heaven.

[I]n the epistle to the Galatians, speaking in terms of reproach to those who believe that they are reading the law and yet do not understand it, and laying it down that they who do not believe that there are allegories in the writings do not understand the law, he [Paul] says: "Tell me, you who desire to be under the law, do you not hear the law? For it is written, that Abraham had two sons, one by the hand-maid and one by the free woman. Howbeit the son by the handmaid is born after the flesh; but the son by the free woman is born through promise. Which things contain an allegory; for these women are two covenants. . . ."[106]

Origen draws on Paul's explanation that Hagar and Sarah represent "two covenants" with God. Origen does not elaborate further on this example, perhaps believing that it speaks for itself or that its allegorical (figurative) meaning is well known by his intended audience of presbyters. Yet, by reviewing Paul's message, it is possible to recognize how Origen understands this passage to be an example of pneumatic meaning.

For Paul, the slave woman, Hagar, represents the "present," earthly "Jerusalem" and "is in slavery with her children,"[107] while the free woman, Sarah, represents "the Jerusalem above," heaven, and "is free" and "our mother."[108] Paul refers to these representations as "allegory,"[109] constituting part of his larger argument that a Gentile who converts to Christianity need not receive circumcision or observe all of the Old Testament laws.[110] The Christian believer is a child

---

[106] *Princ.* 4.2.6 (quoting Gal. 4:21–24a, which refers to Gen. 16:15 and Gen. 21:1–21; Butterworth, 280); Ἀλλὰ μὴν καὶ ἐν τῇ πρὸς Γαλάτας ἐπιστολῇ, οἱονεὶ ὀνειδίζων τοῖς ἀναγινώσκειν νομίζουσι τὸν νόμον καὶ μὴ ουνιεῖσιν αὐτόν, μὴ συνιέναι κρίνων ἐκείνους, ὅσοι μὴ ἀλληγορίας εἶναι ἐν τοῖς γεγραμμένοις νομίζουσι· Λέγετέ μοι φησὶν οἱ ὑπὸ νόμον θέλοντες εἶναι, τὸν νόμον οὐκ ἀκούετε; Γέγραπται γὰρ ὅτι Ἀβραὰμ δύο υἱοὺς ἔσχεν, ἕνα ἐκ τῆς παιδίσκης καὶ ἕνα ἐκ τῆς ἐλευθέρας. Ἀλλ' ὁ μὲν ἐκ τῆς παιδίσκης κατὰ σάρκα γεγέννηται, ὁ δὲ ἐκ τῆς ἐλευθέρας διὰ τῆς ἐπαγγελίας· ἅτινά ἐστιν ἀλληγορούμενα· αὗται γάρ εἰσι δύο διαθῆκαι (SC 268:322, 324). The corresponding Latin texts reads: Ad Galatas uero scribens et uelut exprobrans quibusdam, qui uidentur sibi legere legem nec tamen intellegunt eam, pro eo quod allegorias esse in his quae scripta sunt ignorant, ita cum increpatione quadam ait ad eos: *Dicite mihi uos, qui sub lege uultis esse, legem non audistis? Scriptum est enim quia Abraham duos filios habuit, unum ex ancilla et unum de libera. Sed ille quidem, qui de ancilla natus est, secundum carnem natus est, qui uero de libera, secundum repromissionem: quae sunt allegorica. Haec enim sunt duo testamenta . . .*

[107] Gal. 4:25 RSV.

[108] Gal. 4:26 RSV.

[109] The Greek term translated here as "allegory" comes from the verb ἀλληγορέω, which means to speak figuratively or metaphorically or by way of veiled language.

[110] See esp. Gal. 5.

of the "free woman," Sarah, and, like Isaac, is heir to the covenant that God established with Abraham.

For Origen, Paul employs a pneumatic reading here, because his reading of Sarah and Hagar stress that Christian faith (presumably in the saving effects of the Cross), not physical circumcision, is the true mark of one who is a free heir to God's promises, including ultimately arrival at the Jerusalem above, or heaven. With this example, then, Origen implicitly reaffirms that the pneumatic sense focuses on the Incarnation, the age of the church that emerges from it, and the eschatological hope of salvation, all unified by the central, connecting theme of Christ and his saving power.[111]

G. *Summary of the Definitions*

In brief, Origen views the somatic sense as the literal reading of the text that edifies the hearer by true history or moral instruction. The psychic sense is a figurative reading that speaks to the hearer's duty to live morally. It offers a more general message than that of the moral somatic sense: While the moral somatic sense promotes particular virtues, the psychic sense informs the soul that vice and virtue fight temporally for its possession and, thus, urges Scripture's hearer to grow in virtue generally. Finally, the pneumatic sense centers on Christ, conveying insights about the Incarnation, church and Eschaton. While all three senses contribute to Scripture's salvation story, the pneumatic sense somehow *completes or fulfills* this story.

IV. *The Process of Scripture's Communication*

Having established Origen's understanding of the purpose and basic content of the three senses, that is, *why* and *what* they communicate to Scripture's hearers, we turn to his explanation of their process of

---

[111] This definition of the pneumatic sense stresses its focus on two main saving acts of Christ: the Incarnation and the Eschaton—in other words, Christ's first and second coming. While this work does not cover later, medieval biblical exegesis, it is worth noting here that Origen's three senses arguably translate directly into the four medieval senses: (1) historical/literal, (2) tropological/moral, (3) allegorical, and (4) anagogical. We need only recognize that the last two medieval senses—the allegorical and anagogical—resemble the two focuses of Origen's pneumatic sense: the Incarnational and the eschatological. It may be possible to trace Origen's method of three senses through Evagrius Ponticus and John Cassian ultimately to the medieval practice of four senses.

communication, that is, *how* Scripture communicates their messages to the hearer for his salvation. As discussed above, Origen likely presents the process before the definitions in order to forewarn concerned audience members that all three senses work as an integral whole, and, thus, no part of their content can be deleted or changed. However, we presently will examine the process with the definitions in mind so that we can consider how as a body, soul, and spirit they effect Scripture's spiritual purpose.

Origen's discussion of Scripture's process of communication in *Princ.* 4.2.4 establishes three points: first, all three senses address every individual human soul; second, they edify the soul at its various levels of progress toward a full understanding of Scripture's truths; and, third, they direct this progress by functioning as a body, soul, and spirit.

A. *The Intended Hearer as the Individual Human Soul*

Origen first explains that each hearer is to write the three senses onto his own soul: "[O]ne must therefore portray the meanings of the sacred writings in a threefold way upon one's own soul . . . ."[113] The Greek term νόημα, translated here in the plural accusative form as "meanings," signifies thought, understanding, or mind. Origen employs this word in the plural form, logically referring to all three senses. The phrase τριχῶς or *tripliciter*, "in a threefold way," confirms that "meanings" refers to all three senses. Both parts of the verb translated as "must portray" are significant. The auxiliary verb δεῖ or *oportet*, which in both languages represents the impersonal verb meaning "it is necessary" or "one must," makes the action "to portray" an imperative. The Greek term translated as portray comes from the verb ἀπογράφω, meaning to write out, copy or register. Similarly, the Latin term for this action, *describere*, means to transcribe or copy. The object of this necessary action is "one's own soul," which appears in the Greek as εἰς τὴν ἑαυτοῦ ψυχὴν and in Latin as *in anima sua unumquemque*. Thus, Origen states here that a person must copy upon his *own* soul *all three* meanings, understandings, or minds of Scripture.

---

[112] *Princ.* 4.2.4; (Butterworth, 275); Οὐκοῦν τριχῶς ἀπογράφεσθαι δεῖ εἰς τὴν ἑαυτοῦ θυχὴν τὰ τῶν ἁγίων γραμμάτων νοήματα (SC 268:310). The corresponding Latin text reads: Tripliciter ergo describere oportet in anima sua unumquemque diuinarum intellegentiam litterarum . . .

By addressing this imperative impersonally and generally, Origen suggests that this task is expected of every human person. Scripture's spiritual communication, then, is personal and interactive with every human soul. Greer confirms Origen's interactive view of Scripture, when he states that "Origen virtually identifies the spiritual life with the interpretation of Scripture . . . ," suggesting that spiritual growth occurs through engagement with Scripture.[113] Scripture, through the preacher's interpretation and conveyance of it to believers, is the actual facilitator of the spiritual life by its personal interaction with every believer's soul.

B. *The Progressive Stages of Edification*

Origen describes the progressive stages by which Scripture edifies the hearer and leads him toward a fuller understanding of divine things:

> . . . so that [(1)] the simpler man may be edified by what we call the flesh of the scripture, . . . the obvious interpretation; while [(2)] the man who has made some progress may be edified by its soul . . .; and [(3)] the man who is perfect . . . [that is, possessing] "a wisdom not of this world . . . but . . . God's wisdom in a mystery, even the wisdom that has been hidden, which God foreordained before the worlds unto our glory" . . . may be edified by the spiritual law, which has a "shadow of the good things to come."[114]

---

[113] Greer, *Early Biblical Interpretation*, 180. See also the discussion of Greer's analysis in chapter 1.

[114] *Princ.* 4.2.4 (citing 1 Cor. 2:6–7 and Heb. 10:1, as well as alluding to Rom 7:14; Butterworth, 275–276). The fuller Greek text reads: ἵνα ὁ μὲν ἁπλούστερος οἰκοδομῆται ἀπὸ τῆς οἰονεὶ σαρκὸς τῆς γραφῆς, οὕτως ὀνομαζόντων ἡμῶν τὴν πρόχειρον ἐκδοχήν, ὁ δὲ ἐπὶ ποσὸν ἀναβεβηκὼς ἀπὸ τῆς ὡσπερεὶ ψυχῆς αὐτῆς, ὁ δὲ τέλειος καὶ ὅμοιος τοῖς παρὰ τῷ ἀποστόλῳ λεγομένοις· **Σοφίαν δὲ λαλοῦμεν ἐν τοῖς τελείοις, σοφίαν δὲ οὐ τοῦ αἰῶνος τούτου οὐδὲ τῶν ἀρχόντων τοῦ αἰῶνος τούτου τῶν καταργουμένων, ἀλλὰ λαλοῦμεν θεοῦ σοφίαν ἐν μυστηρίῳ τὴν ἀποκεκρυμμένην, ἣν προώρισεν ὁ θεὸς πρὸ τῶν αἰώνων εἰς δόξαν ἡμῶν, ἀπὸ τοῦ πνευματικοῦ νόμου,** σκιὰν περιέχοντος τῶν μελλόντων ἀγαθῶν (SC 268:310, 312). The corresponding Latin text reads in full: id est, ut simpliciores quique aedificentur ab ipso, ut ita dixerim, corpore scripturarum (sic enim appellamus communem istum et historialem intellectum); si qui uero aliquantum iam proficere coeperunt et possunt amplius aliquid intueri, ab ipsa scripturae anima aedificentur; qui uero perfecti sunt et similes his, de quibus apostolus dicit: *Sapientiam autem loquimur inter perfectos, sapientiam uero non huius saeculi neque principum huius saeculi, qui destruentur, sed loquimur dei sapientiam in mysterio absconditam, quam praedestinauit deus ante saecula in gloriam nostram,* hi tales ab ipsa spiritali lege, quae umbram habet futurorum bonorum, tamquam ab spiritu aedificentur.

All three senses are designed to edify the hearer.[115] Given Scripture's purpose, each sense is to be written upon the soul of the hearer so as to facilitate his progress toward perfection and salvation.

Scripture contains beneficial meaning even for the "simpler" person by way of its "flesh." Origen also refers to this flesh as πρόχειρον ἐκδοχήν, translated here as the "obvious meaning." This Greek phrase means literally the ready, handy, convenient or common understanding or interpretation. The simpler person sees in Scripture what is edifying on its surface, at the literal level of interpretation. The Greek term ἁπλούστερος, translated here as "simpler," derives from the adjective ἁπλοῦς or ἁπλόος, which means simple, onefold, or single-minded. The simpler person comes to Scripture with a single focus, centering on its flesh (σάρξ). While Rufinus employs in the Latin translation the term *corpus* for "body," Origen uses the Greek word σάρξ for "flesh" here rather than σῶμα for "body," perhaps to emphasize that the simpler person cannot yet see anything except the surface of Scripture.[116]

Next, the human soul who "has made some progress" can receive edification from Scripture's "soul," ψυχή or *anima*. The Greek term ἀναβαίνω, translated here as "progress," means to go up, mount or ascend, as in ascending to heaven or to higher knowledge. Origen suggests that the meaning conveyed by Scripture's soul, the psychic sense, can edify the person who already ascends toward the highest truths in Scripture and is at least some distance beyond receiving edification only from its surface meaning.

Finally, the person who has become "perfect" can receive edification from Scripture's πνευματικοῦ νόμου, translated here as "spiritual law," appearing in the Latin as *spiritus*, or "spirit."[117] The Greek term

---

[115] Origen employs here, as in the passage on two and three firkins in *Princ.* 4.2.5 (analyzed above), the Greek term οἰκοδομέω, translated here as "edify." Again, it means literally to build a house, and metaphorically to build up or edify. The corresponding Latin term, *aedificare*, also means to build as well as build up or edify. Origen perceives that Scripture's purpose is to edify hearers in the sense of helping them prepare for and move toward perfection and salvation.

[116] Also, arguably Origen feels free to employ "flesh" synonymously with "body" when speaking of Scripture, since the Holy Spirit wrote Scripture for the benefit of humankind and it contains the words of Christ and, thus, cannot become disordered. The term "flesh," then, holds a negative connotation with regard to the human person that cannot translate over to Scripture's own nature. See the discussion of Origen's anthropology below.

[117] Origen borrows the term "spiritual law" from Rom. 7:14, where Paul stresses that he knows the "law is spiritual," but still he is "carnal" and sins. By using the

τέλειος, translated here as "perfect," also means full, fulfilled, complete, or accomplished, and stems from the noun τέλος (telos), which means the end, purpose, consummation, achievement or attainment of something. Origen suggests here that the person who makes full progress with the senses perceives the end or fulfillment of Scripture's message, which is found in its spiritual law or spirit. This recalls Origen's definition of the pneumatic sense as the fulfillment of Scripture's salvation story.[118]

Origen next presents a passage from Hermas' *The Shepherd* as authority for his view that the three senses edify through progressive stages:[119]

> [I]n The Shepherd . . . Hermas is bidden to "write two books," and after this to "announce to the presbyters of the Church" what he has learned from the Spirit. This is the wording: "You shall write two books, and shall give one to Clement and one to Grapte. And Grapte shall admonish the widows and the orphans. But Clement shall send to the cities without, and you [Hermas] shall announce to the presbyters of the Church."[120]

---

term "spiritual law" interchangeably with "spirit" of Scripture or "spiritual (pneumatic) sense," Origen again implicitly draws on Paul as authority for seeking the figurative, pneumatic sense in Scripture.

[118] By again citing language that he attributes to Paul, Origen offers the same details about the pneumatic sense that he set forth in his definition of it. This perfect person speaks "a wisdom not of this world," "God's wisdom in a mystery" which "has been hidden, which God foreordained before the worlds unto our glory" (1 Cor. 2:6–7). Thus, the fullness or end of Scripture's knowledge and instruction focuses on God's "wisdom," which presents itself to persons in the temporal realm as "mysteries" of the non-temporal realities. This fullness conveys to the perfected temporal hearer the "spiritual law, which has 'a shadow of the good things to come'" (Rom. 7:14 and Heb. 10:1).

[119] Specifically, Origen refers to Herm. *Vis.* 2.4.3. Origen introduces Hermas' work as "a book which is despised by some" (*Princ.* 4.2.4; Butterworth, 276); ἐν τῷ ὑπό τινων καταφρονουμένῳ βιβλίῳ (SC 268:312). The corresponding Latin text reads: qui a nonnullis contemni uidetur. The Greek term for "despise" comes from the verb καταφρονέω, which means to think slightly of, disdain, despise, scorn or condemn. Origen seems to suggest that Hermas' *The Shepherd* is thought slightly of, or not considered authoritative, on divine matters. Butterworth remarks: "Irenaeus and Clement of Alexandria both treated Hermas as an inspired writer, as Origen does here" (Butterworth, 277, n. 1). Origen cites Hermas as authority here and yet seems to warn his audience that they should not assume that this authority will be accepted by all persons. Perhaps Origen uses this controversial text not only because he views it to have the authority of Divinely inspired words, but also because it figuratively portrays God directing the human author of His Words to place within them the three different senses of meaning. Origen seems to consider this imagery so relevant to his theoretical discussion of the three senses that he is willing to employ it even though he is aware that the text at hand is of debatable authority.

[120] *Princ.* 4.2.4; (Butterworth, 276–277); Διὰ τοῦτο ἡμεῖς καὶ τὸ ἐν τῷ ὑπό τινων

The Spirit instructs Hermas to write "two books," but there are three messages and messengers.[121] While the two books are for the first two messengers, Grapte and Clement, Hermas is the third messenger who, receiving his instruction directly, does not need to write a book of instruction for himself. Each of these three messengers is to bring Scripture to a group of souls that reflects a respective level of advancement in understanding Scripture.

This passage discusses four types of souls to receive instruction, but they amount to three progressive levels of the individual soul's ability to understand Scripture:

> Now Grapte, who admonishes the widows and orphans, is the bare letter, which admonishes those child souls that are not yet able to enroll God as their Father and are on this account called orphans, and which also admonishes those who while no longer associating with the unlawful bridegroom are in widowhood because they have not yet become worthy of the true one. But Clement, who has already gone beyond the letter, is said to send the sayings "to the cities without," . . . to the souls that are outside all bodily and lower thoughts; while the disciple of the Spirit [Hermas] is bidden to announce the message in person, no longer through letters but through living words, to the presbyters or elders of the whole Church of God, to men who have grown grey through wisdom.[122]

καταφρονουμένῳ βιβλίῳ, τῷ Ποιμένι, περὶ τοῦ προστάσσεσθαι τὸν Ἑρμᾶν δύο γράψαι βιβλία, καὶ μετὰ ταῦτα αὐτὸν ἀναγγέλλειν τοῖς πρεσβυτέροις τῆς ἐκκλησίας ἃ μεμάθηκεν ὑπὸ τοῦ πνεύματος, οὕτω διηγούμεθα. Ἔστι δὲ ἡ λέξις αὕτη · **Γράψεις δύο βιβλία, καὶ δώσεις ἓν Κλήμεντι καὶ ἓν Γραπτῇ. Καὶ Γραπτὴ μὲν νουθετήσει τὰς χήρας καὶ τοὺς ὀρφανούς, Κλήμης δὲ πέμψει εἰς τὰς ἔξω πόλεις, σὺ δὲ ἀναγγελεῖς τοῖς πρεσβυτέροις τῆς ἐκκλησίας** (SC 268:312, 314). The corresponding Latin text reads: Quod nos etiam in libello Pastoris, qui a nonnullis contemni uidetur, designatum uidemus, cum iubetur Hermas duos libellos scribere et postea ipse denuntiare presbyteris ecclesiae quae ab spiritu didicit. Quod his uerbis scriptum est: *Et scribes inquit duos libellos, et dabis unum Clementi et unum Graptae. Et Grapte quidem commoneat uiduas et orfanos, Clemens uero mittat per omnes ciuitates, quae foris sunt, tu uero annuntiabis presbyteris ecclesiae.*

[121] Grant argues that Origen's use of the Hermas passage constitutes an immediate breakdown in his presentation of a "threefold" method of interpretation by itself presenting a twofold illustration (*The Letter and the Spirit*, 94–95). I will demonstrate that Origen reads the passage from Hermas as promoting *three* separate senses of scriptural meaning.

[122] *Princ.* 4.2.4. (Butterworth 277); Γραπτὴ μὲν γάρ, ἡ νουθετοῦσα τὰς χήρας καὶ τοὺς ὀρφανούς, αὐτὸ ψιλόν ἐστι τὸ γράμμα, νουθετοῦν τοὺς παῖδας τὰς ψυχὰς καὶ μηδέπω πατέρα θεὸν ἐπιγράψασθαι δυναμένους καὶ διὰ τοῦτο ὀρφανοὺς καλουμένους, νουθετοῦν δὲ καὶ τὰς μηκέτι μὲν τῷ παρανόμῳ νυμφίῳ χρωμένας, χηρευούσας δὲ τῷ μηδέπω ἀξίας αὐτὰς τοῦ νυμφίου γεγονέναι. Κλήμης δέ, ὁ ἤδη τοῦ γράμματος ἐξιστάμενος, εἰς τὰς ἔξω πόλεις λέγεται πέμπειν τὰ λεγόμενα, ὡς εἰ λέγοιμεν τὰς ἔξω τῶν σωματικῶν καὶ τῶν κάτω νοημάτων τυγχανούσας ψυχάς. Οὐκέτι δὲ διὰ γραμμάτων, ἀλλὰ διὰ λόγων ζώντων αὐτὸς ὁ μαθητὴς τοῦ πνεύματος προστάσσεται

Grapte is to instruct the first group of souls, which consists of two types: "widows and orphans." They receive the somatic meaning—the "bare letter" of the text and, implicitly, that which in it is edifying—since it will cause them to grow, or "become worthy" of greater truths. Both the widow and orphan represent the simpler, to whom Origen refers above as able to receive the flesh of Scripture. The simpler person is the beginner who is separated from God. The "child" soul is an orphan, because she has not declared God to be her Father and Creator. The "widowed" soul is one who once worshipped false gods or false images of the one God, but has become a widow by rejecting them and must now prepare for real marriage to the one true "Bridegroom," implicitly, Christ. The Spirit directs Hermas to instruct Grapte, Scripture's bare letter,[123] to offer its somatic sense to the orphaned and widowed souls, since union with this first sense is the beginning of union with God.

To the souls in the "cities without," the Spirit instructs Hermas to send Clement, "who has already gone beyond the letter." The souls in these cities have progressed to the extent that they have moved "without" or outside of "all bodily and lower thoughts." These cities recall those who "have made some progress," that is, those who are ready to apprehend meanings of Scripture figuratively, according to Scripture's "soul," or psychic meaning.

Meanwhile, Hermas is the "disciple of the Spirit," the one whom the Spirit has entrusted with the delivery of all of these instructions. While he is to write a book to Grapte and Clement, instructing them to convey somatic and psychic meanings respectively to simpler souls

---

ἀναγγέλλειν τοῖς τῆς πάσης ἐκκλησίας τοῦ θεοῦ πρεσβυτέροις πεπολιωμένοις ὑπὸ φρονήσεως (SC 268:314, 316). The corresponding Latin text reads: Est ergo Grapte quae orfanos iubetur et uiduas commonere, purus ipsius litterae intellectus, per quem commonentur animae pueriles, quae nondum patrem deum habere meruerunt et propterea orfani appellantur. Sed et uiduae sunt, quae ab illo quidem iniquo uiro, cui contra legem iunctae fuerant, recesserunt, uiduae uero permanent ex eo quod nondum profecerunt in hoc, ut caelesti sponso iungerentur. Clemens uero his, qui iam recedunt a littera, in eas quae foris sunt ciuitates mittere iubetur quae dicta sunt, uelut si diceret: ad eas animas, quae per haec aedificatae extra corporis curam et extra desideria carnalia esse coeperunt. Ipse uero quae ab spiritu sancto didicerat non per litteras neque per libellum, sed uiuenti uoce iubetur annuntiare presbyteris ecclesiarum Christi, id est his, qui maturum prudentiae sensum pro capacitate doctrinae spiritalis gerunt.

[123] The name "Grapte" is based on the feminine form of the Greek adjective γραπτή, which means written, or marked with letters (related to the neuter noun γράμμα, meaning a written character or letter, as in the alphabet). Here Grapte represents the literal, straightforward reading of text from which arises the first, obvious—somatic—sense.

and souls who have made some progress, the Spirit instructs Hermas "to announce" his "message in person, no longer through letters but through living words." Hermas' message consists of "wisdom," which recalls the description of the pneumatic sense as the "spiritual law," conveying "God's wisdom in a mystery" "of the good things to come." He should deliver this third message in person, thus inter-acting more intimately with his audience than Grapte and Clement interact with their audiences. Hermas is to convey his message to the "presbyters or elders of the whole Church of God," those "who have grown grey through wisdom." They are souls who have pro-gressed even further than those in the cities without. They are the "perfect" who have achieved the ability to grasp not only the somatic and psychic senses but also the pneumatic sense. They now are able to receive the deepest truths of the pneumatic sense, indeed, the full-ness of Scripture's whole message.[124]

By this interpretation of Hermas and his preceding discussion of Scripture's body, soul and spirit, Origen stresses that Scripture has three senses that edify the soul progressively. However, he does not identify three innately separate groups of people: that is, some who always will be simpler, some who will make only some progress, and others who will reach the fullness of Scripture's knowledge.[125] Rather,

---

[124] I have chosen to discuss Origen's portrayal of the three characters in the pas-sage from *The Shepherd*—Grapte, Clement and Hermas—as the messengers rather than the messages, or senses themselves, since they are given messages to deliver to others. In the case of Grapte, I explained, in n. 123 above, that the Greek mean-ing of that name suggests that he represents the letter of the text, which properly is a messenger, since, as discussed above, the somatic sense and the literal reading of a text are not synonymous terms for Origen: the somatic sense is found only in literal readings that are edifying. However, it is possible that Origen also consid-ered Grapte (with this qualification about the somatic versus literal reading of a text), Clement and Hermas also to represent the senses themselves. If so, Origen's discussion of Hermas' duties are important to note here. He explains that Hermas is to give his message to his audience more directly than are Grapte and Clement. Hermas is to speak his message in person to his respective audience. As the practical texts in the later chapters will emphasize, Origen understands the pneumatic sense to be the most direct rendering of God's own wisdom and secret truths to the advanced soul. In fact, as Origen will explain in *Hom. Num.* 9 (treated in chapter 3), the pneumatic sense alone will continue to edify in eternity, for it embodies God's own wisdom and love, interaction with which corresponds to the activity of salva-tion or heaven itself.

[125] This reading would be Gnostic, resembling Gnostic classifications of those who are not saved, those who will enjoy some kind of partial salvation, and those who will be wholly saved. See the earlier discussion on Origen's use of the terms for "psychic" and "moral" at the end of the definition of the psychic sense. Near the beginning of 4.2.4, Origen already stressed that each person should write Scripture's three senses onto his own soul. In other words, the saving edification of all three

here in 4.2.4, Origen speaks in terms of differing but progressive levels of advancement in the understanding of biblical truths. Scripture meets the soul at its most elementary level of understanding and, through the edification of each sense, builds up that soul for receipt of the next higher sense. By its own structure of three senses, Scripture is accessible and beneficial to every person, speaking to the hearer at whatever level of spiritual maturity he presently maintains, and then helping him to ascend up through its levels of knowledge, or meanings, ultimately to the fullness of God's revealed wisdom.[126]

Origen's language, though, suggests that the senses do not edify in a strictly consecutive way. They are *initially* grasped in a consecutive way: one cannot begin to receive the edification of the psychic sense until he has learned to receive the somatic meaning, nor can he receive the wisdom of the pneumatic meaning until he has learned to grasp the truths of the somatic and psychic senses. Still, there is no reason to assume here that Origen considers the benefits of the prior sense or senses to become useless when the hearer advances to an understanding of the next higher sense. Later chapters on Origen's practice will demonstrate that he understands that the senses build upon each other so that each continues to edify the hearer as he begins to grasp the next higher one.[127] The initial ability to comprehend them occurs hierarchically, but their beneficial effects continue and build. During this life, then, the "perfect" soul enjoys edification from all three senses simultaneously.

Throughout *Princ.* 4.2, Origen uses the term "perfect" in relation to the third, pneumatic meaning. As the examples in later chapters will confirm, although the perfect are teachers of the church, Origen suggests that *all* believers should seek this level of spiritual growth. Also, once a person begins to grasp the pneumatic sense, he will

senses is for everyone (*Princ.* 4.2.4; [Butterworth, 275]; SC 268:310). See also the recent discussion of the intended hearer of Scripture as the individual human soul.

[126] Torjesen explains how Origen presents in *Princ.* 4.2.4 progressive stages of edification for the one (indeed, for each) hearer of Scripture rather than different messages for three separate classes of hearers (*Hermeneutical Procedure*, 40–43; and idem, "'Body,' 'Soul,' and 'Spirit,'" 19–22; and the discussion of Torjesen's views in chapter 1).

[127] In contrast, Torjesen observes that "although there are three stages there is only one movement: from the lower to the higher ones" ("'Body,' 'Soul,' and 'Spirit,'" 21).

continue to grow in his understanding of it, being brought into greater intimacy with it by continued edification from the somatic and psychic senses. The "perfect," then, are not "completed," but are the more advanced among spiritual journeyers. They have become able to receive edification from all three senses, and they now have the privilege to receive more edification as well as the duty to help other souls also to progress in understanding Scripture's edifying truths.[128]

Logic dictates that Origen assumes that his audience of presbyters is among the "perfect" who can grasp all three senses, since he expects them to comprehend his definitions for the three senses and his explanation of how they are to be communicated to others. The elders and presbyters whom Hermas addresses, as well as Grapte and Clement, resemble those of Origen's own audience for this treatise. Origen, like Hermas, claims that he has received the wisdom to instruct presbyters and elders of the church on the deepest truths in Scripture and then to send them out as Graptes and Clements to preach Scripture's meanings to the ordinary folk.

Origen calls his audience of presbyters to expose all three senses to the audiences whom they instruct. They will find themselves preaching to crowds that include believers at beginning, intermediate, and advanced capacities to understand Scripture, and Scripture intends all these believers to eventually receive all of its meanings, its whole mind.[129]

Implicit here is Origen's understanding that Scripture is the first and paradigmatic instructor of souls. It both holds the truths necessary to build up the human soul and is the chief instructor of these truths. While the presbyter conveys the Word to his audience, it is that Word, or Scripture, that holds the instructions on how best to teach the truths that its three senses contain.

---

[128] Later chapters, especially chapter 5, will explore and substantiate these observations about Origen's view of the "perfect" person as continuing to progress spiritually throughout this life.

[129] Torjesen argues these same two points (*Hermeneutical Procedure*, 40–43; idem, "'Body,' 'Soul,' and 'Spirit,'" 20–24; and the discussion of Torjesen's analysis in chapter 1).

C. *The Senses as Body, Soul, and Spirit*

1. *The Anthropological Analogy to Scripture*

In order to explain fully his understanding of Scripture's own instructions for interpretation, Origen identifies the three senses with the
three parts of human nature: body (σῶμα or *corpus*), soul (ψυχή or
anima) and spirit (πνεῦμα or *spiritus*). He offers this analogy in the
following way:

> [J]ust as man consists of body, soul and spirit, so in the same way
> does the scripture, which has been prepared by God to be given for
> man's salvation.[130]

The connecting adverb for this metaphor, in the Greek ὥσπερ and
in the Latin *sicut*, means just as, even as or like. Just as the human
person "consists of" body, soul and spirit, "so in the same way (τὸν
αὐτὸν τρόπον)," or in Latin "so also (*ita etiam*)," does Scripture con-
sist of three such parts.[131] This parallel suggests that one better understands the functions and relation of Scripture's three senses when
one compares them to the functions and relation of the three human
parts.[132]

2. *Anthropology of the Human Person*

Origen explains the functions and relation of the three human parts
in the third book of *De Principiis*, and, thus, arguably sees no need
to reiterate them here in the fourth book. While his views are quite
explicit in the passages analyzed below from *Princ.* 3, it is useful to
consider first the likely precedence for his tripartite anthropology.

Origen most likely draws his understanding of human nature as
comprised of three parts, a body, soul and spirit, from Paul's lan-

---

[130] *Princ.* 4.2.4; (Butterworth, 276); Ὥσπερ γὰρ ὁ ἄνθρωπος συνέστηκεν ἐκ σώματος
καὶ ψυχῆς καὶ πνεύματος, τὸν αὐτὸν τρόπον καὶ ἡ οἰκονομηθεῖσα ὑπὸ θεοῦ εἰς
ἀνθρώπων σωτηρίαν δοθῆναι γραφή (SC 268:312). The corresponding Latin text
reads: Sicut ergo homo constare dicitur ex corpore et anima et spiritu, ita etiam
sancta scriptura, quae ad hominum salutem diuina largitione concessa est.
[131] The Greek term, translated here as "consists of," derives from the perfect
indicative active form of the verb συνίστημι, which in the perfect tense, when relating parts of a thing, means to be put together or composed of those parts.
[132] In his later, extended theory Origen continues to refer to Scripture's three
senses as "the body, the soul, and the spirit" (*Hom. Lev.* 5.5.3 [Rufinus], and the
full analysis of this homily in chapter 3).

guage in 1 Thessalonians: "May the God of peace himself sanctify you wholly (ὁλοτελεῖς); and may your spirit (τὸ πνεῦμα) and soul (ἡ ψυχὴ) and body (τὸ σῶμα) be kept sound and blameless at the coming of our Lord Jesus Christ."[133] The term ὁλοτελής stems from ὅλος for "whole" and τέλος for "end or completion" and, thus, conveys the emphatic concept "quite completely." By this term, Paul suggests that the spirit, body, and soul so completely define the human person that any deletion from or addition to them would change that nature. The order in which Paul mentions them is also important to Origen, since he will explain that the three parts are harmoniously ordered only when the spirit leads the soul and, in turn, the body as well.

Crouzel explains how Origen understands these three terms.[134] He points out that πνεῦμα is Paul's translation of the Hebrew word *ruach*, which means "expressing the action of God."[135] Though some Greeks (namely, Stoics) attributed some materiality to it, for Origen it is immaterial[136] and represents the image or imprint of God within human beings. For Origen, the spirit in the human person is not the same as but is directly drawn from the Holy Spirit.[137] The body, on the other hand, is wholly material and carries the soul. It is not the same as the flesh (σάρξ), but indulges in fleshly passions if not directed by the spirit.[138]

The soul has a complex philosophical history, but Origen departs from prior traditions, which tended to divide it into two or more separate entities, by viewing the soul as a singular element that

---

[133] 1 Thess 5:23 RSV. For the Greek text, see NA[27], 537. Crouzel also suggests that this is the main source for Origen's tripartite anthropology (*Origen*, 87).

[134] Crouzel, *Origen*, 87–92; also Ricardo Sanlés, "Origène," *Dictionnaire de Spiritualité*, (Paris: Beauchesne, 1982), 933–962, esp. 937–941; relying on, among others, J. Dupuis, "L'esprit de l'homme," *Étude sur l'anthropologie religieuse d'Origène* (Collection Museum Lessianum, section théologique 62; Bruges-Paris: Desclée de Brouwer, 1967); and Henri Crouzel, "L'anthropologie d'Origène dans la perspective du combat spirituel," *Revue d'ascétique et de mystique* 31 (Paris: Beauchesne 1955) 364–385.

[135] Crouzel, *Origen*, 88.

[136] Ibid.

[137] In *Dialogue with Heraclides*, when Origen explains the human nature of Jesus Christ, he both affirms the tripartite nature of the human person and stresses that the human spirit is *not* identical with the Holy Spirit but derived from it (*Dial.* 5–8, esp. 6.26–27; Robert J. Daly, trans., *Origen: Treatise on the Passover and Dialogue of Origen with Heraclides and his Fellow Bishops on the Father, the Son and the Soul*, ACW 54 [New York: Paulist, 1992], 61–64, esp. 62). For the Greek, see Jean Scherer, ed. and trans., *Entretien d'Origène avec Héraclide* (SC 67; Paris: Cerf, 1960) 66, 68, 70, 72 and 74, esp. 70).

[138] Crouzel, *Origen*, 90–91; and Sanlés, "Origène," 938–939.

includes a rational part (the mind—νοῦς) and an irrational part
(which, Crouzel explains, is associated in the Bible at times with the
flesh—σάρξ).[139] It exists always in tension, struggling between these
two opposing forces, or tendencies.[140] The mind tends toward the
spirit and its godly ways, while the flesh tends toward the body and
its earthly passions.[141] The soul's internal state of conflict makes sense,
since, as discussed below, Origen understands the soul to be the seat
of choice, that is, the locus of the will.

In *Princ.* 3, Origen discusses the functions of and relations between
the spirit as the breath of God, the soul as the seat of choice, and
the body as the material covering. In this first passage, he stresses
the soul's need to choose the spirit or the flesh as the guide for
living:

> [T]he will of th[e] soul [in a human] is something intermediate between
> the flesh and the spirit, undoubtedly serving and obeying one of the
> two, whichever it has chosen to obey. If it gives itself up to the delights
> of the flesh, it makes men fleshly; if, however, it joins itself to the
> spirit, it causes a man to be 'in the spirit' and on this account to be
> called spiritual.[142]

The human soul (*anima*) does not direct its life of virtue or vice. It
is the seat of choice in the human person, and it must choose between
the person's flesh (*caro*) or spirit (*spiritus*) as its leader in life. The
Latin term *delegare*, translated here as "to choose," also means to delegate, assign or transfer. This term suggests that the human soul
does not possess unbridled choice in life. In other words, the soul

---

[139] Crouzel, *Origen*, 88–89 (referring specifically to Rom. 8:6); and Sanlés, "Origène,"
937–938.
[140] Crouzel explains that, for Origen, the human soul is "tendential" by its nature
(*Origen*, 87–92, esp. 88).
[141] Other systems of thought prior to and contemporaneous with Origen, regardless of how they separated the elements of soul, shared with Origen the concern
to explain its inherent, internal conflict (Crouzel, *Origen*, 88; Sanlés, "Origène,"
937–939). For discussions of other philosophical understandings of the soul, including especially those of Philo and Numenius (to whose works Origen likely had ready
access), as well as Stoics, Platonists, and other Middle Platonists, see John Dillon,
The Middle Platonists: 80 B.C. to A.D. 220 (Ithaca, New York: Cornell University Press,
1977), esp. 174–178, 375–378.
[142] *Princ.* 3.4.2; (Butterworth, 233); SC 268:206. This text is extant only in the
Latin, which reads: Et si ita est, constat quod huius animae uoluntas media quaedam
est inter carnem et spiritum, uni sine dubio e duobus seruiens et obtemperans,
cuicumque obtemperare delegerit, quaeque cum se delectationibus carnis subdiderit,
carnales homines facit, cum uero se spiritui iunxerit, in spiritu esse hominem facit
et propter hoc spiritalem nominari.

cannot choose to be its own leader or master. The extent of the soul's own freedom is its ability to delegate or transfer its allegiance to one of two other parties. The guidance of the flesh leads to destruction by "satiating" the soul over time with vices,[143] but the spirit leads to "salvation."[144]

It makes sense, therefore, that each of Scripture's three senses addresses the human *soul*, not his spirit or body, since it is the seat of choice. The senses direct the soul toward perfection and salvation by *helping it to choose* the person's spirit, rather than his flesh, as his guide for living.

In *Hom. Lev.* 2,[145] Origen again explains the soul's choice between flesh (*caro*) and spirit, but also mentions the "body (*corpus*)" within this dynamic:

> [I]t is not the spirit that sins. . . . [I]t is the soul which either "sows in the flesh" or "in the spirit" and which can go to ruin in sin or be converted from sin. For the body is its result to whatever he chooses; and the spirit is its guide to virtue if he wishes to follow it.[146]

Referring to Paul's words in Galatians, Origen emphasizes that it is the soul, *anima*, that chooses, or "sows" in the flesh, *caro*, or in the spirit, *spiritus*. The spirit has no connection with sin. It neither chooses nor directs vice. If the soul chooses to follow the flesh, then the spirit lies dormant, for it is innately good and cannot be brought to ruin. However, the fate of the body, *corpus*, results from the soul's choice. The body, along with the soul, either suffers the leadership of the flesh into sin, to its own shame and "ruin," or enjoys the benefits of virtue that result from the spirit's guidance.[147]

---

[143] *Princ.* 3.4.3; (Butterworth, 234); *satiata* (SC 268:208).

[144] *Princ.* 3.4.4; (Butterworth, 234); *salus* (SC 268:210).

[145] Extant are sixteen intact homilies on the book of Leviticus, translated into Latin by Rufinus. All English translations are from Gary Wayne Barkley, trans. *Origen: Homilies on Leviticus 1–16* (FC 83; Washington, D.C.: Catholic University of America, 1990). The Latin text is from: Marcel Borret, ed. and trans., *Origène: Homélies sur Le Lévitique* (2 vols.; SC 286, 287; Paris: Cerf, 1981).

[146] *Hom. Lev.* 2.2.7 (referring to Gal 6:8; FC 83:43); Non est ergo spiritus ille, qui peccat. . . . [C]onstat animam esse, quae vel *in carne* vel *in spiritu* seminat, et illam esse, quae vel in peccatum ruere possit vel converti a peccato. Nam corpus sequela eius est ad quodcumque delegerit; et spiritus dux eius est ad virtutem, si eum sequi velit (SC 286:100).

[147] The soul can command the body to submit, along with it, to the spirit. See the following example: "Someone who wants to become stronger should be strengthened only in spirit. Many are strengthened in the flesh, and their bodies become more powerful. But an athlete of God should become more powerful in spirit. Thus

The soul's choice, then, determines whether or not a person enjoys the right ordering of his three parts. When the flesh reigns, all three parts are not in use, suggesting disorder and disharmony. When the spirit reigns, the soul submits to the spirit and the body likewise submits to this choice. As a result of this right order, the fleshly tendencies are properly restrained.[148] In this dynamic, all three parts function and create internal harmony within the human person.[149]

Note here that Origen cannot view the flesh to be inherently evil, since, in his description of three progressive levels of edification just above, Origen refers to the first, obvious meaning of Scripture not as body but as flesh. For Origen, Scripture cannot suffer disorder of its three parts, for, as we will discuss below, the pneumatic sense always leads the other two senses in telling Scripture's salvation story and, thus, bringing the hearer into it. Origen feels free, then, to employ the terms flesh and body interchangeably when speaking of the edifying literal—or somatic—sense in Scripture, even though flesh seems to have a generally negative connotation with regard to the human person.

Still, even in relation to the human person, as Crouzel explains, for Origen, flesh "means more than the attraction to sin," but also "contains natural functions, which are not evil in themselves, and can be spiritualized without being destroyed, when the intellect adheres to the spirit."[150] The flesh is tamed or subdued when the body is in submission to the soul and spirit. Origen seems to relate the flesh to the passions, which pull the soul toward the body and then are

---

strengthened, he will crush the wisdom of the flesh. Spiritual activity will subject the body *to the mind's command*" Hom. Luc. 11.3 (treating Luke 1:80, referring to 2 Tim. 2:3–5 and Rom. 8:5–7, emphasis added; FC 94:45); Qui vult fortior fieri, non debet nisi spiritu confortari. Multi confortantur carne, corpore roborantur; athleta autem Dei spiritu roborandus est et, cum sic fuerit confortatus, sapientiam carnis elidet et spiritalis effectus subdet corpus animi imperio (SC 87:190). Note how in this passage Origen employs the term mind (νοῦς or *animus*) interchangeably with soul (*anima*). This is consistent with Crouzel's explanation that, for Origen, the mind represents the rational part of the soul (Crouzel, *Origen*, 88).
[148] "[T]he spirit has obtained the victory over the flesh," Princ. 3.4.3; (Butterworth 233; *cum spiritus carnem uicerit* (SC 268:208).
[149] Also, for examples of additional works in which Origen stresses that the soul must choose to follow either the ways of the spirit or the flesh and, as a result, either suffers sin and corruption or enjoys righteousness and eternal life, see Comm. Matt. 13.2 and Hom. Jer. 11.1–2.
[150] Crouzel, *Origen*, 89.

played out in the body if given full reign, or are subdued and disciplined whcn the person's soul chooses to follow the spirit. For Origen, then, the flesh is the tendency of the soul toward the body before corruption or the body's corrupting force after the flesh has succeeded in persuading the soul to choose its lead.

3. *The Significance of the Anthropological Analogy to Scripture*

The anthropological metaphor that Origen draws in 4.2.4 supports his definitions for the three scriptural senses, that is, *what* their messages convey, and it suggests *how* they communicate their messages to the human soul for the person's salvation. Here, we consider the significant implications of this analogy to Scripture, which will be substantiated by examples from Origen's extended theory and practice in later chapters.

First, Origen's definitions for the three senses confirm what this metaphor suggests about each sense. Just as the human body provides the outward appearance of the human person and covers over the soul and spirit, the somatic sense is drawn from the obvious interpretation of the biblical text and covers over Scripture's nonliteral meanings. As the human soul is the seat of choice in the person, so the soul of Scripture, the psychic sense, is the transitional sense, moving the hearer's focus, through urging growth in virtue, from earthly to heavenly things. It transports the hearer beyond a merely bodily understanding of Scripture and directs him toward its pneumatic truths. Moreover, as the human spirit is the most noble of human nature's three parts such that the human person is in harmony only when his spirit leads his soul and body, similarly, the spirit of Scripture, the pneumatic sense, is the fullness of Scripture's communication in that it most fully embodies God's wisdom and most directly focuses on the human telos of eternal salvation. The content of the pneumatic sense completes the meaning and significance of the somatic and psychic senses' messages.

Second, the anthropological analogy suggests that the three senses communicate the right order of the three human parts by embodying that order themselves, since the psychic and somatic senses always work to bring the attentive hearer to the fullness of Scripture's salvation story in the pneumatic sense. The three senses will never suffer disorder, because they are the divine word of Christ and construction of the Holy Spirit. The pneumatic sense never lies dormant.

It is never inaccessible to the hearer who is ready to grasp it. Since the other two senses always point the hearer to the pneumatic sense, together all three constitute a perfect model for the right order of the human person's body, soul and spirit.

Because the three senses embody the right order of body, soul and spirit, they have the supreme authority to teach this order to human persons. As the extended theory and practice will demonstrate, Origen understands that, the senses not only model the right order of the hearer's three parts through the interrelationship of their messages, but the message of each also teaches the attentive hearer the right order by direct instruction. Specifically, the somatic sense teaches God's goodness and His specific commands to live by virtue. The psychic sense alerts the hearer to the war that good and evil forces presently wage for possession of his soul and calls him to get involved by growing in virtue and shunning sin generally. The pneumatic sense teaches God's wisdom, especially in regard to God's saving plan through Christ, in the church and at the Eschaton. Together, these three messages call the hearer to grow in "imitation" of God's attributes—the virtues—so that the hearer may "attain to an *increasingly* perfect understanding" of divine knowledge—or wisdom.[151] The virtues, as Origen will emphasize in his practice, are equivalent to the fruits of the Holy Spirit, as listed in Gal. 5, and mastering them leads to a true share in God's wisdom. The three messages, then, teach the virtue and wisdom of God, which are emulated when the hearer's soul chooses to follow his spirit, as the divine imprint within him, which, in turn, will discipline his body to resist fleshly tendencies and direct his mind's focus to God. When perfect harmony in the human person is attained, he has reached the perfection necessary for salvation. Thus, the three senses, as Scripture's body, soul and spirit, are designed to lead the hearer, by way of model and direct instruction, to the perfect ordering of his own three parts as preparation for salvation.

By taking seriously Origen's correlation of Scripture's three senses to human nature's three parts, we begin to understand how Origen

---

[151] *Princ.* 4.4.10; (Butterworth 327, emphasis added). This section is extant only in the Latin. The relevant phrases are *per imitationem dei* and *peruenire ad intellectum perfectiorem quae dicit ad imaginem dei factum esse hominem . . . per omnem denique uirtutum chorum, quae cum in deo insint per substantiam, in homine possunt esse . . . per imitationem dei* (SC 268:426, 428).

views interaction with Scripture—as Christ's word and the Holy Spirit's composition—to be a dynamic, transformative process. When the hearer submits to Scripture, he is reformed into a rightly ordered person who imitates God and, thus, becomes worthy of eternal union with God.[152]

---

[152] Daniélou and Crouzel both stress, as discussed in chapter 1, that Origen imposes this anthropological structure upon Scripture, suggesting that it is a confusing and perhaps even unfortunate aspect of his exegetical theory. The implication is that Origen created an artificial construct that cannot play out in practice and that he perhaps even abandoned in later works. The following chapters' examples of extended theory and practice will confirm the significance of the anthropological analogy. Not only did Origen believe that it is a useful means of understanding the three senses, but also he believed that it essentially reflects Scripture's threefold structure and, thus, the way in which the three senses communicate saving truth to Scripture's hearers. Also, note that in his later, extended theory, Origen refers again to Scripture's three senses as "the body, the soul, and the spirit" (*Hom. Lev.* 5.5.3, and the full analysis of this homily in chapter 3).

CHAPTER THREE

EXTENDED EXEGETICAL THEORY

This chapter examines four homiletic texts in which Origen provides extended exegetical theory that confirms and further develops the definitions for the somatic, psychic and pneumatic senses that he set forth in *Princ.* 4. Because he delivered the homilies some ten years after he composed *De Principiis*,[1] these works demonstrate that his theory was consistent over time as well as carried over to his practical works.

De Lubac refers to two of the texts under review (*Hom. Lev.* 5 and *Hom. Num.* 9) as containing examples of moral/psychic meaning that is non-specific to Christian faith.[2] As discussed in chapter 1, de Lubac argues that Origen does not employ a Christian moral sense in his homilies and commentaries that is separate from the spiritual sense. He claims that when the moral sense is mentioned *before* the spiritual sense it is a moral meaning borrowed from Philo and, thus, is not necessary to *Christian* allegory.[3] De Lubac also argues that when the moral sense follows after the spiritual sense it is merely one theme of the multifocused nonliteral sense.

This work offers a different analysis of the orders in which the psychic and pneumatic senses appear within Origen's practical works. In *Hom. Lev.* 5 and *Hom. Num.* 9, as in *Princ.* 4, Origen mentions the somatic, psychic and then pneumatic sense, so as to emphasize the order in which Scripture's hearer *initially comprehends* the senses. In the other two texts reviewed in this chapter, *Hom. Gen.* 2 and *Hom. Gen.* 11, Origen mentions the somatic, pneumatic and then

---

[1] Refer to the chronology set forth in the Introduction. Origen likely wrote *De Principiis* as early as 229–230 while in Alexandria, but delivered the homilies around 239–242 during his later, Caesarean period.

[2] De Lubac, *Histoire et Esprit*, 141–142.

[3] Hanson agrees with de Lubac that Origen's practical use of a moral sense is borrowed from Philo and not specific to Christian allegory (*Allegory and Event*, 242). With Daniélou, though, Hanson finds that the theoretical precedent from Paul (in *Princ.* 4.2.6) is a borrowing from rabbinical traditions (ibid., 28 and 78–79; and Daniélou, *Gospel Message*, 285, n. 18).

psychic sense, an order also found in his practice when he offers full pneumatic and psychic readings. The practical examples in chapters 4 and 5 will demonstrate that Origen tends in practice to offer the pneumatic reading before the psychic in order to facilitate the *continuing cyclical effect of reinforcement* that these two senses have on each other's messages for the hearer who already has begun to grasp all three senses. In the context of theory, *Hom. Gen.* 2 and *Hom. Gen.* 11 also stress this continuing relationship between the two higher senses for the spiritual benefit of the advanced hearer.

All four examples of extended theory, as well as the practical examples in the later chapters, stress the innately Christian character of the middle, moral/psychic sense. Even if Origen borrowed the idea for this sense from Philonic or rabbinic sources, he applies it in a decidedly Christian way. The psychic sense offers moral exhortation that amounts to imitation of Christ and is designed to prepare Scripture's hearer for reception of Christ himself in the pneumatic sense and ultimately for the eternal union with God made possible only through Christ and the church. De Lubac's two categories for moral meaning, then, will break down upon close analysis of the texts.

Also, Hanson argued that in Origen's exegesis the moral/psychic and spiritual/pneumatic senses are fused or absorbed into one overly-broad and thus meaningless nonliteral sense.[4] The examples in this chapter will stress that these two senses are not only distinct in content or focus but also have separate functions that are essential to the way in which they relate for the effect of spiritually transforming the hearer and thus making him ready for salvation.

In order to recognize the two higher senses in practice and thus appreciate their purposeful relationship, it is necessary to take account not only of the theory in *Princ.* 4 but also the extended theory available in his homilies. This chapter asks the following questions of the four homilies under examination. First, does Origen clearly conceive of the senses, especially the psychic and pneumatic senses, as separate in content and function? Second, do these later discussions of Origen's theory confirm the core elements of the definitions as he presented them in *Princ.* 4? Third, do these later discussions explain

---

[4] Hanson, *Allegory and Event*, 235–237, and 243; and chapter 1's discussion of his views.

how each sense functions and how they relate for the spiritual benefit of Scripture's hearers?

These texts will confirm that Origen recognizes three separate senses in Scripture and continues to hold to the main features of the definitions set forth in *Princ.* 4. These texts also give further insight into how the senses function and relate to effect spiritual transformation in the hearer.

I. *Hom. Gen.* 11: *Three Days at the Well of Vision*

This chapter first treats Origen's discussion of Isaac dwelling at the well of vision in *Hom. Gen.* 11.[5] The passage that Origen analyzes, Gen. 25:11, states that, after the death of Abraham, "[t]he Lord blessed Isaac [his son,] . . . and he dwelt at the well of vision."[6] In this homily Origen describes Scripture as an endless well of God's revelations and declares that God will graciously aid the hearer who strives continuously and with all of his effort to extract the truths conveyed by the three senses. On close analysis, Origen places the greatest emphasis on the psychic sense, stressing that it is the locus of the hearer's active engagement with Scripture.

Origen first explains that the well of vision at which Isaac dwelt is Scripture, and the opportunity to dwell there is for anyone a blessing bestowed by God:

> This is the whole blessing with which the Lord blessed Isaac: that he might dwell "at the well of vision." That is a great blessing for those who understand it. Would that the Lord might give this blessing to me too, that I might deserve to dwell "at the well of vision." . . . And if anyone can know and understand each individual vision or the things which are in the Law or in the prophets, that man dwells "at the well of vision."[7]

---

[5] Sixteen homilies are extant on the book of Genesis by Origen, translated into Latin by Rufinus. All English translations are from Ronald E. Heine, trans. *Origen: Homilies on Genesis and Exodus* (FC 71; Washington, D.C.: Catholic University of America, 1982). I will place the corresponding Latin text in footnote, employing the Latin edition of Louis Doutreleau, ed. and trans., *Origène: Homélies sur La Genèse* (SC 7; Paris: Cerf, 1985).
[6] *Hom. Gen.* 11.3 (quoting Gen. 25:11; FC 71:173); Benedixit . . . Dominus Isaac et habitauit ad puteum uisionis (SC 7:286).
[7] *Hom. Gen.* 11.3 (quoting Gen. 25.11; FC 71:173); Haec est omnis benedictio,

The well represents the truths conveyed in the Law and prophets. To say that Isaac dwells at this well is to say that he knows and understands these truths. By applying the imagery of the "well," *puteus*, to Scripture, Origen suggests that, as a well is deep and unlikely to run dry, so is the understanding concerning divine things contained in Scripture. The knowledge that God imparts through Scripture is a well-spring that continues to bring forth increasingly greater understanding once a person has tapped it. Origen states his desire to enjoy such a blessing, humbly implying that even he depends on God's grace to dwell at the well of Scripture. To "dwell" there is to continue to ponder and take in *all* that Scripture has to offer, to reside *fully* within Scripture's truths. Origen suggests that he does not yet comprehend the full breadth of Scripture's truths.[8]

Origen also suggests that his audience does not yet enjoy this blessing. He urges his audience to consider what they may do in order to deserve the full flow of Scripture's bounty:

> But also consider this more carefully, that Isaac deserved to receive such a great blessing from the Lord that he might dwell "at the well of vision." But when shall we sufficiently deserve to pass by, perhaps, "the well of vision?" He deserved to remain and dwell in the vision; we, what little we have been illuminated by the mercy of God, can scarcely perceive or surmise of a single vision.[9]

Isaac "deserved" God's blessing to dwell at the well of vision and received the fruits of full divine knowledge, indeed, a multitude of visions. Origen describes both himself and his audience as those who can "scarcely perceive or surmise a single vision." Yet, he suggests, the blessing of manifold visions from dwelling upon Scripture is not reserved for Isaac alone. While the ability to understand more and

---

qua Dominus benedixit Isaac, ut habitaret *ad puteum uisionis*. Intelligentibus grandis est ista benedictio. Vtinam Dominus et mihi donet hanc benedictionem, ut habitare merear *ad puteum uisionis* . . . Et si qui potest singulas quasque uisiones, uel quae in lege sunt uel quae in prophetis, scire et intelligere, ille habitat *ad puteum uisionis* (SC 7:286, 288).

[8] This suggests a point that I raised in chapter 2: Origen seems to envision that even the perfected person continues to receive increasing edification from Scripture's senses throughout this life.

[9] *Hom. Gen.* 11.3 (quoting Gen. 25.11; FC 71:173); Sed et hoc diligentius perspice, quod ita magnam benedictionem accipere a Domino meruit Isaac, ut habitaret *ad puteum uisionis*; nos uero quando satis mereri poterimus, si forte transitum habere possimus per *puteum uisionis*? Ille permanere in uisione meruit et habitare, nos parum quid illuminati per Dei misericordiam sentire uel suspicari de unaquaque uisione uix possumus (SC 7:288).

more deeply the truths of Scripture is a blessing and not a right, it
is something that one should strive to deserve. Origen suggests, then,
that to understand Scripture's truths fully requires both divine grace
and human effort.

Origen explains that the person who steadfastly attends to Scripture
is the one who deserves to receive more knowledge from it. The
longer a person stands before the well hoping to be invited to dwell
or reside fully at it, the more familiar with its contents he will become,
and he will be invited to drink increasingly from its living water.
Origen states:

> If, however, I shall have been able to perceive some one meaning of
> the visions of God, I shall appear to have spent one day "at the well
> of vision." But if I shall have been able to touch not only something
> according to the letter, but also according to the spirit, I shall appear
> to have spent two days "at the well of vision." But if also I shall have
> touched the moral point, I shall have spent three days. Or certainly
> even if I shall not have been able to understand everything, if I am,
> nevertheless, busily engaged in the divine Scriptures and "I meditate
> on the Law of God day and night" and at no time at all do I desist
> inquiring, discussing, investigating, and certainly, what is greatest, pray-
> ing God and asking for understanding from him who "teaches man
> knowledge," I shall appear to dwell "at the well of vision."[10]

One dwells at the well of Scripture only if he "busily engages" himself with it, "meditating on" it "day and night" and "praying" con-
tinually that God give him understanding and knowledge from it.
Origen shows that God's grace, which is in some sense *earned* when
the hearer attends to the well and desires its water, enables that
hearer to dwell at the well. God allows Scripture to communicate
its edifying truths to the willing and diligent person.

Origen measures the necessary effort in terms of time spent with
Scripture, comparing the number of days spent at the well to Scripture's
three senses of meaning. One who spends only *one* day at the well

---

[10] *Hom. Gen.* 11.3 (quoting Gen. 25:11 and referring to Psa. 1:2, 94:10; FC
71:173–174); Si tamen potuero unum aliquem intellectum sentire de uisionibus Dei,
unam diem uidebor fecisse apud puteum uisionis. Si uero non solum secundum litteram, sed aliquid et secundum spiritum attingere quiuero, bidui uidebor fecisse
apud puteum uisionis. Quod et si moralem locum contigero, fecerim tridui. Vel certe
etiam si non potuero omnia intelligere, assideo tamen Scripturis diuinis et in lege
Dei meditor die ac nocte et omnino numquam desino inquirendo, discutiendo, trac-
tando, certe, quod maximum est, orando Deum et ab illo poscendo intellectum qui
docet hominem scientiam, uidebor etiam ego habitare *ad puteum uisionis* (SC 7:288).

can perceive visions of God's truths only "according to the letter *(lit-tera)*" of Scripture. In *Princ.* 4, Origen explained that the somatic meaning is conveyed through the letter when the literal reading is historically true and/or morally instructive and thus edifying to the hearer. One who spends *two* days at the well progresses in his ability to understand its messages. He can perceive not only God's truths according to the somatic sense, but also "according to Scripture's spirit *(spiritus)*." Once again, this recalls the theory in *Princ.* 4, where Origen identified the spirit of Scripture with the pneumatic sense. Finally, if one spends *three* days at the well, then he is able "also" to "touch on the moral point *(moralem locum)* of Scripture." The word *et*, or also, effectively distinguishes the moral point of Scripture from its spirit and letter, suggesting that the one who spends three days, or full time, with Scripture will comprehend truths according to the moral point *as well as* those relating to the letter and spirit.

Significantly, Origen mentions the moral point (in Rufinus' Latin, *moralem locum*) separately from the letter and the spirit of Scripture as a third sense of understanding. In *Princ.* 4, Origen described the sense of Scripture's ψυχή, or soul (in Rufinus' Latin, *anima*) as a non-literal reading of biblical text that conveys moral instruction. This third, moral point, then, corresponds to the psychic meaning of *Princ.* 4. Origen maintains here three separate senses of scriptural meaning that correspond to the literal somatic (bodily—edifying literal), psychic (soul's) and pneumatic (spiritual) senses set forth earlier in *Princ.* 4.

Through each sense God's grace approaches the listener based on his own ability to comprehend Scripture. In other words, there is a fruitful message for everyone who meditates on Scripture. Origen assures his audience that if they engage Scripture with diligence and consistency, they will gain at least some understanding, though they may not yet understand according to all three senses or may not yet comprehend the full message of a particular sense. Still, he suggests, the more consistently, thoroughly and carefully one studies Scripture, the more likely he is to understand its truth according to all three senses and the message of each sense more fully.

In terms of grasping fully each sense, Origen lists the moral, psychic sense *after* the pneumatic sense. In the theory of *Princ.* 4 he listed the psychic sense *before* the pneumatic sense and stressed the order in which the hearer *initially comprehends* each sense. Here, however, Origen states that a person begins to "touch something according to" the pneumatic sense after two days of meditating on Scripture, but that he must spend three days in order to touch truths conveyed by the moral or psychic sense. Similarly, in all the examples treated in chapters 4 and 5 where Origen presents readings of both higher senses for the same biblical passage, he treats the psychic sense *after* the pneumatic sense. The theory in this homily, then, mirrors the order in which he tends to employ the two higher senses in practice. Arguably, this ordering suggests that as a person who dwells fully at Scripture begins to comprehend divine wisdom according to the pneumatic sense, he is motivated to continue heeding the psychic call so that he—as he becomes more and more like God—can grasp further truths from the pneumatic sense. The metaphor of days spent at the well emphasizes each sense's *increasing effect of edification* on the hearer who already grasps all three and, thus, progresses toward the desired state of "dwelling"—residing *fully*—at the well of Scripture.[11]

Even more significantly, by this order Origen stresses that the psychic sense is the locus of *active* engagement with Scripture. It is the sense that keeps the hearer involved with Scripture throughout this life and keeps pushing him toward fuller intimacy with it. Implicitly, the psychic sense calls the hearer to increasingly higher degrees of moral perfection so that he, in turn, can comprehend greater depths of pneumatic meaning. The psychic sense is the nagging, difficult coach that never relaxes in driving the scriptural athlete through the kinds of discipline that will lead to saving knowledge of God.

Origen then scolds his audience for neglecting to make the effort necessary to receive the blessing of Scripture's truths:

---

[11] As the analysis of *Princ.* 4 in chapter 2 revealed, the pneumatic sense is the fullness of the story that all three senses tell in Scripture and thus the sense that a hearer *begins* to comprehend *last*. As examination of Origen's practice in later chapters will demonstrate, after the hearer first begins to grasp the psychic sense and respond to it by growing in the virtues, he may begin to comprehend the most basic truth of the pneumatic sense—that the hope of eternal salvation belongs to him. With this goal in mind, the hearer will be motivated to *continue* growing in the virtues at the urgings of the psychic sense, and, in turn, he will be able to understand deeper and deeper truths of God's salvation plan as conveyed by the pneumatic sense. The increase in edification from the two higher senses will continue in a cyclical fashion throughout this life. Thus, the theory of this homily mirrors the order of reception of the two higher senses for the *experienced* hearer of Scripture, as will be substantiated by examples from Origen's practice treated in chapters 4 and 5.

> But if I should be negligent and be neither occupied at home in the word of God nor frequently enter the church to hear the word, as I see some among you, who only come to the church on festive days, those who are of this sort do not dwell "by the well of vision." But I fear that perhaps those who are negligent, even when they come to the church, may neither drink from the well of water nor be refreshed, but they may devote themselves to the occupations and thoughts of their heart which they bring with them and may depart thirsty no less from the wells of the Scriptures.[12]

Origen suggests that his audience does not respect the well-spring of truths that God has made available to them. They dishonor this gift in one or more of three ways: they do not study Scripture in their homes, they do not attend church where they can hear it publicly, or they attend church regularly but do not listen. As a result, such persons remain parched for the true waters of divine knowledge.

Origen's audience does not understand the great reward of dwelling upon Scripture. He urges them:

> [H]asten and act sufficiently that that blessing of the Lord may come to you, that you may be able to dwell "at the well of vision," that the Lord may open your eyes and you may see "the well of vision," and may receive from it "living water," which may become in you "a fountain of water springing up into eternal life."[13]

Recalling his statement of Scripture's spiritual purpose in *Princ.* 4 to prepare persons for salvation, Origen here stresses that Scripture promises "eternal life" to the one who partakes of its "living water." However, he must "hasten and act sufficiently" in order to receive this grace. This also recalls Origen's emphasis in *Princ.* 4 on the personal nature of Scripture's communication,[14] by stressing here that

---

[12] *Hom. Gen.* 11.3 (quoting Gen. 25:11; FC 71:174) Si uero negligam et neque domi exercear in uerbo Dei neque ecclesiam ad audiendum uerbum frequenter ingrediar, sicut nonnullos in uobis uideo, qui diebus tantummodo sollemnibus ad ecclesiam ueniunt, qui huiusmodi sunt non habitant *apud puteum uisionis.* Ego autem uereor ne forte qui ita negligentes sunt, etiam cum ad ecclesiam ueniunt, nec bibant de puteo uitae nec reficiantur, sed occupationibus uacent cordis sui et cogitationibus quas secum deferunt, et discedant nihilominus ab Scripturarum puteis sitientes (SC 7:288, 290).

[13] *Hom. Gen.* 11.3 (quoting Gen. 25.11 and referring to Gen. 26:19 and quoting John 4:10, 11 and 14. FC 71:174). The fuller Latin text reads: "*Festinate ergo uos et satis agite ut ista ad uos Domini benedictio ueniat, qua* apud puteum uisionis *habitare possitis, ut aperiat Dominus oculos uestros et uideatis* puteum uisionis *et percipiatis ex eo* aquam uiuam, *quae fiat in uobis* fons aquae salientis in uitam aeternam" (SC 7:290).

[14] Specifically, recall *Princ.* 4.2.4: "One must ... portray the meanings of the

the hearer cannot benefit from Scripture by listening either partially
or from a distance. Scripture's full, eternal benefits come only to the
hearer who interacts or engages himself with it entirely—for three
days.

Origen points out that Paul himself stressed the eternal reward
for taking in Scripture's truths:

> Do you want me to show you who it is who never withdraws from
> the well of vision? It is the apostle Paul who said: "But we all with
> open face behold the glory of the Lord." You too, therefore, if you
> shall always search the prophetic visions, if you always inquire, always
> desire to learn, if you meditate on these things, if you remain in them,
> you too receive a blessing from the Lord and dwell "at the well of
> vision." For the Lord Jesus will appear to you also "in the way" and
> will open the Scriptures to you so that you may say: "Was not our
> heart burning within us when he opened to us the Scriptures?" But
> he appears to these who think about him and meditate on him and
> live "in his law day and night."[15]

Origen presents Paul as an example of one "who never withdraws
from the well of vision." Origen's audience should listen to Paul,
then, when he says that "we" will "behold the glory of the Lord"
with "open face," if we remain faithful to the study of Scripture. In
other words, the reward will be union with God, or salvation. Origen
then addresses the members of his audience individually (by way of
the second person singular—"you"), emphasizing, as in *Princ.* 4, that
Scripture communicates its meanings to each individual human soul.
Each person in his audience is to make the full effort to understand
Scripture's truth so as to achieve salvation.

Also, in this passage, Origen stresses that the person who remains
faithfully in his efforts will receive the gracious aid of Jesus. He will
find himself visited by Jesus, as was Paul, and Jesus will "open" him

---

sacred writings in a threefold way upon one's own soul . . . for . . . salvation" (trans.
Butterworth, 275–276; SC 268:310, 312).

[15] *Hom. Gen.* 11:3 (quoting Gen. 25:11, referring to 2 Cor. 3:18, quoting Luke
24:32, and referring to Psa. 1:2; FC 71:174–175); Vis tibi ostendam quis est qui
numquam recedit a puteo uisionis? Apostolus Paulus, qui dicebat: *Nos autem omnes
reuelata facie gloriam Domini speculamur.* Et tu ergo si semper scruteris propheticas
uisiones, si semper inquiras, semper discere cupias, haec mediteris, in his permaneas,
percipis et tu benedictionem a Domino et habitas *apud puteum uisionis.* Et tibi enim
apparebit Dominus Iesus *in uia* et aperiet tibi Scripturas, ita ut dicas: *Nonne cor nostrum erat ardens in nobis, cum adaperiret nobis Scripturas?* Apparet autem his qui de ipso
cogitant et in ipso meditantur atque *in lege eius die ac nocte* uersantur (SC 7:290).

up to deeper understandings of Scripture's truths. If the student proves his commitment, then Jesus will teach him, appearing to him and revealing truths that lead to eternal life. Jesus will appear, because to meditate on Scripture is to "meditate on *him*." By this, Origen indicates that Jesus is both the content and teacher of Scripture. Origen's theory in *Princ.* 4 suggested that Scripture, with its three-fold structure of meaning, contains its own internal guide of interpretation, and, by communicating the three senses to the hearer, Scripture is the teacher of the human soul (through the channel of the exegete). This homily additionally emphasizes that Jesus is the ultimate teacher and conveyer of Scripture's divine truths. To meditate on Scripture is to learn from and meditate on Jesus himself.[16]

Here Origen stresses that Scripture comes alive and communicates God's truths in a personal and interactive way to the willing and ready soul. Even more, for the believer who responds to the gracious instruction of Scripture with great effort, Jesus imparts himself as God's truth and wisdom through the somatic, pneumatic and psychic senses. Only the most diligent student of Scripture fully embraces the psychic sense (finding himself at the Bible's well-spring for the full three days), for the psychic sense is Scripture's demanding and disciplining agent during this life. The pupil can only deepen his appreciation of Scripture's pneumatic truths by the continued moral rigor that the psychic sense requires. Only by meeting the psychic call's challenge can a person both enjoy the blessings of companionship with Christ and progress toward eternal life.

---

[16] In all the homiletic examples of theory analyzed in this chapter, Origen will identify Jesus as the ultimate teacher and content of Scripture. This insight builds upon the earlier theory in *Princ.* 4, which, though it identified Scripture with Christ (*Princ.* 4.2.6, 4.2.9), tended to stress the Holy Spirit's construction and inspiration of biblical text. As discussed in chapter 1, Torjesen represents the views of many scholars when she explains that Origen identifies the doctrines in Scripture with Christ's instruction of himself as divine Truth (*Hermeneutical Procedure*, 43–48, 108–124, esp. 119–123; also, idem, "Origen's Interpretation of the Psalms," 954–957; and the discussion of her views in chapter 1). Origen's extended theory as a whole will develop the notion that engagement with Scripture is engagement with Jesus Christ. Specifically, in *Hom. Lev.* 5, which will be treated next in this chapter, Origen refers to Scripture, and especially its pneumatic truths, as the "mind of Christ" (*Hom. Lev.* 5.6.2, quoting 1 Cor. 2:16; FC 83:101; SC 286:232).

II. *Hom. Lev.* 5: *The Three Sacrificial Loaves*

Origen also develops his definitions for the three senses in *Hom. Lev.* 5. In this homily, he interprets Lev. 7:9, which mentions three different cooking vessels, each of which is meant to prepare a loaf for sacrifice to God: "And every sacrifice of the priest who offers it [that is, any offering that the priest makes on behalf of any man], that will be made in an oven, and all that is made in a small gridiron or in a frying pan, will be his [that is, will belong to the priest who offers it]."[17] By relating each sense to a cooking vessel, Origen stresses the ease with which Scripture's hearer comprehends the somatic sense, the patience he must display awaiting deepening understanding of the pneumatic sense, and the difficult and constant effort he must apply to the psychic sense in order to reap its benefits. Also, Origen again will identify Scripture with Jesus, this time emphasizing that he is the priest who causes the three senses to be fully cooked in the human heart so that the hearer may become himself a sacrifice acceptable to God.

Origen first reiterates the theory of three separate senses in *Princ.* 4 by associating each sense with one of the cooking vessels:

> And so, there are these three in which it says the sacrifice ought to be prepared, "in an oven, on a gridiron, in a frying pan." I think that "the oven," by reason of its form, signifies some things more profound which are unmentionable in divine Scriptures. "The gridiron" is those which, if they are frequently and often thought upon, can be understood and explained. But "the frying pan" is those which are well known and are understood without any covering. For often we have said that a triple mode of understanding is to be found in divine Scriptures: the historical, the moral, the mystical. From this we understood the body, the soul, and the spirit. This threefold method of preparation of the sacrifices shows the threefold form of this understanding.[18]

---

[17] *Hom. Lev.* 5.5.1 (quoting Lev. 7:9; FC 83:98–99); Et omne sacrificium, quod fiet in clibano, et omne quod fiet in craticula vel in sartagine, sacerdotis, qui offert illud, ipsius erit (SC 286:226).

[18] *Hom. Lev.* 5.5.3 (quoting Lev. 7:9; FC 83:100); Tria itaque sunt haec, in quibus dicit sacrificia debere praeparari, *in clibano, in sartagine, in craticula*, et puto quod *clibanus* secundum sui formam profundiora et ea, quae sunt inenarrabilia, significet in Scripturis divinis; *sartago* vero ea, quae si frequenter ac saepe versentur, intelligi et explicari possunt; *craticula* autem ea, quae palam sunt et absque aliqua obtectione cernuntur. Triplicem namque in Scripturis divinis intelligentiae inveniri saepe diximus modum: historicum, moralem, mysticum; unde et corpus inesse ei et animam ac spiritum intelleximus. Cuius intelligentiae triplicem formam sacrificiorum triplex hic apparatus ostendit (SC 286:230).

Origen's reference back to his assertions in *Princ.* 4 are explicit. He stresses that the three vessels together constitute the "threefold method of preparation of the sacrifices" that the human person makes when he takes in Scripture's three senses. The method is threefold because there is a "triple mode of understanding . . . to be found in divine Scriptures." The genitive form of "understanding" *(intelligenciae)* here is singular. There is one understanding but three parts to it. Origen explains that these three parts are "the body, the soul and the spirit" of Scripture, recalling Origen's anthropological analogy to Scripture in *Princ.* 4. He also describes these three parts here (in Rufinus' Latin translation) as "the historical, the moral, [and] the mystical" forms of understanding in Scripture. These descriptions recall how in *Princ.* 4 Origen explained the content, respectively, of the somatic, psychic and pneumatic senses.

Here Origen describes the sense related to the frying pan as signifying things "which are well known and are understood without any covering." In *Princ.* 4 Origen defined the somatic sense as the meaning that is found in the letter of the text. As the frying pan needs no covering or lid, so also the somatic sense is uncovered and readily visible, requiring no figurative reading. Origen also defined the somatic sense in *Princ.* 4 as conveying historical information and literal moral instruction. Such things arguably are "well-known," or *palam*, as in "openly or publicly" accessible. They are not difficult to grasp. Here, then, Origen refers to his definition for the somatic sense in *Princ.* 4 by relating this sense to Scripture's body which conveys historical understanding.

Origen describes the sense related to the oven as "signif[ying] . . . things more profound which are unmentionable in divine Scriptures." The Latin term *profundus*, translated here as "profound," also means deep or vast. The Latin term *inenarrabile*, translated here as "unmentionable," also means inexplicable. In *Princ.* 4 Origen presented the pneumatic sense as conveying the wisdom of God in a mystery, thus focusing on eternal, not temporal things. Such eternal truths are deep and not wholly explicable in this life. Metaphorically, they need the thorough cooking that takes place in the enclosed structure of an oven in order for the human person to be able to grasp them and receive edification from them. Here, then, Origen refers to his definition for the pneumatic sense in *Princ.* 4 by relating it to Scripture's spirit which conveys mystical meaning.

Origen describes the sense related to the gridiron as signifying that which "if frequently and often thought upon, can be understood and explained." The Latin term *versare*, translated here as "thought upon," means generally to turn and more specifically to turn over in the mind, think over, meditate, reflect on or consider. This sense conveys truths that are more fully explicable in this life than those of the pneumatic sense, and, yet, unlike those of the somatic sense, require frequent and consistent meditation, indeed, repetitive reinforcement. Here, then, Origen refers to his definition for the psychic sense in *Princ.* 4 by relating it to Scripture's soul which conveys moral understanding.

Elsewhere in this same homily Origen shifts metaphors in order to relate the three senses not to cooking vessels but to the loaves prepared in each of them. He refers to Scripture as "the holy basket of perfection," recalling his explanation in *Princ.* 4 of Scripture's purpose to bring the hearer to perfection and salvation.[19] To this end, the three senses are prepared as loaves in the human heart *for sacrifice to the Lord.* Here the oven represents the human heart (or, in *Princ.* 4, the human soul), and the sacrifice of the three loaves of Scripture's senses are placed deep within the hearer's heart so that he may be transformed into a sacrifice to God.[20] Origen explains that the human heart, however, may be "'ignited for burning'" by vices.[21] If vices

---

[19] *Hom. Lev.* 5.5.4 (referring to Lev. 8:26, and recalling *Princ.* 4.2.7; FC 83:100; SC 286:230). He also explains here that the three loaves contained in Scripture are "as foods applied three times for the hearers." This language recalls that of Prov. 22:20–21, which he employed in *Princ.* 4 as Scripture's own declaration of its three senses of meaning. In addition, he cites Jesus' parable in Luke 11:5–6, which tells of the person who came to his friend's door at midnight asking for three loaves. Origen explains that "midnight" refers to this life and the three loaves are those baked in the oven, gridiron and frying pan and thus represent the three senses. In these ways, Origen stresses that Scripture has three senses and that Scripture itself (through Proverbs and Jesus in the Gospel) endorses the threefold reading of biblical passages, all for the hearer's benefit.

[20] In this homily, Origen identifies the part of the human person that is to receive the three senses of scriptural meaning as the heart, *cor*, while in *Princ.* 4 he identified it as the soul, *anima*. This difference in terminology could be merely a result of Rufinus' translations, or a matter of Origen employing "heart" based on the edition of the Bible upon which he relied (see the next footnote). Nonetheless, this analysis proceeds with the understanding that for his exegesis in this homily Origen correlates these terms, whether he viewed the heart as a faculty of the soul or simply treated these terms synonymously.

[21] *Hom. Lev.* 5.5.1–2 (quoting Hos. 7:4, 6). The full text reads: "[L]et us see according to the spiritual sense, which the Spirit gives the Church, what is this 'sacrifice that is baked in an oven,' or how this 'oven' ought to be understood . . . that I may find in Scriptures 'the oven' where I can bake my sacrifice that God may accept it. Indeed, I think I have found it in Hosea the prophet where he says, 'All adulterers are as an oven ignited for burning.' And again, he says, 'Their hearts

ignite it, then it is the devil who inflames it, making the hearer an adulterer with the devil against God. The devil, though, not being a true lover of the human heart or soul, will burn it up and destroy it. Sins will burn the hearer alive. This analogy reminds us of Origen's anthropology, which views a person's sinful soul as slave to the fleshly passions fully unleashed in the body rather than to the enriching guidance of his spirit.

On the contrary, the soul ignited by Christ burns as a well-fueled oven and bakes the loaves of Scripture deep within it.

> But if that one who said, "I came to send fire into the earth" [, Christ,] should ignite it [my heart], the loaves of the divine Scriptures and of the words of God which I receive in my heart, I do not burn up for destruction but I bake for a sacrifice. And perhaps these that are "interior" and the hidden things which cannot easily be brought forth to the crowds are said to be baked "in an oven." . . . If these things are not baked "in an oven," they cannot be eaten because they are raw. . . . [T]hey are not to be brought forth raw but are to be baked in "the oven" of the heart.[22]

In contrast to the devil, Christ ignites the heart with divine illumination by filling it with an understanding of "the loaves of the divine Scriptures."[23] Note that *panes* (loaves) is plural, reinforcing Origen's identification of the three senses with the three loaves prepared in different cooking vessels. Here Origen suggests that the hearer is to receive *all* three senses in his heart, recalling his statement in *Princ.* 4

---

glowed as an oven.' The human heart, therefore, is 'an oven.' But this heart, if vices ignite it or the devil inflames it, will not bake, but it will burn up." (FC 83:99) The corresponding Latin text reads: Quin potius secundum spiritalem sensum, quem Spiritus donat Ecclesiae, videamus, quod sit *istud sacrificium, quod coquatur in clibano,* vel quis iste *clibanus* intelligi debeat . . . ut inveniam in Scripturis *clibanum,* ubi possim coquere sacrificium meum, ut suscipiat illud Deus. Et quidem invenisse me puto in Osee propheta, ubi dicit: *Omnes moechantes, sicut clibanus succensus ad comburendum, et iterum: Incaluerunt inquit sicut clibanus corda eorum.* Cor ergo est hominis *clibanus.* Istud autem cor si vitia succenderint vel diabolus inflammaverit, non coquet, sed exuret (SC 286:228).

[22] *Hom. Lev.* 5.5.2 (quoting Luke 12:49; FC 83:99–100); Si vero ille id succenderit, qui dixit: *Ignem veni mittere in terram,* panes Scripturarum divinarum et sermonum Dei, quos in corde suscipio, non exuro ad perditionem, sed coquo ad sacrificium. Et fortassis illa coqui dicuntur *in clibano,* quae *interiora* sunt et recondita nec proferri facile ad vulgus possunt. . . . Haec si *in clibano* non coquantur, comedi ita, ut sunt cruda, non possunt. . . . [N]on sunt cruda proferenda, sed in cordis *clibano* sunt coquenda (SC 286:228, 230).

[23] Though Rufinus' Latin does not state the name of Christ, Origen explicitly identifies him as the one to ignite the heart of the hearer by quoting him from Luke 12:49.

that all three senses are to be written onto each hearer's soul. Implicitly, the hearer is to consume all three senses so that Christ then will bake each one appropriately within his heart or soul. The resulting sacrifice acceptable to God, then, is the hearer himself.

In this same passage, Origen then turns his audience's attention specifically to the interior and hidden things in Scripture which must be baked in order to be consumed, recalling his descriptions of the pneumatic sense. Since elsewhere in this homily Origen relates the pneumatic sense to "the mind of Christ,"[24] he suggests here that the hearer who comprehends the pneumatic sense consumes Christ's mind and thus becomes like him. In this way he becomes an acceptable sacrifice to God, and it is Christ who facilitates this process. Similar to *Hom. Gen.* 11 where Origen identified Jesus as the content and teacher of Scripture's truths, here he suggests that Christ is the priest and offering of the sacrifice that the human soul makes to God. Christ bakes the senses, and most significantly the pneumatic sense, in the hearer's heart so that the hearer can become like him before God.

In the conclusion to this homily, Origen confirms that the hearer is made into the sacrifice prepared for God by becoming like Christ. In fact, the hearer becomes part of Christ's self-sacrifice on the Cross. Origen explains that Jesus Christ is the "eternal high priest" who makes sacrifices acceptable to God and who "sees fit to make us worthy that we may, through a pure heart and good work, have a part in the divine sacrifice" that he administers.[25]

In this homily, then, Origen builds upon his exegetical theory in both *Princ.* 4 and *Hom. Gen.* 11. He continues the theory by stating that Scripture contains three separate senses that represent its body,

---

[24] *Hom. Lev.* 5.6.2 (quoting 1 Cor. 2:16). The fuller English text reads: "I do not doubt that there are many things which are concealed from us and that surpass our understanding. For we are not worthy of these so that we too can say, 'But we have the mind of Christ.' For it is only this 'mind' to which all things lie open which are contained in the laws of sacrifices within the secret of the letter" (FC 83:101); Non autem dubito multa esse, quae nos lateant et sensum nostrum superent. Non enim sumus illius meriti, ut et nos dicere possimus: *Nos autem sensum Christi habemus.* Ipse enim solus est *sensus*, cui pateant universa, quae in legibus sacrificiorum intra litterae continentur arcanum (SC 286:232). Origen relates the "secret of the letter," or the deepest, pneumatic meanings in Scripture, to the mind of Christ. Note that Rufinus employs the term *sensus* for mind, the same term employed for sense or meaning. The pneumatic meaning is Christ's own meaning.

[25] *Hom. Lev.* 5.12.9 (FC 83:115); in qua dignos nos facere dignetur, ut pro cordis puritate et operum probitate in divino sacrificio habere participium mereamur, per aeternum pontificem Dominum et Salvatorem nostrum Iesum Christum (SC 286:266).

soul and spirit and convey, respectively, historical, moral and mystical meanings. They are designed to lead the hearer to perfection. The somatic sense edifies by the literal, historical meaning in biblical text. It is obvious and easy to grasp. The pneumatic sense is the most hidden, mysterious sense, conveying the mysteries of God's wisdom. One must wait patiently for full comprehension of its meaning. The psychic sense conveys moral instruction and requires constant meditation. The hearer is called to involve himself frequently with the psychic sense.

Here, as in *Hom. Gen.* 11, Origen points to the psychic sense as the locus of active engagement with Scripture. It demands the hearer's continuous attention and keeps the hearer involved in Scripture's transforming process. Christ, though, is the one who bakes the three senses in the human heart in order to make a sacrifice acceptable to God. This sacrifice consists in making the hearer an imitator of Christ, for to consume the pneumatic sense (and, thus, all three senses) is to take on the mind of Christ. The attentive hearer who wrestles with the psychic sense's moral instruction and strives to comply will take in pneumatic truths and, correspondingly, become a participant in Christ's self-sacrifice on the Cross. Through the tutelage of Christ in Scripture, he will consume the three senses and become before God a likeness to Christ.

III. *Hom. Num.* 9: *The Three Parts of the Almond*

Origen develops his definitions for the somatic, psychic and pneumatic senses further in *Hom. Num.* 9,[26] providing new insights concerning their interrelationship. In *Hom. Num.* 9, he treats Num. 17:1–5 and 8, in which God instructs Moses to collect the rods from the leaders of every tribe so that God may declare, through a sign, that Aaron and his tribe of Levites are divinely ordained as the official priests of the Israelites. After Moses collects the rods, God makes

---

[26] Twenty-eight homilies on Numbers by Origen are extant in Latin, translated by Rufinus. Any English quotations used later within this work from Origen's *Hom. Num.* 27 are from Greer, *Origen*, 245–269. English text from all the other homilies on Numbers by Origen, including the present one—*Hom. Num.* 9—constitute my own translation from the Latin. I will place the corresponding Latin texts in footnote, employing the edition by W. A. Baehrens (GCS, 30; Leipzig: J. C. Hinrichs'sche, 1921).

Aaron's rod "sprout forth . . . producing leaves, bringing forth flowers and sprouting forth almonds."[27] Origen interprets the almond as a figure for Scripture's three meanings by relating each of its parts, the husk, shell and center, to one of the three senses.[28]

Origen first describes the almond's three parts:

> What then is the fruit that he brought forth? "Almonds," it says, which is a bitter fruit indeed at the first [outer] covering; it is protected and concealed by the next [layer] that follows; [and] thirdly, with respect to the richest part, it feeds and nourishes.[29]

---

[27] Origen's fuller recitation of these verses reads as follows: "And the Lord spoke to Moses saying: 'speak to the sons of Israel and take twelve rods from them, from every chief the rod of the home of his family; and write the name of each one of them on his rod. And write the name "Aaron" on the rod of Levi; for there is one rod per tribe; they will give to you one for each home of his family. And place them in the tabernacle of witnesses opposite to the threshing-floor; that I might acknowledge these things to you from there. And the man whom I will choose, his rod will sprout forth; and I will remove from you the complaints of the sons of Israel, those things which they are saying against you. . . .' And behold, the rod of Aaron in the home of Levi sprouted forth . . . and produced leaves, brought forth flowers and sprouted forth almonds" (*Hom. Num.* 9.7–8, quoting Num. 17:1–5, 8; my trans.). Et locutus est Dominus ad Moysen dicens: loquere filiis Istrahel, et accipe ab iis virgam per domos familiarum ipsorum ab omnibus principibus ipsorum, duodecim virgas; et uniuscuiusque eorum nomen scribe in virga sua. Et nomen Aaron scribe in virga Levi; est enim virga una, per tribum, per domos familiarum suarum dabunt tibi. Et pones eas in tabernaculo testimonii contra aream, ex quibus agnoscar tibi inde. Et erit homo, quemcumque elegero, virga eius germinabit; et auferam a te murmurationem filiorum Istrahel, in quibuscumque ipsi murmurant de vobis. . . . [E]t ecce, germinavit virga Aaron in domo Levi . . . et produxit frondes et protulit flores et germinavit nuces (GCS 30:63, 65).
[28] Keep in mind two matters regarding Origen's treatment of the nut in this homily. First, Origen speaks of a *nux*, or generically a "nut." Yet, he makes much of the fact that its outer covering is *amara*, or "bitter." The Latin phrase *nux amara* traditionally refers to an almond. Moreover, the RSV translation of Num. 17:8 reads as "ripe almonds." Therefore, this analysis will often use the more specific term "almond."
Second, Origen views the almond's three layers, from its exterior to its interior, as (1) the husk, hull or calyx—that outer part that attaches to the tree (in Latin, *cortex*), (2) the hard shell (in Latin, *testa*), and (3) the soft center. In the analogy to the three senses within this homily, Origen does not speak about the skin inside the shell that hugs the soft center. This inside skin typically can be peeled away if the nut is heated, or it can be eaten along with the center. The term *cortex* can be translated as skin or shell, as well as bark, rind, or hull, and, figuratively, as the outward part or covering, as in the body, or *corpus*, of the human person. With regard to a nut, *cortex* most precisely refers to the husk *over, or outside*, the shell of a nut. Also, *testa*, means shell as in skull, shell of a shell-fish, a piece of bone, or covering of ice. Thus, *testa* definitely refers to the *hard* shell when regarding a nut. Therefore, this study will translate *cortex* as husk and *testa* as shell. It will understand Origen either to include implicitly the *inner*, thin layer of skin when discussing the nut's soft center or to disregard it altogether from this metaphor to Scripture's three senses.
[29] *Hom. Num.* 9.7 (quoting Num. 17:8). Quis autem iste est fructus, quem attulit?

Origen explains that the almond's "first covering" is "bitter," the "following" layer "protect[s] and conceal[s]" its core, and the "richest part," the core, "feeds and nourishes" the one who eats it. These descriptions respectively bring to mind the almond's husk, hard shell and soft center.

Origen points out that the husk is a "covering." The Latin term *indumentum* is also the term that Rufinus employed in his translation of Origen's discussion of the somatic sense in *Princ.* 4, where he described "the body *(corpus)* of Scripture" as "the outer covering of the letter *(litterae indumentum)*" that acts as a "veil on the spiritual meanings *(uelamen spiritalium sensuum)*."[30] As stated in chapter 2, *indumentum* means garment, clothing, covering, or even body, as that which covers over the soul and spirit of the human person. Though Origen presents this husk as a covering, he does not attribute to it any cover or protection of its own. This first covering is *amarus*, or bitter, as in raw, sour or unpleasant to the taste. It describes the husk of the nut, which never ripens in taste.

Origen then refers to that which follows, *sequenti*, as the part of the almond that protects and conceals its core. Since the husk is the first covering, this "next layer" is a second covering, also an *indumentum* of the nut. The Latin verb *munire*, translated in this passage as "protect," also means to build a wall around or defend with a wall, as in fortify, guard, secure or shelter. This second covering is also a barrier, like the husk, that further protects the inner core of the almond from outside elements. The second verb *tego*, translated here as "conceal," also means to cover, hide, veil or keep secret, or, synonymously with *munire*, to defend, protect or guard. The shell of

---

« Nuces » inquit, qui fructus primo quidem indumento amarus est, sequenti munitur ac tegitur, tertio sumentem pascit ac nutrit (GCS 30:63).

[30] *Princ.* 4.2.8 (Butterworth, 285, and the discussion in chapter 2 on Origen's description of the somatic sense). In *De Principiis*, Origen's articulation reads (translated from the Latin): "Further, by a marvellous example of wisdom, in the writings of the law the law of truth is implanted and prophetically indicated; and all these are by the divine skill and wisdom woven together to form a kind of outer covering and veil for spiritual meanings, which is what we meant by the body of holy scripture; with the result that even through this that we have called the outer covering of the letter, woven by the art of wisdom, very many readers may be edified and make progress, who otherwise could not do so." The Latin text reads: Sed et in scriptura legali per ammirandam sapientiae disciplinam lex ueritatis inseritur et prophetatur; quae singula diuina quadam arte sapientiae uelut indumentum quoddam et uelamen spiritalium sensuum texta sunt; et hoc est quod diximus scripturae sanctae corpus: ut etiam per hoc ipsum quod diximus litterae indumentum, sapientiae arte contextum, possent quam plurimi aedificari et proficere, qui aliter non possent (SC 268:334).

an almond surrounds that which lies within it as a fortress, veiling
it and keeping it safe and hidden from outside influences.

Origen refers to the third part of the nut as the "richest part,"
which feeds and nourishes the person who consumes it. The Latin
term *sumentem*, translated here as "the richest part," comes from the
word *sumen*, meaning, literally, the breast of a woman or a sow's
udder, and, figuratively, the fat part or richest portion of a thing.
Metaphorically, then, this part produces milk, that which is essential to the recipient for sustenance and growth. The Latin verb *pascere*,
translated here as "feeds," also means to cause to eat or supply with
food. The Latin verb *nutrire*, translated here as "nourish," also means
to nurse, feed, bring up or rear, as well as support, sustain, take
care of, and even heal. The core of the almond, then, nourishes the
recipient regardless of whether or not he himself knows what he
needs—just as a babe at the mother's breast—and, specifically, it
causes growth, provides healing and sustains health.

By stressing that the almond's husk is an inedible covering, the
shell a protection that is necessary for the survival of the nut's core,
and its core the nutrition of the nut, Origen demonstrates that all
three parts are significant to the nut. Yet, even more than the husk,
the shell is vital to ensuring that the core reaches its recipient and
provides him with all of its nutritional value. While the core is the
essence of the nut, there is no core without a shell. With these rela-
tionships established between the nut's parts, Origen will identify the
husk, shell and core, respectively, with the somatic, psychic and pneumatic senses.[31]

---

[31] As in *Princ.* 4 and *Hom. Lev.* 5, Origen again in this homily refers to Prov.
22:20–21 as Scripture's own authority for claiming three separate senses of meaning: "In this manner then the plan of all the Scriptures passes through the stages
of this threefold mystery. And in this way Wisdom instructs, as 'we describe this
in a threefold way in the heart in us', 'in order to answer,' it says, 'the word of
truth regarding these things, which they spoke to us'" (*Hom. Num.* 9.7, quoting Prov.
22:20–21). Rufinus' Latin translation reads: Hoc igitur modo in omnibus scripturis
triplicis huius sacramenti ratio percurrit. Sic et Sapientia monet, ut « describamus
ea nobis in corde tripliciter », « ad respondendum » inquit « verbum veritatis his,
qui proposuerint nobis » (GCS 30:64). Origen also mentions the three wells that
Isaac dug as representative of the three senses: "So the patriarch Isaac dug three
wells, of which only the third one is called by that 'breadth' and 'grandeur'" (*Hom.
Num.* 9.7, referring to Gen. 26:15–22); Sic tres puteos fodit Isaac patriarcha, quorum solus ille tertius ab eo « latitudo » vel « amplitudo » nominatur (GCS 30:64).
In these ways, Origen clarifies that he continues in this homily, as he did in *Princ.*
4, to view Scripture as containing *three* senses of meaning, each of which is to be
written onto the heart or soul of the hearer.

A. *Somatic Sense*

First, Origen relates the almond's husk to the "outward appearance of the letter" in Scripture:

> Such then in the school of Christ is the doctrine of the Law and Prophets: the first outward appearance of the letter is sufficiently bitter, which orders the circumcision of the flesh, which gives orders of sacrifices and the rest, by which are designated the "letter that kills." All these things one will throw away as the bitter husk of an almond.[32]

In Christ's school of Scripture, one first finds the letter. As the nut's husk is bitter to taste, *amara*, this letter is bitter and hard to follow in its strict and unyielding demands. Origen points to the literal commands set forth in the "Law and Prophets" of the Old Testament, citing, as examples, commands to submit to circumcision and regulations for making sacrifices to God. He identifies these literal commands with Paul's statement, "'the letter that kills.'" The letter is the whip that either brings forth discipline and obedience or exposes the guilt of disobedience and brings the offender to the due penalty, death. This letter, then, is bitter to the one who tries to follow the commands, finding them difficult and demanding, as well as to the one who ignores the commands, finding himself subject to God's wrath. By directly citing Paul's words "the letter that kills," Origen may also suggest that the somatic sense is condemning (especially when it occurs through the Law). It is so difficult to follow that it makes Scripture's hearer aware of his sinful nature and the need to submit to a full cleansing by Christ (as through submission to the psychic sense's call to virtue). In *Princ.* 4, Origen described the somatic sense as the meaning that is found in the letter of Scripture and edifies. While his examples of circumcision and altar sacrifice are no longer relevant for God's faithful to follow (that is, no longer edifying), these literal commands were necessary to follow *before* the Incarnation in order to obey God. Thus, with these examples, Origen relates the husk of the almond to the somatic sense.

Significantly, by employing these examples here, he stresses the transitory nature of the somatic sense. He states that this sense, like

---

[32] *Hom. Num.* 9.7 (quoting 2 Cor. 3:6); Talis ergo est in auditorio Christi doctrina legis et prophetarum: prima litterae facies satis amara est, quae circumcisionem carnis praecipit, quae de sacrificiis mandat et cetera, quae per « occidentem litteram » designantur. Haec omnia tamquam amarum nucis corticem proice (GCS 30:63).

the husk of the almond, will be thrown away. The Latin verb *proicere* also means to fling, cast out, expel or banish, or renounce or reject. By this term Origen suggests that the somatic sense will at some time be cast out and rejected. It can even cease to edify the hearer *during* this life, as circumcision and sacrifice were important for the Israelites to follow *before* the Incarnation, but are no longer needed.[33]

These two examples do not suggest that *all* literal readings of Scripture, even moral ones, have ceased or will cease to edify before the end of time.[34] Yet, in conjunction with the absence of the somatic sense from some passages of Scripture, certain literal readings, at least in relation to certain formerly significant commands, have ceased to edify. This clarification is important because Origen next will distinguish the psychic sense as a meaning that remains fully edifying to the attentive hearer during this life but will cease to be useful at the resurrection.

B. *Psychic Sense*

Origen speaks at the greatest length about the sense that resembles the almond's hard shell lying just beneath the bitter husk. It is the sense that gives moral instruction in a less direct way than does the letter:

> Secondly, you will come to the protection of the shell, in which is signified either moral instruction or motivation for self-control. These things indeed are necessary for the protection of those things that are kept inside; and yet, when these things are broken into pieces, they are no doubt destroyed. For example, let us speak of the fasting from foods and the mortification [or restraint] of the body, [for] they are without a doubt necessary so long as we are in this corruptible and passible body; but when it will have been broken into pieces and weakened, at the time of the resurrection it will be restored from corruptible to incorruptible and from a physical to spiritual body, no longer in the labor of affliction or the punishment of fasting, but by the property itself, the corruption [seduction] of the body will no longer dominate. Thus, now the reason for fasting seems necessary, yet soon it will not be necessary to pursue.[35]

---

[33] Though a past event cannot become historically untrue, a command can become morally irrelevant.

[34] For example, in his earlier theory, Origen stresses that the literal reading of the Ten Commandments continues to be morally necessary to follow and thus edifying (*Princ.* 4.3.4; Butterworth, 295; SC 268:358, 360).

[35] *Hom. Num.* 9.7; Secundo in loco ad munimenta testae pervenies, in quo vel

In *Princ.* 4, Origen presented the psychic sense as the meaning in Scripture that gives moral instruction and is found not in the letter but through a figurative reading of the text. From this passage it is apparent that Origen relates the second scriptural, psychic sense to the hard shell of the almond. This sense gives *moralis doctrina*, moral instruction, or *ratio continentiae*, motivation for self-control.

Origen points out that, as the almond's shell guards and protects its soft, nutritional center, the moral instructions of the psychic sense "are necessary for the protection *(custodiam)* of those things that are kept inside" of Scripture. The Latin term *custodia* conveys not only the idea of protecting and guarding but also of confining something so that it cannot escape. That which lies at the center of Scripture's meanings is held securely within by this shell of moral instruction. The psychic sense, then, both bars undesirable forces from reaching the core of Scripture and also restricts that core from getting out. By this, Origen suggests that the deepest truths of Scripture must be kept away from persons not yet ready to understand them properly, for it is somehow dangerous for the simpler hearer to be exposed prematurely to advanced lessons in God's wisdom.

Moreover, Origen explains that, like the almond's shell, the messages of the psychic sense will be "broken into pieces" and "destroyed" at some point in time. Like the husk or somatic sense, the shell or psychic sense will cease to be useful. Indeed, it will have fulfilled its purpose at the end of time, that is, "at the resurrection." Origen explains that the psychic sense's moral directives are useful as long as the human person lives in a body that is "corruptible" and thus is susceptible to its "seductions." He explains (likely referring to 1 Cor. 15:42–56) that at the resurrection, when the body becomes incorruptible, this seduction of the body "will no longer dominate." Thus, though the psychic sense, like the corruptible human body, will be broken down at the resurrection, the psychic sense, unlike

---

moralis doctrina vel ratio continentiae designatur. Quae necessaria quidem sunt ad custodiam eorum, quae servantur intrinsecus, frangenda tamen quandoque et sine dubio dissolvenda sunt. Ut si verbi causa dicamus, abstinentia ciborum et castigatio corporis, donec sumus in corpore isto corruptibili et passibili, sine dubio necessaria est; cum autem confractum fuerit ac resolutum et resurrectionis tempore incorruptibile ex corruptibili redditum atque ex animali spiritale, non iam labore afflictionis nec abstinentiae castigatione, sed qualitate sui, nulla iam corpori corruptela dominabitur. Sic ergo et nunc necessaria abstinentiae ratio videtur et postmodum non quaerenda (GCS 30:63–64).

the human body, will be destroyed rather than transformed into
something incorruptible.

During this life, however, a person needs to discipline the body
with activities such as fasting. While the somatic sense offers moral
direction through specific literal precepts that may cease to be relevant and necessary to follow even during this life, the psychic sense
more generally urges control over the desires of the body so as to
keep it in check until the end of time when it no longer will be corruptible. At the resurrection, both the somatic and psychic senses
will be discarded, leaving only the messages of the pneumatic sense
lying at the core of Scripture.

C. *Pneumatic Sense*

Origen likens this core of Scripture to the center of the almond, that
is, the richest part that feeds and nourishes the one who consumes it:

> Moreover, in the third place, you will find concealed and hidden . . . a
> sense of the mysteries of "the wisdom and knowledge of God," by
> which the souls of the saints are sustained and nourished and not only
> in the present life but also in the future. For that is the pontifical fruit
> [or fruit of the High Priest], by which it is promised to them that
> "they who hunger and thirst for righteousness will be satisfied."[36]

In *Princ.* 4, Origen defined the pneumatic sense as the one that conveys God's wisdom in a mystery. Here he identifies the almond's
core with Scripture's "sense of the mysteries of 'the wisdom and
knowledge of God.'" This pneumatic sense is what is hidden and
protected by the somatic and psychic senses.

As Origen explained earlier in the homily that the almond's center feeds and nourishes the one who consumes it, here he describes
the pneumatic sense as the meaning that "sustain[s] and nour-
ishe[s] . . . the souls of the saints *(animae sanctorum)*." Rufinus uses the
same Latin terms *pascere* and *nutrire* that he used earlier for Origen's
description of the almond's core. The pneumatic sense is the milk
of Scripture. It brings up and rears as well as heals and sustains the
soul of the believer.

---

[36] *Hom. Num.* 9.7 (quoting Col. 2:3 and Matt. 5:6); Tertio autem loco recondi-
tum in his invenies et secretum mysteriorum « sapientiae et scientiae Dei » sensum,
quo nutriantur et pascantur animae sanctorum non solum in praesenti vita, sed
etiam in futura. Iste enim est pontificalis fructus, de quo promittitur his, « qui esuri-
unt et sitiunt iustitiam, quia saturabuntur » (GCS 30:64).

Moreover, Origen points out that the pneumatic sense will nourish and sustain the believer "not only in the present life but also in the future." Unlike the somatic and psychic senses, the pneumatic sense will not become useless at the resurrection. It serves the human person in the temporal life *and* in the future of eternity, by eternally "'satisf[ying]'" his "'hunger and thirst for righteousness.'"

Also in this passage Origen describes the pneumatic sense as the "pontifical fruit *(pontificalis fructus)*," meaning that which comes from the high priest. In another passage of this homily, Origen identifies Christ as the High Priest of believers, as Aaron is designated the high priest of Israel:

> Whereas yet, as we hold out repeatedly, Christ is the true pontiff [High Priest], it is he alone, whose rod, the Cross, has not only sprouted forth, but also bloomed and brought forth all the fruit to those among the more believing people.[37]

By identifying Christ as the High Priest of the church ("the more believing people"), Origen suggests that Christ is the ultimate teacher of souls. Implicitly, church leaders, like Origen, are priests who serve Christ on earth, as the other Levites served under Aaron. They bring Scripture before the church, so that Christ then can place its fruit within each soul.

Origen also likens Aaron's rod to the Cross. The Cross has "sprouted forth" and caused to "bloom . . . all the fruit" that is to benefit all those who are "more believing." If the parts of the almond represent the three senses, then the almond that sprouts forth from the Cross is Scripture itself. This fruit of the Cross is designed to edify the believer according to the three senses and, ultimately, to nourish him with the pneumatic sense.

If Scripture is the fruit of the Cross, it also is Christ himself. Recalling the imagery in *Hom. Lev.* 5, Christ is the priest who bakes the three senses in the heart of the hearer, thereby making a sacrifice acceptable to God, an offering that is Christ himself. Here, again, Origen stresses, as he did in *Hom. Gen.* 11 and *Hom. Lev.* 5, that Christ both teaches Scripture's truths and is its content. According to the imagery of the nut, when the hearer takes in Scripture, he

---

[37] *Hom. Num.* 9.7; Verum quoniam, ut saepe ostendimus, verus pontifex Christus est, ipse solus est, cuius virga crucis non solum germinavit, sed et floruit et omnes hos credentium populorum attulit fructus (GCS 30:63).

takes in Christ's own essence. More specifically, when he consumes its core, pneumatic truths, he consumes Christ. Elsewhere in the homily Origen, again referring to Christ as "the Great Priest," states that "Christ is the life in the mystery of the 'nut.'"[38] Christ, then, is the pneumatic sense, and the pneumatic sense nourishes by giving life. Origen again stresses, as he did in *Hom. Lev.* 5, that the soul who takes in the devil and his teachings consumes an "'inflamed cauldron'" that can bring only death, while the one who takes in Christ at Scripture's nutritional core will receive life.[39]

Indeed, it is eternal life that the pneumatic core of Scripture provides. For, as Origen has explained, the hard shell of the psychic sense will nourish until the end of time, and yet the soft, pneumatic center of Scripture will feed the believer for eternity. Origen impresses upon his audience this great abundance of life that is to be found in Scripture, emphasizing that God always gives more than God promises:

> God promised only fruit in the rod and he gave more. . . . [E]ven though the sprouting alone was promised, see that God grants much more, such that not only has a bud [shoot] "been produced," but also "leaves," and not only leaves, but also "flowers," and not only flowers, but also "fruit". . . . [T]he generosity of God is even more abundant than his promises; if we also can examine and investigate boldly from them that ineffable goodness of God, which in the letter of Scripture

---

[38] The fuller passage reads: "Since, on the other hand, the priestly mystery is the rod of the nut, for that reason, I judge, also Jeremiah, who was one 'from the priests of Anathoth', 'to see a rod of nut' and to prophesy from it what was written either from the 'rod of nut' or from 'the cauldron' or 'that which was inflamed', as if he would show by this that life was in the 'rod of nut' and death in the 'inflamed cauldron'; for 'life' and 'death' are placed 'before our face' and indeed Christ is the life in the mystery of the 'nut' while death is the devil in the figure of the 'inflamed cauldron'. If therefore you sin, you place your portion into the 'inflamed cauldron'; yet if you do justly, your portion is shown in 'the rod of nut' with the Great Priest" (*Hom. Num.* 9.7, referring to Jer. 1:1, 11–13 and Deut. 30:15); Quia autem sacramentum sacerdotale est virga nucis, idcirco arbitror etiam Hieremiam, qui erat unus « ex sacerdotibus ex Anathoth », « vidisse virgam nuceam » et prophetasse de ea illa, quae scripta sunt vel de « virga nucea » vel de « lebete » sive « olla succensa », quasi si ostenderet per haec in « virga nucea » esse vitam et in « lebete succenso » esse mortem; « vita » enim et « mors » ponitur « ante faciem nostram », et est vita quidem Christus in sacramento « nucis », mors autem diabolus in figura « lebetis succensi ». Si ergo peccaveris, portionem tuam pones cum « lebete succenso »; si autem iuste egeris, efficietur portio tua in « virga nucea » cum magno pontifice (GCS 30:64).
[39] Ibid.

is always hidden, then we would see that there is more abundance in the obtaining than in the promising.[40]

God not only makes great promises and keeps them but also delivers more than the promises suggest. God promises only that the rod of the one chosen for priesthood will "sprout forth." Then it sprouts forth not only a shoot, but also leaves and flowers and fruit. Origen urges his audience to consider how much more lies hidden within Scripture than the appearance of the letter suggests.[41] Eternal life awaits the one who tears away the husk, cracks the shell and consumes Christ at Scripture's core.

In this homily, Origen has confirmed that Scripture contains three separate senses of meaning. The husk of Scripture, or its literal sense, holds somatic instruction, which, when morally exhortative, is hard to follow and, indeed, condemns the sinfulness in the hearer, calling him to submit to a general cleansing from sin and cultivation of the virtues through disciplines called for by the psychic sense. This somatic sense, then, will not always be necessary to the soul of the hearer. Hidden just beneath the husk is Scripture's hard shell, the psychic sense, which morally directs the hearer to subdue the tendencies of the body that lead to sin. Throughout this life, the hearer needs to grow more effective at following the directives of the psychic sense, but it, like the somatic sense, eventually will cease to be useful to the hearer. At the end of time, when the resurrection takes place and the body ceases to be corruptible, only the divine mysteries of the pneumatic sense will be left to edify the hearer throughout eternity.

---

[40] *Hom. Num.* 9.7–8 (quoting Num. 17:5, 8); [U]num promisit Deus futurum in virga et plura dedit. . . . Cum . . . de solo germine fuisset promissum, vide quanta largitur Deus, ut non solum germen « produxerit », sed et « frondes », et non solum frondes, sed et « flores », et non solum flores, sed et « fructus » . . . . Sed attendite diligentius, si forte possumus liberalitatem Dei largiorem etiam ipsis suis promissionibus edocere; si forte et ex his illam ineffabilem bonitatem Dei, quae in Scripturae littera semper tegitur, rimari atque investigare poterimus, cum eum largiorem in praestando quam in promittendo videamus (GCS 30:64–65).

[41] Origen also stresses the abundance of God's gifts in another passage in which he refers to the Bride in *The Song of Songs* who "'descends' 'into the garden of the nut', where . . . she finds with the priestly nuts in a certain measure an abundance of fruit trees" (*Hom. Num.* 9.7 [referring to Cant 6:11, 7:12–13]; Sed et in Canticis Canticorum sponsa « descendere » dicitur « in hortum nucis », ubi etiam pariter cum nucibus sacerdotalium quodammodo pomorum copiam perscribitur invenisse (GCS 30:64).

This pneumatic sense likely needs the double protection of the husk and shell in this life for the same reason that it is the one that remains effective after temporal existence: it contains the most direct and profound truths about Christ himself and, indeed, is his essence. As the hearer grows in understanding of this pneumatic sense, he receives the nourishment that he needs and becomes more healthy and prepared for eternal union with God. More specifically, he becomes more and more familiar with Christ himself and, thus, more and more like Christ. Because of this Christ-centered, eternal focus, the pneumatic sense needs the protective cover of the somatic and psychic senses during this life so that hearers first grasp it only once they are ready for its truths and then increasingly comprehend it at a manageable pace.

This representation of the somatic and psychic senses serving the pneumatic sense during this life recalls Origen's anthropological analogy to Scripture, suggesting that the three senses relate in the way that the three parts of the rightly ordered human person relate. As the soul in the rightly ordered person chooses to follow the spirit for how to live and the body likewise submits to the spirit, the psychic and somatic senses point toward and submit to the pneumatic sense as Scripture's ultimate source of nourishment for the hearer. They will cease to edify at the resurrection, when the human body becomes incorruptible, because then the human person will have reached a perfect ordering of his body, soul and spirit. He will have achieved a perfect reflection of the order enjoyed by Scripture's three parts. This rightly ordered person will have achieved a perfect imitation of Christ, for he will have reached fully the pneumatic sense, the essence of which is Christ. The somatic and psychic senses will fall away, leaving only that sense to which these two were pointing all along. Eternity, as the enjoyment of and participation in God's wisdom, will be the activity of sharing fully in the pneumatic sense and, thus, in Christ himself.

Though this homily stresses the central and lasting role of the pneumatic sense, it also emphasizes the indispensability of the psychic sense. As the shell of Scripture, it is the part with which the hearer must actively struggle during this life. He must wrestle to break it, for he cannot fully consume the pneumatic core until he does so. This striving will not cease until the resurrection. He may begin to crack the psychic shell and tap into the nutritional, pneumatic core, but he will not tear that shell away completely until the end of time. For all of temporal life, then, the shell of Scripture will exact more and more effort from the hearer. Only as he grows more and more virtuous will he come nearer to the full imitation of Christ that is equal to complete consumption of the pneumatic sense. As in the other homilies, here Origen portrays the psychic sense as the locus of active engagement with Scripture. There is no getting to the entire core without getting past the shell, and getting past it completely is a lifelong struggle.

IV. *Hom. Gen.* 2: *The Two and Three Decks of Noah's Ark*

In the last of the four homilies treated in this chapter, Origen reiterates his commitment to three separate senses as defined in *Princ.* 4 and the other homilies and, in addition, stresses that the relationship between the psychic and pneumatic senses is particularly significant to his exegetical method. In *Hom. Gen.* 2, Origen treats Gen. 6 in which God gives the specifications for the ark to Noah. Origen reviews these specifications in detail and renders somatic, psychic and pneumatic readings of them. While the next chapter will examine fully his different readings, this analysis concentrates on his explanation of how language within the biblical passage supports his claim to three separate scriptural senses.

Origen cites the relevant biblical language as follows: "'And the Lord said to Noah,' . . . 'Make . . . yourself an ark. . . . You shall make two lower decks in it and three upper decks.'"[42] Likening the ark to Scripture, Origen interprets the "*three* upper decks" as representative of Scripture's *three senses* of meaning and the "*two* lower decks" as representative of the two higher, nonliteral senses for passages that do not contain a somatic meaning.[43]

First, Origen interprets the "three decks" as supporting his view that, in addition to literal (or historical) and mystical senses, Scripture also contains a moral sense:

---

[42] *Hom. Gen.* 2.1 (quoting from Gen. 6:14–16, esp. 6:16; FC 71:72); Et dixit, *inquit*, Dominus ad Noe: . . . Fac ergo tibi arcam . . . inferiora bicamerata et tricamerata superiora facies ea (SC 7:76, 78).

[43] Regarding the senses, Origen does not draw significance from the fact that the "three decks" are "upper" decks and the "two decks" "lower" decks in the ark. Rather, he concentrates on the language of "two" and "three" for his analogy of the ark's decks to Scripture's senses.

For the historical meaning . . . is placed first as a kind of foundation at the lower levels. This mystical interpretation was second, being higher and loftier. Let us attempt, if we can, to add a moral exposition as the third level. . . . For "with three decks" denotes this threefold exposition.[44]

The *three senses* are the "historical meaning," "mystical interpretation," and "moral exposition."

The Latin term *historica* recalls Origen's description of the somatic sense in *Princ.* 4 as the literal meaning that is historically accurate and thus informative for the hearer. He describes this sense as the lowest of the three decks, the one that "serves as a kind of foundation at the lower levels." The Latin term *fundamentum*, translated here as "foundation," also means the bottom, basis or ground-work of a structure. It supports that which lies above it. Thus, Origen refers to the somatic sense here as the foundation of Scripture's entire structure of meaning, suggesting that it is the first to be grasped and helps to prepare the hearer for reception of the other senses.

The "mystical interpretation" serves as the second level, or deck, and is the "higher and loftier" meaning. The Latin term *mystica*, also means of or belonging to secret rites or mysteries. In *Princ.* 4, Origen defined the pneumatic sense as the meaning in Scripture that contains and conveys the mysteries of God's wisdom. He describes it here as *superior et excelsior*, or higher and loftier. The Latin term *excelsior* means that which is more elevated in station or position, as well as that which is more distinguished, excellent or noble. Origen speaks of the pneumatic sense, then, as more elevated in excellence and honor. This pneumatic sense offers a greater amount or sharper quality of edification than does the somatic sense, though the latter is the supportive foundation of the former.

Origen identifies the third "level" of the ark with the "moral exposition" of Scripture. The Latin term *moralis* is the same term that Rufinus employed in his translations of the other three homilies for the descriptions of the psychic sense.[45] Here, Origen says nothing

---

[44] *Hom. Gen.* 2.6 (quoting Gen. 6:16; FC 71:85); Prima enim, quae praecessit, historica est ueluti fundamentum quoddam in inferioribus posita. Secunda haec mystica superior et excelsior fuit. Tertiam, si possumus, moralem temptemus adicere, . . . Nam *tricamerata* triplicem hanc expositionem designat (SC 7:106, 108).

[45] Here *moralis* occurs in the accusative singular form as *moralem*; also *Hom. Gen.* 11.3 (FC 71:173–174, SC 7:288); *Hom. Lev.* 5.5.3 (FC 83:100, SC 286:230); and *Hom. Num.* 9.7 (GCS 30:63–64).

else about this third sense, but does identify it with the third, highest deck, since he begins with the ark's foundation and thus moves upward in his description of its three levels.

On close analysis, the order of these three senses gives greatest significance to the pneumatic sense. On the ark, it is nestled between the other two senses. As Origen, in *Hom. Num.* 9, presented the pneumatic sense as the nut's center, surrounded and protected by the outer husk of the somatic sense and hard shell of the psychic sense, so here the pneumatic sense lies between the somatic and psychic senses. According to this imagery, the pneumatic sense is exposed neither to the water below the ship nor the air above it, because it is surrounded and protected from all outside elements by the other two senses. Also, this positioning of the pneumatic sense as the middle deck makes it the center, or core of the ship, as in *Hom. Num.* 9 it is the center, or core of the almond. Thus, Origen lists the psychic sense third, as the top level of the ark, because the metaphor of the ark calls for this order as a way of emphasizing that the pneumatic sense is the one that holds the greatest ultimate significance.

This observation reflects a common theme through Origen's imageries of the pneumatic sense as the middle deck of the ark, the core of the almond and the loaf that must be baked in the complete enclosure of the oven. All these images of the pneumatic sense suggest that it requires complete cover or encasement in order to be able to exist for and impact those who reside within this temporal world. Its edification is a prerequisite to eternal life and yet it is the sense among the three that is most eternal in character. The human soul needs temporally that which is eternal within Scripture. The somatic and psychic senses encase the pneumatic sense, making the eternal accessible temporally to the attentive hearer as he becomes ready to receive it.

Also, by listing the psychic sense, and not the pneumatic sense, as the third, highest deck, Origen suggests that it enjoys its fullest effects on the hearer *after* he has *begun* to take in the pneumatic meaning.[46] In chapters 4 and 5, we will see that Origen tends in practice to present the psychic reading of a biblical passage *after* its pneumatic reading in order to offer the advanced hearer—the one

---

[46] Recall that Origen similarly stressed in *Hom. Gen.* 11 that three days at the well of Scripture will bring on the full effects of the psychic sense.

who is able to recognize all three senses—the fullest effect of edification from the two higher senses' messages (while the less advanced hearers benefit as they are able).

Later in the homily, Origen stresses the distinctive focus of each sense:[47]

> If . . . you build an ark [within your heart], if you gather a library, gather it from the words of the prophets and apostles or of those who have followed them in the right lines of faith. You shall make it "with two decks" and "with three decks." From this library learn the historical narratives; from it recognize "the great mystery" which is fulfilled in Christ and in the Church. From it also learn how to correct habits, to curtail vices, to purge the soul and draw it off from every bond of captivity, setting up in it "nests and nests" of the various virtues and perfections."[48]

Origen discusses the focus of each sense by describing the content of three books, or lessons, in Scripture. Note that the three senses are found in "the words of the prophets and apostles or of those who have followed them in the right lines of faith." Arguably, this recalls Origen's statement in *Princ.* 4 that the three senses are handed down by the rule of faith and have the authority of divine teaching according to apostolic succession.

While Origen only reiterates the "historical" focus of the somatic sense, he describes the pneumatic sense more fully. Above he described the pneumatic sense as the "mystical sense" that is higher and more noble than the somatic. Here, he adds that it contains "'the great mystery' which is fulfilled in Christ *and in the Church.*" In *Princ.* 4 he explained that Christ is the central focus of the pneumatic sense, yet here he also mentions the church. In the reexamination of *Princ.* 4

---

[47] This passage occurs in Origen's analysis of the psychic meaning of the ark as representing the human heart, into which the hearer is called to gather a library of divine truths rather than secular teachings. He explains that the hearer is to build the library with two and three decks. He then relates each sense to a different subject matter that one is to store within this library.

[48] *Hom. Gen.* 2.6 (quoting Gen. 6:16 and referring to Eph. 5:32; FC 71:87); Tu ergo si facis arcam, si bibliothecam congregas, ex sermonibus propheticis et apostolicis uel eorum qui eos rectis fidei lineis secuti sunt congrega, *bicameratam* et *tricameratam* facito eam. Ex ipsa narrationes historicas disce, ex ipsa mysterium magnum, quod in Christo et in Ecclesia impletur, agnosce; ex ipsa etiam emendare mores, resecare uitia, purgare animam atque exuere eam omni uinculo captiuitatis intellige, nidos in ea et nidos diuersarum uirtutum et profectuum collocans (SC 7:110). In chapter 4, I will explore this passage again and in even greater detail in relation specifically to Origen's psychic reading of the ark.

in chapter 2, we observed that the pneumatic sense focuses specifically on the events to which Christ is central: aspects of the Incarnation and Eschaton, that is, Christ's first and second coming. We considered that, to the extent that the age of the church is made possible by the Incarnation and brought to completion at the Eschaton, non-literal readings that speak about or to the church render pneumatic meaning. Here, Origen confirms this understanding: the mystery conveyed by the pneumatic sense is "fulfilled" in Christ *and* in the church. No doubt, he refers to the fulfillment of God's salvation plan at the end of time, for which Christ is the administrator and the church the beneficiary.

Also, in this passage, Origen describes at length the psychic sense as teaching "how to correct habits," "curtail vices," and "purge the soul *(anima)*." The Latin term *emendare*, translated here as "correct," also means to free from faults or improve, even to chastise or correct by punishment. The message of the psychic sense directs the hearer to improve his *mores*, "habits," or manners, morals or character by stinging admonition. The Latin term *resecare*, translated here as "curtail," also means to cut off, stop or restrain. The hearer is to cut himself off from the vices that have grafted themselves onto him through previous faults of character and habits. The term *purgare* signifies the act of cleansing from a crime or sin and bestowing atonement on a person. The psychic readings teach the hearer how to purge his soul of past sins, cut himself off from the vices that cling to him and correct his behavior so that he can ward off temptations to sin during the remainder of his life and receive forgiveness.

Origen also states here that the psychic sense helps the hearer to "set up" in his soul "the various virtues and perfections." In *Princ.* 4, Origen stated that the purpose of Scripture is to bring the hearer to perfection and salvation.[49] While Rufinus employed the Latin term *perfectio* for perfection in his translation of *Princ.* 4, which also means a completion or finishing, in his translation of this homily he employs a noun formed on the participle *profectus* from the verb *proficere*. This noun signifies all of the following: an advance, progress, effect, increase, growth, profit, success and improvement. Thus, Rufinus understands

---

[49] *Princ.* 4.2.7, 4.2.4 (Butterworth, 283, 276; SC 268:328, 312). Also, see the discussion in chapter 2 of Scripture's spiritual purpose as Origen explained it in *Princ.* 4.

Origen to state here that the psychic sense's directives effect in the willing hearer growth in virtues and progress toward perfection and salvation. Recalling the discussion of anthropology in chapter 2, the human soul learns from the psychic sense to cut itself off from the reign of fleshly passions in the body and seek the spirit's holy direction for living. This choice is essential to the hearer's achievement of perfection, which is marked by the harmonious ordering of his body, soul and spirit.

In one additional passage, Origen focuses on the separate phrases of "two decks" and "three decks" for the ark, offering insight into the relationship between the senses. He explains that the mention of two rather than three decks refers to the occasions in Scripture where the somatic sense is missing, leaving available to the hearer edification only from the passage's psychic and pneumatic senses:

> But the historical succession cannot always be established in the divine Scriptures, but sometimes is lacking . . . . Because of these things, . . . the ark is constructed not only "with three decks," but also "with two decks," that we might know that there is not always a triple explanation in the divine Scriptures because a historical explanation does not always follow for us, but sometimes only the mingled meaning of the double explanation.[50]

Here, as in *Princ.* 4, Origen states that the edifying literal or historical meaning, or the somatic sense, is absent from some biblical passages in order to direct the hearer to seek edification from "the mingled meaning of the double explanation *(duplicis . . . sensum expositionis insertum)*," implicitly, that of the psychic and pneumatic senses. The Latin term *insertum*, translated here as "mingled," modifies *sensum* (meaning or sense). It stems from the verb *inserere*, which means to bring into, introduce, mix or mingle with or join with something else. The two senses, when the somatic is absent, are joined together, or mingled, as the full edification of the text. However, Origen explains, the psychic and pneumatic senses remain "double *(duplicis)*" in "explanation *(expositionis)*" and thus separate in meaning or sense *(sensum)*.[51] Since Origen states that where there are only "two decks"

---

[50] *Hom. Gen.* 2.6 (quoting Gen. 6:16; FC 71:86); Sed quia non semper in Scripturis diuinis historialis consequentia stare potest, sed nonnumquam deficit, . . . propter haec . . . , non solum *tricamerata*, sed *et bicamerata* arca contextitur, ut sciamus in Scripturis diuinis non semper triplicem, quia non semper nos historia sequitur, sed interdum duplicis tantummodo sensum expositionis insertum (SC 7:108).
[51] This "mingling" of senses that nevertheless remain separate is different from

they are the psychic and pneumatic senses, he informs his audience that the occasional absence of the somatic sense is Scripture's way of focusing the hearer on the relationship between the two higher senses. This suggests that for Origen the height of Scripture's intended meaning occurs through a distinction between the two figurative senses and not principally between a literal and nonliteral meaning. Chapters 4 and 5 will review examples from Origen's homilies and commentaries where he focuses principally on separate psychic and pneumatic readings for the same biblical passage. In all these examples their separate messages will mingle, or relate, so that each increases the edifying effects of the other for the hearer.

In this homily, Origen has confirmed his commitment to three separate senses of meaning and defined them in conformity with *Princ.* 4 and the other homiletic explications of theory. As Scripture's foundation, the somatic sense is the first that the hearer grasps, and it prepares him to comprehend the others. As Scripture's center, the pneumatic sense is the most precious meaning. It is the ultimate reward for the attentive and diligent hearer. As Scripture's top deck, the psychic sense (as stressed in *Hom. Num.* 9) is essential for protecting the pneumatic sense, helping to prepare the hearer for it and making it accessible only when he is ready for its truths. It is Scripture's call for the hearer to purge his soul of sins and grow in virtue. It punishes the submissive hearer into purity. Again, as with all the other homilies, Origen here presents the psychic sense as the locus of active engagement with Scripture. It is the difficult sense with which one must wrestle if he is to reach the prize of understanding Scripture's pneumatic truths in their fullness and being ever edified by them.

It makes sense, then, that Origen considers the relationship between the psychic and pneumatic senses to be of primary significance to his exegesis. In this homily, he explains that they are double—that is, separate but mingled—for the effect of edifying the hearer. Even where the somatic sense is absent, these two nonliteral senses are present and interact for the hearer's benefit.

---

the "fusion" or "absorption" of which recent scholars such as Hanson have accused Origen. Specifically, Hanson argues that in practice Origen fuses the moral/psychic and spiritual/pneumatic senses together in a seemingly inadvertent way, losing sight of the middle, "moral" sense and ending up with only one overly broad "spiritual" sense to be contrasted from the literal sense (*Allegory and Event*, 235–243; and the discussion of Hanson's views in chapter 1).

V. *The Main Developments*

In all four homilies Origen reaffirms his theory of three separate senses of scriptural meaning and confirms and builds upon their definitions as set forth in *Princ.* 4.

These homilies together confirm *Princ.* 4's description of the somatic sense as Scripture's body which conveys historical information or moral instruction through literal readings of the text. It is the first sense, indeed, the most obvious and thus easiest to grasp. It acts as clothing or a cover over the other senses, but it is not present in every passage of Scripture. Building upon these basic elements, these homilies additionally stress that, as a cover, the somatic sense helps to hide and protect the other senses from those who are not ready for their deeper truths. Though it is easy to grasp, it is condemning (especially through the Law) and, thus, bitter to accept. At least one way in which it prepares the hearer for the other senses, then, is by persuading him that he sins and needs the moral discipline provided by the psychic sense if he ever is to learn more deeply about God and salvation. Its aid is temporary, and, while it may cease in some passages to edify during this life, its usefulness will be wholly spent by the resurrection.

These homilies together also reaffirm *Princ.* 4's definition of the psychic sense as Scripture's soul which conveys moral instruction through figurative readings of the text. To this general description, these homilies add that this moral direction is general and holistic, disciplining the hearer to restrain the flesh, cleanse his soul of *all* vice, and grow in *all* virtue. It is the hardest sense with which to deal in this life, for it is the locus of active engagement with Scripture. Its message calls the hearer to interact with Scripture, to meditate on it with consistency and diligence. It exacts moral correction from the hearer and, thus, keeps him engaged in the constant struggle toward perfection. The psychic sense, then, will hound the persevering student of Scripture for this whole life, remaining fully edifying until the resurrection. Like the somatic sense, the psychic sense covers and protects the pneumatic sense from those who are not yet ready for its deepest truths and at the same time prepares them for it. It is the indispensable way to initial as well as deepening comprehension of the pneumatic sense prior to the resurrection.

Finally, these homilies together also, consistently with *Princ.* 4, describe the pneumatic sense as the spirit of Scripture which gives insights about God's wisdom. These truths are so focused on the eternal that they are not fully explicable. The pneumatic sense is a figurative reading of text and is revealed to the hearer only slowly as he becomes more and more ready through the other two senses to make contact with its eternal truths. It is the fullness of Scripture's story that all three senses help to convey. It centers on Christ, his Incarnation, his faithful church, and his final victory at the Eschaton. In addition, these homilies emphasize that when the somatic and psychic senses cease wholly to edify, at the end of time, the pneumatic sense alone will remain. It sprouts forth from the rod of the Cross and reflects both Christ's authority and God's generosity. It will never cease to edify, because it will unfold as the activity of heaven. It is the mind of Christ and is his essence. It is, then, the nutritional core of Scripture, the eternal food, an endlessly abundant reward for the student who perseveres to the end.

This extended theory also builds upon the implication in *Princ.* 4 that Origen draws his method out of Scripture's own structure. The Holy Spirit built Scripture with three parts that reflect the tripartite human nature. These homilies suggest that the three senses relate in a way that is reflective of Origen's portrayal of the rightly ordered person. As a person's soul and body properly submit to his spirit as the guide for living, so also do the psychic and somatic senses protect and promote, indeed point toward, the pneumatic sense. As the pneumatic sense is Scripture's full story, the psychic and somatic senses are the chapters that lead up to the conclusion. They make the pneumatic sense's eternal message increasingly comprehensible to temporally bound persons.

These homilies also stress that the attentive hearer will meet Jesus Christ in Scripture. While in *Princ.* 4 Origen tended to stress the Holy Spirit's role as chief architect of Scripture, who constructed it with a body, soul and spirit, in these texts he underscores that the core content of Scripture is Christ himself. Jesus is the teacher and the content of Scripture. He is the high priest and the offering sacrificed in it. Jesus will match the diligent student's effort with his gracious aid. He will bring that student into his own sacrifice on the Cross and make him also a sacrifice acceptable to God. The hearer will become an offering to God by becoming conformed to the image of Christ. As he takes in the pneumatic truths, he will consume Christ and, ultimately, achieve an imitation of him.

If this is the goal of Scripture, then it becomes clear why for

Origen the relationship between the two nonliteral senses, rather than between a literal and one nonliteral sense, holds the greatest significance in his exegesis. The psychic sense demands full commitment to the study of Scripture, a full three days. It requires frequent turning and attention. It is the shell that must be cracked fully before the hearer can wholly consume Scripture's core, pneumatic truths. It requires the lifelong commitment of struggling to cut off vice, refrain from new sins and take on all the virtues. Its demands will never let up in this life, for it is the nonnegotiable means of preparing for a *full* understanding of the pneumatic sense's eternal truths.[52] While the pneumatic sense is the reward of Origen's method, the psychic sense is its key player.[53] As the practical examples in the next chapters will demonstrate, these two higher senses are separate and yet relate, or are mingled, in a way that marks the height of Origen's exegetical effort to bring his hearers to Scripture's goals of perfection and salvation.

---

[53] Since, for Origen, the psychic sense will continue to edify each hearer until the end of time, he presumably understands that throughout temporal life every person continues to make progress but does not reach completely the perfection that is necessary for salvation. Even the "perfected" one who is the most advanced in grasping all three meanings—indeed, every church leader, such as Origen himself—continues to struggle with the psychic sense and its call to perfect virtue. This helps to explain why Origen in *Hom. Gen.* 11 on the well of vision admitted that he did not yet enjoy the *full* blessings from dwelling at Scripture. It will also help to explain why in places such as *Hom. Num.* 27 (analyzed in the next chapter) he admits, albeit with frustration, that he does not yet understand the deeper, pneumatic reading of certain passages. The remaining chapters will explore further this qualified understanding of "perfected" persons within Origen's thought.

[54] In addition to the homilies treated in this chapter, Origen also stresses that there are three separate senses and that the figurative moral, psychic sense is necessary—indeed, vital—preparation for comprehension of the mystical, pneumatic sense in the brief passage in *Comm. Matt.* 10:14 (ANF 9:421–422; Robert Girod, ed. and trans., *Origène: Commentaire sur L'Évangile selon Matthieu* [SC 162; Paris: Cerf, 1970] 1:194–202); and Erich Klostermann and Ernst Benz, eds., *Origenes Matthäuserklärung* [*Origenes Werke* 10; GCS 40; Leipzig: J. C. Hinrichs'sche, 1935] 1:16–18). Without the aid of the psychic sense, hearers of Scripture will remain at the level of its bare letter with no access to its highest truths. In the original Greek for *Comm. Matt.* 10:14, Origen employs forms of τροπολογέω and τροπολογία (tropological or moral) for the psychic sense and forms of πνευματικόν (spiritual) and ἀναγώγιον (anagogical or mystical) for the pneumatic sense.

CHAPTER FOUR

THE PSYCHIC AND PNEUMATIC SENSES IN PRACTICE

The homilies examined in the prior chapter demonstrated that Origen carries over his threefold theory of scriptural meaning from *Princ.* 4 and develops it further in his later, exegetical works. He remains committed in his theory to the nonliteral psychic sense as distinct from both the somatic and pneumatic senses. Still, his exegetical works do more than continue and develop the theory; they put it into practice.

This chapter analyzes five homilies in which Origen presents both the psychic and pneumatic senses for the same biblical passage. Together, they demonstrate the following points: (1) Origen employs each higher sense as a separately functioning message for his audience; (2) each message individually edifies the hearer, that is, aids him in his pursuit and/or understanding of salvation; (3) the separate meanings of the psychic and pneumatic senses facilitate a complementary relationship between their messages such that, when Origen presents both higher readings for a single passage side-by-side, they collaborate to edify Scripture's hearer more completely; and (4) the psychic sense is profoundly Christian in character, which is especially evident when viewed in its relation to the pneumatic sense.

I have chosen to treat these five homilies, because in them Origen not only offers a full reading for both senses but also explicitly labels the transitions between them. Of course, other works of Origen also display separate psychic and pneumatic readings for the same biblical passage, including works on New Testament passages as well as commentaries, but frequently they do not include explicit labels for each reading and the readings are not always presented in full.[1]

---

[1] For further research and substantiation of the findings in this chapter and the work as a whole, see Origen's psychic and pneumatic readings in the following texts: the historical text in *Hom. Josh.* 6–7 (on the battle of Jericho); the prophetic texts (also extant in Greek) in *Hom. Jer.* 1 (on the Lord's announcement of the "uproot[ing] and demolish[ing] of nations and kingdoms") and *Hom. Jer.* 16 (on the sins of Judah); and the New Testament texts in *Comm. Jo.* 10 (on the city of Jerusalem

This chapter sets forth the most complete examples of Origen's presentation of the two higher senses for the same scriptural text. These examples will act as the guide for continuing research into the various ways in which Origen reads Scripture pneumatically and psychically throughout his extant works.

Finally, at the end, this chapter offers a brief review of the well-known *Hom. Num.* 27, in which Origen likens the journey of the Israelites through the desert toward the promised land to the soul's journey to God. In this homily, although he presents only the psychic reading, he describes how the pneumatic reading would differ if presented. His contrasting outlines for the two readings in this sixth homily significantly substantiate the findings of the five homilies treated fully in this chapter. Also, in *Hom. Num.* 27 Origen arguably expresses frustration over his own self-perceived inability to grasp fully the pneumatic sense of the biblical passage at hand. This frustration suggests why Origen does not always present both higher readings for all biblical passages within his extant works: he may not be able as yet to grasp sufficiently the pneumatic sense of some passages.[2]

I. *Hom. Gen.* 2: *The Two Upper Decks of Noah's Ark*

We have already reviewed Origen's theoretical treatment of Noah's ark in *Hom. Gen.* 2, in which he interprets the "*three* upper decks" of the ark as the three senses, and the "*two* lower decks" as the psychic and pneumatic sense for biblical passages that do not contain a somatic meaning. The analysis here concentrates on Origen's practical use—full readings—of the senses in this homily.

---

and the cleansing of the temple). For a text outside the homilies and commentaries, see Origen's *Treatise on the Passover* (or *De Pascha*) (available in Greek) for figurative meanings of the Passover. These examples of additional texts where Origen offers psychic and pneumatic readings do not constitute an exhaustive list, but they provide a starting point for further consideration of the findings of this work. I suggest that when examining additional texts, the student of Origen should be open to the possibility that he may sometimes offer more than one psychic and/or pneumatic reading for the same biblical passage and, in other instances, may approach a biblical passage by reading some of its concepts pneumatically and others psychically. (For an example of the latter scenario, see *Comm. Matt.* 14:6–14 on Jesus' parable regarding the debt of the King's servants in Matt. 18:23–35.)

[2] Of course, in some cases he may refrain from offering full readings of both higher senses because of constraints of time and/or considerations of the immediate needs or capabilities of his audience.

At the beginning of the homily, Origen recites the relevant biblical verses:

> And the Lord said to Noah . . . "the critical moment of every man has
> come before me, since the earth is filled with iniquity by them; and
> behold, I shall destroy them and the earth. Make, therefore, yourself
> an ark of squared planks; you shall make nests in the ark, and you
> shall cover it with pitch within and without. And thus you shall make
> the ark: the length of the ark three hundred cubits and the breadth
> fifty cubits and its height thirty cubits, you shall assemble and make
> the ark, and you shall finish it on top to a cubit. And you shall make
> a door in the side of the ark. You shall make two lower decks in it
> and three upper decks." . . . And Noah did everything which the Lord
> God commanded him, thus he did it.[3]

Origen begins by offering a somatic reading of the text, in which
he principally defends the historical veracity of the ark's dimensions.
Then, he presents a pneumatic reading, interpreting the ark as the
church, the architect as Christ, and the flood as the final, eschatological destruction of the earth. Lastly, he gives a psychic reading,
interpreting the ark as a structure that his audience is to build within
their hearts to house Scripture's divine truths and the flood as Christ's
temporal cleansing of the soul from sin and vice.

A. *The Somatic Reading: The Historical Veracity of the Ark*

Origen defends the literal, historical veracity of the text in order to
contradict the heresy of Apelles, a student of Marcion, who claimed
that the writings of Moses are not divinely inspired. As an example,
Apelles argued that so many animals, some of enormous size, could
not abide in the small space specified in the text with all the necessary food and for so long a time.[4] Origen refutes Apelles' view in
two ways. First, he explains that Moses was schooled in Egyptian

---

[3] *Hom. Gen.* 2.1 (quoting Gen. 6:13–16, 22; FC 71:72); Et dixit . . . Dominus ad
Noe: Tempus omnis hominis uenit ante me, quoniam impleta est terra iniquitati-
bus ab iis; et ecce, ego disperdam illos et terram. Fac ergo tibi arcam de lignis
quadratis, nidos et nidos facies in arca, et bituminabis eam ab intus et a foris bitu-
mine. Et sic facies arcam: trecentorum cubitorum longitudinem arcae et quinquaginta
cubitorum latitudinem et triginta cubitorum altitudinem eius colligens facies arcam,
et in cubitum consummabis eam in summo. Ostium autem arcae facies ex latere,
inferiora bicamerata et tricamerata superiora facies ea. . . . Et fecit . . . Noe omnia
quaecumque praecepit ei Dominus Deus, sic fecit (SC 7:76, 78).
[4] *Hom. Gen.* 2.2; FC 71:75–76; SC 7:84, 86.

geometry, which has its own units of measurement. With these meas-
urements, Origen argues, the ark was able to contain all of the animals large and small.[5] Second, he argues that these specifications
lent the ark a logical structure that allowed the separations necessary
to ensure proper sanitation and physical safety of all inhabitants.[6]

Origen claims that the making of the ark for its intended use, as
recorded, is historically true. The historical possibility and logic of
the literal reading support the position that Moses' writings are from
God. This defense of the ark's historicity suggests that the literal
reading of its dimensions edifies the hearer, offering some kind of
historically true information about God's involvement with humankind
and, thus, it contains a somatic sense. Implicitly, Origen stresses, by
this somatic reading, that God's harsh justice and saving mercy are
historically verifiable.

B. *The Pneumatic Reading of the Ark*

Origen announces that after considering the "historical account," he
and his audience can "ascend *(adscendere)*" to the "spiritual meaning
(spiritalis intelligentiae)" of the ark's dimensions.[7] In this spiritual reading, he interprets the ark as the church and places the soul's journey of ascent within it, tracing this ascent from the church's lowest
parts to its highest point where Christ resides as head. Framing this
whole reading is Origen's focus on the church's safety at the eschatological return of Christ.

Origen parallels the flood in Noah's time to the end of the world:

> I think . . . that that flood which nearly ended the world at that time
> contains a form of that end of the world which really will be. Because
> also the Lord himself announced saying: "For just as in the days of
> Noah they were buying, they were selling, they were building, they
> were marrying, they were giving in marriage, and the flood came and
> destroyed them all; so shall also the coming of the Son of man be."

---

[5] *Hom. Gen.* 2.2; FC 71:76–77; SC 7:86, 88.
[6] *Hom. Gen.* 2.1; FC 71:73–74; SC 7:78–82.
[7] *Hom. Gen.* 2.1. The full English texts reads: "[W]e can ascend from the historical account to the mystical and allegorical understanding of the spiritual meaning and, if these contain anything secret, we can explain it as the Lord reveals
knowledge of his word to us" (FC 71:72); . . . ab historiae textu possimus adscendere ad spiritalis intelligentiae mysticum et allegoricum sensum et, si quid in iis
arcanum continetur, aperire Domino nobis uerbi sui scientiam reuelante (SC 7:76).

> In this statement the Lord clearly represents that flood which preceded
> and the end of the world which he says is to come as one and the
> same kind of flood.[8]

According to Rufinus' translation, Origen presents the flood in Noah's
time as a *forma* of the eschatological flood. As support for this likeness, Origen refers to Jesus' prophetic words in the Gospels that,
when the "Son of man" comes, the world will be found iniquitous
and thus will be destroyed by flood, as in Noah's day. Yet, Noah's
flood is a mere likeness to the final reality, not a duplicate of it.
The Latin term *forma* means form, figure, image or type. Noah's
flood is but an image of the great flood that will destroy the world
completely and bring it to its ultimate end, *finis*.[9]
Origen identifies the "Son of man" with Christ himself and Noah
as a type or prefigurement of him:

> Therefore, just as it is said at that time to that Noah that he make
> an ark and bring into it along with himself not only his sons and
> neighbors, but also diverse kinds of animals, so also it is said by the
> Father in the consummation of the ages to our Noah, the Lord Jesus
> Christ, who alone is truly just and perfect, that he make himself an
> ark of squared planks and give it dimensions filled with heavenly
> mysteries.[10]

Origen refers to "the consummation of the ages." The Latin term
consummatio, even more than *finis*, denotes the completion or finishing of a thing, a summing up of something so that what has pre-
ceded will cease to be. He speaks, then, of the end of the world.

---

[8] *Hom. Gen.* 2.3 (quoting Luke 17:26–27, or Matt. 24:37–39, and referring to
Gen. 6:5, 11–13; FC 71:77–78); Puto . . . quod illud diluuium, quo paene finis tunc
datus est mundo, formam teneat finis illius qui uere futurus est mundi. Quod et
ipse Dominus pronuntiauit dicens: *Sicut enim in diebus Noe emebant, uendebant, aedificabant,
nubebant, et nuptum tradebant, et uenit diluuium, et perdidit omnes: ita erit et aduentus Filii
hominis.* In quo euidenter unam eandemque forman diluuii, quod praecessit, et finis
mundi, quem uenturum dicit designat (SC 7:88).
[9] This inexact likeness between Noah's flood and the eschatological flood upon
Christ's return coincides with the meaning of *forma*—type or image—as a mere historical foreshadowing of another, separate event. This, then, is a typological reading of text that is characteristic of early Christian exegesis.
[10] *Hom. Gen.* 2.3 (FC 71:78); Sicut ergo tunc dictum est ad illum Noe ut faceret
arcam et introduceret in eam secum non solum filios et proximos suos, uerum etiam
diuersi generis animalia, ita etiam ad nostrum Noe, qui uere solus iustus et solus
perfectus est, Dominum Iesum Christum, in consummatione saeculorum dictum est
a Patre ut faceret sibi arcam ex lignis quadratis et mensuras ei daret caelestibus
sacramentis repletas (SC 7:88, 90).

When the world comes to an end, "our Noah, the Lord Jesus Christ," will keep "his sons and neighbors" safe from that final flood within the protective walls of his ark. Christ will give his ark "dimensions filled with heavenly mysteries." This ark is the church, and Christ is the "architect of the Church."[11] Christ's "sons and neighbors" are the faithful people of the church. Origen states, "This people . . . which is saved in the Church, is compared to all those whether men or animals which are saved in the ark."[12] Thus, Christ's faithful people will survive the world's final destruction in the eschatological flood, because they will be safe within the church.

Believers are housed within the strong walls of the church. Origen explains that teachers, leaders, and zealots for the faith are the ark's strong walls, or "squared planks":

> Let us see . . . what the squared planks are. . . . Those are the planks which bear all the weight either of the animals within or the floods without. I think these are the teachers in the Church, the leaders, and zealots of the faith who both encourage the people who have been placed within the Church by a word of admonition and the grace of the teaching, and who resist, by the power of the word and the wisdom of reason, those without, whether heathens or heretics, who assail the Church and stir up floods of questions and storms of strife.[13]

The church's planks, teachers, leaders and zealots, are firm enough to hold all the faithful at their different levels of personal progress. These exemplars of the faith both encourage the progress of those within the church and hold at bay those "heathens" and "heretics" who confuse and manipulate matters of faith.[14]

As Noah's ark had various decks to hold and separate the peo-

---

[11] *Hom. Gen.* 2.4 (FC 71:81); architectus Ecclesiae Christus (SC 7:96).

[12] *Hom. Gen.* 2.3 (FC 71:78); Confertur ergo populus hic, qui saluatur in Ecclesia, illis omnibus siue hominibus siue animalibus quae saluata sunt in arca (SC 7:90).

[13] *Hom. Gen.* 2.4 (FC 71:80); Videamus . . . quae sunt quadrata ligna. . . . Ista sunt ligna quae omne pondus uel animalium intrinsecus uel fluctuum extrinsecus ferunt. Quos ego arbitror doctores esse in Ecclesia et magistros atque aemulatores fidei, qui et populos intrinsecus positos uerbo commonitionis et doctrinae gratia consolantur et impugnantibus extrinsecus uel gentilibus uel haereticis et quaestionum fluctus ac procellas certaminum commouentibus uirtute uerbi ac sapientia rationis obsistunt (SC 7:94).

[14] As discussed at the end of chapter 3, as Origen likens the three upper decks of the ark to Scripture's three senses with the somatic and psychic senses holding the pneumatic sense inside away from those not ready for it and keeping those outside who would dangerously misread it, so here he suggests that the perfected—the teachers and leaders—within the church keep heathen outside and the faithful safely inside.

ple from the animals and the different types of animals from each other, so also the church contains various "decks" to accommodate the people of varying levels of advancement in faith:

> But since neither the merit of all nor the progress in faith is one, therefore, also that ark does not offer one abode for all, but there are two lower decks and three upper decks and compartments are separated in it to show that also in the Church, although all are contained within the one faith and are washed in the one baptism, progress, however, is not one and the same for all, "but each one in his own order."[15]

There is but one faith and one baptism that unites all the members of the church. However, each member at any given time during this life exhibits his own level of faith. The church is designed to hold them all.

Origen explains how the interior of the church holds a spectrum of progress in faith:

> These . . . who live by rational knowledge and are capable not only of ruling themselves but also of teaching others, since very few are found, represent the few who are saved with Noah himself and are united with him in the closest relationship, just as also our Lord, the true Noah, Christ Jesus, has few intimates, few sons and relatives, who are participants in his word and capable of his wisdom. And these are the ones who are placed in the highest position and are gathered in the uppermost part of the ark. A multitude of other irrational animals or even beasts is held in the lower decks, and especially a multitude of those beasts whose fierce raging the charm of faith has not tamed. But of this group those are a little superior which, though falling short in reason, nevertheless, preserve more simplicity and innocence.[16]

---

[15] *Hom. Gen.* 2.3 (referring to Gen. 6:16 and quoting 1 Cor. 15:23; FC 71:78). Verum quoniam non est omnium unum meritum nec unus in fide profectus, idcirco et arca illa non unam praebet omnibus mansionem, sed bicamerata sunt inferiora et tricamerata superiora, et nidi distinguuntur in ea, ut ostendat quia et in Ecclesia, licet omnes intra unam fidem contineantur atque uno baptismate diluantur, non tamen unus omnibus atque idem profectus est, *sed unusquisque in suo ordine* (SC 7:90).

[16] *Hom. Gen.* 2.3 (referring to 2 Tim. 2:2; FC 71:78–79); Hi quidem qui per rationabilem scientiam uiuunt et idonei sunt non solum semetipsos regere, sed et alios docere, quoniam ualde pauci inueniuntur, paucorum, qui cum ipso Noe saluantur et proxima ei propinquitate iunguntur, tenent figuram, sicut et Dominus noster, uerus Noe, Christus Iesus, paucos habet proximos, paucos filios et propinquos, qui uerbi eius participes sunt et sapientiae capaces. Et hi sunt qui in summo gradu positi sunt et in summitate arcae collocantur. Ceterum multitudo irrationabilium animalium uel etiam bestiarum in inferioribus locis habetur, et eorum maxime quorum feritatis saeuitiam nec fidei dulcedo molliuit. Superiores uero aliquantulo ab his sunt qui, licet minus rationis, plurimum tamen simplicitatis innocentiaeque custodiunt (SC 7:90, 92).

Those who reside at the lowest levels of the church are as "beasts . . . not tamed." They need to leave behind the irrational ways of the flesh in order to learn to follow the ways of the spirit. Conversely, those who are most advanced in the faith and share the closest unity with the architect, Christ, serve him by "teaching others" within the church. These advanced believers live "by rational knowledge" and rule themselves properly, in contrast to those whose faith is in some degree irrational. According to Origen's anthropology,[17] the human person is well-ordered if his soul has chosen to follow the ways of the spirit over the body's fleshly ways. One mark of this right internal order is that the person follows the dictates of reason and is rational in his thoughts, words and actions. The rightly ordered, rational person rules himself well and can teach others how to rule themselves by reason and choose the ways of the spirit. Because of their progress in faith, the advanced abide in the "uppermost part of the ark," that is, in the highest positions within the church, and are closest in holiness and authority to Christ. Those who fall in between the teachers and brutes are those who as yet have not learned to follow reason but do possess a "simplicity and innocence" that makes them more gentle than the brutes. Still, all of these people, having some degree of faith, dwell within the church—on different levels of the ark—that Christ has built for their protection and deliverance to safety at the end of the world.[18]

---

[17] See the latter portion of chapter 2.

[18] Note that there is a rough parallel between this passage's three types of faithful within the church and Origen's description of three types of scriptural hearers in *Princ.* 4.2.4, as analyzed in Chapter 2. There Origen spoke of the perfected, those who have made some progress, and the simpler ones. Here Origen speaks of the most advanced in reason—teachers, those who are not too untamed in their rationality—the simple and innocent, and those whose reason is as yet wholly untamed—the brutes. While he speaks more roughly of the least advanced group here than he does in *Princ.* 4.2.4, here he includes them among those who reside within the church as similarly in 4.2.4 he equates the lowest group with those who are able to take in at least the bodily meaning of Scripture. This homiletic passage is significant to a clearer understanding of *Princ.* 4.2.4, since, as follows below, Origen's explanation of it stresses that full advancement toward union with Christ is the goal of every group. He does not intend to divide the faithful into fixed classes some of which are barred from full progress in faith and perfection. The full resources of the church are intended for every human soul's perfection and salvation. As this and every other practical work treated in chapters 3, 4 and 5 stress (see especially just below how Origen's psychic reading of the ark finds context within and gives context to this pneumatic reading), Scripture is the heart of the church's resources. Christ has entrusted Scripture, and more specifically its three senses of meaning, to the church to hold securely and distribute in an effective way ultimately to *every* person.

Origen generally urges his audience to strive to be among the most advanced, rational believers and thus come most near to Christ. He does not present these various levels of progress as fixed states of being. Rather, arguably, Origen suggests that everyone who resides in the church should strive for increasing advancement in faith, the perfection of which will bring him to full union with Christ:

> And thus by ascending through the individual levels of the dwellings, one arrives at Noah himself, whose name means rest or righteous, who is Christ Jesus. . . . But if you look to our Lord Jesus Christ of whom it is said: "Behold the lamb of God, behold him who takes away the sin of the world," . . . it is said to this spiritual Noah who has given rest to men and has taken away the sin of the world: "You shall make yourself an ark of squared planks."[19]

Christ is the captain of the ship, sitting at the uppermost peak of the ark. Union with Christ is the telos of every believer, which is accomplished through ascending the levels of faith within the church.

The believer "ascends" toward Christ by progressing in faith along a path paved by Christ's descent to earth in the Incarnation:

> [L]et us see what this is which Scripture calls length and breadth and height. The Apostle, in a certain passage, when he was speaking very mystically about the mystery of the cross, says as follows: "That you might know what is the length and breadth and depth." Now depth and height mean the same thing except that height appears to measure space from the lower regions to the higher, but depth begins from the higher and descends to the lower. . . . [T]he spirit of God discloses figures of great mysteries through both Moses and Paul. For since Paul was preaching the mystery of the condescension of Christ, he used the term depth as if Christ comes from the upper regions to the lower. But Moses is describing the restoration of those who are recalled by Christ from the lower regions to the higher and celestial ones, from the destruction and ruin of the world, as from the violent death of a flood. For this reason Moses does not speak about depth, but height in the measure of the ark, as it were, where one ascends from the earthly and lowly regions to the heavenly and exalted ones.[20]

---

[19] *Hom. Gen.* 2.3 (quoting John 1:29 and Gen. 6:14; FC 71:79–80); Et sic per singulos habitationum gradus adscendentibus peruenitur ad ipsum Noe, qui interpretatur requies uel iustus, qui est Christus Iesus. . . . Si uero respicias ad Dominum nostrum Iesum Christum, de quo dicitur: *Ecce agnus Dei, ecce qui tollit peccatum mundi,* . . . [h]uic . . . spiritali Noe, qui requiem dedit hominibus et tulit peccatum mundi, dicitur: *Facies tibi arcam ex lignis quadratis* (SC 7:92, 94).

[20] *Hom. Gen.* 2.5 (referring to Gen. 6:15 and quoting Eph. 3:18; FC 71:82) [H]oc quod dicit longitudinem et latitudinem et altitudinem, quale sit uideamus. Apostolus in quodam loco, cum de mysterio crucis sacratius loqueretur, ita ait: *Vt sciatis quae*

By relating Moses' term "height" for the ark to Paul's term "depth" for Christ's condescension to earth, Origen points out that the believer's path of ascent is paved by Christ's descent. The height of ascent is possible because of the depth of Christ's condescension. Therefore, Christ is not only the goal but also the way of ascent. Christ's *descent* is the believer's *ascent*, and this two-way path is found only within the church.

Note also that Origen refers to this insight as the disclosure of the "figures of great mysteries" and centers specifically on the "mystery" of the Incarnation. In his exegetical theory, Origen defined the pneumatic sense as the meaning that focuses directly on Christ, the church and the "heavenly mysteries."[21] Thus, by its language and focus, Origen indicates that this interpretation is his pneumatic reading of Noah's ark.

This pneumatic reading of Noah's ark brings into focus for Origen's audience the telos, or fulfillment of human existence: Christ himself. Union with Christ is salvation, achieved by ascending up the downward path created by Christ within the ark of the church. Implicitly, for Origen, to exercise faith in Christ is to walk the path of the Incarnation from its most mundane elements to its most mystical beginnings. As Origen states, "all things hasten to the one goal of the perfection of God."[22]

This discussion of the spiritual progress and ascent of different human souls is part of a pneumatic reading of the text, because it focuses on the church as the proper structure within which this advancement is possible and on Christ as both the map for and goal of this ascent. Having established this focus, Origen now shifts to a psychic reading of the ark's dimensions, recasting the figurative import

---

sit longitudo et latitudo et altitudo et profundum. Profundum autem et altitudo idem significant, tantum quod altitudo spatium de inferioribus uidetur ad superiora metiri, profundum uero de superioribus incipere et ad inferiora descendere. Consequenter igitur Spiritus Dei et per Moysen et per Paulum ingentium sacramentorum figuras enuntiat. Nam Paulus quoniam descensionis Christi mysterium praedicabat, profundum nominauit quasi de superioribus ad inferiora uenientis; Moyses uero, quia restitutionem designat eorum qui per Christum de interitu et perditione saeculi tamquam de nece diluuii ex inferioribus ad superna et caelestia reuocantur, in mensura arcae non profundum memorat sed altum, tamquam ubi de terrenis et humilibus ad caelestia et excelsa conscenditur (SC 7:98, 100).

[21] See especially *Princ.* 4.2.6–7, the treatment of *Hom. Gen.* 2 in chapter 3, and generally the discussion of the pneumatic sense in the conclusions of chapters 2 and 3.

[22] *Hom. Gen.* 2.5 (FC 71:83); *ad unum perfectionis Dei finem cuncta festinant* (SC 7:102).

of the same biblical concepts of Noah, the ark and the flood. He can now discuss specifically what is required of each person who wishes to reside within the safe walls of the church and make progress toward his natural telos, Christ.

C. *The Psychic Reading of the Ark*

Origen makes his transition to the psychic sense explicit by announcing that he will set forth a "third," "moral" reading of the text. He now interprets the ark as a construction within the believer's individual "heart," or soul,[23] in which he should store the divine truths of Scripture:

> Let us attempt, therefore, to discuss also a third exposition at the moral level. If there is anyone who, while evils are increasing and vices are overflowing, can turn from the things which are in flux and passing away and fallen, and can hear the word of God and the heavenly precepts, this man is building an ark of salvation within his own heart and is dedicating a library, so to speak, of the divine word within himself. . . . He raises the height of hope to heavenly and exalted places. For while he walks upon the earth he has his "citizenship in heaven." But he brings the sum of his acts back to one. For he knows that "all indeed run, but one receives the palm of victory," of course, being that one who was not changeable with a variety of thoughts and instability of mind.[24]

The "moral *(moralis)*" reading directs the individual believer to "hear the word of God." Inevitably, the believer first comes to the healing truths of Scripture with a soul that is infiltrated with and surrounded by "evils" and "vices." Still, he must make every effort to hear Scripture's "divine word." If he can bring it "within himself" and gather it together there as a "library" of divine truths, then he

---

[23] Origen speaks here of the heart, but he confirms later in this psychic reading of the text that he means also the human soul (*Hom. Gen.* 2.6; FC 71:87–88; SC 7:110, 112). See Origen's text in footnote 27 below.

[24] *Hom. Gen.* 2.6 (referring to Phil. 3:20 and quoting 1 Cor. 9:24; FC 71:86); Temptemus igitur et tertiam expositionem disserere secundum moralem locum. Si quis est, qui crescentibus malis et inundantibus uitiis conuertere se potest a rebus fluxis ac pereuntibus et caducis et audire uerbum Dei ac praecepta caelestia, hic intra cor suum arcam salutis aedificat et bibliothecam, ut ita dicam, intra se diuini consecrat uerbi, . . . altitudinem spei ad caelestia erigit et excelsa; super terram enim ambulans *in caelis* habet *conuersationem.* Summam uero actuum suorum refert ad unum. Scit enim quia *omnes quidem currunt, sed unus accipit palmam,* scilicet qui cogitationum uarietate et instabilitate mentis non fuerit multiplex (SC 7:108, 110).

will make within his heart an "ark of salvation." In this reading, then, Noah, represents the believer, whom God calls to build an ark of saving truths within his own "heart," or soul.

This ark, holding the library of Scripture's truth, occupies the believer's heart and raises his "hope" to the "height" of heaven. Origen gives particular emphasis to those truths in Scripture that are "heavenly precepts," bringing to mind the lessons of the pneumatic sense. These truths direct the believer's vision toward heaven and, implicitly, cause him to focus on and follow the ways of the spirit, the guidance of which will make him strong against the urgings of the flesh. His hope takes on the form of an upward gaze toward heaven and the telos of salvation, placing into plain view before him the path that he is called to climb.

By pursuing this ascent, the believer reserves for himself, during this temporal life, a "citizenship in heaven." The goal of eternal union with Christ—taught by the pneumatic sense—becomes his singular focus and frees him from the "variety of thoughts and instability of mind" that previously immobilized him and reflects a more rational faith.

Yet, in order to become more stable and rational in faith, the believer must heed the psychic call to store the appropriate material within his heart's library:

> But he does not construct this library from planks which are unhewn and rough, but from planks which have been squared and arranged in a uniform line, that is, not from the volumes of secular authors, but from the prophetic and apostolic volumes. For these authors, who have been hewn by diverse temptations, all vices having been curtailed and excised, contain life which has been squared and set free in every part. For the authors of secular books . . . speak indeed in a lofty manner and use flowery eloquence; they have not, however, acted as they have spoken. They cannot, therefore, be called "squared planks" because life and speech will by no means be equal in them.[25]

---

[25] *Hom. Gen.* 2.6 (referring to Gen. 6:14; FC 71:86–87); Sed hanc bibliothecam non ex agrestibus et impolitis, sex ex quadratis et secundum aequitatis lineam directis construit lignis, id est non ex saecularium auctorum, sed ex propheticis atque apostolicis uoluminibus. Ipsi enim sunt qui diuersis temptationibus edolati, resecatis omnibus uitiis et excisis, quadratam continent uitam et ex omni parte libratam. Nam auctores saecularium librorum . . . illi loquuntur quidem excelsa et florida utuntur eloquentia, non tamen ita egerunt ut locuti sunt; et ideo non possunt *ligna quadrata* nominari, quod in iis nequaquam uita et sermo collibret (SC 7:110).

The psychic interpretation separates the merits of Scripture from the dangers of secular books by focusing on the qualities of their respective authors. "Secular" authors are those whose speech is "lofty" and filled with a "flowery eloquence" that covers over their lack of experience with holding off vice and, implicitly, growing in virtue. They cannot speak authoritatively about the life of virtue, because they are not squared planks.

On the other hand, the divine books "from the prophetic and apostolic volumes" have been transcribed through human authors who cleansed themselves of "vices" and learned to resist the "diverse temptations" of this life. Implicitly, these holy authors built up their lives with virtue, hewing the rough edges and becoming squared planks that fit together to reinforce their defenses against sin and permit them to pursue perfection in virtue. Their messages are true and righteous, because they are themselves straightforward and firm as squared planks. The scriptural authors, then, have written the definitive books on the divine truths. While in the pneumatic reading the squared planks are the church's leaders, who direct the faithful within and keep the heretics without, in this psychic reading the words of the prophets and apostles are the squared planks, which form the strong walls of the soul's interior ark of salvation by keeping vice out of it and cultivating virtues within it.

Origen explains that the divine truths by which the prophets and apostles direct the believer's progress in virtues are those conveyed according to Scripture's three senses of meaning:

> If, therefore, you build an ark, if you gather a library, gather it from the words of the prophets and apostles or of those who have followed them in the right lines of faith. You shall make it "with two decks" and "with three decks." From this library learn the historical narratives; from it recognize "the great mystery" which is fulfilled in Christ and in the Church. From it also learn how to correct habits, to curtail vices, to purge the soul and draw it off from every bond of captivity, setting up in it "nests and nests" of the various virtues and perfections.[26]

---

[26] *Hom. Gen.* 2.6 (referring to Gen. 6:16 and Eph. 5:32; FC 71:87); Tu ergo si facis arcam, si bibliothecam congregas, ex sermonibus propheticis et apostolicis uel eorum qui eos rectis fidei lineis secuti sunt congrega, *bicameratam et tricameratam* facito eam. Ex ipsa narrationes historicas disce, ex ipsa *mysterium magnum*, quod in Christo et in Ecclesia impletur, agnosce; ex ipsa etiam emendare mores, resecare uitia, purgare animam atque exuere eam omni uinculo captiuitatis intellige, *nidos in*

By this extended theory of three senses (which was examined in full in chapter 3), Origen explains how we are to extract the meanings from Scripture that yield a life of Christian virtue. He describes the somatic sense as the "historical narratives" of Scripture, the pneumatic sense as the hidden "mysteries" that are "fulfilled in Christ and in the Church," and the psychic sense as Scripture's instructions to "correct habits," "curtail vices," and "purge the soul." The three senses of Scripture direct the believer during this temporal life to pursue eternal salvation by cultivating the virtues.

In order to take full advantage of the aids offered by Scripture's truths, the believer must be a "doer" as well as "hearer" of the three senses:

> Let us pray . . . the mercy of the omnipotent God to make us "not only hearers of" his "word," but also "doers" and to bring upon our souls also a flood of his water and destroy in us what he knows should be destroyed and quicken what he knows should be quickened, through Christ our Lord and through his Holy Spirit.[27]

Origen challenges his audience to place the truths of the divine books within their hearts, or souls. He urges them also to pray that God, through Christ and the Holy Spirit, "bring upon [their] souls" the "flood" that eventually will abolish within them all that "should be destroyed," all vices and tendencies to sin.[28] This is a temporal flood

---

ea et *nidos* diuersarum uirtutum et profectuum collocans (SC 7:110). Origen relates the three types of divine books to the three senses of Scripture. See chapter 3 for his theoretical explication of the ark's "three decks."

[27] *Hom. Gen.* 2.6 (referring to Jas. 1:22; FC 71:88); Omnipotentis . . . Dei misericordiam deprecemur, qui nos *non solum auditores uerbi* sui faciat, sed et *factores* et inducat super nostras quoque animas diluuium aquae suae et deleat in nobis quae scit esse delenda et uiuificet quae iudicat esse uiuificanda, per Christum Dominum nostrum et per Spiritum suum sanctum (SC 7:112).

[28] Directly before this exhortative ending to the homily, Origen considers the fact that Noah placed "unclean" as well as "clean animals" in the ark. Origen interprets the unclean animals as the vices that "are in every soul," such as "concupiscence and wrath." He explains that the presence of these unclean animals in the soul aids the purification process and progress toward perfection in virtue. Their presence prompts the necessary "correction and discipline" of the soul, and, if the soul learns to resist consciously their tempting urges, it will become increasingly stronger as a storehouse for virtues. Thus, Origen suggests that his audience should not fret the presence of vices during the temporal life, but they should let them be used to aid and strengthen, rather than hinder, their growth in virtue and, thus, progress toward perfection and salvation. The cleansing flood will destroy the vices' hold on the soul during this life, and, ultimately, in eternity, they will cease to be present within the soul.

that Christ and the Holy Spirit are ready to administer within every soul as a necessary aid toward perfect virtue and salvation.[29]

D. *Summary of the Psychic and Pneumatic Readings in Hom. Gen. 2*

In this homily, Origen presents psychic and pneumatic senses of Noah's ark, by setting forth distinct readings of the text. While the pneumatic sense analogizes the ark to the church, Noah to Christ, and the ancient flood to the Eschaton, or end of the world, the psychic sense compares the ark to a structure within the human heart, or soul, that stores Scripture's truths, Noah to the individual believer,

---

The relevant text reads: "In this ark, therefore, let us place, meanwhile, at the moral level, either that library of divine books or a faithful soul. You ought also to bring in animals of every kind not only clean but also unclean. Now we can easily say that the clean animals indeed can be understood as memory, learning, understanding, examination and discernment of those things which we read, and other things like these. But it is difficult to speak about the unclean animals which also are named 'two by two.' Nevertheless we can, in such difficult passages, dare so much: I think that concupiscence and wrath, which are in every soul, are necessarily said to be unclean in the sense that they serve to make man sin. But in the sense that neither succession of posterity is renewed without concupiscence nor can any correction or discipline exist without anger, they are said to be necessary and must be preserved" (*Hom. Gen.* 2.6, referring to Gen. 6:19; FC 71:87–88).

The corresponding Latin text reads: In hanc ergo arcam, siue eam bibliothecam diuinorum librorum siue animam fidelem secundum moralem interim locum ponamus, introducere debes etiam animalia ex omni genere non solum munda sed et immunda. Sed munda quidem animalia facile possumus dicere quod memoria, eruditio, intellectus, examinatio et iudicium eorum quae legimus aliaque his similia intelligi possint. De immundis uero pronuntiare difficile est, quae et *bina bina* nominantur. Verumtamen quantum in tam difficilibus locis audere possumus, puto quod concupiscentia et ira, quia inest omni animae, necessario istae, secundum hoc quod ad peccandum homini famulantur, immundae dicuntur; secundum hoc uero quod neque posteritatis sine concupiscentia successio reparatur neque emendatio ulla sine ira potest neque disciplina constare, necessariae et conseruandae dicuntur (SC 7:110, 112).

[29] According to Rufinus' translation, near the end of the homily Origen speculates that his most recent words may sound more "natural *(naturali)*" than "moral *(morali)*." Origen does not hereby suggest that the "third" reading, which he has labeled "moral" according to Rufinus's translation, is actually not "moral." Rather, he acknowledges that the discussion has focused on the very *structure* of the soul, speaking of the "ark" that is to be built in the "heart" and the "library" of divine words that is to be stored within this internal ark. To this extent he is speaking about the "nature" of the soul, yet still, as he points out, he has related this psychic reading to his hearers for their "moral" edification.

The relevant passage reads: "And although these things discussed may now appear not to be in the moral but in the natural sense, nevertheless, we have treated for edification the ideas which could occur to us at present" (*Hom. Gen.* 2.6; FC 71:88). The corresponding Latin text reads: Et quamuis haec iam non morali sed naturali ratione discussa uideantur, tamen quae ad praesens occurrere potuerunt, pro aedificatione tractauimus (SC 7:112).

and the flood to the temporal cleansings from sin that Christ and
the Holy Spirit conduct on each willing soul. These different metaphorical readings lead naturally to independently edifying messages. The
pneumatic message informs Origen's audience that the church is the
only safe place in which to reside and that its very structure provides the means of achieving the telos of human existence: a perfection in faith that is rewarded by union with Christ. The believer
need not feel overwhelmed by this task, since the path of this ascent
within the church has been paved already by Christ's descent to
Incarnate form. The psychic message urges each believer to progress
in virtue by apprehending all of Scripture's truths so that Christ may
cleanse his soul of sin, leaving only the strengthening material of
God's truth.

Even though each reading offers its own edifying message, Origen's
consideration of them side-by-side shows that, in relation, they more
completely edify his audience. The psychic sense explains the way
in which the believer may pursue temporally the eternal salvation
that the pneumatic sense presents as a goal. Only through the psychic sense does the human person in this life have the means to
actively pursue the pneumatic hope of eternal union with Christ.
Likewise, only within the context of the pneumatic message does the
psychic call to virtue through engagement with Scripture take on
real significance and purpose. Separately, each reading offers divine
truth, but together they give the hearer both the reason for and the
means of reaching salvation.

On closer analysis the psychic sense emerges as a profoundly
Christian sense, when viewed alongside the pneumatic sense. First,
it is the means of approaching an eternal union with Christ. Second,
the path of ascent traveled by shunning vice and growing in virtue
is available only because Christ descended, indeed condescended,
into human form, by the Incarnation. Christ's descent is the believer's
ascent to Christ, and the steps of that ascent are formed by heeding the psychic call to virtue. Third, believers are assured of safe

---

It is possible that, rather than Origen, Rufinus added this comment into his Latin
translation of the homily after finding that Origen's "moral" reading of the ark
focuses very specifically on the nature of the human soul. Perhaps he acknowledges
that Origen's third reading of the ark is more than simple moral instruction, since
it regards the soul's right make-up, achieved by its temporal duty to build within
the heart a structure of Scripture's truths that will facilitate the acquisition of virtues
and, thus, readiness for eternal salvation.

and successful travels along this path, since Christ placed it within the secure walls of the church. In sum, the psychic call to virtue has both meaning and possibility of success only within the context of Christ's guidance.

Together, then, the two higher readings underscore that Christ is both the goal of human existence and the way of attaining it. The pneumatic sense focuses on Christ as the goal and the psychic sense on Christ as the way. They each hold significance only because of the Incarnation, and together they stress to the hearer the end that will fulfill him *and* the way to that end. It is not simply that the psychic sense becomes Christian within the context of the pneumatic reading. Rather, each sense provides Christ-centered context for the other: the pneumatic reading stresses *that* the believer's ascent to Christ is possible within the church and necessary for salvation, while the psychic sense explains specifically *how* the person, together with Christ, can pursue this ascent temporally. (Later practical examples will stress that the psychic call to virtue is essentially the call to imitate Christ.)

Recalling the positions of de Lubac and others as set forth in chapter 1, we have found that in this homily Origen provides a psychic reading that is Christian in focus as well as more than a "moral" aspect of the one, pneumatic reading. Though de Lubac points specifically to *Hom. Gen.* 2 as an example of moral meaning that is part of the one, broad spiritual meaning,[30] in this homily Origen develops the psychic sense in a distinctive reading from the pneumatic sense's Christological, ecclesiastical and eschatological themes. Origen treats the nonliteral, moral focus of the psychic sense separately from the other nonliteral themes, because it provides the *temporal* means of pursuing the *eternal* goal that is brought into focus by the unified themes of the pneumatic sense. Thus, only by recognizing Origen's separate treatments of the two higher senses can we perceive how they relate for a more complete edification of his audience.

---

[30] De Lubac, *Medieval Exegesis*, 145; idem, *Histoire et Esprit*, 141–142, n. 13; 145, n. 32; and the discussion of de Lubac's views in chapter 1. Note that de Lubac also cites other texts treated within this chapter as examples of Origen's employment of a moral theme as an extension of the one nonliteral (spiritual) sense (*Medieval Exegesis*, 142–150; *Histoire et Esprit*, 139–150). This chapter will demonstrate that in all these texts Origen is able to *relate* the psychic and pneumatic senses for the spiritual benefit of his audience *because* he views them as *separately* functioning and independent, Christian meanings for the same biblical passage.

II. *Hom. Exod.* 3: *The Two Types of Three-Day Journeys*

In *Hom. Exod.* 3,[31] Origen presents separate pneumatic and psychic readings of the phrase "journey of three days" in Exod. 3:18 (and repeated in Exod. 5:3). This passage refers to a portion of the Israelites' exodus from Egypt. First, Moses and Aaron inform Pharaoh that God wants the Israelites to leave Egypt and serve Him in the wilderness: "'Thus says the Lord, Send my people out that they may serve me in the wilderness.'"[32] After this, Moses explains to the Israelites: "'We will go . . . a journey of three days into the wilderness and there we will sacrifice to the Lord our God.'"[33] Wanting his audience to relate this passage to themselves, Origen asks: "What is the 'journey of three days' which *we* are to go, that going out from Egypt we can arrive at the place in which *we* ought to sacrifice?"[34]

Origen offers two answers, one by a pneumatic reading and the other by a psychic reading of the three-days' journey. The pneumatic reading points toward the "third day" that Christ's death and resurrection have made possible: the Eschaton, when the saved will offer eternal praise to God. The psychic reading stresses the journey of three temporal days that the believer is called to travel by cleansing all three parts of his human nature: body, soul, and spirit. This purification is facilitated by meditation on Scripture, which is itself an offering of temporal praise to God.

---

[31] Thirteen intact homilies on Exodus by Origen are extant in Latin, translated by Rufinus. For English translations of Origen's homilies on Exodus, I employ Ronald E. Heine, trans., *Origen: Homilies on Genesis and Exodus* (FC 71; Washington, D.C.: Catholic University of America, 1982). The corresponding Latin text is from Marcel Borret, ed. and trans., *Origène: Homélies sur L'Exode* (SC 321; Paris: Cerf, 1985).

[32] *Hom. Exod.* 3.3 (quoting Exod. 5:1; FC 71:252–253); Haec dicit Dominus: dimitte populum meum, ut seruiat mihi in eremo (SC 321:98).

[33] *Hom. Exod.* 3.3 (quoting Exod. 3:18 or Exod. 5:3; FC 71:253); Viam, . . . trium dierum ibimus in eremo et ibi immolabimus Domino Deo nostro (SC 321:100).

[34] *Hom. Exod.* 3.3 (emphasis added; FC 71:253); Quae est uia trium dierum quae nobis incedenda est, ut exeuntes de Aegypto peruenire possimus ad locum in quo immolare debeamus? (SC 321:100).

A. *The Pneumatic Reading of the "Three Days"*

Origen first gives the "mystical meaning [or, understanding]" of traveling three days to the place of sacrifice to the Lord.[35] It treats Jesus Christ as the "way" of the journey, the "third day" as the Eschaton, and the "sacrifice" as the praise that the saved will lift up eternally to God:

> I understand "way" to refer to him who said, "I am the way, the truth, and the life." We are to go this way for three days. For he who "has confessed with his mouth the Lord Jesus and believed in his heart that God raised him from the dead" on the third day, "will be saved." This, therefore, is "the way of three days" by which one arrives at the place in which the "sacrifice of praise" is sacrificed and offered to the Lord.[36]

Here, Origen relates the "third day" of the journey to the believer's resurrection at the Eschaton by referring to Jesus' resurrection on the third day: As God raised Jesus on the third day, so will he raise, or "save" the one who "confesses" his belief in Jesus. This faithful person "will be saved," finding himself at the "place where the sacrifice of praise" is eternally offered to God. This is the telos and proper goal of human existence.

Jesus' three days in the tomb, then, constitute a blueprint for this three-day human journey. Jesus is the *via*, the way or road, on which the believer travels to salvation. These themes of Christ's saving action and the Eschaton fall within Origen's theoretical descriptions of the pneumatic sense. They also recall the theme presented in Origen's description of the pneumatic sense in *Hom. Gen.* 2 (on Noah's ark) that the path for the believer's ascent to God has been paved by Christ's condescension into Incarnate form.

---

[35] *Hom. Exod.* 3.3 (FC 71:253); Haec, quantum ad mysticum pertinet intellectum (SC 321:100).

[36] *Hom. Exod.* 3.3 (quoting John 14:6 and referring to Rom. 10:9 and Ps. 50:14; FC 71:253); Ego uiam illum intelligo qui dixit: *Ego sum uia, ueritas et uita. Haec uia triduo nobis incedenda est.* Qui enim *confessus fuerit in ore suo Dominum Iesum, et crediderit in corde suo quod Deus illum suscitauit a mortuis tertia die, saluus erit.* Haec ergo est tridui uia per quam peruenitur in locum in quo Domino immoletur et reddatur *sacrificium laudis* (SC 321:100).

B. *The Psychic Reading of the "Three Days"*

Origen next turns to the "moral meaning" of the three-day journey, focusing on the travels that the believer is called to pursue temporally:

> But if we also require a place for the moral meaning which is very useful for us, we travel a "journey of three days" from Egypt if we thus preserve ourselves from all filth of soul, body, and spirit, that, as the Apostle said, "our spirit and soul and body may be kept whole in the day of Jesus Christ." We travel a "journey of three days" from Egypt if, ceasing from worldly things we turn our rational, natural, moral wisdom to the divine laws. We travel a "journey of three days" from Egypt if, purifying our words, deeds, or thoughts—for these are the three things by which men can sin—we would be made "pure in heart" so that we could "see God."[37]

According to this moral reading, Egypt represents "worldly things," or the ways of the world. By making the three-day journey, the hearer "preserve[s]" his "soul (*anima*)," "body (*corpus*)," and "spirit (*spiritus*)" from "all filth." The Latin term *conservare*, translated here as "preserve," also means to leave safe or unhurt. The hearer is called during this life to keep all three parts of his human nature protected from the filth of sin, so that they "may be kept whole in the day of Jesus Christ." Origen's audience already understands from the pneumatic sense that this "day of Jesus Christ" is the eschatological "third day," when the believer will be "saved" and join in an eternal praise of God. Origen considers this "moral"[38] reading *perutilis*, or "very useful," to his audience, likely because it provides the means to pursue *presently* the eschatological third day of eternal praise.

The hearer makes a temporal three-day journey from worldly Egypt by "turning" all of his wisdom, in its rational, natural and

---

[37] *Hom. Exod.* 3.3 (referring to Exod. 3:18 or 5:3; quoting 1 Thess. 5:23 and Matt. 5:8; FC 71:253–254); Si uero etiam moralem, qui nobis perutilis est, requirimus locum, iter tridui de Aegypto proficiscimur, si ita nos ab omni inquinamento animae, corporis ac spiritus conseruemus ut, quemadmodum dixit Apostolus, *integer spiritus noster et anima et corpus in die Iesu Christi seruetur*. Tridui iter proficiscimur de Aegypto, si rationalem, naturalem, moralem sapientiam de rebus mundialibus auferentes ad statuta diuina conuertimus; tridui iter de Aegypto proficiscimur, si purificantes in nobis dicta, facta uel cogitata—tria sunt enim haec, per quae peccare homines possunt—efficiamur *mundi corde*, ut possimus *Deum uidere* (SC 321:100, 102).

[38] The Latin term for "moral meaning" is the familiar term *moralis*, in the substantive adjective form.

moral parts, to the "divine laws." The Latin term *convertere*, translated as "turn," also means to turn around or turn in any direction. The Latin term *sapientia*, translated as "wisdom," also means good sense or discernment. The hearer is to turn his discernment of rational, natural and moral matters in the direction of "the divine laws," or Scripture's teachings, just as he is called, according to *Hom. Gen.* 2, to fill the ark within his soul with Scripture's truths. The three-day journey, then, involves seeking the guidance of Scripture, which will lead the hearer to "purify" his words, deeds and thoughts from all forms of sin. If the hearer is cleansed in all three ways, then the hearer will "be made pure in heart," and, thus, as the beatitude promises, he will "see God." This focus on purification from sin recalls Origen's theoretical descriptions of the psychic sense.

Furthermore, the psychic sense is more than simply "moral" (even though it is labeled as such in Rufinus' Latin), since it urges the hearer to seek Scripture's aid in discerning not only moral but also rational and natural matters. This reading urges the hearer to submit *all* aspects of the soul in this life to Scripture's guidance. Origen's anthropology stresses that human nature is rightly ordered when the soul chooses to submit to the spirit to live and the body follows this choice by subduing the flesh. When so ordered (naturally, rationally and morally), the believer can enjoy resurrection and salvation as established through Jesus Christ. Therefore, this psychic reading directly calls the hearer to rightly order his "soul, body, and spirit," or to be "kept whole" on the day of Jesus Christ, that is, up to and at the Eschaton.

In this introduction to the psychic reading of the passage, Origen suggests its distinction from and relationship with the preceding pneumatic reading. First, in contrast to the pneumatic reading, which interprets Jesus Christ as the way, the third day of the journey as the Eschaton, and the sacrifice as the eternal praise of the saved, the psychic reading treats Scripture as the way, the three days of the journey as the process of purifying oneself wholly—in body, soul, and spirit—and the sacrifice as submission to Scripture. Second, in this psychic interpretation Origen reminds his audience that the body, soul and spirit await "'the day of Jesus Christ,'" recalling the idea, described in the pneumatic sense, that the "third day," or Eschaton, is marked by Jesus' resurrection on the third day. In addition, he reminds his audience of the promise that the obedient hearer will "see God." By doing so, Origen makes more vivid the reward at the Eschaton: the beginning of an eternal intimacy with God. Thus, by presenting the pneumatic reading first, Origen provides his audience with motivation to heed the psychic call to purification from sin in words, thoughts and deeds that he now sets before them.

Origen emphasizes that this journey of purification is not one of "space," or physical distance, but, rather, an "advanc[e] in faith," for it has to do with not "'lov[ing] the world [ ]or those things in the world'":

> [W]e must go forth from Egypt. We must leave the world behind if we wish "to serve the Lord." I mean, however, that we must leave the world behind not in space, but in the [mind or rational principle of the] soul; not by setting out on a [physical] journey, but by advancing in faith. Hear John saying these same things: "Little children, do not love the world nor those things which are in the world, since everything which is in the world is the desire of the flesh and the desire of the eyes."[39]

The hearer must travel away from the ways of Egypt, the "flesh (*caro*)," if he is "to serve the Lord" either now or perpetually. This journey is not one of distance or space but occurs *animo*, in the mind—or rational principle of the soul. It occurs within the soul during this life as an "advanc[e] in faith." The Latin term *proficere*, translated here as "advance," is the root for the noun *profectus*, which, as in Origen's theoretical discussions of the psychic sense, means an advance, progress, increase, growth, or improvement. This temporal journey is the soul's progress or growth in faith. If the hearer puts his full faith in Christ and Scripture, then he will "'not love the world'" or the ways of the flesh. Instead, he will choose to submit his soul and body to the divine imprint, or spirit, within him and, in so doing, subdue the flesh.

Origen explains that each day of this three-day, temporal journey refers to that portion of the hearer, his words, deeds, or thoughts, that he successfully keeps out of Satan's reach:

---

[39] *Hom. Exod.* 3.3 (referring to Exod. 5:1 and quoting 1 John 2:15–16; FC 71:253); Exeundum igitur nobis est de Aegypto; relinquendus est mundus, si uolumus Domino seruire. Relinquendus autem, dico, non loco, sed animo, non itinere proficiscendo, sed fide proficiendo. Audi haec eadem Iohannem dicentem: *Filioli, nolite diligere mundum neque ea quae in mundo sunt; quoniam omne quod in mundo est, desiderium carnis est et desiderium oculorum* (SC 321:98).

Do you wish to see, however, that this is what the Holy Spirit indicates in the Scriptures? When this Pharaoh, who is the prince of Egypt, sees that he is strongly pressed to send the people of God out, he wishes to effect by this inferior place that "they not go farther away," that they not travel the full three days. He says, "Go not far away." He does not wish the people of God to be far from himself. He wishes them to sin, if not in deed, certainly in word: to fail, if not in word, certainly in thought. He does not want them to travel a full three days from himself. He wishes to have one day at least in us as his own. In some he has two days, in others he possesses the full three days. But blessed are those who withdraw a whole three days from him and he possesses no day in them as his own.[40]

Pharaoh represents Satan and the fleshy ways of this world. Origen warns his audience that Satan desires to shorten as much as possible a person's journey of purification from sin and keep the "people of God" near him. Satan tries to ensure that they do not progress a "full three days" from him. Sinning in any one of words, deeds, or thoughts forfeits the distance of a whole day's journey from Satan, and sinning in any two of these ways forfeits two days' distance from Satan. Sinning in all three ways is to make no journey at all but to remain within Satan's presence and grip. Origen warns his audience against falling short of the whole three days' distance. The truest victory over Satan is to travel the full three days of advance in faith by purifying one's words, deeds *and* thoughts, implicitly through cultivation of the virtues. This reading underscores the psychic sense's nature as a general call to *all* virtues, rather than to specific virtues as with the moral somatic reading.

Origen next stresses that hearing and understanding Scripture "spiritually *(spiritaliter)*" is the only sure way to defeat Satan's persistent threats. Like *Hom. Gen.* 11 (in which he likens the three senses to three days spent at the well of vision, or Scripture),[41] Origen presents

---

[40] *Hom. Exod.* 3.3 (referring to Exod. 5:2, quoting Exod. 8:28; FC 71:254); Vis autem uidere quia huiusmodi sunt quae in Scripturis indicat Spiritus sanctus? Pharao hic, qui est princeps Aegypti, ubi se uidet uehementius perurgeri ut dimittat populum Dei, secundo loco hoc cupit impetrare ne longius abeant, ne totum triduum proficiscantur, et dicit: *Non longe abeatis.* Non uult longe a se fieri populum Dei; uult eum si non in facto, uel in sermone peccare; si non in sermone, uel in cogitatione delinquere. Non uult ut totum a se triduum proficiscantur. Vult in nobis uel unun diem suum habere; in aliis duos, in aliis totum triduum ipse possidet. Sed illi beati qui integrum ab eo triduum secedunt, et nullam in iis suam possidet diem (SC 321:102).

[41] See chapter 3 for Origen's reading of Isaac's three days at the well of vision as representative of Scripture's three senses of meaning.

the journey of three days from Satan as effected only by a person's full engagement with Scripture's truths:

> Do not suppose, therefore, that Moses led the people out of Egypt only at that time. Even now Moses, whom we have with us—"for we have Moses and the prophets"—that is, the Law of God, wishes to lead you out of Egypt. If you would hear it, it wishes to make you "far" from Pharaoh. If only you would hear the Law of God and understand it spiritually, it desires to deliver you from the work of mud and chaff. It does not wish you to remain in the activities of the flesh and darkness, but to go out to the wilderness, to come to the place free from the confusions and disturbances of the world, to come to the rest of silence. For "words of wisdom are learned in silence and rest."[42]

Origen stresses that the guidance of Scripture, and particularly its "spiritual" meanings, is necessary in order to flee the ways of the flesh and remain outside their influence. Origen may emphasize the spiritual meanings because he faces critics, either in his audience or known by his audience, who disfavor figurative readings of Scripture or, perhaps, to warn his audience against the Jewish error of reading Scripture, especially the Law of the Old Testament, only according to the letter of the text. Of course, he might also do so because his audience is less than diligent in their spiritual meditation upon Scripture.

Origen speaks of the "spiritual (*spiritaliter*)" understanding of Scripture generally, likely referring to both higher senses, the pneumatic and the psychic meanings. Scripture summons believers to come before it in a state of "silence and rest," leaving behind the noise and distraction of the world and the flesh. Only in such quiet can the hearer "learn" God's "words of wisdom." In this way, Origen uses the psychic sense to direct his audience to focus on Scripture, hear it, understand both its pneumatic and psychic meanings and be transformed by them. By doing so, they may learn to shun sin and rest in the

---

[42] *Hom. Exod.* 3.3 (referring to Luke 16:29 and Eccl. 9:17; FC 71:254); Non ergo putetis quia tunc tantummodo eduxit Moyses populum de Aegypto: et nunc Moyses, quem habemus nobiscum—*habemus enim Moysen et prophetas*—id est lex Dei uult te educere de Aegypto; si audias eam, uult te longe facere a Pharaone; eruere te cupit de opere luti et palearum, si tamen audias legem Dei et spiritaliter intelligas. Non uult te in carnis et tenebrarum actibus permanere, sed exire ad eremum, uenire ad locum perturbationibus et fluctibus saeculi uacuum, uenire ad quietem silentii. *Verba enim Sapientiae in silentio et quiete discuntur* (SC 321:102).

presence of God's wisdom. This psychic reading, then, calls his audience to meditate upon, indeed, intimately engage with Scripture.

Origen suggests that those who come before Scripture and learn
its spiritual meanings in silence and rest can "sacrifice" praises to
God not only in eternity but also *during this life*:

> When you come to this place of rest, therefore, you will be able "to
> sacrifice to the Lord" there. You will be able to know the Law of God
> and the virtue of the divine voice there. For that reason, therefore,
> Moses desires to bring you out of the midst of vacillating daily busi-
> ness and from the midst of noisy people. For that reason he desires
> you to depart from Egypt, that is from the darkness of ignorance that
> you might hear the Law of God and receive the light of knowledge.[43]

Moses, that is, Scripture's "divine voice," leads the person who departs
from the noise and business of the world to understand its spiritual
truths and enjoy God's wisdom. When the hearer takes in Scripture's
transformative truths, he offers "sacrifices to the Lord" now, indeed,
temporal sacrifices of praise that are rehearsals for the eternal sacrifice
of praise in heaven that defines salvation.

C. *Summary of the Psychic and Pneumatic Readings in Hom. Exod. 3*

In this homily, the mystical, pneumatic reading treats Egypt as this
physical world, the pilgrim as the believer, the third day of the journey as the eschatological goal of union with God, Jesus Christ as
the pathway, and the place of sacrifice as the eternal act of prais-
ing God. The moral, psychic reading treats Egypt as this world's
fleshly ways (and Pharaoh as Satan), the pilgrim as the believer's
soul, each day of travel as a purification from sins (and, implicitly,
a cultivation of virtues) in words, deeds, and thoughts, Scripture as
the pathway, and the place of sacrifice as full meditation of Scripture
amidst the filth and noise of this world. Each reading, therefore,
provides a separately edifying message. The pneumatic sense stresses
that Jesus' resurrection on the third day makes possible the final resurrection of humanity. Christ provides hope for those still trapped

---

[43] *Hom. Exod.* 3.3 (referring to Exod. 5:3; FC 71:254–255); Ad hunc ergo locum
quietis cum ueneris, ibi poteris *immolare Domino*, ibi legem Dei et uirtutem diuinae
uocis agnoscere. Propterea ergo cupit te Moyses eicere de medio fluctuantium nego-
tiorum et de medio perstrepentium populorum. Propterea cupit te exire de Aegypto,
id est de tenebris ignorantiae, ut legem Dei audias et lucem scientiae capias (SC
321:102, 104).

in this world of evil and sin. The hearer is assured that his belief
in Christ will lead him to the salvation of eternal praise to God.
Independently, the psychic sense urges the hearer to study Scripture
diligently, with the promise that its guidance will lead him away
from Satan's grip by purifying him wholly in all his words, thoughts
and deeds and thus bring him to a quiet, restful place of medita-
tive praise even during this life.

As with *Hom. Gen.* 2, when read together, each of the two higher
senses in this homily complements the other. For the advanced
believer (who can grasp even pneumatic meanings), by hearing the
pneumatic sense in this homily first, he already has in mind the eternal goal of salvific praise to God when he learns from the psychic
sense how to pursue and practice this goal temporally—through the
purifying meditation of Scripture. Together, the two higher senses
point the hearer toward salvation *and* provide him the means of
preparing for it now.

Finally, in this passage, the psychic sense is innately *Christian*,
because it is faith in the Incarnate Christ's death and resurrection
that makes the psychic call to purification meaningful and possible.
By believing in Christ, the hearer surrenders to the truths of Scripture,
which prompt his purification in words, thoughts and deeds (implicitly, his growth in virtue) and, thus, his spiritual transformation. In
this homily, Christ again emerges as both the way and the goal of
the struggle for purity, or virtue. As Christ traveled three days from
death to resurrection, so the believer is to travel three days from
Satan to the full purification of his body, soul and spirit by meditation on Scripture. To travel the way of the virtues is to travel the
way of Christ. Origen's two readings together suggest that progress
in virtue is a three-day journey into the passion, death and resurrection of Christ. The psychic sense calls the hearer to travel with
Christ. Christ makes possible the way both to temporal rest in
Scripture and eternal rest in God.

Moreover, the psychic sense is temporal, while the Christological
and eschatological themes of the pneumatic sense offer one, unified
picture of the hope of eternal salvation. Through the psychic sense
Origen emphasizes the *temporal* means of recognizing that a pneumatic meaning exists and understanding how to progress toward and
rehearse now its salvific goal of eternal praise: through submission
to Scripture's purifying effects and increasing communion with its
wisdom.

III. *Hom. Gen.* 12: *The Two Sets of Nations in Rebecca's Womb*

In *Hom. Gen.* 12, Origen offers separate pneumatic and psychic readings of the "two nations" in Rebecca's womb, represented by the twins Esau and Jacob. He recites the relevant biblical passage as follows:

> Therefore the Lord said to her [Rebecca]: "Two nations [or peoples] are in your womb, and two peoples shall be divided out of your womb. And one people shall overcome the other, and the elder shall serve the younger."[44]

Origen focuses on how the two nations are "divided" and how the younger "shall overcome" the elder. Literally, the two nations refer to the descendants of Jacob, the younger born twin, and those of Esau, the elder, first-born twin. Jacob's progeny is blessed by taking from Esau's descendants what by birthright belonged to them. Origen first interprets the two nations or twins pneumatically as the church and Synagogue, explaining how the former has become the new chosen people of God because of their belief in Christ. Then he reads the two nations psychically as the virtues and vices that temporally struggle for dominance within the human soul.

A. *The Pneumatic Reading of the "Two Nations"*

Origen reads the two nations pneumatically as follows:

> How "one people has risen above the other," that is, the Church over the Synagogue, and how "the elder serves the younger" is known even to the Jews themselves although they do not believe.[45]

In this reading, Origen explains that the aggregate of Christian believers "has risen above" the people of Israel. The Jewish people are represented by Esau, the elder of Rebecca's twins, and the Christians by Jacob, the younger. Whereas the Jews do not "believe," by implication, the church does. Origen assumes his audience understands

---

[44] *Hom. Gen.* 12.3 (quoting Gen. 25:23; FC 71:178–179); Dixit ergo ei Dominus: *Duae gentes in utero tuo sunt, et duo populi de uentre tuo segregabuntur. Et populus populum superabit et maior seruiet minori* (SC 7:298).

[45] *Hom. Gen.* 12.3 (referring to Gen. 25:23; FC 71:179); Quomodo *populus populum superauerit*, id est Ecclesia Synagogam, et quomodo *maior seruiat minori*, etiam ipsis Iudaeis licet non credentibus notum est (SC 7:298).

the object of this belief, the Incarnation of Christ, which distinguishes
the Christians from the Jewish people. Because Christians believe in
Christ's saving death and resurrection, the church has become the
new chosen people of God. The church supplants the position previously held by the people of Israel, as, through Rebecca's aid, Jacob
the younger received the paternal blessing from Isaac that was reserved
for the elder son.[46] Christians become the rightful heirs of all God's
promises, even those announced previously to the Israelite patriarchs.

This focus on the church recalls Origen's theoretical descriptions
of the pneumatic sense as conveying God's mysteries, which are
"fulfilled in Christ and in the Church."[47] Consistent with his theory,
this pneumatic reading relates figuratively to the role of the church.
Origen finds this pneumatic reading to be "well known and very
commonplace to everyone."[48] Thus, rather than developing its details,
he sets forth its theme as a context for the psychic reading of the
same passage. This context is that of God's grace toward believers
and the church's faithfulness toward God. Because of the church's
belief in the Incarnation, God has chosen to reward the church's
faithfulness by transferring His blessing of the first-born, Jewish people to the Christian faithful. Thus, Origen reminds his audience in
this pneumatic reading that God offers His grace and favor to those
who respond faithfully to His divine plans.

B. *The Psychic Reading of the "Two Nations"*

Having established the pneumatic context, Origen shifts to a psychic reading of the two nations by announcing that he will "add"
a reading that can "edify and instruct" each individual who listens
to the biblical words:

> Let us add this, if it is agreeable, which can edify and instruct each
> of us who hear these words. I think that this can be said also of us
> as individuals, that "two nations and two peoples are within us."[49]

---

[46] See Gen. 27.
[47] *Hom. Gen.* 2.6; FC 71:87; SC 7:110. Also, see the discussion of this explanation in chapter 3.
[48] *Hom. Gen.* 12.3 (FC 71:179); De his ergo, quae palam sunt et ualde omnibus
trita, dicere superfluum puto (SC 7:298).
[49] *Hom. Gen.* 12.3 (referring to Gen. 25:23; FC 71:179); Illud, si placet, addamus,
quod unumquemque nostrum, qui haec audit, aedificare et instruere queat. Ego
puto quod et de singulis nobis hoc dici potest quia *duae gentes et duo populi* sint intra
nos (SC 7:298).

Origen stresses that this added reading builds up and informs "each of us," because its message can be applied "also" to "us as individuals." He explains that there are "two nations and two peoples . . . within us," that is, within each individual person.

Origen interprets the two nations as the virtues and vices that reside within the human person and struggle for dominance therein:

> For there is both a people of virtues within us and there is no less a people of vices within us. "For from our heart proceed evil thoughts, adulteries, thefts, false testimonies," but also "deceits, contentions, heresies, jealousies, revelings and such like." Do you see how great a people of evils is within us? But if we should deserve to utter that word of the saints: "From fear of you, Lord, we have conceived in the womb and have brought forth; we have wrought the spirit of your salvation on the earth," then also another people, begotten in the spirit, is found within us. For "the fruit of the spirit is love, joy, peace, patience, goodness, gentleness, temperance, purity" and such like.[50]

Origen informs his audience that *intra* or "within" each person resides two nations: a "people of virtues" and a "people of vices" or "evils." The people of vices are made up of the sins conducted by the individual through his words, deeds, and thoughts—"evil thoughts, adulteries, thefts, [and] false testimonies," and proceed from the "'heart *(cor)*.'" The "other people . . . begotten in the spirit" are made up of good words, deeds and thoughts, that is, virtues, which Origen identifies with the fruit of the Holy Spirit, as listed in Gal. 5. This psychic interpretation is similar to the psychic call in *Hom. Exod.* 3 to move wholly away—or three full days—from Satan by purifying oneself in all three aspects of word, deed and thought. We are to take the virtues, or fruit of the Spirit, "into the womb" of our heart, or implicitly our soul, recalling Origen's theoretical representation of the heart, or soul, in *Hom. Lev.* 5 as the oven in which the divine loaves of Scripture are baked, burning away vice and causing the virtues to grow in their place.

---

[50] *Hom. Gen.* 12.3 (referring to Gen. 25:23; and quoting, in order, Matt. 15:19. Gal. 5:19–21, Isa. 26:18, and Gal. 5:22–23; FC 71:179); Nam et uirtutum populus intra nos est et uitiorum nihilominus populus intra nos est: *De corde enim nostro procedunt cogitationes malae, adulteria, furta, falsa testimonia*, sed et *doli, contentiones, haereses, inuidiae, comessationes et his similia*. Vides quantus malorum populus intra nos est? Si uero mereamur illam uocem dicere sanctorum: *A timore tuo, Domine, in utero concepimus, et peperimus, spiritum salutis tuae fecimus super terram*, tunc et alius intra nos populus inuenitur in spiritu generatus. *Fructus enim spiritus est caritas, gaudium, pax, patientia, bonitas, mansuetudo, continentia, castitas* et his similia (SC 7:298).

In Origen's analysis, the people of vices relate to Esau the elder
and the people of virtues to Jacob the younger. He explains that
the vices are "elder" because they have been more numerous than
virtues within and among individual hearts, or souls:

> You see another people which is also itself within us. But this one is
> less, that one greater. For there are always more evil than good peo-
> ple and vices are more numerous than virtues.[51]

As Esau claims the birthright by being the first-born son, the vices
claim superiority and possession over souls on the basis that they
have been more numerous both within and among individual souls
than have the virtues. Origen warns his audience that if they are
not attentive, they will come more and more under the control of
the vices.

As in *Hom. Gen.* 2 and *Hom. Exod.* 3, Origen here stresses that the
guidance of Scripture is both the necessary and available means of
causing the virtues to supplant the vices within the soul:

> But if we should be such as Rebecca and should deserve to conceive
> from Isaac, that is, from the word of God, "one people shall over-
> come the other and the elder shall serve the younger" even in us, for
> the flesh shall serve the spirit and vices shall yield to virtues.[52]

Origen wants his audience to identify with Rebecca, who conceived
her children by union with Isaac, who, in turn, represents Scripture,
"the word of God." Intercourse with Scripture's truths gives birth
to and eventually perfects all virtues within the human soul. If the
believer attends to Scripture and allows it to lay the seeds of virtue
within the womb of his soul, then the vices that have resided there
for so long will be forced to "yield" to the increasingly numerous
virtues.[53] The vices give their ground in the soul to the virtues when

---

[51] *Hom. Gen.* 12.3 (referring to Gen. 25:23; FC 71:179); Vides alium populum
qui et ipse intra nos est; sed iste minor est, ille maior. Semper enim plures sunt
mali quam boni et uitia numerosiora uirtutibus (SC 7:298).
[52] *Hom. Gen.* 12.3 (quoting Gen. 25:23; FC 71:179); Sed si tales simus qualis
Rebecca, et mereamur de Isaac, id est de Verbo Dei, habere conceptum, etiam in
nobis *populus populum superabit et maior seruiet minori*; seruiet enim caro spiritui et uitia
uirtutibus cedent (SC 7:298).
[53] The Latin term *cedere*, translated here as "yield," also means, when accompanied by the dative form as it is here, to give ground to or submit to something.
Above, in n. 28, in the treatment of *Hom. Gen.* 2 on the ark, I pointed out that
near the end of that homily Origen briefly offers a psychic reading of the "unclean
animals" that Noah placed into the ark in addition to the clean animals (*Hom. Gen.*

that person consistently interacts with Scripture. Again, then, the psychic reading calls the hearer to intimate engagement with Scripture as the means of becoming virtuous and thus ready for union with God. Indeed, by this interaction, the person will move toward perfection and salvation.

Origen here reminds his audience of his anthropology by stating that through union with Scripture a believer conceives a right internal order among the three parts of his human nature, such that the "flesh serves the spirit." This means that the properly-ordered soul follows the ways of the spirit rather than that of the flesh. This notion is consistent with our prior observations about Origen's anthropology, which suggest that the soul needs to choose the guidance of the spirit rather than fleshly tendencies in order to enjoy harmony among these three parts. If the spirit leads, then the soul follows the spirit and the body resists fleshly tendencies and submits to the soul's allegiance to the spirit. Once again, we may conclude that, according to Origen, Scripture leads hearers to the right ordering of body, soul and spirit that is necessary for salvation, because this right order is equivalent to perfection in the virtues.

As discussed previously, this psychic reading calls the hearer to cultivate virtues generally within his soul, in light of the temporal struggle for its possession by good and evil forces. The psychic sense, again, is more than the simple call to a set of virtues as with the moral somatic sense. It is a call to take on *all* the virtues through meditation on Scripture. Here, as in *Princ.* 4, Origen emphasizes that Scripture promotes and exemplifies the virtues, since they are the fruit of its author, the Holy Spirit. By spending time with Scripture, the human soul comes into contact with the Holy Spirit and learns to recognize and submit to the Holy Spirit's ways (and, thus, the ways of his own spirit), thereby increasing in the virtues.

2.6, referring to Gen. 6:19; FC 71:87–88; SC 7:110, 112). There Origen likens the unclean animals to the vices "which are in every soul." They are unclean because "they serve to make man sin." However, they are beneficial to the individual human soul to the extent that their presence brings "correction or discipline." Thus, he explains, they are "necessary and must be preserved" along with the clean animals, or virtues, during this temporal life. Here, in *Hom. Gen.* 12, note that Origen speaks of the vices "yielding *(cedere)*," or "giving ground to" the virtues, rather than being obliterated. The virtues begin to outnumber the vices during this life, but, as Origen suggests in *Hom. Gen.* 2 with the concept of "unclean animals" and here with the word *cedere*, no individual human soul will destroy *all* the vices within his soul until the end of his temporal existence.

Origen assures his audience that this can occur within each individual person: "even within us." If the believer diligently and submissively listens to Scripture, then, as suggested by the pneumatic reading, God graciously will reward his faithfulness—specifically, by directing him into a virtuous life marked by internal harmony between his body, soul, and spirit.

C. *Summary of the Psychic and Pneumatic Readings in Hom. Gen. 12*

In this homily, the pneumatic message informs Origen's audience that God graciously favors the church for its belief in His divine plans, implicitly, the Incarnate Christ's life, death and resurrection. After this reminder that God rewards faithfulness, Origen informs his audience through the psychic reading that their souls are the focus of a very real, temporal struggle between virtue and vice. To be victorious in this struggle, his audience member is encouraged to expose himself to the guiding truths of Scripture. From Scripture, he will learn to submit his own body and soul to the virtuous ways of his spirit (which is the divine imprint within him of Scripture's author, the Holy Spirit). Thus, each higher reading offers independently edifying messages.

Together, though, the two nonliteral readings offer a more complete edification to Origen's audience. First, in relation, the two senses stress that God will reward the faithful hearer of Scripture with growth in virtue and internal harmony, just as God has rewarded the faithful church with divine favor. Second, together, the two senses suggest that God will provide the faithful hearer of Scripture with membership in the divinely-favored church and, thus, a share in the promise of eternal salvation. In sum, God's favor toward the church gives hope to the individual believer: As God rewards the faithfulness of the church, so He will reward the faithfulness of each individual believer. As the church is held together by God's grace, so the faithful believer will achieve, by grace through Scripture, a strong constitution among his body, soul and spirit. Inasmuch as the individual believer recognizes that God has rewarded the church's faithfulness, so should he trust that God will reward his own personal faithfulness and include him in the church's favor. Origen's audience now should have every incentive to give due attention and deference to Scripture.

Again, the psychic reading in this homily is *Christian*. By viewing the psychic reading in its relation to the pneumatic sense, we have

THE PSYCHIC AND PNEUMATIC SENSES IN PRACTICE

found that the psychic reading instructs the individual believer how to share in the church's reward for belief in the Incarnate Christ. The goal of the psychic call to virtue, then, is Christ. Also, the way of the psychic call is Christ. Christ is the way by which both the individual and the church find favored union with God, and Scripture is the medium by which Christ teaches his own attributes, which are the virtues, or fruits of the Holy Spirit.[54] Again, then, Origen's psychic reading presents growth in virtue as a uniquely Christian pursuit.

Still, while the two senses draw context from each other, their themes reflect different—eternal and temporal—focuses. In this homily, the pneumatic senses' explicit ecclesiastical and implicit Christological themes together point to God's gracious, *eternal* favor of the church for its belief in Christ, while the psychic sense informs the individual believer of the specific *temporal* steps he can take in order to share in this favor which God grants to the church. Hence, because of their distinct themes, each sense provides crucial context for the other.

IV. *Hom. Lev.* 1: *Two Whole Burnt Offerings*

In *Hom. Lev.* 1, Origen offers two separate, figurative readings of the specifications set forth in Lev. 1:1–9, especially 1–5, for making a "whole burnt offering" to God. He recites the relevant verses as follows:

> The Lord called Moses and spoke to him from the Tent of Meeting[:] . . . "If a person should bring an offering to the Lord, then he should make the offering from cattle[,] . . . a calf [male] without blemish from the herd as a whole burnt offering . . . acceptable before the Lord . . . at the door of the tabernacle. . . . And he will lay his hand upon the head of the offering and will kill the calf before the Lord, and the sons of Aaron the priest will offer the blood and pour it out while going around the altar which is at the door of the Tent of Meeting."[55]

---

[54] For Origen's identification of Scripture's ultimate content and teacher as Christ, see *Princ.* 4.2.6, 4.2.9; the discussion in chapter 2; and chapter 3 generally.

[55] *Hom. Lev.* 1.2.1–3.1 (quoting Lev. 1:1–5; FC 83:31–33); [V]ocavit Dominus Moysen et locutus est illi de tabernaculo testimonii[:] . . . Si homo munus offeret Deo, offeret ex bobus [,] . . . holocaustum offerat vitulum [masculum] ex bobus sine macula . . . acceptus contra Dominum . . . ad ostium tabernaculi. . . . Imponet manum suam . . . super caput hostiae et iugulabunt vitulum contra Dominum, et offerent filii Aaron sacerdotis sanguinem, et effundent sanguinem ad altare in circuitu, quod est ad ostium tabernaculi testimonii (SC 286:70–76).

In this passage, God gives Moses instructions for making a *holocaustum*, or "whole burnt offering," which Moses is to relay to the people of Israel. As we have observed in the previous examples, Origen first interprets the whole burnt offering pneumatically, viewing it as Christ's self-sacrifice on the Cross for the sins of the world. Second, he interprets the whole burnt offering psychically as the believer's sacrifice of his own flesh to God through growing in virtue.

A. *The Pneumatic Reading of the Whole Burnt Offering*

Origen first calls his audience to discern the "spiritual sense" in Scripture. He explains that Scripture has a "*spiritual sense* hiding within," a "divinity . . . covered . . . with the veil of the letter," its "flesh," just as the Incarnate Christ possessed the "proper clothing" or flesh of his humanity so as to keep "the knowledge of his divinity" visible only to "the few."[56] Origen urges his audience to look beyond the flesh of Scripture—the clothing of its divinity—and "inwardly see the divine spirit that is concealed in the veil of the letter."[57] He assures his audience that the person who "bring[s] [the] clean ears of [his] inner person" to Scripture will hear its hidden truths.[58]

---

[56] *Hom. Lev.* 1.1.1 (referring to 2 Cor. 3:14–18). The fuller English text reads: "For the sight of his flesh was open for all to see, but the knowledge of his divinity was given to the few, even the elect. So also when the Word of God was brought to humans through the Prophets and the Lawgiver, it was not brought without proper clothing. For just as there it was covered with the veil of flesh, so here with the veil of the letter, so that indeed the letter is seen as flesh but the *spiritual sense* hiding within is perceived as divinity" (FC 83:29; emphasis added). The corresponding Latin text reads:—carnis namque adspectus in eo patebat omnibus, paucis vero et electis dabatur divinitatis agnitio—, ita et cum per prophetas vel legislatorem Verbum Dei profertur ad homines, non absque competentibus profertur indumentis. Nam sicut ibi carnis, ita hic litterae velamine tegitur, ut littera quidem adspiciatur tamquam caro, latens vero intrinsecus spiritalis sensus tamquam divinitas sentiatur (SC 286:66).

[57] *Hom. Lev.* 1.1.1 (referring to Luke 10:23). The fuller English text reads: "But perchance the worthy and the unworthy see and hear these things according to the letter, which is, as it were, the flesh of the Word of God and the clothing of its divinity. But 'blessed are those eyes' which inwardly see the divine spirit that is concealed in the veil of the letter. . . ." (FC 83:29). The corresponding Latin text reads: Sed haec secundum litteram, quae tamquam caro Verbi Dei est et indumentum divinitatis eius, digni fortassis vel adspiciant, vel audiant et indigni. Sed *beati sunt illi oculi*, qui velamine litterae obtectum intrinsecus divinum Spiritum vident . . . (SC 286:66).

[58] *Hom. Lev.* 1.1.1. The fuller English text reads: "[B]lessed are they who bring clean ears of the inner person to hear these things" (FC 83:29) The corresponding Latin text reads: et beati sunt, qui ad haec audienda mundas aures interioris hominis deferunt (SC 286:66).

Consistent with his theory, "spiritual sense *(spiritalis sensus)*" often refers to the pneumatic sense, and the letter acts as an *indumentum*, or "covering" over it.[59] Thus, here Origen describes the pneumatic sense.

Origen explains the pneumatic sense of this biblical passage by identifying the "whole burnt offering" with Christ: "[W]hat is as 'acceptable' as the sacrifice of Christ 'who offered himself to God?'"[60] Origen suggests that no sacrifice is more appropriately "accepted before the Lord" than the offering of Christ on the Cross:

> [I]t is "a male without blemish." It is truly "a male" which does not know the sin which is of female fragility. Therefore, only that "male," only he is "without blemish," who "did not sin and guile was not found in his mouth" and who "acceptable before the Lord," is offered "at the door of the tabernacle."[61]

Origen suggests two ways in which the Incarnate Christ represents the "male without blemish" that is to be sacrificed. First, he is "truly 'a male *(masculus)*.'" Here, Origen refers not to Christ's human gender. Rather, he means that Christ never suffered the "fragility" or weakness toward "sin" that Origen associates with the term "female." He possessed a strong resolve against the temptations of sin during his life, because he was *masculus*, which means manly, vigorous, or bold. Origen understands "male" to represent any person, man or woman, who shows resolve and strength against evil. Thus, Christ is the archetypal male, since he not only possessed great strength against the threats of sin while walking the earth, but his own power overshadowed the powers of sin. Second, Christ also was "without blemish *(sine macula)*," because he not only "did not know" weakness toward sin but also did not sin. The Latin term *macula* also means a stain or blot, and, more specifically, a fault in character. Origen stresses that Christ never had any such fault. Thus, Christ, with his strong and spotless character, is the quintessential male without blemish with respect to sin. Pneumatically speaking, Christ is the offering who is archetypally "acceptable before the Lord."

Origen next explains the significance of finding this offering "at the door of the tabernacle":

---

[59] See *Princ.* 4.2.8; Butterworth, 285; SC 268:334; and *Hom. Num.* 9.7; GCS 30:63.

[60] *Hom. Lev.* 1.2.8 (referring to Lev. 1:3 and Heb. 9:14; FC 83:33); quid tam *acceptum* quam hostia *Christi, qui se ipsum obtulit Deo?* (SC 286:76).

[61] *Hom. Lev.* 1.2.8 (quoting Lev. 1:3 and Isa. 53:9; FC 83:33); Est . . . *masculus sine macula. Masculus* vere est, qui peccatum, quod est femineae fragilitatis, ignorat. Solus ergo ille *masculus,* solus *sine macula* est, qui *peccatum non fecit, nec dolus inventus est in ore eius, et qui acceptus contra Dominum* offertur *ad ostium tabernaculi* (SC 286:74).

"At the door of the tabernacle" is not inside the door but outside the
door. For Jesus was outside the door, "for he came to his own and
his own did not receive him." Therefore, he did not enter into that
tabernacle to which he had come but "at the door of it" he was offered
for a *whole burnt offering*, since he suffered "outside the camp." . . . This,
therefore, is what is offered "at the door of the tabernacle, acceptable
before the Lord."[62]

Origen points out that *ad* or "at" the door means "outside *(extra)*,"
rather than "inside *(intra)*," the door. No one stood outside the door
of this world's acceptance more than Jesus himself, since "'his own
did not receive him.'" As a result of this rejection, he "suffered" and
was offered up. Origen suggests to his audience that they, as all
humans, are responsible for rejecting Jesus and causing his death,
which made him the whole burnt offering.

Origen next explains that Jesus Christ not only was the offering
on the Cross, but he also was the priest who administered the offering.
In other words, Christ made a self-sacrifice:

"[H]e placed his hand upon the head of the calf;" that is, he placed
the sins of the human race upon his own body, for he himself is the
head of his body, the Church.[63]

The biblical passage indicates that the priest who administers the
sacrifice is to "lay his hand upon the head of the offering."[64] Origen
explains that Christ placed his hand upon his *own head*, when "he
placed the sins of the human race upon his own body" on the Cross.
This gesture indicates that Christ administered the offering himself.
Because "he himself is the head of his body" and that body is the
church, Christ not only made a *self*-sacrifice on the Cross but took
on "the sins of the human race." He freed the church from its own
and the world's sins through his cleansing self-sacrifice.

Origen next explains that Jesus' self-sacrifice was a "double sacrifice,"
because he offered himself not only for those on earth but also for

---

[62] *Hom. Lev.* 1.2.8 (quoting John 1:11; Lev. 4:12, 1:3; FC 83:33); Ad ostium tabernaculi *non est intra ostium, sed extra ostium. Extra ostium etenim fuit Iesus, quia* in sua pro-
pria venit, et sui eum non receperunt. *Non est ergo ingressus tabernaculum illud, ad quod
venerat, sed* ad ostium *eius oblatus est* holocaustum, *quia* extra castra *passus est.* . . . *Hoc est
ergo quod offertur* ad ostium tabernaculi acceptum contra Dominum . . . (SC 286:74, 76).
[63] *Hom. Lev.* 1.3.1 (quoting Lev. 1:4 and referring to Eph. 1:22–23; FC 83:33);
"*Posuit ergo et manum suam super caput vituli,* hoc est peccata generis humani imposuit
super corpus suum; ipse est enim caput corporis Ecclesiae suae (SC 286:76).
[64] Lev. 1:4.

those in heaven. Origen draws the idea of a "double" sacrifice out of the biblical text by pointing out that it twice mentions that the offering is made "at the door of the Tent of Meeting."[65] The first reference places the "offering" at the door, but the second places the "altar" at this door, the altar on which the "blood" from the offering will be thrown. Origen relates these two statements to Christ's self-sacrifice in the following way:

> [I]t rightly names a second time "the altar that is at the door of the Tent of Meeting," because the sacrifice of Jesus was offered not only for those on earth but also for those in heaven. Indeed, here, he poured out the very bodily matter of his blood for men; but in heavenly places, if there are those who minister as priests there, he offered the vital strength of his body as some kind of spiritual sacrifice. However, do you want to know how there was a double sacrifice in him, suitable for those on earth and appropriate for those in heaven? The Apostle, writing to the Hebrews, says, "through the veil, that is, his flesh." And again he interprets the inner veil, "heaven," which Jesus "penetrated" that he "may now stand before the face of God for us," as he says, "always living to intercede for these." If, therefore, two veils are understood which Jesus, as it were, entered as high priest, in the same way we are to understand a double sacrifice through which he will have saved both those on earth and those in heaven.[66]

Origen explains that Jesus' sacrifice was both a physical sacrifice of the life force of his bodily matter, his blood, for those on earth, and a spiritual sacrifice of the "strength of his body" for those in heaven. Regarding the latter sacrifice, the Latin term *virtutem*, which is often translated as "virtue" or "excellence," is translated here as "strength" and also means valor, courage and fortitude or manliness. Origen already pointed out that Christ is male (*masculus*), signifying his surpassing strength against sin and its powers. Here, Origen suggests

---

[65] Lev. 1:3, 5.
[66] *Hom. Lev.* 1.3.2–3 (quoting Lev. 1:5; Heb. 10:20, 9:24, 7:25; FC 83:34); Recte ergo secundo nominat *altare, quod est ad ostium tabernaculi testimonii*, quia non solum pro terrestribus, sed etiam pro caelestibus oblatus est hostia Iesus, et hic quidem pro hominibus ipsam corporalem materiam sanguinis sui fudit, in caelestibus vero, ministrantibus—si qui illi inibi sunt—sacerdotibus, vitalem corporis sui virtutem velut spiritale quoddam sacrificium immolavit. Vis autem scire quia duplex hostia in eo fuit, conveniens terrestribus et apta caelestibus? Apostolus ad Hebraeos scribens dicit: *Per velamen, id est carnem suam.* Et iterum interius velamen interpretatur *caelum*, quod *penetraverit* Iesus, et *adsistat nunc vultui Dei pro nobis, semper inquit vivens ad interpellandum pro his.* Si ergo duo intelliguntur velamina, quae velut pontifex ingressus est Iesus, consequenter et sacrificium, duplex intelligendum est, per quod et terrestria salvaverit et caelestia (SC 286:76, 78).

that Jesus offered for those in heaven this character of his human form—he offered up his strength against evil for their sake. Also, Christ offered up his physical body and, more specifically, its blood, for those on earth. Thus, according to Origen, Christ's death on the Cross effected a double sacrifice, conquering evil for heavenly inhabitants and sin and death for earthly inhabitants.[67]

Origen's "spiritual" reading of Lev. 1:1–5 corresponds to his theoretical descriptions of the pneumatic sense as conveying the mysteries that are "fulfilled in Christ and in the Church."[68] By it, he assures his audience that Christ's death has freed the church and, for its sake, facilitated victory over sin.

B. *The Psychic Reading of the Whole Burnt Offering*

Origen then makes an explicit transition to a separate figurative reading of Lev. 1:1–5 by announcing that he now will read the passage *ad moralem locum*, or "in the moral sense," in which the priest represents the individual believer and the offering his flesh:

> But if you wish to understand these things in the moral sense, then you have "a calf" which you ought to offer. The "calf" is your flesh and it is indeed exceedingly proud. If you wish to present it as an offering to the Lord, then you keep it spotless and pure, bring it "to the door of the Tent," that is, where it can hear the divine books.[69]

Origen addresses his audience, urging each member to offer his own "flesh *(caro)*" to God. This flesh is *superbus*, or "proud," which also

---

[67] In order to provide another look at this double sacrifice of Christ, Origen draws on New Testament language from Hebrews, which he attributes to Paul. This passage mentions two kinds of "veils." First, there is the veil of Christ's flesh, and, second, there is the "inner veil [of] 'heaven.'" Origen states that "Jesus 'penetrated'" this inner veil of heaven so "that he 'may now stand before the face of God for us . . . always living to intercede for these.'" Christ has "'penetrated *(penetrare)*,'" or entered into, the veil over heaven as well as "pierced" the veil of his flesh, exposing the divinity lying behind both veils (H. Lev. 1.3.2–3 quoting Heb. 10:20, 9:24, 7:25); FC 83:34; SC 286:76, 78). In these ways, he brings the power of salvation to humans and angels alike.

[68] *Hom. Gen.* 2.6; FC 71:87; SC 7:110; Also, see the discussion of this explanation in chapter 3.

[69] *Hom. Lev.* 1.5.1 (referring to Lev. 1:3; FC 83:37); Verum si haec etiam ad moralem locum inclinare velis, habes et tu *vitulum*, quem offerre debeas. *Vitulus* est et quidem valde superbus caro tua; quam si vis munus Domino offerre, ut eam castam pudicamque custodias, adduc eam *ad ostium tabernaculi*, id est ubi divinorum librorum suscipere possit auditum (SC 286:84).

means arrogant or overbearing. Recalling Origen's anthropology, we recognize this flesh as the tendency toward sin, which, when unleashed in the body, directs the human person's life in a way opposite to that of the spirit. It is proud and arrogant in the sense that it wishes to direct the person's life away from God. Given the opportunity, it is overbearing, insisting upon directing all of the person's decisions.

In his anthropology, Origen stresses that the soul of the person must choose to follow the spirit so as to subdue the flesh (*caro*) and put the body (*corpus*) in its proper position of subordination to both the soul and spirit. According to this psychic reading, in order to effect this right internal order the person must present his flesh as an offering to God, that is, serve it up to God, and thereby convert the allegiance of his soul from the ways of the flesh to the divine ways of the spirit. When the flesh does not govern, the body, like the soul, will be spotless and pure, following the ways of the spirit.

In order to accomplish this kind of sacrifice, the person must bring his flesh "'to the door of the Tent,'" which Origen interprets as a church service, where he "can hear the divine books," or Scripture, and expose his flesh to them. The Latin literally states that the person is to bring his flesh to where it "can receive, acknowledge or take upon itself (*suscipere*) the hearing of the divine books." Origen suggests that the flesh "receive or take onto itself" Scripture's truths.

As discussed in Chapter 2, Origen understands that the Holy Spirit has designed Scripture through the interrelationship of its own bodily, soul's and spiritual meanings as a model for the human person's right internal ordering. By exposing his flesh to Scripture, then, the hearer will begin to reorganize his nature's three parts properly: his body, and his fleshly tendencies, will learn to submit to his soul's choice to follow his spirit's lead in the decisions of this life. Origen interprets the whole burnt offering psychically as the believer's submission of his flesh to Scripture's truths, which in turn will bring his soul and body into proper submission to his spirit, the divine imprint within him. This act is the human person's form of self-sacrifice.

This "moral" reading of the whole burnt offering reinforces the main theme promoted in the psychic readings of the previously reviewed homilies. It calls for the hearer to engage with Scripture intimately, since exposure to it makes the flesh "pure and spotless," or, implicitly, promotes growth in virtues. These virtues will bring his body, soul and spirit into the harmonious order that leads to salvation.

Origen next explains that by heeding this call to cleanse himself of fleshly tendencies through exposure to Scripture, the believer will transform himself into the state that is necessary for self-sacrifice. He will become a "male without blemish":

> Your offering should be "a male." It should not know a female; it should avoid concupiscence; it should shun weakness. It should require nothing dissolute or effeminate.... Kill it [cut its throat] "before the Lord," that is, place a bridle of continence on it and do not remove the hand of discipline from it just as that one placed the hand on his own flesh, that one who said, "I torture my body and subject it to slavery lest, perchance, when I have preached to others, I should myself become reprobate." And kill it "before the Lord" mortifying without wavering your "limbs" which are upon the earth.[70]

Origen urges his audience to become like Jesus, a "male." Specifically, he must "avoid concupiscence" and "shun weakness" and thus be a strong force against the tendencies of the flesh. Then he will begin to be "without blemish," without sin. By placing the "hand of discipline" on his flesh, he effectively lays his own hands on it as a priest marking it for sacrifice. The person administers the sacrifice of his own flesh, as did Paul, all in imitation of Jesus on the Cross. By pointing to the example of Paul's own imitation of Jesus, Origen clarifies that his audience is not to literally imitate the physical death of Jesus. Their sacrifice is the suppression of fleshly tendencies and, implicitly, the submission of the body to the spirit. The person "kills" the ways of the flesh within himself when he disciplines the body. If the person subdues the urgings of his flesh, then he becomes a male without blemish, no longer tainted by sin but a strong force against it.

Likening the person's self-sacrifice to that of Jesus, Origen also explains the psychic meaning of "double sacrifice." The person not only should offer his body (*corpus*) to God through suppression, or discipline, of the flesh (*caro*), but he also should offer his spirit (*spiritus*) to God and, thus, his whole being:

---

[70] *Hom. Lev.* 1.5.1 (quoting Lev. 1:3, 5; I Cor. 9:27; and referring to Col. 3:5; FC 83:37); *Masculinum* sit munus tuum, feminam nesciat, concupiscentiam respuat, fragilitatem refugiat, nihil dissolutum requirat aut molle.... [E]t iugula illam *contra Dominum*, hoc est impone ei continentiae frenum et manum disciplinae ne auferas ab ea, sicut imposuit manum carni suae ille, qui dicebat: *Macero corpus meum et servituti subicio, ne forte, cum aliis praedicavero, ipse reprobus efficiar.* Et iugula eam *contra Dominum*, mortificans sine dubio *membra* tua, *quae sunt super terram* (SC 286:84).

> And "the sons of Aaron the priest" should offer its blood. The priest,
> and his sons, is in your mind which is also its understanding in you
> who are rightly called a priest and "sons of a priest," for they are the
> only ones who perceive God and are capable of the knowledge of
> God. Therefore, the divine word desires that you offer your flesh to
> God in purity with reasonable understanding.... To offer blood on
> the altar through the priest or the sons of the priest is to be made
> pure both in body and spirit.[71]

As Jesus offered both his blood and his strength, so, too, is the
believer called to offer both his "body and spirit" to God. The
believer offers both parts to God when he makes them *castus*, or
"pure," which also means clean, chaste or holy. Origen has already
explained that the believer makes his body pure by disciplining the
flesh and becoming "male," or strong against sin, by submitting to
the spirit.

As for the spirit, according to Origen's anthropology, it is not susceptible to corruption.[72] If the soul follows the fleshly tendencies
unleashed in the body, then the spirit lies dormant. To make the
spirit "pure," then, is simply to bring it out of dormancy, so that it
can take its rightful lead within the person. Origen suggests that the
level of "understanding (*sensus*)" in the believer's "mind (*mens*)" reflects
either the strength or dormancy of his spirit. The Latin term *sensus*
also means "judgment or perception." The believer's spirit is strong
and pure, if his judgments and perceptions are based on *ratio*, "reason,"
or "consideration or calculation." A "reasonable understanding" or
right "judgment" reflects a strong spirit. Since the spirit is the rightful guide and counsel of the whole human person, it makes sense
that sound judgment reflects the spirit's leadership. In *Hom. Gen.* 2,
discussed earlier in this chapter, Origen identified the most advanced
in the faith as the most rational and the least advanced as the most
irrational. The most rational believer employs his reason in all facets
of his life; this is the mark of a strong spirit that leads the soul and
body in all decisions and actions. Here, Origen explains that when

---

[71] *Hom. Lev.* 1.5.1 (quoting Lev. 1:5; FC 83:37); Sed et *filii Aaron sacerdotis* offerant
sanguinem eius. Sacerdos in te est et filii eius mens quae in te est et sensus eius,
qui merito sacerdos vel *filii sacerdotis* appellantur; soli enim sunt, qui intelligant Deum
et capaces sint scientiae Dei. Vult ergo sermo divinus, ut rationabili sensu carnem
tuam in castitate offeras Deo.... Et hoc est per sacerdotem vel filios sacerdotis
offerre sanguinem ad altare, cum et corpore et spiritu quis castus efficitur (SC
286:84, 86).
[72] See the discussion of Origen's anthropology in the second half of chapter 2.

the spirit properly leads the person, his judgment acts as the priest
who performs the sacrifice of his own flesh to God.

Origen warns his audience that there are some persons who may
appear disciplined in the body but whose judgments are full of sin:

> For there are also others who offer their flesh as a whole burnt offering
> but not through the ministry of the priest. They offer neither know-
> ingly nor according to the Law which is in the mouth of the priest.
> They are indeed pure in body but are found to be impure in the
> mind [the rational principle of the soul] (*animo*). For either they are
> defiled with the concupiscence of human glory, or they are polluted
> with the lust of greed, or they grow filthy by the misfortune of jeal-
> ousy and malice, or they are tormented by being mad with hatred
> and with an excess of rage.[73]

Origen explains that some persons "offer their flesh (*caro*)" by openly
disciplining it, and appear "pure in body (*corpus*)," but they do not
do it "knowingly" or "according to the Law," as a "priest." The
proper guide of the soul and body is the person's spirit, and the
proper guide of his spirit is "the Law," the divine truths of Scripture.
Right judgments and reasonable understandings reflect the leadership of the spirit within the person. Origen warns his audience that
a person is "impure in the rational principle of his soul," that is,
unreasonable in his mind, or understandings and judgments, if he
has not submitted himself to Scripture and, thus, has given into
prideful glory, greed, jealousy, hatred or rage. Scripture directs purity
both inwardly and outwardly—the cultivation of reasonable judgments as well as bodily disciplines.

Origen explains that the person who is not inwardly pure, that
is, in his judgments and motivations, cannot act as priest of his
sacrifice to God and, thus, cannot make a *self*-sacrifice:

> Yet, they do not offer their whole burnt offerings through the hands
> and ministry of the priest. For they do not have in them the counsel

---

[73] *Hom. Lev.* 1.5.2 (referring to Lev. 1:3–5; FC 83:37–38); Sunt enim et alii, qui
offerunt quidem holocaustum carnem suam, sed non per ministerium sacerdotis.
Non enim scienter nec secundum legem quae in ore sacerdotis est, offerunt, sed
sunt quidem casti corpore, animo autem inveniuntur incesti. Aut enim gloriae
humanae concupiscentia maculantur aut cupiditate avaritiae polluuntur aut invidiae
ac livoris infelicitate sordescunt vel furentis odii et irae immanitate vexantur (SC
286:86). For *animo . . . incesti*, the English translator Gary Wayne Barkley uses "impure
spirit"; however, it is most literally translated as "impure mind," as a principle of
the soul. The literal meaning makes more sense, since in Origen's anthropology the
spirit of the human person cannot be corrupted or tainted, only the soul and body.

and the prudence with which to perform the priestly function in the presence of God. . . . Hence, the continence of the flesh alone is not able to reach to the altar of the Lord if it is lacking the remaining virtues and the priestly ministry.[74]

The person who appears outwardly pure in his body does not necessarily make a sacrifice of his flesh, for the "priestly function," also required, is marked by "counsel and prudence." The Latin term *consilium*, translated here as "counsel," also means consultation, judgment and understanding. The term *prudentia*, translated here as "prudence," also means foresight, knowledge and discretion. These terms signify sound judgment and wise discretion. Only the soul that consciously avoids the sins of greed, rage and the like, will take on these good qualities. Thus, in addition to disciplining the flesh, the person who wishes to make a whole burnt offering of himself to God must also offer his spirit by forming good internal judgment and wise discretion—more exactly, by submitting his soul and body to the lead of his spirit—which is the natural result of exposing himself to Scripture. Only then does he cultivate *all* of the virtues and present himself to God as a "whole" and, thus, "acceptable" offering. Hence, we see why Origen's psychic readings always call his hearer to intimate engagement with Scripture.

C. *Summary of the Psychic and Pneumatic Readings in Hom. Lev. 1*

Once again, in this homily each higher sense interprets the main biblical concepts differently and provides an independently edifying message for the hearer. The pneumatic reading encourages the hearer to acknowledge the sacrifice that Christ made on the Cross, which has freed the church from sin. The psychic reading urges the hearer to seek strength from sin in both his body and his internal judgments during this life. It explains that he may accomplish this by exposing his spirit to its proper guide, Scripture, since its author is the Holy Spirit. As a result, he will be led to discipline the body and subdue fleshly tendencies in obedience to his spirit. By submitting

---

[74] *Hom. Lev.* 1.5.2 (referring to Lev. 1:3–5; FC 83:38); [T]amen non offerunt holocausta sua per manus et ministerium sacerdotis. Non est enim in iis consilium et prudentia, quae sacerdotio fungitur apud Deum. . . . [Q]uoniam sola carnis continentia ad altare dominicum non potest pervenire, si reliquis virtutibus et sacerdotalibus ministeriis deseratur (SC 286:86).

himself to Scripture's guidance, he is freed of sin both inwardly and outwardly and, thus, becomes a whole burnt offering to God.

As with the previous homilies, here Origen's placement of the two readings side-by-side effects a more complete edification of the hearer by allowing the interrelation of their messages. In fact, Origen ends this homily with a statement that focuses directly on this relationship between the two readings. He stresses that a person should pursue the psychic call to purity and strength against sins both inwardly and outwardly as an *imitation* of Christ's self-sacrifice on the Cross:

> And therefore, we who read or hear these things should attend to both parts—to be pure in body, upright in mind, pure in heart, reformed in habits. We should strive to make progress in deeds, be vigilant in knowledge, faith, and actions, and be perfect in deeds and understanding in order that we may be worthy to be conformed to the likeness of Christ's offering, through our Lord Jesus Christ himself. . . .[75]

Origen encourages his audience to pursue the psychic call to purity and virtue during this life, by assuring them, through the pneumatic reading, that they do not forge a new path. Christ precedes them as the archetypal whole burnt offering to God. The pneumatic sense presents Christ as the model for answering the psychic call to make a self-sacrifice to God.

Essentially, the call is to make oneself "worthy to be conformed to the likeness (*ad similitudinem*) of Christ's offering, through (*per*) our Lord Jesus Christ himself"—to become, like Christ, a "male without blemish." By hearing the pneumatic sense first, the hearer heeds the psychic call to grow in purity and virtue with the understanding that he is part of the church that Christ already has freed from the bondage of sin. He also has Christ in clearer view as the pattern to follow in these efforts. Together, the two higher senses give the hearer an assurance of escape from sin and a way to affect this escape through a temporal imitation of Christ's self-sacrifice. Christ emerges as both the means of and model for achieving salvation.

Also, again, the psychic sense is essentially *Christian* in character. The psychic reading of the whole burnt offering is a call to sacrifice one's flesh temporally and thereby become a "whole burnt offering"

---

[75] *Hom. Lev.* 1.5.3 (FC 83:38); Et ideo qui haec legimus vel audimus, in utramque partem operam demus casti esse corpore, recti mente, mundi corde, moribus emendati, proficere in operibus, vigilare in scientia, fide et actibus, gestis et intellectibus esse perfecti, ut ad similitudinem hostiae Christi conformari mereamur per ipsum Dominum nostrum Iesum Christum (SC 286:86, 88).

along *with* Christ. Its purpose or reward is enjoyment of the church's victory over sin, which Christ already has accomplished. In addition, growth in outward and inward purity and the resulting right order of spirit, soul and body occur only if one submits to Christ's teaching in the Word of God. The psychic call to engage with Scripture is a call to imitate Christ. If Scripture models the human person's rightly ordered nature, it is because Scripture reflects the perfection of Christ himself. In fact, Christ has paved the way for the believer's ascent to God by modeling the virtues, which are summed up in his self-sacrifice on the Cross. As Origen stressed in *Hom. Gen.* 2, Christ's descent—condescension to incarnate life and death—is the pathway for the believer's ascent to God.

The pneumatic focus on the church and Christ stands apart from the psychic call to virtue, since the latter provides the *temporal* means of entering into the church's eternal victory over sin and death by imitating now Christ's *eternally* effective self-sacrifice. In this way, the psychic sense makes the hearer able to understand the pneumatic sense of the text and pursue its eternal hope now.

V. *Hom. Gen.* 8: *The Two Isaacs*

In *Hom. Gen.* 8, Origen offers pneumatic and psychic readings of Gen. 22:1–14, in which God commands Abraham to sacrifice his son Isaac, Abraham responds obediently, and then God spares Isaac.[76]

---

[76] Origen recites the biblical passage as follows: "God tested Abraham and said to him: 'Abraham, Abraham.' And he said: 'Here I am.' . . . 'Take your dearest son Isaac, whom you love, and offer him to me. Go, . . . into the high land and there you shall offer him for an holocaust on one of the mountains which I shall show you.' . . . Abraham arose . . . in the morning and saddled his ass, and cut wood for the holocaust. And he took his son Isaac and two servants and came to the place which God had said to him, on the third day. . . . Abraham . . . looking about saw the place afar off. And he said to his servants: 'Stay here with the ass, but I and the boy will go as far as yonder, and when we have worshipped, we will return to you.' . . . Abraham took the wood for the holocaust and laid it on Isaac his son, and he took the fire in his own hands and a sword, and they went off together. . . . Isaac . . . said to Abraham, his father: 'Father.' . . . 'What is it, son?' And Isaac says, 'Behold the fire and the wood. Where is the sheep for the holocaust?' Abraham responded . . . 'God himself will provide himself a sheep for the holocaust, son.' . . . They both proceeded, therefore, and came to the place which God had said to him. . . . And Abraham put forth his hand . . . to take the sword and slay his son. And an angel of the Lord from heaven called him and said: 'Abraham, Abraham.' And he said: 'Here I am.' And he said: 'Do not lay your hand on the boy nor do anything to him. For now I know that you fear God. . . . You spared not your beloved son

Origen reads Isaac pneumatically as a type of Christ who later is sacrificed on the altar of the Cross. Then, he interprets Isaac psychically as the individual human soul that God calls each person to offer freely through faithful obedience to God's commands. Like the psychic and pneumatic readings of the whole burnt offering in *Hom. Lev.* 1, the two higher readings in this homily stress the themes of self-sacrifice and imitation of Christ. However, they do so with more specific application to historical persons and with particular emphasis on the theme of God's abundant love for humankind.

A. *The Pneumatic Reading of Isaac*

Origen first treats Isaac as a prefiguration of the Crucified Christ:

> [T]he text says, "Abraham took the wood for the holocaust and laid it on Isaac his son, and he took the fire in his own hands and a sword, and they went off together." That Isaac himself carries on himself "the wood for the holocaust" is a figure, because Christ also "himself carried his own cross," and yet to carry "the wood for the holocaust" is the duty of a priest. He himself, therefore, becomes both victim and priest. But what is added also is related to this: "And they both went off together." For when Abraham carries the fire and knife as if to

because of me.' And looking back with his eyes . . . Abraham saw, and behold a ram was held by its horns in a bush *Sabec*. . . . And he took the ram . . . and offered it for a holocaust instead of his son Isaac. And Abraham called the name of that place: *the Lord saw*" (*Hom. Gen.* 8.1–10 [quoting Gen. 22:1–14; FC 71:136–146]); [T]entauit Deus Abraham et dixit ad eum: Abraham, Abraham. At ille dixit: Ecce ego. . . . Accipe filium tuum carissimum quem diligis, Isaac, et offer mihi eum. Vade, . . . in terram excelsam, et ibi offer eum holocaustum in uno ex montibus, quem ostendero tibi. . . . Surrexit ergo Abraham mane, et strauit asinam suam, et concidit ligna ad holocaustum. Et accepit filium suum Isaac et duos pueros, et peruenit ad locum quem dixit ei Deus die tertia. . . . Respiciens . . . Abraham uidit locum de longe et dixit ad pueros suos: Sedete hic cum asina, ego autem et puer ibimus usque illuc, et cum adorauerimus, reuertemur ad uos. . . . [A]ccepit . . . Abraham ligna ad holocaustum et superposuit ea Isaac filio suo, et accepit ignem in manibus suis et gladium, et abierunt simul. . . . Dixit . . . Isaac ad Abraham patrem suum: Pater. . . . Quid est, fili? . . . Ecce . . . ignis et ligna, ubi ouis ad holocaustum? . . . Deus prouidebit ipse sibi ouem ad holocaustum, fili. . . . Perrexerunt ergo ambo et uenerunt ad locum quem dixerat ei Deus. . . . Et extendit . . . Abraham manum suam ut acciperet gladium et iugularet filium suum. Et uocauit eum angelus Domini e caelo, et dixit: Abraham, Abraham. At ille dixit: Ecce ego. Et dixit: Non inicias manum tuam super puerum neque facias ei quicquam. Nunc enim cognoui quoniam times tu Deum. . . . Non pepercisti filio tuo dilecto propter me. Et respiciens . . . Abraham oculis suis uidit, et ecce aries tenebatur cornibus in uirgulto sabec. . . . Et accepit . . . arietem et obtulit eum holocaustum pro Isaac filio suo, et uocauit Abraham nomen loci illius: Dominus uidit (SC 7:212–232).

> sacrifice, Isaac does not go behind him, but with him, that he might
> be shown to contribute equally with the priesthood itself.[77]

Origen interprets Isaac as Christ who made a self-sacrifice on the
Cross. As he interpreted the whole burnt offering in *Hom. Lev.* 1
pneumatically as referring to Christ, he treats Isaac, whom his father
Abraham is to sacrifice to God, pneumatically as Christ. As Christ
is both victim and priest of his self-sacrifice according to *Hom. Lev.*
1, so Isaac is both victim and priest of this sacrifice. Origen points
out that Isaac carries the wood to the place of offering, just as Christ
carried the wooden Cross to his Crucifixion. Thus, pneumatically,
Isaac is a prefigurement of Christ, who, at his Father's will, carried
the wood to be used in his own death.

Origen emphasizes to his audience that Isaac is a figure only, not
Christ himself. Here, Origen interjects the literal, somatic reading of
the passage, emphasizing that God, in the end, called off the sacrifice
of Isaac. Origen effectively relates the somatic and pneumatic readings in order to give even greater emphasis to the pneumatic sense.
By stopping the sacrifice, God demonstrates that God's love for
humankind far exceeds what any human can or is expected by God
to offer in return. In the end, God did not ask Abraham to follow
through with the sacrifice of his only son, for God alone performs
a loving act of such magnitude. That is why God had an angel stop
the sacrifice and inform Abraham that he had shown proper fear of
God.[78] Origen explains:

> But grant that these words are spoken to Abraham and he is said to
> fear God. Why? Because he did not spare his son. But let us com-
> pare these words with those of the Apostle, where he says of God:
> "Who spared not his own son, but delivered him up for us all." Behold
> God contending with men in magnificent liberality: Abraham offered
> God a mortal son who was not put to death; God delivered to death
> an immortal son for men. What shall we say to these things? "What
> shall we render to the Lord for all the things that he has rendered to

---

[77] *Hom. Gen.* 8.6 (quoting Gen. 22:6 and John 19:17; FC 71:140–141); *Post haec
accepit*, inquit, *Abraham ligna ad holocaustum et superposuit ea Isaac filio suo, et accepit ignem
in manibus suis et gladium, et abierunt simul.* Quod ipse sibi *ligna ad holocaustum* portat
Isaac, illa figura est, quod et Christus *ipse sibi baiulauit crucem*, et tamen portare *ligna
ad holocaustum* sacerdotis officium est. Fit ergo ipse et hostia et sacerdos. Sed et quod
additur *et abierunt ambo simul*, ad hoc refertur. Cum enim Abraham uelut sacrificaturus
ignem portaret et cultrum, Isaac non uadit post ipsum, sed cum ipso, ut ostendatur
cum ipso pariter fungi sacerdotio (SC 7:222).

[78] Gen. 22:11–12.

us?" God the Father, on account of us, "spared not his own son."
Who of you, do you suppose, will sometime hear the voice of an angel
saying: "Now I know that you fear God, because you spared not your
son," or your daughter or wife, or you spared not your money or the
honors of the world or the ambitions of the world, but you have
despised all things and "have counted all things dung that you may
gain Christ," "you have sold all things and have given to the poor
and have followed the Word of God?"[79]

The historical truth of the somatic sense—that God, in the end, did
not require the sacrifice of Isaac—adds emphasis to the pneumatic
message that God's love for His creatures exceeds any form of love
that they can or are expected to demonstrate toward Him. By this
pneumatic reading, Origen urges his audience to give the full measure of their love and obedience to God, since God has shown,
through the Cross, that His love for them is greater than anything
He asks from them or that they can return to Him.[80]

Having established the general pneumatic context, Origen next
focuses on the individual state of Abraham in what almost appears
to be a psychic reading of the text but, in fact, completes the pneumatic reading by focusing on the notion of ascent (as did *Hom. Gen.* 2).

---

[79] *Hom. Gen.* 8.8 (quoting Rom. 8:32, Ps. 116:12, Gen. 22:12, Phil. 3:8, and Matt
19:21; FC 71:144–145); Verum haec dicta sint ad Abraham, et pronuntiatus sit
timere Deum. Quare? Quia non pepercit filio suo. Nos uero conferamus haec cum
Apostoli dictis, ubi dicit de Deo: *Qui proprio filio non pepercit, sed pro nobis omnibus tradidit illum.* Vide Deum magnifica cum hominibus liberalitate certantem: Abraham
mortalem filium non moriturum obtulit Deo; Deus immortalem filium pro hominibus
tradidit morti. Quid nos ad haec dicemus? *Quid retribuemus Domino pro omnibus, quae
retribuit nobis?* Deus Pater propter nos *proprio filio non pepercit.* Quis uestrum, putas,
audiet aliquando angeli uocem dicentis: *Nunc cognoui quoniam times tu Deum, quia non
pepercisti filio tuo* uel filiae tuae uel uxori, aut non pepercisti pecuniae uel honoribus
saeculi et ambitionibus mundi, sed omnia contempsisti et *omnia duxisti stercora, ut
Christum lucrifaceres, uendidisti omnia et dedisti pauperibus et secutus es Verbum Dei*? (SC
7:228, 230).

[80] Origen also gives a pneumatic reading of the "ram" that God provided for
Abraham as a substitute burnt offering in place of Isaac (*Hom. Gen.* 8.9, quoting
Gen. 22:13; John 1:14, 29; and 1 Cor. 15:42; FC 71:145; SC 7:230). Like Isaac,
the ram also represents Christ. Isaac, whom God first requested as a sacrifice but
later withheld from this fate, represents the divine part of Christ that lived on after
the Crucifixion without corruption, that is, the imperishable nature of Christ. The
ram that God provided for the actual sacrifice represents the perishable part of
Jesus Christ, the human nature that suffered and died on the Cross. While earlier
Origen explains that Isaac, as Christ, acts as both victim and priest in a self-sacrifice,
since he himself carries the wood to the place of sacrifice, here, in view of the fact
that God spares Isaac and provides the ram for the actual sacrifice, Origen reads
Isaac as the priest, the divine nature in Christ, and the ram as the victim, the
human nature in Christ.

Origen acknowledges the difficulty of the call to return to God the fullest love humanly possible. He emphasizes that God's call for Abraham's obedience represents the call of every believer to "ascend the mountain," which leads, implicitly, to resurrection and eternal union with God:

> But first it is said to him that he ought to offer his son, and then he is ordered to go "into the high land" and ascend the mountain. For what reason? That while he is walking, while he is making the journey, throughout the whole trip he might be torn to pieces with his thoughts, that hence he might be tormented by the oppressing command, hence he might be tormented by the struggling true affection for his only son . . . [;] that in all these things there might be a period of struggle between affection and faith, love of God and love of flesh, the charm of things present and the expectation of things future. He is sent, therefore, "into the high land" and the high land is not sufficient for a patriarch about to accomplish so great a work for the Lord, but he is also ordered to ascend a mountain, of course that, exalted by faith, he might abandon earthly things and ascend to things above.[81]

The physical climb through the "high land" that Abraham must make in order to reach the place of sacrifice symbolizes the struggle of ascending to God. This struggle results from forces pulling Abraham in opposite directions: attraction to the things of this world and the "expectation of things future." Like Abraham, each person must decide to "abandon earthly things and ascend to things above." The future expectation to which Origen refers here is the force that causes Abraham, and any person, to leave behind earthly attractions and ascend toward God: it is the knowledge that God has an eschatological plan of resurrection and salvation for every believer. The believer, like Abraham, then, must ascend from the loves of this world toward the promise of eternal life, toward union with God.

Origen explains that Abraham and Isaac journeyed for a period of three days to reach the place where he was to sacrifice Isaac.

---

[81] *Hom. Gen.* 8.3 (referring to Gen. 22:2; FC 71:139); Sed prius ei dicitur quia offerre debet filium suum et tunc iubetur ire in terram excelsam et adscendere in montem. Quo hoc spectat? Vt dum ambulat, dum iter agit, per totam uiam cogitationibus discerpatur, ut hinc perurgente praecepto, hinc uero unici affectu obluctante crucietur. . . . ut in his omnibus spatium certaminis accipiant affectus et fides, amor Dei et amor carnis, praesentium gratia et expectatio futurorum. Mittitur ergo *in terram excelsam* et non sufficit patriarchae tantum opus Domino peracturo terra excelsa, sed et montem iubetur adscendere, silicet ut fide elatus terrena derelinquat et ad superna conscendat (SC 7:218).

Origen relates the eschatological resurrection of believers to the concept of the "third day" (as in *Hom. Exod.* 3):

> "And he [Abraham] came," the text says, "to the place which the Lord had said to him, on the third day." . . . I consider the wisdom and intention of the one who tempts him. . . . [A] journey is prolonged for three days and during the whole three days the parent's heart is tormented with recurring anxieties, so that the father might consider the son in this whole lengthy period, that he might partake of food with him, that the child might weigh in his father's embraces for so many nights, might cling to his breast, might lie in his bosom? Behold to what an extent the test is heaped up. The third day, however, is always applied to mysteries. For also when the people had departed from Egypt, they offer sacrifice to God on the third day and are purified on the third day. And the third day is the day of the Lord's resurrection.[82]

Abraham travels alone with Isaac for three days to the place of sacrifice. This close and constant interaction between father and son is sure to make it even harder for Abraham to follow through with the sacrifice on the third day. Origen relates this third day to the "mysteries" of the "Lord's resurrection": God actually did sacrifice His Only Son, but then raised him from the dead on the third day. Origen suggests here, as in *Hom. Exod.* 3, that the third day pneumatically refers to Christ's resurrection and, implicitly, to the eschatological resurrection of believers. Origen urges his audience to consider that although the life of faith is metaphorically a difficult ascent, its goal is sure.

While the latter portion of this pneumatic reading seems to stress psychic themes such as individual obedience and human effort, Origen clearly views them here as part of the pneumatic sense. While he may speak of individual struggle and progress, he emphasizes the ultimate goal, or reward, of faithfulness: ascension to God and resurrection. Origen's focus is eschatological. Thus, the fact that a read-

---

[82] *Hom. Gen.* 8.4 (quoting Gen. 22:3–4; and referring, in order, to Exod. 5:3; 19:11, 15, 16; 24:5; Matt. 27:63; and Mark 8:31; FC 71:139–140); *Et peruenit*, inquit, *ad locum quem dixerat ei Dominus die tertia* . . . [S]apientiam et consilium tentantis intueor . . . [P]er triduum iter protenditur et per totum triduum recursantibus curis paterna uiscera cruciantur, ut omni hoc spatio tam prolixo intueretur filium pater, cibum cum eo sumeret, tot noctibus puer penderet in amplexibus patris, inhaereret pectori, cubitaret in gremio. Vide in quantum tentatio cumulatur. Tertia tamen dies semper apta fit sacramentis. Nam et populus cum exisset de Aegypto, tertia die offert sacrificium Deo et in die tertia purificatur; et resurrectionis Domini tertia est dies (SC 7:220).

ing addresses individualistic concerns does not necessarily make it a psychic reading.

Of course, Origen has in mind the psychic reading which follows and wishes to prepare the hearers who have grasped this pneumatic reading for the more specific focus on growth in virtues, including faithful obedience, that will occupy the psychic reading. As with the pneumatic readings in *Hom. Gen.* 2 and *Hom. Exod.* 3, here Origen discusses the notions of ascent and telos within the context of the pneumatic reading. In all three cases, these pneumatic discussions clearly establish context for the subsequent urgings of the psychic sense toward virtue and, thus, individual inclusion within this general ascent toward salvation. The contextualizing effects of the pneumatic readings show how Origen "mingles" but does not "fuse" the two higher senses.[83]

B. *The Psychic Reading of Isaac*

Later in the homily, Origen focuses specifically on the steps of the difficult ascent with a psychic reading of the sacrifice of Isaac. He refers to this psychic reading as "spiritual" (in Rufinus' Latin, *spiritalis*): "A clear way of spiritual understanding is opened for those who know how to hear these words."[84] While the pneumatic reading is also a "spiritual" reading of the text, Origen clarifies that this next reading is a second kind of spiritual reading. While also an edifying figurative reading, it interprets the same biblical concepts differently and holds its own distinct focus and message, centering on the virtues that the individual soul is to cultivate. Here Isaac represents the human soul.

Origen calls his audience to "beget a son Isaac in the spirit" by working to grow in virtue. After stating that God spares Isaac and provides Abraham with a ram to sacrifice in his place, Origen explains that the "Isaac" that the believer is called to offer to God is a soul full of virtue:

> "And he took the ram," the text says, "and offered it for a holocaust instead of his son Isaac. And Abraham called the name of that place:

---

[83] See chapter 1 for the discussion of Hanson's criticism that Origen fuses the two higher senses into one reading; and the end of chapter 3 for Origen's language in *Hom. Gen.* 2 regarding the "mingling" of the two higher senses.
[84] *Hom. Gen.* 8.10 (FC 71:146); Scientibus haec audire intelligentiae spiritalis euidens panditur uia (SC 7:232).

the Lord saw." . . . For everything which has been done reaches to the vision, for it is said that "the Lord saw." But the vision which "the Lord saw" is in the spirit so that you too might see these things in the spirit which are written and, just as there is nothing corporeal in God so also you might perceive nothing corporeal in all these things, but you too might beget a son Isaac in the spirit, when you begin to have "the fruit of the Spirit, joy, peace."[85]

Origen calls each member of his audience to beget, as Abraham, a son Isaac "in spirit" by cultivating "the fruit of the Spirit" in his soul. As in *Hom. Gen.* 12, Origen here refers to the "virtues" by mentioning the "fruit of the Spirit" listed in Gal. 5. The believer who manifests faith like Abraham will beget a son Isaac, a soul that bears the fruit of God's Spirit. Origen motivates his audience to heed this psychic call to virtue by assuring them that God will reward them with "the vision" of the things of God. Implicitly, they will see God.

Origen explains that the believer will take on the faithfulness of Abraham that makes possible this eternal vision, if he makes his soul like Isaac through the cultivation of the virtues:

Which son, however, you will at length so beget if, as it is written of Sara: "It ceased to be with Sara after the manner of women," and then she bore Isaac, so the things after the manner of women should cease also in your soul, so that you no longer have anything womanish or effeminate in your soul, but "you act manfully" and manfully gird your loins. You will beget such a son if your breast is "protected with the breastplate of justice; if you are armed with the helmet of salvation and the sword of the Spirit." If, therefore, the things after the manner of women cease to be in your soul, you beget joy and gladness as a son from your wife, virtue and wisdom. Now you beget joy if "you count it all joy when you fall into various temptations" and you offer that joy in sacrifice to God.[86]

---

[85] *Hom. Gen.* 8.10 (quoting Gen. 22:13–14 and referring to Gal. 5:22–23; FC 71:145–146); *Et accepit,* inquit, *arietem et obtulit eum holocaustum pro Isaac filio suo, et uocauit Abraham nomen loci illius: Dominus uidit.* . . . Omnia enim quae gesta sunt ad uisionem peruenunt; dicitur namque quia *Dominus uidit.* Visio autem quam *Dominus uidit* in spiritu est, ut et tu haec quae scripta sunt in spiritu uideas et, sicut in Deo corporeum nihil est, ita etiam tu in his omnibus nihil corporeum sentias, sed in spiritu generes etiam tu filium Isaac, cum habere coeperis *fructum Spiritus, gaudium, pacem* (SC 7:232).
[86] *Hom. Gen.* 8.10 (quoting Gen. 18:11, Deut. 31:6, Eph. 6:14, 17 and Jas. 1:2; FC 71:146); Quem tamen filium ita demum generabis, si, ut de Sarra scriptum est quia *defecerunt Sarrae muliebria* et tunc genuit Isaac, ita deficiant et in anima tua muliebria, ut nihil iam muliebre et effeminatum habeas in anima tua, sed *uiriliter agas* et uiriliter *praecingas lumbos tuos,* si sit pectus tuum *thorace iustitiae munitum, si galea salutari et gladio spiritus accingaris.* Si ergo deficiant muliebria fieri in anima tua, generas filium de coniuge tua, uirtute et sapientia, gaudium ac laetitiam. Generas autem

Each person bears a son, that is, a soul, either of God's Spirit or of weakness, sin and temptation. As in *Hom. Lev.* 1, Origen here relates the weak soul metaphorically to the female gender and the strong, virtuous soul to the male gender. The soul that is not of God's Spirit is "womanish" or "effeminate," weak in the ways of the Spirit. The soul that is strong in the ways of the Spirit is "manly," full of divine attributes such as justice, the hope of salvation and the power of God's Word.

The person with a manly soul is like Abraham who joined himself to Sarah, who represents "virtue and wisdom." Such a union for Abraham and Sarah resulted in Isaac, who represents a soul filled with and directed by the fruits of divine "joy and gladness." If the individual believer joins himself with God's virtue and wisdom— which we know from the prior homiletic examples is found by interacting with Scripture—then he too will bear the fruits of God's Spirit, the virtues. By cultivating these attributes of the Holy Spirit, such a soul will choose to follow the ways of his own spirit and discipline the body and subdue the flesh.[87] In this way, he will show the faithfulness of Abraham by sacrificing his whole nature to the Holy Spirit's transforming power and so make an offering of himself that is acceptable to God.

C. *Summary of the Psychic and Pneumatic Readings in* Hom. Gen. *8*

Each figurative reading in this homily interprets the biblical concepts differently, lending separately edifying messages. Pneumatically, Isaac prefigures Christ on the Cross. Psychically, Isaac represents the human soul adorned with virtue and wisdom. Alone, the pneumatic reading directs the hearer to focus on God's sacrifice of His own Son on the Cross for the sins of the human race. In this way, it emphasizes God's love for humankind and the promise of resurrection as the reward for ascending away from the things of this world toward God. Alone, the psychic sense informs the hearer how to make this ascent: he can offer his soul to God presently by growing in virtue through interaction with Scripture.

---

gaudium, si *omne gaudium existimaueris, cum in tentationes uarias incideris* et istud gaudium offers in sacrificium Deo (SC 7:232).

[87] Note how Origen stresses that temptations can be offered to God as sacrifice, turning sins and inclinations toward them to good, much as Origen spoke of their usefulness in his metaphorical reading of clean and unclean animals in *Hom. Gen.* 2 (*Hom. Gen.* 2.6; FC 71:87–88; SC 7:110, 112). See also n. 28 above.

By presenting both readings together, Origen facilitates an inter-relation between them that effects a more complete edification for his audience. His listeners are motivated to make the difficult ascent to God by attending to the virtues now, because the struggle will prove to be small compared to the reward of God's generous love. At the end of the homily, Origen articulates this interrelationship between the pneumatic and psychic readings in the following way:

> For when you have approached God joyfully, he again gives back to you what you have offered and says to you: "You will see me again, and your heart shall rejoice, and no man shall take your joy from you." So, therefore, what you have offered to God you shall receive back multiplied. . . . So, therefore, we appear at least to engage in business for the Lord, but the profits of the business go to us. And we appear to offer victims to the Lord, but the things we offer are given back to us. For God needs nothing, but he wishes us to be rich, he desires our progress through each individual thing. . . . Do you see what it means to lose something for God? It means to receive it back multiplied. But the Gospels promise you something even more, "a hundred-fold" is offered to you, besides also "life eternal" in Christ Jesus our Lord. . . . [88]

In this statement, Origen brings together the psychic and pneumatic readings of Isaac. As Christ sacrificed himself on the Cross, out of divine love for the world, so each person is called to offer his soul to God by becoming virtuous. Though less explicitly than in *Hom. Lev.* 1, this again is a call to *imitate* Christ.

In calling the hearer to imitate Christ, the two higher readings together stress the reward of this difficult task. Though it is an offering of oneself to God, God needs nothing. The benefit of the offering reverts back to the offeror. By imitating Christ, the believer will enjoy "'life eternal' in Christ Jesus." He will be united for eternity with Christ. Also, Origen stresses, this is more than a transference

---

[88] *Hom. Gen.* 8.10 (quoting John 16:22, referring to John 16:17; and quoting Matt. 19:29; FC 71:146–147); Cum enim laetus accesseris ad Deum, iterum tibi reddit quod obtuleris, et dicit tibi quia: *Iterum uidebitis me, et gaudebit cor uestrum, et gaudium uestrum nemo auferet a uobis.* Sic ergo quae obtuleris Deo, multiplicata recipies. . . . Sic ergo uidemur quidem Domino negotiari, sed nobis cedunt negotiationis lucra; et uidemur offere Domino hostias, sed nobis, quae offerimus, redonantur. Deus enim nullius indiget, sed nos uult diuites esse, nostrum desiderat per singula quaeque profectum. . . . Vides quid est amittere aliquid pro Deo, hoc est multiplicata recipere tibi. Tibi autem et amplius aliquid Euangelia promittunt, centupla tibi pollicentur, insuper et *uitam aeternam* in Christo Iesu Domino nostro (SC 7:232, 234).

of the mere offering back to the offeror. He will receive back even more than he offers to God: he will "receive it back multiplied."[89]

In addition, the sacrifice of a virtuous soul remains a small offering of love compared to the love that the believer receives from God. God did not require Abraham to follow through on the sacrifice of Isaac, but did sacrifice His only child. Since God *will* accept the believers' sacrifice of a virtuous soul, that sacrifice is, by implication, not as difficult as that of sacrificing one's son. More to the point, it is not as generous an offering as God's sacrifice of Christ on the Cross. Thus, the two higher readings together stress that the hearer should gladly offer himself up to God, according to the psychic sense's instruction, because, as the pneumatic reading stresses, God's generosity of love and life makes the believer's faithful growth in virtue, in comparison, a small and easy task.

In this way, each higher sense makes the other's message more meaningful for and more accessible to the hearer. However, the reinforcing nature of their relationship does not occur only one time, but builds over time. By pointing to God's surpassing love and rewards, the pneumatic sense gives incentive and motivation for following the psychic call to virtue. In turn, the psychic call to imitate Christ's self-sacrifice on the Cross through growth in virtue increases the hearer's understanding of the depths of God's love, as conveyed by the pneumatic sense. Thus, the pneumatic sense gives purpose to the psychic sense, which, in turn, makes the eternal truths and hope of the pneumatic message increasingly accessible and meaningful to the hearer now.[90]

As with all the preceding examples, in this homily the psychic sense's relation to the pneumatic sense makes more clear its innately Christian character. The psychic call to virtue is revealed to be a call to imitate Christ. This *temporal* call to virtue is centered on and made possible by Christ, since to grow in virtue is to imitate Christ, as well as to make oneself a worthy recipient of God's bountiful, *eternal* love, as exemplified on the Cross and articulated by the pneumatic sense.

---

[89] Recall Origen's similar observation in *Hom. Num.* 9 (on the three layers of the almond) that God delivers on His promises with greater abundance than the original promises themselves suggested (see chapter 3).

[90] Of course, Origen believed, then, that the person who repeatedly exposes himself to biblical passages will yield ever-ripening fruit from them.

VI. *Hom. Num.* 27: *Two Types of Exodus*

In *Hom. Num.* 27,[91] Origen treats Num. 33, which mentions forty-two places through which the Israelites traveled during their exodus from Egypt to the promised land. Origen dedicates the entire homily to a psychic reading of the names of these locations, interpreting each as a stage in the human soul's temporal journey toward perfection in virtue. He does not present a pneumatic reading of the locations, because, he seems to suggest, he is not able to do it justice.[92] However, he describes how its focus would offer a different message if presented. Because *Hom. Num.* 27 is a well-known homily among students of Origen, it is worth considering briefly his descriptions of both higher readings of Numbers 33.

Origen finds it significant that the name of each place is mentioned twice within the biblical passage, first when the Israelites arrive at the location and a second time when they move on from that place:

> [W]e see what great care the Lord took in describing those stages so that their description would be introduced in a second place. For those names are recounted, granted with some differences, at the point when the children of Israel are said to have left each different place *and* to have camped at it. . . . The stages are repeated twice in order to show two journeys for the soul.[93]

Origen considers this twofold reference to be an explicit invitation by Scripture to interpret the places according to two separate non-literal senses of meaning. He describes these two distinct interpretations several times. He explains that this biblical passage holds "a double line of interpretation" by which "our soul may make progress," learning "*either* how we ought to live the life that turns from error and follows the Law of God *or* how great an expectation we have

---

[91] For the English translation of *Hom. Num.* 27, see Greer, *Origen*, 245–269. References to *Hom. Num.* 26 are based on my own translation. For Rufinus' Latin text of *Hom. Num.* 26 and 27, see Baehrens (GCS 30:242–280).

[92] *Hom. Num.* 27.4, 13; Greer, 250–252, 268–269; GCS 30:260–262, 279–280. For a fuller consideration of why Origen does not set forth the pneumatic reading in detail in this homily, see the final discussion at the end of this analysis.

[93] *Hom. Num.* 27.6 (Greer, 253, emphasis added); [M]axime cum videamus tantam fuisse curam Domino de istis mansionibus perscribendis, ut descriptio earum secundo iam hoc divinis legibus inderetur. Commemorata sunt enim nomina ista, licet in nonnullis immutata, iam tunc, cum per loca singula elevasse dicuntur filii Istrahel de illo loco et applicuisse in illo loco. . . . [B]is enim repetuntur, ut duas animae ostenderent vias . . . (GCS:263–264).

of the future hope that is promised on the basis of the resurrection."[94] Elsewhere, he explains that these two readings constitute "in
a spiritual sense . . . a double exodus from Egypt, *either* when we leave
our life as Gentiles and come to the knowledge of the divine Law
or when the soul leaves its dwelling place in the body."[95] In still
another place, Origen describes the two readings as signifying:

> two journeys for the soul. *One* is the means of training the soul in
> virtues through the Law of God when it is placed in flesh[ ] and by
> ascending . . . from virtue to virtue . . . uses these progressions as stages.
> And *the other* journey is the one by which the soul, in gradually ascend-
> ing to the heavens after the resurrection, does not reach the highest
> point unseasonably, but is led through many stages . . . illumined at
> each stage by the light of Wisdom, until it arrives at the Father of
> lights Himself.[96]

---

[94] *Hom. Num.* 27.6 (Greer, 253, emphasis added). The fuller Latin text reads:
Duplici igitur expositione utentes omnem hunc, qui recitatus est, considerare debemus
ordinem mansionum, ut ex utroque sit animae nostrae profectus, agnoscentibus ex
his, vel haec vita, quae ex conversione erroris legem Dei sequitur, qualiter agi
debeat, vel futurae spei, quae ex resurrectione promittitur, quanta sit exspectatio
(GCS 30:263).

[95] *Hom. Num.* 27.2 (Greer, 248, emphasis added). The fuller Latin text reads:
Superior disputatio, cum nobis occasionem dicendi de profectione filiorum Istrahel
ex Aegypto praebuisset, dupliciter diximus videri posse spiritaliter exire unumquemque
de Aegypto: vel cum relinquentes gentilem vitam ad agnitionem divinae legis acced-
imus, vel cum anima de corporis huius habitatione discedit. Ad utrumque ergo istae
mansiones, quas nunc per verbum Domini Moyses describit, adspiciunt (GCS 30:258).
Note that Origen uses "spiritual sense" here to refer simultaneously to both higher
senses. As we discussed in chapter 2 on Origen's theory in *Princ.* 4, Origen employs
the term πνευματικός (in the Latin, *spiritalis*) both to refer to the third, pneumatic
sense and sometimes also to the two higher, figurative readings together. The com-
bined reference in this homily *(spiritaliter)* does not suggest that the two readings
are one, since the very point of his remarks in this homily is that he will not offer
the pneumatic reading but only a psychic reading of the biblical text.
  Also, note that it is possible that Origen envisions a non-bodily resurrection of
the human person in this and his other descriptions of the pneumatic reading in
this homily. However, it is not conclusive, and this controversial part of Origen
studies is not the focus of this work.

[96] *Hom. Num.* 27.6 (referring to Jas 1:17; Greer, 253, emphasis added). The fuller
Latin text reads: [B]is enim repetuntur, ut duas animae ostenderent vias: unam,
qua in carne posita per legem Dei in virtutibus exercetur et per gradus quosdam
profectuum adscendens pergit, ut diximus, « de virtute in virtutem » et ipsis pro-
fectibus quasi mansionibus utitur; aliam vero, qua post resurrectionem adscensura
ad coelos non subito nec importune ad summa conscendit, sed per multas deduci-
tur mansiones, in quibus illuminata per singulas et augmento semper splendoris
accepto in unaquaque mansione illustrata sapientiae lumine usque ad ipsum per-
veniat « luminum patrem » GCS 30:264.

Based on all these descriptions, Origen observes two spiritual, or edifying nonliteral, interpretations of each location's name. The first
regards the moment when the Israelites *reach the location*, focusing on
the human person's conversion to Christianity and resulting struggle to shun sin and grow in virtue through coming to knowledge of
the Law of God during this temporal life.[97] The second interpretation regards the moment when the Israelites *leave the location*, focusing
on the human person's continued ascent after departing from this
life, which culminates in a full communion with God's own wisdom.[98]
We recognize the first interpretation, with its focus on the temporal
growth in virtue, as a psychic reading of the text, and the second,
with its focus on a post-resurrection ascent of the believer's soul to
God and, thus, its eschatological and eternal emphases, as a pneumatic reading of the text.

Origen stresses that both journeys are "ascents" of the human soul
toward God. As in *Hom. Gen.* 2, here Origen emphasizes that the
believer is called to ascend the path to God that Christ paved by
his descent into human form: Humans are to "ascend through the
stages by which Christ descended."[99] He further explains that Christ's
Incarnation traversed eternity as well as temporality, and his descent
is the way and guide of *both* ascents.[100] The psychic reading focuses
on the soul's temporal ascent toward God through the cultivation of
virtues.[101] Instruction for this ascent is found in both the Law and
Prophets of the Old Testament and the Gospel of the New Testament.[102] Like the prior examples, the psychic reading here calls for
engagement with Scripture. In contrast, the pneumatic reading focuses
on the soul's ascent "from the Egypt of this life ... to heaven and
the mystery of the resurrection from the dead,"[103] that is, "after the

---

[97] For additional descriptions of the first, temporal journey of the soul's growth
in the virtues, see *Hom. Num.* 26.4; GCS 30:249; and *Hom. Num.* 27.5; Greer, 252;
GCS 30:263.

[98] For an additional description of the second, post-temporal (final) journey to
the ultimate "promised land," heaven, see *Hom. Num.* 26.4; GCS 30:249–250.

[99] *Hom. Num.* 27.3 (alluding to Eph. 4:10; Greer, 250); incipiamus per ea, quae
descendit Christus, adscendere (GCS 30:260).

[100] *Hom. Num.* 27.3; Greer, 249–250; GCS 30:259–260; also *Hom. Num.* 27.2;
Greer, 248–249; GCS 30:258–259.

[101] *Hom. Num.* 27.3; Greer, 250; GCS 30:260.

[102] *Hom. Num.* 26.4; GCS 30:249–250; and *Hom. Num.* 27.6; Greer, 253; GCS
30:263–264.

[103] *Hom. Num.* 27.4 (Greer, 250–252); de Aegypto vitae huius ... ad coelum et
resurrectionis ex mortuis sacramentum (GCS 30:260–262).

resurrection."[104] It is the human person's mysterious journey to God that continues after this life. Like the prior examples, the pneumatic reading here focuses on things eternal, and even implies (as was made explicit in *Hom. Num.* 9 regarding the almond—treated in chapter 3) that the pneumatic sense is an *eternally* abiding truth. Both ascents retrace a portion of the path that Christ paved by condescending to human form.

Since Origen only describes and does not develop the second, pneumatic ascent of the soul, we cannot know what details he would give to it, how he would employ it to edify his audience, or how he would envision the full presentations of both nonliteral interpretations to relate in a mutually enhancing way for the benefit of his audience. However, we can make a few observations that are relevant to the findings of this chapter. First, Origen observes two separate, nonliteral readings and describes each in a way that recalls his theoretical descriptions and other practical applications of the psychic and pneumatic senses. Second, the pneumatic sense brings the hearer's attention to *eternal* contemplation of God, while the psychic sense directs him toward *temporal* growth in virtues, as spurred on by the study of Scripture. Third, even the psychic sense is *Christian* in focus, since Origen expressly describes it as drawing the hearer onto a path of ascent that spans a portion of Christ's own descent into human form. Finally, while each sense edifies according to its own function and focus, together they provide the hearer with both the eternal goal of his existence *and* the means, or way, of pursuing it now. Therefore, Origen's general descriptions of both senses in this homily lay the foundation for a presentation of the two higher readings that is similar to those that we observed in previous examples: one that establishes a relationship of mutual reinforcement based on separate focuses and functions, all for the spiritual transformation of Scripture's hearer.

Origen was intrigued enough by the possibility of this dynamic exegesis of Num. 33 to describe both nonliteral interpretations repeatedly, but, for reasons he does not fully explain, he decided that the pneumatic reading would be too difficult to offer in detail. His repeated descriptions of the pneumatic reading and his plea at the end of the homily for "any who are wise" to seek understanding at

---

[104] *Hom. Num.* 27.6 (Greer, 253); post resurrectionem adscensura ad coelos (GCS 30:264).

the "more divine" level[105] suggest that he wanted to consider the pneumatic reading further. He does not leave us with the impression that he simply thought his audience too immature for the pneumatic reading of this text. Rather, earlier in the homily, he questions whether any preacher could do it justice, wondering aloud "[w]ho will be found worthy and so understanding of the divine mysteries that he can describe the stages of that journey? . . ." that is, the "stages . . . by which the soul journeys from earth to heaven."[106] Of this second ascent, Origen states: "I do not know who would dare to explain the stages one by one and also to guess at the special properties of the stages by contemplating their names."[107] By these statements, he suggests that this pneumatic reading of post-resurrection contemplation is so mysterious that it is even beyond his own ability to render with authority. Still, his plea to anyone wise to explore it further reveals that he does not simply view it to be a pneumatic reading so deep that it, unlike others, cannot be tapped in this life. Also, even if he thinks that this pneumatic reading is too eternal to offer to audiences that include members less advanced in the faith, the amount of time that he spends on it, the wonder that he expresses about it, and his plea for anyone wiser to explore it further strongly suggest that he wished for a deeper understanding of it himself and was perhaps frustrated to not have grasped as yet more of its edifying meaning.

This preoccupation with the pneumatic reading of the forty-two stages and seeming desire to understand it better arguably shed light on why we do not see Origen offer both higher senses fully in all of his treatments of biblical texts. In addition to concerns about time limits and the appropriateness of occasions, as well as the abilities of his audience members at hand, he also simply does not

---

[105] *Hom. Num.* 27.13 (Greer, 269); The fuller Latin text reads: Illam vero aliam expositionis partem prudentibus quibusque ex ista coniciendam et contemplandam relinquo. « Sapientibus » enim sufficit « occasiones dedisse » . . . . [I]mmo et aliquid perspicacius ac divinius contempletur (GCS 30:280, quoting Prov. 9:9).

[106] *Hom. Num.* 27.4 (Greer, 251). The fuller Latin text reads: Istae ergo mansiones sunt, quibus iter e terris agitur ad coelum. Et quis ita invenietur idoneus et divinorum conscius secretorum, qui possit itineris istius et adscensionis animae describere mansiones et uniuscuiusque loci vel labores explicare vel requies? (GCS 30:261).

[107] *Hom. Num.* 27.4 (Greer, 251). The fuller Latin text reads: Sed haec, ut dixi, qui per singulas mansiones audeat aperire et pro contemplatione nominum qualitates quoque conicere mansionum, nescio si aut sensus dicentis ad mysteriorum pondus sufficiat aut auditus capiat audientium (GCS 30:261–262).

comprehend the full import of some passages' pneumatic meaning. This inability, of course, is understandable, because the pneumatic sense focuses on things beyond the temporal world. Some such meanings will surely be even more mysterious and challenging than others. This supports Origen's theoretical view that the "perfected"—teachers and leaders in the church—continue to grow in understanding Scripture's senses, especially the pneumatic sense, throughout this life, as well as afterwards.

VII. *Conclusion*

The five full-length examples in this chapter present separate psychic and pneumatic readings for the same scriptural passage, each representing the same biblical concepts differently. The analyses of these homilies have demonstrated the following core insights: First, each reading, by its focus and representations, is recognizable as either a psychic or pneumatic reading in accordance with Origen's theoretical descriptions of each sense. Second, each reading offers a message that, on its own, edifies the hearer, providing him with information, hope, instruction or encouragement for his Christian pursuit of salvation. Third, when Origen presents both psychic and pneumatic readings for the same passage, with the pneumatic reading offered first, it becomes apparent that each message enhances the beneficial effects of the other for a more complete edification of the hearer.

This examination more specifically has established that the focus of the middle, psychic sense is functionally separate from the related themes of the pneumatic sense, and these functional differences recall Origen's theoretical descriptions of the senses as set forth in chapters 2 and 3. His pneumatic reading consistently centers on Christ's saving power, focusing specifically on (1) Christ's Incarnation, sacrifice on the Cross or resurrection, (2) the church as the first beneficiary of Christ's saving power and the medium through which this power is conveyed, (3) the eschatological fruition of Christ's saving act, and/or (4) the path on which the believer can ascend toward salvation, paved by Christ's descent to human form and found only within the church. In contrast, Origen's psychic reading consistently centers on the individual human soul's need to shun sin and grow in the virtues, and it directs him to intimately engagement with Scripture in order to learn how to do this. These different focuses

allow each higher sense independently to edify the hearer, that is,
aid him in his pursuit of salvation. The pneumatic sense directs the
hearer to focus on the telos of salvation, helping him to see beyond
the temporal realm to things eternal and giving him hope and informing him of God's love. In contrast, the psychic sense informs the
hearer that good and evil forces fight for possession of his soul and
that he needs to become involved if good is to prevail.

As a correlative point, the psychic sense itself is distinctively *Christian*,
contrary to de Lubac who suggests that Origen likely borrowed the
notion of the middle, moral sense from Philo's natural notion of
virtue. The examples in this chapter show that even if Origen draws
upon extra-Christian notions of the quest for virtue, he recasts it
entirely within the Gospel message. Origen's psychic readings instruct
the hearer how to access the path of ascent to perfection and salvation. The believer makes this ascent by purifying his soul from sin
and growing in virtue through exposure to the Word of God. In
this way, his soul takes on the mind of Christ. He becomes like
Christ in the virtues, and, by offering God a virtuous soul, the believer
imitates Christ's sacrifice of love on the Cross. Moreover, the whole
significance of the psychic sense rests on the fact that it is the means
of pursuing eternal union with Christ. Christ, then, is the model,
way *and* goal of the quest to which the psychic sense summons
Scripture's hearer.

By presenting the two senses *together*, with the pneumatic reading
offered first, Origen shows the transformative effect of their interrelationship on the hearer. As discussed in chapter 2, Origen's early
theory in *Prin.* 4 envisions the *initial* reception of the three senses in
the following order: Scripture's hearer first grasps the somatic sense,
then the psychic sense, and only lastly does he achieve an initial
comprehension of the pneumatic sense. However, in the examined
homilies, Origen presents the pneumatic reading before the psychic
reading. Arguably, not only did Origen perceive some advanced
members in the audiences for these homilies—people who already
could comprehend all three senses to some extent, or at least recognize them[108]—but, obviously, Origen believed that the psychic sense
continues to edify even the hearer who comprehends pneumatic

---

[108] Also, recall the discussion in chapter 2 suggesting Origen's desire through
the text of *Princ.* 4.2.4 to urge all preachers and exegetes to offer all 3 (or 2) senses
of a biblical passage when it is likely that the members in their audiences repre-

meanings. By presenting the pneumatic reading first, Origen brings his mature audience members to the psychic reading with their focus already on salvation. Duly motivated by this eternal telos, they learn from the psychic reading *how* temporally to pursue it. As they persevere in this temporal pursuit, they will come to understand the pneumatic sense in an ever-deepening way.

As discussed in chapter 1, Greer finds within the prologue to *Comm. Cant.* that Origen—at least in theory—understands Scripture to be aimed generally at promoting the spiritual growth of the hearer through a dialectic between contemplation and action (or the life of virtue).[109] As these examples demonstrate, Origen accesses this dialectic in practice through the interrelationship between the two higher senses. Similarly, the reinforcing moral and mystical pedagogies of Scripture that Torjesen observes to be important to Origen are in fact embodied by these two separate and yet related higher senses of meaning.[110]

The thematic and functional differences of the two higher senses are essential to the effectiveness of their interrelationship. De Lubac suggests that even where the middle, moral sense takes on a Christian cast within Origen's practice, it is an extension of one spiritual sense.[111] Moreover, Hanson claims that the two higher senses are "fused" together, or the moral sense is "absorbed" into the spiritual sense.[112] Yet, the examples in this chapter reveal that the middle, psychic sense is separate in focus and function. While the Christological, ecclesiastical and eschatological themes of the pneumatic sense are joined by their central focus on Christ's salvific power, the psychic sense provides a *temporal means* to pursue the *eternal hope* conveyed by these collective pneumatic themes.

Origen's *primary* exegetical concern, then, is with the two figurative, psychic and pneumatic senses, *not* literal and nonliteral readings of

---

sent the full range of learning and growth in faith, so that each member may receive the full benefit of the scriptural text at hand according to his own capacity. With this in mind, Origen arguably presents the pneumatic sense before the psychic sense in such cases so that the more advanced in his audience may receive not only both messages of the two higher senses but the fuller benefits of their interrelationship as well.

[109] Greer, *Early Biblical Interpretation*, 191; and the discussion of Greer's views in chapter 1.

[110] Torjesen, *Hermeneutical Procedure*, 120–123; and the discussion of Torjesen's views in chapter 1.

[111] De Lubac, *Histoire et Esprit*, 139–150; and, idem. *Medieval Exegesis*, I:142–150.

[112] Hanson, *Allegory and Event*, 235–237 and 243.

Scripture. His exegetical aim is best described as his effort to direct the believer toward salvation and provide him with lessons by which he can pursue it. The goal is eternal, but the task of achieving it must begin now. Thus, the height of this exegetical effort to transform his audience is the interrelationship between these two separately-focused senses.

Moreover, Origen's exegetical practice reflects his understanding of Scripture's own internal structure. The three senses—somatic, psychic and pneumatic—constitute this structure, and, in turn, convey Scripture's own internal interpretive guide. For Origen, the Holy Spirit designed Scripture according to these three senses in order to bring believers to salvation. He has designed and applied an exegetical method that he believes reflects Scripture's own pedagogy for salvation. Origen describes a threefold method of interpretation *because* he observes a threefold structure in Scripture.

Because Origen views the three senses as Scripture's own map of instruction for the exegete, he tends to stress in his psychic readings the central role of Scripture in facilitating the hearer's temporal exposure to Christ and growth in virtue. This is because the messages and interrelationships of the separate senses direct the hearer toward the right internal order of his body, soul and spirit. Since, for Origen, the Holy Spirit transmits Scripture for the salvation of the human person and its message is Christ's word, meditation on Scripture enables interaction with the Holy Spirit and Christ. Exposure to the Holy Spirit and Christ inevitably strengthens the leadership of the human person's own spirit over his soul and body. The person learns from the messages of the three senses to follow (as well as how to follow) the spirit and cause the body to resist enslavement by fleshly tendencies.[113] Scripture's body, soul and spirit—the somatic, psychic and pneumatic senses—interrelate in a way that models the person's right internal order. The somatic and psychic senses—and most fully the psychic sense—serve the pneumatic sense, by offering a temporal means to increasingly understand and prepare for its eternal truths. Origen's anthropology, then, keeps coming to mind (and is explicit in *Hom. Gen.* 12 and *Hom. Lev.* 1) through the psychic call to spend time with Scripture, since the interrelationship between the senses' messages points to the human person's right internal order.

---

[113] See the discussion regarding Origen's anthropology in the second half of chapter 2.

CHAPTER FIVE

THE TEMPORAL MEANS TO THE ETERNAL HOPE

The texts examined in the prior chapter established the following points about the interrelationship between the two higher senses. First, for Origen the psychic sense is more than a Philonic or philosophical natural moral sense. Origen presents this call to virtue as a call to grow like Christ, through exposure to Scripture, and toward union with him. As with the pneumatic sense, the defining reference of the psychic sense is Christ.[1] Second, the two higher senses are distinct and yet related. Using Origen's own words, their relationship is a purposeful and productive "mingling"[2] that facilitates the hearer's advancement toward salvation. Third, Origen effects this fruitful mingling by presenting the psychic sense as the temporal means of pursuing the eternal hope that the pneumatic sense conveys.

To explore the interrelationship between the psychic and pneumatic senses in greater depth, this chapter analyzes Book 1 of Origen's *Commentary on the Song of Songs*. Not only does this work establish that Origen applies and relates the two separate pneumatic and psychic senses in the wisdom literature (in addition to the legal and historical, or Pentateuchal, books) of the Bible[3] and within the commentary (in

---

[1] Building upon Young's notion of "reference," this work shows that Origen not only shifts the reference of his textual reading to Christ when setting forth a pneumatic meaning, but he also makes imitation of Christ the essential reference for the psychic sense. See Young, *Biblical Exegesis*, generally. As the following reading of *Comm. Cant.* 1 will show, the reference of the psychic sense can be none other than Christ since Christ is, in fact, equal to all the virtues.

[2] The Latin term *insertum*, meaning "mingled," occurs in Rufinus' Latin translation of Origen's *Hom. Gen.* 2.6, where Origen explains that some biblical passages contain no edifying literal meaning but only the two moral and mystical, or spiritual, meanings. In that text, Origen refers to the two higher senses as *duplicis . . . sensum expositionis insertum*, or the "mingled meaning of the double explanation." This phrase and the overall passage were reviewed near the end of chapter 3. As I explained there, as well as demonstrated in chapter 4 and will explore further in this chapter, Origen treats the two higher senses in theory and practice as separate and yet related, or "mingled."

[3] The best practical examples for this overall work came from Origen's treatments of Old Testament texts. The best examples were those where Origen presented full readings of both higher senses for the same biblical passage using terminology that made explicit his transition from one reading to the other. Still,

addition to the homiletic) format.[4] It also substantiates and builds upon the above insights through a complex, multi-layered application of psychic and pneumatic readings especially designed to address Origen's audience of other church leaders (preachers and teachers) like himself. For this text, his audience members, individually, are "perfected" souls, because they have begun to grasp pneumatic meanings in Scripture. Collectively, they represent the church, for they are its "squared planks" which hold together the aggregate faithful (as discussed in *Hom. Gen.* 2 on the ark).[5]

To this audience, Origen presents a psychic reading that reaches beyond a simple call to cultivate virtues in oneself. It urges his audience members, as leaders, to help their congregations of less advanced believers to recognize and understand pneumatic meanings in Scripture. The ability of church leaders to grasp pneumatic meanings yields a continuing duty to lead others to the same privilege. Helping others becomes for the "perfected" persons in the church a means to a more perfect imitation of Christ during this life.

The psychic sense, then, though "moral" in character, is more accurately described as the call to "temporal" imitation of Christ, facilitated by an ever-enriching exposure to him in the pneumatic sense. This psychic sense, in addition to the pneumatic sense, continues to edify even the advanced hearer throughout this life. For this reason, the cyclically reinforcing interrelationship between these

---

we learned in chapter 2 that Origen speaks broadly about his threefold theory in *Princ.* 4.2, making explicit its relevance to New Testament texts, both gospels and epistles, as well as the variety of Old Testament texts. With the basic observations of this work set forth and thus the means established for identifying the separate senses, future studies can search for applications of one or both of the two higher senses in Origen's works on the New Testament, as well as other types of Old Testament, texts—even where explicit transitions between readings are lacking. Future studies also can explore the various ways in which Origen plays out their interrelation, as well as the independent edification of each sense, within the varied contexts of these biblical genres. For direction, see the footnote at the beginning of chapter 4, which lists various other texts in Origen's works where he at least describes, if he does not fully treat or explicitly label, psychic and pneumatic readings for the same biblical passages.

[4] As the compiled information and time chart at the end of the Introduction reflect, Origen likely wrote *Comm. Cant.* 1 after (if not during) the time period in which he delivered the transcribed homilies. Comparing the findings of this chapter with those of chapters 3 and 4, Origen seems to have applied the same standards of exegesis, that is, the same conception of the three senses, to both his homilies and this commentary.

[5] See the analysis of the pneumatic reading of *Hom. Gen.* 2 at the beginning of chapter 4.

two nonliteral senses emerges as the central focus of Origen's exegetical effort to prepare Scripture's hearers for salvation.

I. *An Overview of Comm. Cant. 1: Two Brides and Bridegrooms*

In *Comm. Cant.* 1,[6] Origen interprets Cant. 1:2–4, which records a Bride's initial expressions of longing and love for her Bridegroom, as well as exclamations by the Bride's companions, the maidens. He recites the verses (extant in Rufinus' Latin) as follows, with the added dividers marking the four portions of the passage that he treats separately:

> [2]Let Him kiss me with the kisses of His mouth./For Your breasts are better than wine. [3] The fragrance of Your ointments is above all spices. Your name is as ointment emptied out./Therefore have the maidens loved You, [4] have they drawn You. We will run after You into the fragrance of Your ointments./The King has brought me into His chamber. Let us rejoice and be glad in You. We will love Your breasts more than wine. Equity has loved You.[7]

He reads the four divided portions literally in the following ways: First, the Bride, longing for the Bridegroom's presence and kisses, prays that God bring him to her. Second, the Bride realizes that the Bridegroom already stands before her giving her kisses. Third, the Bride, though admitted into the Bridegroom's presence, condescends to run with the maidens in order to help them become worthy also to share the honor of his presence. Fourth, the Bride, after having run some distance with the maidens, finds herself within the

---

[6] Extant are a prologue, three intact books and a substantial portion of a fourth book of Origen's Commentary on the Song of Songs, in the Latin by Rufinus. I employ an English translation of treated passages from the Commentary within the text of this work and provide the corresponding Latin in footnote. For the English, I employ Lawson, *Origen: The Song of Songs Commentary* (ACW 26); and for the Latin, Luc Brésard, Henri Crouzel, and Marcel Borret, trans. and eds., *Origène: Commentaire sur le Cantique des Cantiques* (vol. 1; SC 375, Paris: Cerf, 1991).

[7] Cant. 1:2–4 (ACW 26:58, 62, 70, 74, 84). The Latin by Rufinus reads: Osculetur me ab osculis oris sui, quia bona sunt ubera tua super vinum, / et odor unguentorum tuorum super omnia aromata. Unguentum exinanitum nomen tuum. / Propterea iuvenculae [adulescentulae] dilexerunt te, traxerunt te; post te in odorem unguentorum tuorum curremus. Introduxit me rex in cubiculum suum; exsultemus et iucundemur in te. Diligemus ubera tua super vinum. Aequitas dilexit te (ACW 26:323; SC 375: 176, 190, 220, 242, 250, 252). The numbering of the verses within this translation corresponds with those in the RSV.

Bridegroom's chamber, while the maidens, seeing this honor bestowed upon her, increasingly long for the same achievement.

For each portion, Origen interprets the Bride, Bridegroom and maidens in two different ways: on the one hand, as the church, Incarnate Christ and young churches in the world and, on the other hand, as the individual, "perfected" soul, the Word of God and young souls who are not yet perfected. In the latter scenario, the perfected soul is one who has grown in the virtues enough to be able to grasp all three senses of Scripture. In contrast, the young, maiden souls are those not yet proficient in gleaning edification from Scripture's highest, pneumatic truths. The analysis below will explore how Origen develops the two interpretations as separate pneumatic readings (about the church, Christ and young churches) and then psychic readings (about the perfected soul, the Word of God and young souls) for each segment, as well as how they work together for the spiritual transformation of his audience.[8]

II. *The Unifying Theme of Love*

Before treating each of the four segments, Origen explains that the whole biblical text promotes love for God.[9] He states that "passionate love" for God is natural to humans: the "only laudable love" is that which is "found first in God" and then "implanted in the human soul by the Creator's kindness" so that the soul possesses the "power" to "direct" this love back "to God."[10] Origen considers this theme

---

[8] R. P. Lawson employs, as I will, the labels "pneumatic" and "psychic" when describing Origen's two representations of the Bride as church and soul in this commentary ("Introduction," *Origen: The Song of Songs Commentary*; ACW 26:10). Still, no one as yet has offered a treatment of this text that seeks the distinction and inter-relationship between these pneumatic and psychic readings.

[9] *Comm. Cant.* Prol. 2; "Before we come to consider the things that are written in this book . . . it seems to me necessary to say a few things first about love itself, which is the main theme of this Scripture . . ." (ACW 26:23); Igitur necessarium mihi videtur, antequam ad ea quae in hoc libello scripta sunt discutienda veniamus, de amore prius ipso, qui est scripturae huius causa praecipua, pauca disserere . . . (SC [Prol. 1.8] 375:86).

[10] *Comm. Cant.* Prol. 2 (ACW 26:36); Sed et hoc scire oportet quod impossibile est ut non semper humana natura aliquid amet. . . . Verum nonnulli hunc amoris affectum, qui animae rationabili insitus est beneficio conditoris. . . . Si enim, quod bonum est, hoc et probabile est, bonum autem proprie non erga usus corporeos, sed in Deo primum et in virtutibus animi intelligitur, consequenter ergo solus ille

of love for God to be the "spiritual intent"[11] of the whole biblical passage. The task of the exegete is to draw out this theme fully for his audience.

Origen announces that he will bring out this theme of love through two different figurative readings of the biblical text:

> [W]e shall get from it [this book—*The Song of Songs*] according to our powers a simple record of events[,] [a]nd the spiritual interpretation too, [for which] the appellations of Bride and Bridegroom denote either the Church in her relation to Christ, or the soul in her union with the Word of God.[12]

Origen promises a "spiritual interpretation" of the biblical passage that consists of two distinct readings. The term *spiritalis*, translated here as "spiritual," is identical to Rufinus' Latin translation of πνευματικόν for the pneumatic sense in *Princ.* 4. However, here, Origen applies it generally to two different figurative readings in contrast to the text's literal, "simple record of events." One "spiritual" reading relates the Bride and Bridegroom to the church (*ecclesia*) and Christ, while the other relates them to the soul (*anima*) and Word of God. These two spiritual readings, taken together, facilitate the text's overall theme of love for God.

Throughout his exegesis of this biblical text, Origen develops the idea that the church and individual soul share the same *telos*: love for God manifested in union with Him. Here he articulates this unifying theme:

> The Scripture before us . . . speaks of this love with which the blessed soul is kindled and inflamed towards the Word of God; it sings by the Spirit the song of the marriage whereby the Church is joined and allied to Christ the heavenly Bridegroom, desiring to be united to Him. . . .[13]

Both the church and the individual soul naturally possess a passionate love for God and find fulfillment only in union with God.

---

amor probabilis est qui Deo et virtutibus animi coaptatur (SC [Prol. 2.39–40] 375: 118, 120).

[11] *Comm. Cant.* Prol. 2; (ACW 26:24); *spiritaliter* (SC [Prol. 2.3] 375:92).

[12] *Comm. Cant.* 1.1; (ACW 26:58); Haec ergo erit totius libelli species, et secundum hanc pro viribus historica a nobis aptabitur expositio. Spiritalis vero intelligentia, . . . vel de ecclesia ad Christum sub sponsae vel sponsi titulo vel de animae cum Verbo Dei coniunctione dirigitur (SC [1.1.2] 375:176).

[13] *Comm. Cant.* Prol. 2 (ACW 26:38); Hunc . . . amorem loquitur praesens scriptura, quo erga Verbum Dei anima beata uritur et inflammatur, et istud epithalamii carmen per Spiritum canit, quo ecclesia sponso caelesti Christo coniungitur ac sociatur, desiderans misceri ei (SC [Prol. 2.46] 375:122).

However, as Origen's exegesis will reveal, the paths to this telos are different, though complementary, for each type of Bride: the church enjoys union with Christ as a reward for faithfully guarding and passing on the teachings that he has given to her, while the individual soul enjoys an intimate union with the Word of God, in whose image she was made, as a reward for faithfully submitting to these teachings' promptings to grow in virtue and become like Christ and teach others to do the same.

As stated above, the individual soul addressed throughout this work is a "perfected" soul, one who is able to grasp at least some pneumatic meanings in Scripture. Origen assumes that the audience for this commentary can grasp pneumatic meanings and, thus, are "perfected" souls—like himself. Given the focus of Book 1 on the perfected soul's duty to teach others, it becomes clear that Origen addresses this exegesis to other church leaders like himself. The psychic readings address them individually as perfected souls and the pneumatic readings address them collectively as the church itself.

At the end of *Comm. Cant.* 1, Origen unites both sets of spiritual (pneumatic and psychic) interpretations to convey that the perfected soul reaches salvation through teaching others. He places the reading of the Bride as the individual soul within the context of the Bride as the church so as to emphasize the perfected believer's duties as a leader of the faithful. These duties involve both preaching the Word to other souls *and* increasing one's own intimacy with God. In the first instance, the perfected soul follows Origen's lead as an exegete by bringing the two higher senses to his own congregation of believers, and, in the second, the perfected soul provides an example of growth in perfection and the unfolding enjoyment of its fruits.[14] This fruitful union of the two spiritual interpretations represents the pinnacle of Origen's exegetical practice, reflecting the height of his method's intended effectiveness at facilitating the spiritual transformation of his audience that leads to salvation.

---

[14] In a more general way, Crouzel also observes an interrelationship between the two readings of "Bride" in *Comm. Cant.* He finds that the two "ideas . . . [of] the Church as Bride . . . [and] the soul as bride . . ." are "complementary," stressing that "salvation is both personal and ecclesial." He observes that "the faithful soul is bride of Christ because she forms part of the Church which is the Bride; and the more she behaves as a bride in the perfection of her Christian life, the more the Church is the Bride" (*Origen*, 77).

III. *The Bride Awaits the Bridegroom*

Origen offers no somatic, or *edifying* literal, sense of this text, since, as he suggests in the Prologue, this text arguably lacks this first type of meaning. In fact, a literal interpretation of the type of passionate love portrayed here, he warns, is likely to incite fleshly passions within those who are immature of faith.[15] Origen, then, merely outlines the plot and characters in each passage so as to draw figuratively on the details. Origen first describes the Bride's disposition when she begs to receive the Bridegroom's kisses: "Let Him kiss me with the kisses of His mouth."

> Reading it as a simple story, then, we see a bride . . . having received for her betrothal and by way of dowry most fitting gifts from a most noble bridegroom; but, because the bridegroom delays his coming for so long, she, grieved with longing for his love . . ., seeing that she can neither be quit of her love, nor yet achieve what she desires, [she] betakes herself to prayer and makes supplication to God, whom she knows to be her Bridegroom's Father. After this manner, then, let us consider her . . . aflame with longing for her Spouse, vexed by the inward wound of love, pouring out her prayer to God . . . and saying concerning her Spouse: "Let Him kiss me with the kisses of His mouth." This is the content of the actual story, presented in dramatic form.[16]

---

[15] The English text reads: (*Comm. Cant.* Prol. 1 referring to Heb. 5:12 and 1 Pet. 2:2; ACW 26:22): ". . . to those who are at the stage of infancy and childhood in their interior life—to those, that is to say, who are being nourished with milk in Christ, not with strong meat, and are only beginning *to desire the rational milk without guile*—it is not given to grasp the meaning of these sayings." The Latin text reads: ita nec ad capienda quidem verba haec parvula et infantilis interioris hominis aetas admittitur, illorum scilicet qui *lacte* in Christo aluntur *non cibo forti*, et qui nunc primum *rationabile et sine dolo lac concupiscunt* (SC [Prol. 1.4] 375: 82). Origen further explains that a babe in the faith may experience neither gain nor harm from hearing this biblical text, but, if this person lives in a fleshly way, he will surely read this drama of passionate love as an endorsement to indulge his own lustful desires. Thus, Origen suggests that no edifying somatic reading exists here, but it in fact is an example of biblical text that lacks a somatic meaning so as to urge on those who are capable to grasp figurative understandings of passionate human love. The literal readings that Origen sets forth here are merely dramatic renditions of the text to which he intends to apply figurative readings that will edify his listeners. (See chapter 2's explanation of the somatic sense, specifically why the "literal" reading of the text is not the same as the "somatic" meaning of the text.)

[16] *Comm. Cant.* 1.1 (quoting Cant. 1:2*a*; ACW 26:58–59); Introducatur ergo nunc per historiae speciem sponsa quaedam, quae susceperit quaedam sponsaliorum et dotis titulo dignissima munera ab sponso nobilissimo, sed plurimo tempore moram faciente sponso, sollicitari eam desiderio amoris eius, . . . Quae, quoniam differri amorem suum nec adipisci se posse quod desiderat, videt, convertat se ad orationem

Origen stresses the dramatic state of the Bride as she waits for the Bridegroom. She longs for his kisses, hardly able to contain her passion. The "betrothal gifts" no longer satisfy her as a substitute for his presence. She is so desperate to be with him that she prays to God for the Bridegroom's arrival. She knows that God is the Father of this Bridegroom and that it is within His power to bring the Bridegroom to her. It is a "simple" reading because it does not explain why or how one properly develops such depth of love. Still, even in this otherwise straightforward narration, Origen reveals that, figuratively, the Father of the Bridegroom is God. With the characters and plot established, Origen next provides his audience with two separate figurative interpretations for their edification.

A. *The Pneumatic Reading: The Church Awaits Christ*

Like the homiletic examples examined in the previous chapter, Origen offers each pneumatic reading first followed by the separate but related psychic reading. In his Latin translation, Rufinus labels this first figurative reading as the "interior meaning *(interior intellectus)*" of the Bride's impatient and burning love for the Bridegroom. In this reading, Origen identifies the Bride with the church and the Bridegroom with Christ:

> But let us see if the interior meaning also can be fittingly supplied along these lines. Let it be the Church who longs for union with Christ; but the Church . . . is the whole assembly of the saints. So it must be the Church as a corporate personality who speaks and says: 'I am sated with the gifts which I received as betrothal presents or as dowry before my marriage. For of old, while I was being prepared for my wedding with the King's Son and the Firstborn of all creation, His holy angels . . . [brought] the Law as a betrothal gift. . . . [A]lso . . . [the] prophetic voice proclaimed to me about His coming; filled with the Holy Spirit, they foretold His countless acts of power and His mighty works. His beauty also they described, His charm and gentleness, that I might be inflamed beyond all bearing with the love of Him by all these things.[17]

---

et supplicet Deo, sciens eum Patrem esse sponsi sui. Consideremus ergo eam . . . aestuantem vero desiderio sponsi et interno vulnere amoris agitatam, orationem . . . fundere ad Deum et dicere de sponso suo: *Osculetur me ab osculis oris sui.* Haec sunt quae dramatis in modum composita historica continet explanatio (SC [1.1.3–4] 375:178).

[17] *Comm. Cant.* 1.1 (referring to 1 Cor. 14:23, Matt. 22:1–4, Rev. 19:6–9 and Col. 1:15; ACW 26:59–60); Interior vero intellectus videamus si hoc modo poterit

Though the Latin translation does not employ the equivalent term of πνευματικόν, *spiritalis*, this interior meaning focuses on Christ and the church. Such references resemble Origen's theoretical characterization of the pneumatic sense, which conveys the mysteries of God fulfilled in Christ and in the church.[18]

Origen defines the church as "the whole assembly of the saints" and the "corporate personality," which we may understand as the aggregate faithful. He identifies this church specifically with the community of God's faithful *before* the Incarnation. This church became impatient with her betrothal gifts, the Law and the Prophets. The Law offered a foretaste of Christ's teachings, and the Prophets foretold his coming. In response, the church's longing for Christ's direct teaching and actual presence grew stronger over time: she grew more and more "inflamed" with "long[ing] for union with Christ."

This pre-Incarnational church prayed to God the Father that he might bring Christ to her so that she could experience the "kisses of His mouth," his direct teachings:

> But, since the age is almost ended and His own presence is not granted me, . . . I pour out my petition to You, the Father of my Spouse, . . . to have compassion at last upon my love, and to send Him, that He may no longer speak to me only by His servants the angels and the prophets, but may come Himself, directly, and kiss me with the kisses of His mouth—that is to say, may pour the words of His mouth into mine, that I may hear Him speak Himself, and see Him teaching.[19]

---

competenter aptari. Ecclesia sit desiderans Christo coniungi; ecclesiam autem coetum omnium adverte sanctorum. Haec ergo ecclesia sit quasi omnium una persona, quae loquatur et dicat: omnia habeo, repleta sum muneribus quae sponsaliorum vel dotis titulo ante nuptias sumpsi. Dudum enim cum praepararer ad coniugium filii regis et *primogeniti omnis creaturae*, obsecuti sunt et ministraverunt mihi angeli sancti eius deferentes ad me legem sponsalis muneris loco . . . [E]tiam . . . denuntiaverunt mihi propheticis vocibus de adventu eius, et de innumeris virtutibus operibusque eius immensis repleti sancto Spiritu praedicaverunt. Pulchritudinem quoque eius et speciem ac mansuetudinem descripserunt, ita ut ex omnibus his ad amorem eius intolerabiliter inflammarer (FC [1.1.5–6] 375:178, 180).

[18] See *Hom. Gen.* 2 on the ark and the discussion of exegetical theory in this homily in chapter 3, as well as *Princ.* 4.2.6 and the discussion of Origen's theoretical definition for the pneumatic sense in chapter 2.

[19] *Comm. Cant.* 1.1 (quoting Cant. 1:2a; ACW 26:60); Sed quoniam saeculum iam paene finitum est et ipsius quidem praesentia non datur mihi, . . . propter hoc ad te Patrem sponsi mei precem fundo et obsecro, ut tandem miseratus amorem meum mittas eum, ut iam non mihi per ministros suos angelos dumtaxat et prophetas loquatur, sed ipse per semet ipsum veniat et *osculetur me ab osculis oris sui*, verba scilicet in os meum sui oris infundat, ipsum audiam loquentem, ipsum videam docentem (SC [1.1.7] 375:180, 182).

This Bride church prayed to God to have mercy on her longing, because Christ's absence caused her pain that could only be relieved by his arrival. She no longer wanted the servants, angels and prophets who had been coming to her on his behalf. She could only be satisfied by him. She asked to receive "the words of His mouth" directly, that Christ would come and "pour" his "teaching" from his mouth directly into her mouth.

By presenting this unsatisfied state of the pre-Incarnational Bride church to his audience of church leaders, Origen places them within the long history of God's faithful on earth. They are part of that church that spans human history. God's plan of salvation involves a church that loved Christ even before Christ's descent to human form and, thus, was ripe for receiving his direct teachings. This pneumatic reading causes the church leaders in Origen's audience to acknowledge that in the historical event of the Incarnation God graciously provided the means of fulfilling the church's burning desire for Christ's presence, which, in turn, should reassure them that God also will fulfill their present longing for Christ's return.

B. *The Psychic Reading: The Soul Awaits the Word of God*

Having established for his audience of church leaders the pneumatic understanding that they, as the church, are reassured of Christ's return in the future, Origen offers a reading of the Bride as the individual soul. He introduces it as "the third point in our exposition" in which "[we] bring in the soul." It is a third reading, coming after the simple, literal explanation of a Bride's burning love and the interior, pneumatic reading of that Bride as the pre-Incarnational church. This third reading is the other "spiritual interpretation" about which Origen spoke in the Prologue to *Comm. Cant.* and at the beginning of Book 1. Although in his Latin translation Rufinus does not employ his usual term for the psychic sense, *moralis*, the text does mention as its central focus *anima*, or the soul, which is consistent with Origen's label for and descriptions of the middle, psychic sense in *Princ.* 4 and his other theoretical discussions.

Origen's practice of treating first the pneumatic sense of the text and then the psychic meaning is now familiar to us. Now that his audience members have in mind the church's longing for Christ, he asks each member, as an individual believer, to turn inward and recognize the natural longing of his soul for the Word of God:

> As the third point in our exposition, let us bring in the soul whose only desire is to be united to the Word of God and to be in fellowship with Him, and to enter into the mysteries of His wisdom and knowledge as into the chambers of her heavenly Bridegroom. . . . [J]ust as the Church's dowry was the volumes of the Law and the Prophets, so let us regard natural law and reason and free will as the soul's betrothal gifts. . . . But, since she does not find in these the full and perfect satisfaction of her desire and love, let her pray that her pure and virginal mind may be enlightened by the illumination and the visitation of the Word of God Himself. For, when her mind is filled with divine perception and understanding without the agency of human or angelic ministration, then she may believe she has received the kisses of the Word of God Himself.[20]

As the church before the Incarnation longed for union with Christ, so the individual soul yearns "to be united to the Word of God." Yet, it is the soul who has a "pure and virginal mind" that desires this union with the Word of God. Origen speaks here, then, of the Bride soul—one who is single-minded in her devotion toward God and purified from things that distract, such as sin. Origen expects his audience of church leaders to identify with this type of soul, a soul advanced in virtue and appropriately motivated toward God, but, of course, still seeking fuller union with Him.

This soul, Origen explains, longs to "enter into the mysteries of His wisdom and knowledge," which Origen likens to "the chambers of her heavenly Bridegroom." As the church, before Christ's condescension into human form, was given the Law and Prophets as a temporary substitute for his direct teachings, the soul has been given the faculties of "natural law and reason and free will" as temporary substitutes for the "illumination" and "understanding" that the Word of God can bestow directly upon her. As the church grew tired of the precursor gifts, so does the soul. This advanced soul longs for the direct kisses of the Word of God, which are "divine perception and understanding" that come to the mind "without . . . human or angelic" mediation.

---

[20] *Comm. Cant.* 1.1 (ACW 26:60–61); Tertio vero expositionis loco introducamus animam, cuius omne studium sit coniungi et consociari Verbo Dei et intra mysteria sapientiae eius ac scientiae veluti sponsi caelestis thalamos intrare . . . Sicut enim ecclesiae dos fuit legis et prophetarum volumina, ita huic lex naturae et rationabilis sensus ac libertas arbitrii dotalia munera deputentur. . . . Sed quoniam in his non est ei plena et perfecta desiderii sui et amoris expletio, deprecetur ut mens eius pura et virginalis ipsius Verbi Dei illuminationibus ac visitationibus illustretur. Cum enim nullo hominis vel angeli ministerio divinis sensibus et intellectibus mens repletur, tunc oscula ipsius Verbi Dei suscepisse se credat. (SC [1.1.9–10] 375:182).

Origen now makes explicit his identification of the Bride as the "perfected soul," pointing out the plural form of "kisses" and suggesting that each illumination of the mind directly received is a kiss bestowed by the Word of God upon such a soul:

> Moreover, the plural, "kisses," is used in order that we may understand that the lighting up of every obscure meaning is a kiss of the Word of God bestowed on the perfected soul. . . . And let us understand that by the "mouth" of the Bridegroom is meant the power by which He enlightens the mind and, as by some word of love addressed to her—if so she deserve to experience the presence of power so great—makes plain whatever is unknown and dark to her. And this is the truer, closer, holier kiss, which is said to be granted by the Bridegroom—Word of God to the Bride—that is to say, to the pure and perfect soul. . . .[21]

For the soul a kiss from the Word of God is the "lighting up of [an] obscure meaning." Whenever the Word of God "enlightens the mind" of the soul, "mak[ing] plain whatever is unknown and dark to her," he gives her a kiss directly. He bestows such direct kisses upon—enlightens or illuminates with knowledge—only a "pure and perfect soul." The more kisses, or insights into the mysteries of the Word's own wisdom and knowledge, that the soul enjoys, the more "perfect" she becomes. Thus, a perfected soul can become still more perfect in understanding the Word's mysteries and so increase her intimacy with him.

To this end, Origen urges his audience of perfected souls to pray that God will help them to understand the direct teachings of His Word that still elude them, that is, receive more of the Word's own kisses:

> As often, therefore, as we find some problem pertaining to the divine teachings and meanings revealed in our heart without instructors' help, so often may we believe that kisses have been given to us by the Bridegroom—Word of God. But, when we seek the meaning of something of this sort and cannot find it, then let us make this prayer our

---

[21] *Comm. Cant.* 1.1 (ACW 26:61–62); Ideo autem et pluraliter oscula posuit, ut intelligamus uniuscuiusque obscuri sensus illuminationem osculum esse Verbi Dei ad animam perfectam delatum. . . . Os autem sponsi intelligamus virtutem dici qua illuminat mentem, et velut sermone quodam amoris ad eam facto, si tamen capere mereatur tantae virtutis praesentiam, incognita quaeque sibi et obscura manifestat, et hoc est verius propiusque et sanctius osculum, quod ab sponso Dei Verbo porrigi dicitur sponsae, purae scilicet animae ac perfectae (SC [1.1.12–13] 375:184).

own and beg from God the visitation of His Word, saying: "Let Him kiss me with the kisses of His mouth." For the Father knows each single soul's capacity and understands the right time for a soul to receive the kisses of the Word in lights and insights of this sort.[22]

If a believer understands "divine teachings and meanings" "without instructors' help," that is, without human or angelic intervention, then he has received *direct* kisses from the Word of God. Origen encourages every member of his audience to pray to God for such direct enlightenment concerning divine truths—implicitly, the Word of God's wisdom hidden in Scripture—that he still does not understand. By such a prayer, the believer requests the "visitation of His Word" upon his soul. God answers such prayers in the most beneficial way for each petitioner, for God knows the "capacity" of each soul and the "right time" for her to grasp each divine truth. Thus, Origen assures his audience of church leaders that God will lead their perfected souls into increasing perfection and intimacy with the Word of God at the pace and by the means appropriate to each of them.

In this first set of pneumatic and psychic readings Origen encourages his audience of church leaders to identify with each type of Bride. In one respect, they are the church that once longed for Christ's arrival and now longs for Christ's return. In the other respect, they are the perfected souls who long for increased intimacy with the Word of God. They are hungry for God, and, taking the two readings together, they are assured that God will faithfully satisfy them. Not only can the church be assured of Christ's return, but the individual, perfected soul can be assured that God will answer her pleas for increased understanding of divine truths. By placing the pneumatic reading of the church first, Origen establishes the context of the assurance of God's faithfulness and places the psychic reading within this context: the individual soul may trust that the Word of God *will* satisfy her longings for intimacy just as the Incarnation satisfied the church's longing for Christ. Yet, in the meantime, they

---

[22] *Comm. Cant.* 1.1 (quoting Cant. 1:2*a*; ACW 26:62); Quotiens ergo in corde nostro aliquid quod de divinis dogmatibus et sensibus quaeritur, absque monitoribus invenimus, totiens oscula nobis data esse ab sponso Dei Verbo credamus. Ubi vero quaerentes aliquid de divinis sensibus invenire non possumus, tunc affectu orationis huius assumpto petamus a Deo visitationem Verbi eius, et dicamus: *Osculetur me ab osculis oris sui*. Scit autem Pater uniuscuiusque animae capacitatem, et novit in tempore cui animae quae oscula Verbi porrigere in intellectibus dumtaxat et sensibus debeat (SC [1.1.14–15] 375:184, 186).

208 CHAPTER FIVE

must continue to strive for deeper understandings of God's truths in
Scripture with the trust that God will grant them the desired increase
in intimacy with God's Word.[23]

IV. *The Bride Finds Herself in the Bridegroom's Presence*

Developing a theme of love rewarded and longing satisfied with
regard to the church and the soul, Origen explains the Bride's excla-
mation of praise about the Bridegroom's "breasts" and "the fragrance
of [his] ointments":

> While she is thus praying to the Father . . . "Let Him kiss me with the
> kisses of His mouth," . . . even as she began to utter those words, the
> Bridegroom was present and standing by her as she prayed, and . . . He
> revealed His breasts to her, and appeared as Himself anointed with
> splendid ointments, possessed of fragrance such as befits a Spouse. The
> Bride, having seen that He, for whose coming she was praying, was
> already present, and that even as she spoke He offered her the thing
> for which she asked, and that the kisses that she had demanded had
> been given her, is rendered thereby glad indeed; and, moved deeply
> by the beauty of His breasts and by the fragrant odor of Himself, she
> alters the form of her prayer . . . [and] now continues, speaking to the
> Bridegroom's present Self: "Your breasts are better than wine, and the
> fragrance of Your ointments is above all spices."[24]

The Bride's perspective and disposition have now changed. While
praying to God for the kisses of her Bridegroom, she realizes that
the one for whom she yearns stands directly in front of her. He
"reveals His breasts to her," and, because he is "anointed with splen-
did ointments," he emits a fragrance that she cannot ignore. She
recognizes that he is "already present" and has been kissing her even
as she was praying. The Bride turns from plea to praise, marveling

---

[23] Later in this exegesis, Origen will explain that to receive the Word's or Christ's
kisses, or direct teaching, is to grow in understanding truths conveyed by the pneumatic sense in Scripture.

[24] *Comm. Cant.* 1.2 (quoting Cant. 1.2*a* and 1.2*b*–3*a*; ACW 26:63); Dumque haec
orat ad Patrem: . . . *Osculetur me ab osculis oris sui,* . . . in hoc principio sermonis affuisse
sponsus et oranti ei adstitisse ac revelasse ubera sua, ipsumque sponsum unguentis
magnificis et quibus fraglare sponsum decebat constitisse delibutum. Sponsa vero,
ubi adesse vidit eum pro quo orabat ut adesset, et adhuc loquenti sibi praestitum
quod orabat, ac data sibi ab ipso oscula quae poposcerat, laeta pro hoc reddita, et
decore uberum ac fraglantiae ipsius odore permota, propositae orationis sermonem
convertit . . . ad praesentem iam sponsum loquens: *Bona ubera tua super vinum, et odor
unguentorum tuorum super omnia aromata* (SC [1.2.1–2] 375:190, 192).

that his "breasts are better than wine" and the "fragrance of [his] ointments is above all spices."

A. *The Pneumatic Reading: The Church Finds Christ Present*

Origen first interprets the Bride as the church who has received the joy of the Incarnation and thus begun to receive Christ's teachings directly. Again, Origen refers to this reading as the "interior meaning (*intellectus interior*)" of the text,[25] and, although he does not mention the word "church" here, he carries over the same concepts and themes from the previous pneumatic reading, which expressly applied to the church.

Origen again mentions the church's betrothal gifts of the Law and Prophets, when he explains how the Bride compares the Bridegroom's breasts to wine:

> By wine is meant the ordinances and teachings which the Bride had been wont to receive through the Law and Prophets before the Bridegroom came.... So, realizing now that the instructions and the knowledge that are found in the Bridegroom are of high eminence, and that a much more perfect teaching than that of the ancients issues from His breasts, she says: "Your breasts are better than wine." ... The breasts of the Bridegroom ... are good, because treasures of wisdom and knowledge are hidden in Him; and these, when they have been opened and revealed to the eyes of the Bride, will seem to her much more excellent than was that wine of the Law and the teaching of the Prophets, which she had before.[26]

Origen interprets the wine as the "ordinances and teachings" found in "the Law and Prophets," which were the betrothal gifts to the church. Upon Christ's Incarnation, the Bride church could enjoy his breasts—his direct revelation—which hold the "treasures of wisdom and knowledge ... hidden in Him." These "issues from his breasts" constitute "a much more perfect teaching" and, thus, in all ways are

---

[25] *Comm. Cant.* 1.2 (ACW 26:63); Nunc vero, quid intellectus interior habeat, requiramus (SC [1.2.2] 375:192).

[26] *Comm. Cant.* 1.2 (referring to Matt. 7:12, quoting Cant. 1:2b, and referring to Col 2:3; ACW 26:65, 69); Vinum autem illa intelligenda sunt dogmata et doctrinae, quae per *legem et prophetas* ante adventum sponsi sumere sponsa consueverat.... Videns ergo nunc multam esse eminentiam dogmatum et scientiae apud sponsum et longe ex eo perfectiorem quam fuit apud antiquos emanare doctrinam, dicit: *Bona sunt ubera tua super vinum....* Bona sunt ... ubera sponsi; *thesauri* enim sunt *sapientiae et scientiae in eo absconditi*, qui cum aperti et revelati fuerint oculis sponsae, multo praestantiores ei videbuntur quam fuit prius illud vinum legis et doctrina prophetica (SC [1.2.8–9, 22] 375:196, 204).

"more excellent" than the wine of the Law and Prophets. Likely drawing upon Paul's notion of milk as the food of babes in the faith,[27] here Origen implicitly relates the truths provided directly from Christ's breasts to mother's milk. By this, Origen suggests to his audience that Christ's truths are his own essence, and he nourishes his children, those who are ready, with no external substitute.[28]

Now, Origen analyzes the Bride church's praise for the "fragrance" of Christ's "ointments":

> The Bridegroom has . . . certain ointments also, and with their fragrance the Bride has been delighted; so she says: "The fragrance of Your ointments is above all spices." . . . The Bride had the use and the knowledge of spices—that is, of the words of the Law and the Prophets, by which, though only to a moderate extent, she was instructed and practiced in the service of God before the Bridegroom came, she being then yet a little child and under tutors . . . for . . . *the Law was our pedagogue to Christ.* All these things, then, were the spices with which . . . she was nourished and made ready for her Spouse. *But when the fullness of the time was come,* and the Bride was grown up, and the Father had *sent His Only-begotten Son into this world,* . . . then, having perceived the fragrance of the divine ointment and realizing that all the spices she employed before are vastly inferior when set beside the sweetness of this new and heavenly ointment, she says: "The fragrance of Your ointments is above all spices."[29]

Origen interprets the "spices" as the words that the Law and Prophets spoke to the church about Christ before the Incarnation, indicating his divinity and holiness. Now that Christ has come to earth and stands before his Bride church, she recognizes the "fragrance" of his

---

[27] See 1 Cor. 3:1–2. For other New Testament references which Origen may also have had in mind, see Heb. 5:12–14 and 1 Pet. 2:2.

[28] Origen's explanation that Christ's more direct and perfect teachings issue from his breasts recalls for us his description of the pneumatic sense as the milk-like nourishment of the almond's core in *Hom. Num.* 9.7 (GCS:63–64); and the discussion of this homily in chapter 3.

[29] *Comm. Cant.* 1.3 (quoting Cant. 1:3a; and referring to Matt. 7:12; Gal. 3:24, 4:4; and 1 John 4:9; ACW 26:70–71); Sunt . . . etiam unguenta quaedam sponsi, quorum fraglantia delectata est sponsa et dicit: *Odor unguentorum tuorum super omnia aromata.* . . . Sponsa ergo habuit quidem usum et notitiam aromatum, hoc est verborum *legis et prophetarum,* quibus ante adventum sponsi, mediocriter licet, instrui tamen videbatur *et exerceri* ad cultum Dei, utpote *parvula* adhuc et *sub curatoribus* . . ., *lex* . . . *paedagogus noster fuit ad Christum.* Haec ergo omnia aromata fuerant, in quibus enutriri visa est et sponso suo praeparari. Sed *ubi venit plenitudo temporum* et adolevit atque *Unigenitum suum Pater* . . . *misit in hunc mundum,* odorata sponsa divini unguenti fraglantiam sentiensque quod illa omnia aromata, quibus prius usa videbatur, longe inferiora sunt ad comparationem suavitatis novi huius et caelestis unguenti ait: *Odor unguentorum tuorum super omnia aromata* (SC [1.3.1–2] 375:208).

own "ointments"—the presence of his actual divinity and holiness. She exclaims that the fragrance rising forth from the closeness of his divinity is far "sweet[er]" than the mere descriptions of them by the Law and Prophets.

When the church was "yet a little child and under [the] tut[elage]" of the Law and Prophets, she needed their less intense lessons. However, over time she became ready to receive Christ's teachings directly and enjoy his own presence. Therefore, "when the fullness of the time was come," Christ finally came into the church's presence through the Incarnation. The church now finds Christ's direct teachings and the presence of his divinity far more satisfying than she could have predicted from the Old Testament's preliminary lessons and descriptions of Christ's coming glory. Those dried spices are no substitute for the fragrant ointment that comes forth from the source itself.

While the previous pneumatic reading stressed God's faithfulness in bringing Christ to the church in the Incarnation, and implicitly assured the church that God too will faithfully bring Christ's return, in this pneumatic reading Origen emphasizes for his audience of church leaders that God has entrusted them with the direct teachings and holy presence of Christ. As the church, they are stewards of these treasures.

B. *The Psychic Reading: The Soul Finds the Word of God Present*

Origen again announces a "third explanation," focusing on the individual "soul" and "Word of God," thus signaling a psychic reading of text. He describes the soul who discovers the Word of God standing directly before her:

> But if we ought to understand these things according to a third explanation, with reference to the perfect soul and the Word of God, then we may say in this connection that as long as a person is a child and has not yet offered himself wholly to God, he drinks the wine which that field produces, which holds within itself the hidden treasure too; and he is gladdened by the wine he drinks. But, when he has offered and vowed himself to God and . . . has found the hidden treasure and come to the very breasts and fountains of the Word of God, then he will no longer drink wine and spirit, but with reference to these treasures of wisdom and knowledge that are hidden in the Word of God, he will say to Him: "Your breasts are better than wine."[30]

---

[30] *Comm. Cant.* 1.2 (referring to Heb. 5:13, 9:14; Luke 1:15; Col. 2:3; and quoting

Here, Origen explains, when the perfected soul was still a child—
not yet perfected—she drank the wine of the fields. Now, however,
she has "offered [her]self wholly to God" and thus is no longer a
"child." Origen does not define "perfect" here, but he indicates that
the perfected soul—the one who has "offered and vowed [her]self
to God"—is the only type of soul capable of entering directly into
the presence of the Word of God. She turns to the "hidden trea-
sure" in the Word of God and drinks from his "breasts and foun-
tains," relying upon them as the source of her own sustenance.
Significantly, these hidden treasures that the perfected soul enjoys
are the same treasures that the church enjoys after the Incarnation:
"the wisdom and knowledge" of God. As the church enjoys direct
nourishment from the Incarnate Christ, so the perfected soul enjoys
direct teachings of God's Word. Here, Origen implicitly relates (and
will explicitly relate later in this exegesis) the Word of God to
Scripture, the very soil ready to provide life and growth to the
implanted soul. This recalls the consistent psychic call, as witnessed
in the homiletic examples in the previous chapter, to immerse oneself in Scripture as the guide to and beginning of union with God
and God's truths. The soul here finds that the direct teachings from
God's own Word are more satisfying than all previous, preparatory
lessons.

Origen next interprets spices psychically, relating them to those
preparatory lessons, and again implicitly connects the Word of God
with Scripture:

> We shall make use of a like interpretation whenever we transfer these
> words to every individual soul that is fixed in the love of the Word
> of God and in desire for Him; a soul that will have traversed in order
> all the sorts of instruction in which she was exercised and taught before
> she attained to the knowledge of the Word of God, whether those
> teachings be based on ethics or on natural philosophy. For all those
> things were so many spices for that soul, in that by their means an
> agreeable disposition and improvement of behavior are acquired, and

Cant. 1:2*b*; ACW 26:69–70); Sed et si tertia expositione de anima haec perfecta et
Verbo Dei sentire debeamus, possumus dicere in his quia, donec quis parvulus est
et nondum *semet ipsum ex integro obtulit Deo*, bibit vinum quod affert *ager ille* qui habet
intra se etiam *thesaurum absconditum*, et bibens laetificatur ex vino. Cum autem *obtu-
lerit et devoverit semet ipsum Deo* . . . atque *invenerit thesaurum absconditum* et ad ipsa ubera
fontesque pervenerit Verbi *Dei, vinum et siceram iam non bibet* dicens ad ipsum Dei
Verbum de his *thesauris qui in ipso sapientiae et scientiae reconditi sunt: Quia bona sunt ubera
tua super vinum* (SC [1.2.23–24] 375:204).

because in them the vanity of the world is discovered and the deceitful marvels of perishable things are rejected. All these things were,
then, as spices and perfumes, cosmetics as it were for the soul.[31]

"[E]very individual soul" who comes to love the Word of God first
grows in knowledge of him through "instruction" in "ethics" or "natural philosophy," which are the "spices" of this world. This type of
training facilitates a disposition of moral conduct in the soul and
teaches the soul that the world is "vain" and that "perishable" things
are "deceitful" and fleeting. The soul learns these things through her
faculties of "natural law and reason and free will," which Origen
described above as the soul's betrothal gifts. As a result, she grows
virtuous in her behavior. Yet, these betrothal gifts remain only "cosmetics (*pigmenta*)," or "ornaments" for the soul. They make the soul
presentable to God, bringing her only to the point of being worthy
and ready to turn to the Word of God and begin to receive directly
the wisdom and knowledge hidden in his breast.

The language here of "ethics" and "natural philosophy" may seem
to support the hunch of some scholars that Origen borrowed his
idea of the psychic sense at least in part from Philonic or other philosophical notions of a natural morality.[32] Yet, this psychic reading
calls the individual believer to seek lessons in virtue that will prepare him for the presence of God's own Word. The natural and
secular lessons have value to Origen only because they will help to
prepare the soul for the presence of the Word of God and the receipt
of his direct teachings, which, as the pneumatic reading above clarified,
Christ has entrusted to the church and renders to the individual soul
by way of Scripture. Thus, the proper goal of secular learning is to
make the person ready to begin recognizing and growing in the
understanding of Christ's wisdom (in Scripture) within the church,
so that he can begin ascending the path to union with Christ that

---

[31] *Comm. Cant.* 1.3 (ACW 26:73); Simili autem expositione utimur, etiam si ad
unamquamque animam in amore et desiderio Verbi Dei positam transferatur hic
sermo, cui fuerint omnes doctrinae per ordinem decursae, in quibus ante agnitionem
Verbi Dei exercitata videtur et erudita, sive ex moralibus descendentes sive ex naturalibus scholis. Erant enim ei ista omnia aromata quaedam pro eo quod in his
institutio probabilis et morum conquiritur emendatio, quod deprehenditur in his
vanitas saeculi, et caducarum rerum respuuntur falsa miracula. Erant ergo haec
omnia velut aromata et odoramenta quaedam animae pigmenta (SC [1.3.12] 375:214).
[32] See the discussion of scholars' views of Origen's exegesis, especially those of
Hanson and Daniélou, in chapter 1.

Christ has paved by his own descent to human form.[33] Implicitly, then, the psychic sense promotes only the types and amounts of secular learning that help to facilitate this intimacy with Christ.

Origen next relates the fragrance of the Word's ointments to the hidden truths in God's Word:

> But when she [the soul] has come to knowledge of the mysteries and the divine judgments, when she has reached the gates of . . . the very wisdom of God which is discoursed upon among the perfect, and . . . the soul ascends to recognition of this so great secret, she has cause to say: "The fragrance of Your ointments"—that is, the spiritual and mystical meaning—"is above all spices" of moral and natural philosophy.[34]

The person who rejects this world's ways will know "the mysteries and the divine judgments" that constitute "the very wisdom of God." Such descriptions recall Origen's theoretical definition of the pneumatic sense. This type of knowledge is what the "perfect" person contemplates, causing his soul to "ascend[ ]" to the "great secret" of God's truths. When the person's soul turns to the pneumatic truths in Scripture, which Origen identifies elsewhere with "the mind of Christ,"[35] he perceives the fragrance of the Word's ointments, a scent that is sweeter than that of the spices of ordinary "moral and natural philosophy." The latter were only preparatory to the ointments of God's Word, and they have no value apart from helping to prepare the soul to receive it. Indeed, as the soul progresses in understanding these secular, natural lessons, she learns that they are not enough to satisfy her hunger. She realizes that she needs the Word of God's direct, pneumatic lessons.

Origen identifies the sweeter truth of God's Word—the Word of God's direct lessons, or kisses—with the "spiritual and mystical meaning (spiritalis . . . intelligentia et mystica)," which, again, recalls Origen's theoretical terminology for Scripture's pneumatic meaning. He acknowledges that in some translations of the scriptural passage at hand (in

---

[33] Recall this theme of ascent in Origen's *Hom. Gen.* 2 on Noah's ark, which is treated fully in chapter 4.

[34] *Comm. Cant.* 1.3 (referring to I Cor. 2:6–7 and Col. 1:26; quoting Cant. 1:3a; ACW 26:73); Sed ubi ad agnitionem mysteriorum et divinorum dogmatum scientiam ventum est, ubi ad ianuas ipsius sapientiae . . . ad ipsam Dei *sapientiam* quae *inter perfectos* disseritur, et . . . anima ad agnitionem tanti huius adscendit arcani, merito dicit: *Quia odor unguentorum tuorum*—spiritalis scilicet intelligentia et mystica—*super omnia aromata* moralis naturalisque philosophiae (SC ([1.3.13] 375:214, 216).

[35] *Hom. Lev.* 5.6.2 (quoting 1 Cor. 2:16; FC 83:101; SC 286:232). Also, see the discussion of this homily in chapter 3.

Cant 1:2*b*) the text reads "Your *sayings* are better than wine," putting
"sayings (*loquelae*)" in place of "breasts (*ubera*)."[36] He states that "sayings" is the "plainer meaning (*evidentius significasse*)" but that he prefers
to follow the Septuagint's term, "breasts," since it keeps better hidden the "spiritual interpretation (*spiritali interpretatione*)" of this text.[37]
By this aside, Origen makes explicit the fact that he speaks of the
perfected soul's ability to grasp the mysteries conveyed by Scripture's
pneumatic sense. The psychic sense's achievements, then, are the
soul's ability to begin and continue to receive Scripture's ever-deeper,
pneumatic truths.

Origen's audience of church leaders—perfected souls—understands
from this psychic reading that Christ has been offering them his
direct kisses in the pneumatic meanings that they are already able
to grasp within Scripture. This is the presence of the Word of God
for which they yearn, and, indeed, they have begun to be privileged
recipients of it already.

In this set of readings, then, Origen's audience first learns from
the pneumatic reading that they, as church leaders, have been
entrusted with Christ's direct teachings. Then, from the psychic reading of "every individual soul," Origen suggests that they enjoy these
teachings personally when they grasp pneumatic meanings in Scripture.
As both perfected souls and the church, it is their privilege to increasingly understand God's pneumatic truths.

Moreover, these readings together suggest that the process of
preparing for and growing in understanding of pneumatic truths can
only occur within the church, where the divine teachings of Scripture
are kept and guarded. Thus, the psychic call to virtue, within the
context of its relation to the pneumatic message, is a Christian call
to expose oneself to Scripture's pneumatic meanings as the treasury
of Christ's wisdom and knowledge, indeed, his direct, most transformative teachings.

V. *The Bride Runs with the Maidens: Two Types of Maidens*

Origen now interprets the third portion of the biblical passage, which
reads: "Therefore have the maidens loved You, have they drawn

---

[36] *Comm. Cant.* 1.3, emphasis added (ACW 26:74; SC [1.3.14] 375:216).
[37] Ibid.

You. We will run after You into the fragrance of Your ointments."
The Bride explains that, although she can enjoy the presence of her
Bridegroom and his kisses, breasts and fragrance, she chooses to run
with the young maidens in *their* pursuit of him.

Unlike the two stages of analysis above, Origen does not begin
with a dramatic rendering of the text's letter here, but proceeds
directly to a pneumatic reading of the Bride as the church and then
a psychic reading of the Bride as the individual soul. Perhaps he
considers the dramatic character of the literal language to be obvious: a *true* love, as the Bride holds for her Bridegroom, is not selfish
but wishes for others also to enjoy such great intimacy.

A. *The Pneumatic Reading: The Individual Churches*

Origen's pneumatic reading explains how the Bride church runs with
the young maidens, the individual local churches in the world, to
make them perfect for God and, ultimately, united with the church
in faith:

> We may well see in these words a certain prophecy, uttered by the
> Bride herself concerning Christ, to the effect that at Our Lord and
> Savior's coming . . . His name should be so spread abroad throughout
> the globe and over the whole world, as to make it an odor of sweet-
> ness in every place. . . . [T]he maidens, namely, draw Christ to them-
> selves—this surely must be taken as referring to the churches, which
> are one Church when perfected, but many "maidens" while they are
> still under instruction and advancing on their way. These, then, draw
> Christ to themselves through faith . . . [and] by their unity of mind.[38]

When the Bride church received the Incarnate Christ's presence and
direct teachings, she became responsible not only for guarding and
protecting these teachings but also delivering them to individual
churches throughout the world. The Bride church, which Origen
has defined as the assembly of the saints,[39] or the aggregate mature

---

[38] *Comm. Cant.* 1.4 (ACW 26:74–75, 76); Potest sane in his prophetia quaedam
videri ex persona sponsae prolata de Christo quod futurum esset, ut in adventu
Domini et Salvatoris nostri nomen eius ita per orbem terrae et per universum
mundum diffunderetur, ut fieret odor suavitatis in omni loco. . . . [T]rahunt ad se
Christum adulescentulae, siquidem de ecclesiis intelligatur, quae una quidem est,
cum perfecta est, multae vero sunt adulescentulae, cum adhuc instruuntur et proficiunt.
Istae ergo ad se trahunt Christum per fidem . . . et unanimitate provocatus (SC
[1.4.2, 1.4.6] 375:220, 222, 224).
[39] *Comm. Cant.* 1.1 (referring to 1 Cor. 14:23; ACW 26:59–60; FC [1.1.5–6]
375:178, 180).

in faith, runs with the maiden churches toward Christ. Though already enjoying his presence and direct teachings, she fulfills her temporal duty of directing young, individual churches—those pockets of believers who are less mature in faith—to embrace and grow in their devotion to Christ. The Bride church, as the steward of Christ's teachings, spreads his name throughout the world, bringing his fragrance, the "sweetness" of his divinity, to "every place."

As a result, local, "maiden" churches "draw Christ to themselves" by accepting the "faith" and joining in the "unity of mind" that the Bride church enjoys. These local churches continue to be maidens as long as they remain "under instruction" in the things of God. Yet, when they finally embrace the faith in full and enter into a complete unity of mind with the Bride church, they will be "perfected" like the Bride church and become "one" with her.

With this pneumatic reading, Origen impresses upon his audience that their privilege as church leaders to keep and guard Christ's pneumatic truths establishes a responsibility to build up communities of believers by conveying these teachings to them. It is their duty to establish unity in teaching and in faith.

B. *The Psychic Reading: The Young, Less Advanced Souls*

Origen now turns to the "third explanation," or psychic sense, relating the Bride and Bridegroom to the soul and Word of God. He explains why the perfected soul runs with the young, maiden souls, even though she has achieved the honor of residing in his presence. Yet, first Origen turns his audience's focus to the needs of their own congregations of young, maiden souls by explaining what draws the Word of God to any soul, that is, what makes a soul worthy (or perfected enough) to begin enjoying his intimate presence:

> If . . . on the third explanation it behooves us to take this passage as referring to the soul that is following the Word of God, to every soul that has been first instructed in ethics and then practiced in natural philosophy, then the Word of God is drawn by means of all those things which, as we showed just now, are taught in the aforesaid studies—namely, amendment of manners, knowledge of affairs, and uprightness of conduct. And He is willing to be drawn, and comes very gladly to instructed souls. . . .[40]

---

[40] *Comm. Cant.* 1.4 (ACW 26:76–77); Si vero tertia expositione de anima Verbum Dei sequente intelligi haec oportet, quaecumque anima fuerit erudita primo in moralibus, secundo etiam in naturalibus exercitata, per illa omnia quae in his disciplinis

"[E]very soul" who receives instruction in "ethics" and practice in "natural philosophy" begins to learn "amendment of manners, knowledge of affairs, and uprightness of conduct." In other words, she begins to acquire the virtues. The Word of God is attracted, or drawn in, to a soul who has received such instruction. Psychically, then, the maiden is the young soul "growing up in years and beauty"— growing in the virtues, hoping that the Word of God will be attracted to her.[41]

Origen next points out that each soul progresses in the virtues according to her own "capacity and faith." Not every soul advances in the same time or at the same pace. Yet, when a young soul draws sufficiently near to the Word of God, she begins to understand her telos, salvation, and that which facilitates it, the Word of God's love as manifested in the Incarnation and on the Cross—that is, she begins to understand Scripture's pneumatic truths, and, with that, she increasingly hungers for more:

> [E]very soul draws and receives to itself the Word of God according to the measure of its capacity and faith. But when souls have thus drawn the Word of God to themselves, and have engrafted Him into their minds and understandings, and have experienced the pleasantness of His sweetness and odor, when they have received the fragrance of His ointments and have grasped at last the reason for His coming, the motives of the Redemption and Passion, and the love whereby He, the Immortal, went *even to the death of the cross* for the salvation of all men, then these maiden souls, attracted by all this as by the odors of a divine and ineffable perfume and being filled with vigor and complete alacrity, run after Him and hasten to the odor of His sweetness. . . .[42]

---

edoceri supra ostendimus, ipsa morum emendatio et eruditio rerum ac probitas disciplinae trahit ad se Verbum Dei; et libens trahitur, gratissime enim ad eruditas animas venit . . . (SC [1.4.7] 375:224).

[41] *Comm. Cant.* 1.4 (referring to 2 Cor. 4:16 and Eph. 4:24; ACW 26:75); *adulescentulae in augmento scilicet aetatis et pulchritudinis positae animae* (SC [1.4.3–4] 375:220, 222).

[42] *Comm. Cant.* 1.4 (referring to Phil. 2:8; ACW 26:75–76); Trahit enim unaquaeque anima et adsumit ad se Verbum Dei pro capacitatis et fidei suae mensura. Cum autem traxerint ad se animae Verbum Dei et sensibus suis atque intellectibus inseruerint ac dulcedinis eius et odoris sumpserint suavitatem, ubi unguentorum eius fraglantiam ceperint, rationem dumtaxat adventus eius et redemptionis ac passionis causas caritatemque eius agnoverint, qua pro salute omnium *usque ad mortem crucis* immortalis accessit, et his omnibus velut divini cuiusdam et ineffabilis unguenti odoribus invitatae *adulescentulae* istae, animae plenae vigoris atque alacritatis effectae, currunt post ipsum atque in odorem suavitatis eius . . . festinant. . . . (SC [1.4.4–5] 375:222).

Each maiden soul progresses at her own pace, but the fruits of such progress are the same for all souls: they draw near to the Word's divine presence and, thus, his more direct teachings. Upon drawing near to him, they hasten even faster to his side, for they now understand that he has effected their redemption and salvation. This realization intensifies their love and desire for full union with the Word of God. In other words, having tasted pneumatic truth, the soul naturally quickens her pace in striving to become more deeply intimate with it.

Here, we see the psychic and pneumatic senses collaborate to inform Origen's audience of their specific responsibilities to the maiden souls in their own congregations. The process that Origen explains by which souls advance toward the Word of God depends on continuing growth in virtue at the behest of the psychic sense, which, in turn, brings a deepening understanding of pneumatic truths. Origen's audience needs to facilitate this process in their own congregations.

Origen now shifts focus from the maidens (his audience's congregations) to the Bride, or perfected soul (his own audience of church leaders). He discusses the psychic meaning of the Bride's condescension to run with the maidens. This mature soul already enjoys union with God's Word and yet is willing to "run with" the maiden souls who have not yet been admitted into his presence. Origen explains: "[T]he reason why she herself runs with the maidens after Him is that the perfect always *become all things to all men, that they may gain all.*"[43] The perfected Bride soul condescends to run with the less mature souls, because she wants to help them reach the levels of perfection that she is privileged to enjoy. By running with the less advanced souls, she becomes "an example" to them:

> The Bride had drawn her Bridegroom's attention to the fact that the maidens, attracted by His fragrance, were running after Him, and that she herself likewise was going to run with them; so that in all things she might set them an example.[44]

---

[43] *Comm. Cant.* 1.4 (quoting 1 Cor. 9:22; ACW 26:83); Quod vero etiam ipsa cum adulescentulis currit post ipsum, hanc esse causam quod perfecti quique *omnibus omnia fiunt, ut omnes lucrifaciant.* . . . (SC [1.4.30] 375:238).

[44] *Comm. Cant.* 1.5 (referring to 1 Thess. 1:6–7; ACW 26:84); Cum indicasset sponso suo sponsa quod adulescentulae odore eius captae currerent post ipsum, cum quibus etiam ipsa cursura esset, ut eis *formam* praeberet in *omnibus* (SC [1.5.1] 375:242).

The Bride soul runs with the younger—less perfect—maiden souls to provide them with an example of the perfected soul. By communing with them along their path of progress, she can keep straight their paths toward the Word of God and encourage them at each step of the way. Thus, Origen challenges his audience to assist their maiden congregations to grow along the path to union with God's Word.

In this third portion of his analysis, Origen presents the Bride church and the perfected soul as both condescending from their enjoyment, respectively, of Christ's and the Word of God's presence in order to help young churches and souls progress toward this same goal. The Bride church, entrusted with Christ's teachings, is called to reach out to the localities of the world to raise up churches in the faith and bring them to a "unity of mind" with her. The perfected soul is called to reach out to other souls, directing them to the same intimacy with the Word that she enjoys. This perfected soul grasps pneumatic meanings in Scripture (as established by the prior psychic reading on the Bride's recognition of the Word's presence), but, instead of spending her full energies meditating on these divine truths, she spends some of her time and attention helping less advanced souls grasp and grow in understanding pneumatic truths themselves.

Implicitly, the Bride church and perfected soul pattern their condescensions after the Word of God's descent into the Incarnate Christ. The Bride church and the perfected soul both know of the Word's condescension, because Christ has entrusted the Bride church with Scripture's pneumatic truths, which center on the fact of the Incarnation and Christ's salvific powers, and the perfected soul has achieved some understanding of them. His descent to human form has established the path of ascent along which the church and each soul is to rise to salvific union with him. While the path is within the Bride church (according to *Hom. Gen.* 2 on the ark, as treated in chapter 4), the Bride church arguably enjoys fuller intimacy with Christ as each of her members enjoys increased intimacy with the Word of God. The perfected soul's (and, in the aggregate, the Bride church's) great advancement in this ascent is marked by a willingness to descend in order to draw others up toward the Word of God, or Christ. They have achieved enough love for God to become true imitators of Christ. Origen's audience members, as perfected souls, constitute the Bride church on earth. They are the Bride called to strengthen maiden churches and souls in virtue and expose them to God's pneu-matic truths. They are to run with the maidens and, thus, be as Christ to the less mature in faith.

By this combination of readings, Origen effects a deliberate and productive mingling of the two higher senses that emerges from their distinct functions. Origen shows his audience that the psychic call provides the means for them, as individuals, to fulfill the task of the Bride church described in the pneumatic sense. The Bride church holds the pneumatic truths that are to be taught to those less advanced in faith. The perfected souls—perfected because they can grasp pneu-matic meanings in Scripture—have the duty to teach less advanced souls. Their progress in virtue and scriptural understanding obligates them to act as preachers and teachers. This duty is called for by the psychic sense, and, in relation to the pneumatic sense, it is an ecclesial duty. Their private privilege (as perfected souls) becomes their communal responsibility (as the Bride church) during this life. This duty is made possible by Christ and is to be exercised within the Bride church, since she holds and guards the treasury of Christ's wisdom in Scripture.

Also, this psychic exhortation underscores the core, identifying character of the psychic sense: it provides the *temporal* way of pur-suing the *eternal* hope conveyed by the pneumatic message. The pneu-matic sense focuses on the goal, unity of all believers with Christ, as well as the place in which to pursue it, the Bride church, while the psychic sense explains *how* Origen's audience, the perfected souls, proceed temporally toward this eternal end, by practicing imitation of Christ's self-giving through teaching others.

VI. *The Bride Enters the Bridegroom's Chamber*

In the fourth and final analysis of *Comm. Cant.* 1, Origen interprets the Bride's entrance into the Bridegroom's or "King's chamber." Although he does not treat separately his readings of the Bride as church and perfected soul, the two readings are distinguishable within his analysis, each giving context and direction to the other.

We find in this last portion of Book 1 a culmination of the three prior sets of readings. The entire book is a crescendo of the inter-relationship between the two higher readings, providing a sophisti-cated example of how Origen intends the two senses to mutually

reinforce one another for the spiritual transformation of his audience. Origen brings together the two higher senses, not as a fusion,
but as a deliberate mingling of them, showing that the duty *and*
reward of the advanced soul occurs within the church. Only within
the church, with help from more advanced souls, can a soul pursue
and reach the Bridegroom's chamber—Christ's own mind—and begin
advancing toward the full intimacy with Christ that characterizes
eternal bliss. The believer's goal is not simply a private union between
his soul and the Word of God but, rather, between his soul, as a
member of the church, and God's Incarnate Word. While the previous sets of higher readings aligned Christ with the church and the
Word of God with the soul, this final set of readings reveals that
the Christ who appears to the church in history is the Incarnate
pre-existent Word (manifest in the very structure and content of
Scripture) who teaches individual souls.

Origen begins this final analysis of text with a dramatic rendering of its letter:

> But now, as though she has already attained the reward of her labor
> in thus running with the runners [young maidens], she tells us that
> the King has brought her into His chamber, that she may see there
> all the royal riches. And this gives her good reason for gladness and
> rejoicing, in that she has now beheld the secrets of the King and hid-
> den mysteries.[45]

Origen explains that the Bride who enters into the Bridegroom's
chamber enjoys his secrets and the hidden mysteries stored within
it, indeed, the royal treasures of a king. In one respect, this enjoyment is a reward for her work in running with the young maidens.
In another respect, the Bride has not yet completed her duties to
the maidens, since, Origen states, it is only "*as though* she has already
attained the reward of her labor in thus running with the runners."
Origen draws a picture of the perfected soul's dual existence during
this life. On the one hand, the Bride enjoys the intimacy of private
communion with the Bridegroom in his chamber, but, on the other
hand, she still has the duty to continue helping the younger maidens
achieve such intimacy.

---

[45] *Comm. Cant.* 1.5 (ACW 26:84); [N]unc quasi laboris sui consecuta iam palmam, pro eo quod concurrerit currentibus, introductam se dicit ab sponso *rege in
cubiculum* eius, ut ibi videret cunctas opes regias. In quo utique merito iucundatur
et exsultat, utpote quae secreta iam regis et arcana prospexerit (SC [1.5.1–2] 375:242).

In developing the figurative meanings of this passage, Origen stresses that love for God, during this life, involves both private, individual intimacies with God as well as communal responsibilities toward others. Indeed, Origen will reveal that even his audience's private intimacies are a part of their communal duties to others.

A. *The Pneumatic and Psychic Readings: Private Intimacies*

Origen emphasizes that both the Bride church and the perfected soul enjoy the same treasures of God's wisdom and knowledge, for the mind of Christ and the Word of God are one and the same:

> But since the reference is either to the Church who comes to Christ, or to the soul that cleaves to the Word of God, how should we understand Christ's chamber and the storehouse of the Word of God into which He brings the Church or the soul thus cleaving to Him—you can take it either way—except as Christ's own secret and mysterious mind? Of this Paul also said: *We have the mind of Christ, that we may know the things that are given us from God.* These things are those that *eye has not seen, nor ear heard, neither has it entered into the heart of man, what things God has prepared for them that love Him.* So, when Christ leads a soul to understand his mind, she is said to be brought into the King's chamber, *in which are hid the treasures of His wisdom and knowledge.*[46]

Origen refers both to "Christ's chamber" and the "storehouse of the Word of God." The Bride church enters into the former and the perfected soul into the latter. His audience is now to understand that both refer to Christ's, or the Incarnate Word's "own secret and mysterious mind." Here, Origen mingles the two higher senses by stressing that the church and individual soul enjoy the same telos. Both enter into union with the mind of Christ, God's Word. This union is equivalent to intimacy with God. The term *sensus*, translated here as "mind," also means understanding or reason. Within Christ's mind,

---

[46] *Comm. Cant.* 1.5 (quoting, in order, 1 Cor. 2:16, 2:12, 2:9; alluding to Isa. 64:4; referring to Cant. 1:4; quoting Col. 2:3; ACW 26:84–85); Sed quoniam, cui res agitur, ecclesia est ad Christum veniens vel anima Verbo Dei adhaerens, quod aliud *cubiculum* Christi et *promptuarium* Verbi Dei credendum est, in quo vel ecclesiam suam vel animam cohaerentem sibi *introducat*, nisi ipse Christi arcanus et reconditus sensus? De quo et Paulus dicebat: *Nos autem sensum Christi habemus, ut sciamus quae a Deo donata sunt nobis.* Haec illa sunt quae *oculus non vidit nec auris audivit nec in cor hominis adscendit, quae praeparavit Deus his qui diligunt eum.* Cum igitur animam Christus in intelligentiam sui sensus inducit, *in cubiculum regis introducta dicitur,* in quo *sunt thesauri sapientiae ac scientiae eius absconditi* (SC [1.5.3–4] 375:242, 244).

the Bride can begin to understand the things that Christ knows and comprehends. These are the "treasures of His wisdom and knowledge," specifically God's "secret and mysterious" truths. The term *arcanus*, translated here as "secret," also means private. The term *reconditus*, translated here as "mysterious," also means hidden or concealed. These private and hidden truths suggest the mysteries of Scripture's pneumatic sense, which Origen has referred to elsewhere as the mind of Christ.[47] Christ has invited the Bride church, and, individually, the perfected soul, into his mind, by providing them with the ability to comprehend Scripture's pneumatic truths.

Now Origen's audience can see how Christ and the pneumatic sense are one and the same, for the Incarnate Word of God offers himself through the pages of Scripture, at the core of which lies the pneumatic truths. Since Christ is the content of Scripture and is eternal, the pneumatic sense, as Scripture's core content and full story, is eternal.[48]

Here, Origen informs his audience of church leaders that, as both the Bride church and perfected souls, they are to take in Christ, the Word of God, through increasing intimacy with Scripture's deepest, pneumatic truths. As the leaders of the church, their own progress is also the church's progress. As each leader grows more intimate with Christ's mind, so does the Bride church become stronger.

B. *The Pneumatic and Psychic Readings: Temporal, Communal Duties*

After stressing the private intimacies with Christ that the Bride church and perfected soul enjoy, through increasingly greater comprehension of Scripture's pneumatic truths, Origen explains how his audience's progress strengthens the church not only at its leadership level but also at its core, which is made up of less advanced, maiden churches and souls. By seeing the Bride church and perfected soul enjoying this union with Christ, the maidens' desires to pursue the same reward increase. From afar, they see the Bride "brought into

---

[47] *Hom. Lev.* 5.6.2 (quoting 1 Cor. 2:16; FC 83:101; SC 286:232). See the discussion of *Hom. Lev.* 5 in chapter 3.
[48] The understanding of Christ as Scripture's content is discussed in the context of *Princ.* 4 (4.2.6, 4.2.9) in chapter 2 and in great detail throughout chapter 3. Also, see chapter 1 for Torjesen's explanation of this notion within Origen's thought. For the notion of the pneumatic sense as eternally abiding, see the discussion of *Hom. Num.* 9 in chapter 3.

the chamber of the King, and . . . made the queen. . . ."[49] The maidens celebrate her coronation, because their passion and hope for their own crowning is inflamed by witnessing it: "[T]hey rejoice with her, because they look forward to becoming partakers of her joy and gladness."[50]

Origen explains that when the maidens exclaim, "We *will* love Your breasts more than wine," they speak in the future tense,[51] because they still are striving to enjoy similar intimacies with the Bridegroom:

> The Bride herself, after she has been found worthy to receive kisses from the Bridegroom's own mouth, and to enjoy His breasts, says to Him: "Your breasts are above wine." But the maidens, who had not yet reached that degree of blessedness, nor attained the summit of perfection, nor yet had so produced the fruits of perfect charity in conduct and works as to enable them to say from experience that His breasts are good, these . . . seeing the Bride . . . drink the cups of heavenly teaching, promise and say, as those who copy her perfection and desire to follow in her steps: "We *will* love Your breasts more than wine." . . . They promise . . . that when the fullness of the times has come and Christ in them has advanced in age and wisdom, . . . they will then love the Bridegroom's breasts, which now they love after the manner of children, "more than wine"— . . . they will be apter students of Christ's full and perfect teachings than ever they were of their ordinary studies, or of the teachings of the Law and the Prophets.[52]

[49] *Comm. Cant.* 1.5 (ACW 26:86); Introducitur *ergo* in cubiculum regis *et efficitur regina* (SC [1.5.9] 375:246).

[50] *Comm. Cant.* 1.5 (quoting Cant. 1:4; ACW 26:87); The fuller Latin text reads: Vel etiam ad sponsam potest dictum videri ab adulescentulis congratulantibus ei et promittentibus, quod participes fiant exsultationis eius et laetitiae, *Diligemus ubera tua super vinum* (SC [1.6.2] 375:250).

[51] Cant. 1:4b.

[52] *Comm. Cant.* 1.5 (quoting Cant. 1:2*b*, 4; and referring to Gal. 4:4 and Luke 2:52; ACW 26:87–88); Sponsa quidem, posteaquam oscula meruit ab ipso sponsi ore suscipere et uberibus eius perfrui, ait ad eum: *Bona sunt ubera tua super vinum*; adulescentulae vero, quae nondum in id beatitudinis venerant neque summam perfectionis acceperant neque usu et operibus fructus perfectae caritatis expleverant, ut quasi expertae pronuntiarent de uberibus eius quia *bona sunt*, videntes tamen sponsam . . . pocula caelestis doctrinae sumentem, tamquam imitatrices perfectionis eius et desiderantes iisdem vestigiis incedere promittunt et dicunt: *Diligemus ubera tua super vinum.* . . . Sed ubi *advenit* iam *plenitudo temporum* et Christus in iis *profecit aetate et sapientia* . . . promittunt quia *plus quam vinum*, quod nunc tamquam parvulae diligunt, dilecturae sint ubera sponsi, . . . propensiores futurae erga perfecta et in omni plenitudine decreta Christi dogmata, quam sive in communibus studiis sive in legis *et prophetarum* visae sunt institutionibus exstitisse (SC [1.6.3, 5] 375:250, 252).

The maiden churches and souls witness the Bride church and per-fected soul enjoy the "blessedness" attained upon reaching the "sum-mit of perfection," that is, the degree of growth in virtue and wisdom that makes possible reception of pneumatic truths (or the Word of God's direct kisses) and, thus, intimacy with Christ. This achieve-ment has brought the Bride church and soul to the place where they "drink the cups of heavenly teaching," that is, they are now able to take in still deeper pneumatic truths about God's wisdom and love. The maidens see the Bride's enjoyment of increasing wisdom through intimacy with Christ, and they long also to enter the chamber of Christ's "full and perfect teachings." They "promise" that "when the fullness of the times has come" within them—when "Christ *within* them has advanced in age and wisdom," that is, when they too exhibit the growth in virtue and wisdom necessary for these advanced blessings—they too will love Christ's breasts more than wine. They will love his direct teachings more than the natural, "ordinary stud-ies" (for maiden souls) or the lessons of the Law and Prophets (for the maiden churches) that have been their preparatory, betrothal gifts.

We learn from this passage that even when the Bride church or perfected soul is *not* "running with" the local churches or less advanced souls, she continues to be an example and inspiration to them. The church's leaders (Origen's audience), though they are responsible in this life to the less advanced in faith, must step away from service at times to permit Christ to work within them for their own con-tinued advancement in understanding God's highest, pneumatic truths. For in so doing, they continue to aid others by example.

For this reason, Origen now exhorts his audience members—in psychic fashion—to continue their *own* growth in virtue and corre-sponding increase in wisdom so that they can continue to be good examples as well as teachers to their maiden congregations. Perhaps not to risk a condescending tone, Origen begins this exhortation by continuing to direct his comments to the "maidens." He speaks of maidens feeling shame for not yet having reached the "perfection of spiritual and mystical teaching":

> "Equity has loved You." I think this, too, is spoken by the maid-
> ens. . . . The words imply self-blame: the maidens have not yet so cast
> away iniquity with respect to everything and come to equity, as to be
> able to love the Bridegroom's breasts more than wine now; and they
> know that it is wholly unfitting for any trace of iniquity to remain in

a person who has reached the perfection of spiritual and mystical teaching. Therefore, because the height of perfection consists in charity, and
charity allows nothing of iniquity—and where there is no iniquity,
there surely is equity—it is rightly said to be Equity that loves the
Bridegroom.[53]

Origen explains that even the *maiden* churches and souls know that
to reach the "perfection"—or fulfillment—of Christ's teachings in
Scripture it is necessary to increase equity and decrease iniquity. The
term *aequitas*, translated here as "equity," also means fairness or justice, but most literally evenness. *Iniquitas*, translated here as "iniquity," also means unfairness or injustice, but most literally unevenness.
The maidens know that they do not yet possess the "even" spirit,
implicitly, the fullness of the virtues, that is found in those who have
attained "the perfection of spiritual and mystical teaching *(ad perfectionem spiritalis et mysticae doctrinae)*," which we recognize as referring
to the *full depth* of Scripture's pneumatic truths, indeed, the *telos or
full story* of Scripture, which, in turn, is the telos or fulfillment of the
human person.

Here, it seems, Origen targets his own audience of church leaders. Since even the perfected still have progress to make in this life,
church leaders too must continue attending to their own increase in
virtue and deepening understanding of Scripture's pneumatic truths.
And their maiden congregations know this! As a psychic exhortation, Origen wishes his church leaders to feel the shame ("self-blame")
of maidens, if they have been at all negligent in advancing their own
growth in virtue and wisdom. Certainly, they are able to take in
pneumatic meanings and, thus, have the duty to teach others. However,
their ability to teach and lead others to the same privileges wanes,
if they do not continue to grow toward the fullness of pneumatic
understanding through continued growth in virtue and deepening
exposure to Scripture. If they have stagnated—or perhaps not con-
centrated sufficiently on their own continued improvement—they

---

[53] *Comm. Cant.* 1.5 (quoting Cant. 1:4; referring to Col. 3:14 and 1 Cor. 13; ACW
26:88–89); *Aequitas dilexit te.* Etiam hoc videntur mihi adulescentulae proloqui. . . .
Est ergo vox ista velut incusantium semet ipsas, quasi quae nondum abiecta omni
iniquitate pervenerint ad *aequitatem*, ut possint iam *diligere super vinum ubera* sponsi,
scientes inconveniens omnino esse ut aliquid adhuc resideat iniquitatis in eo qui ad
perfectionem spiritalis et mysticae doctrinae pervenerit. Quia ergo summa perfectionis in caritate consistit, caritas autem nihil iniquitatis admittit—ubi autem nihil
iniquitatis est, ibi sine dubio est aequitas—, merito ergo *aequitas* esse dicitur quae
diligit sponsum (SC [1.6.6–8] 375:252, 254).

should feel shame not only because their duty to others depends
upon it but also because their maiden congregations are always
watching them. The maidens will know if the perfected are making
the progress that the perfected urge of them. Therefore, the perfected souls' own private intimacies with Christ determine the strength
and progress of the Bride church on earth.

For this reason, here Origen states that each person (including,
and with special haste, the perfected church leader) must continue
the process of purging from himself "*any* trace of *iniquity*" if he is
eventually to reach the telos, or fulfillment, of pneumatic truths, and,
in the meantime, bring others onto this same path. The person who
has grown in equity has reached the pneumatic level of understanding, and he should continue to advance in it. As he grows closer
to Christ and his wisdom, in Scripture's pneumatic truths, he must
advance still further in equity, spurred on by increasing love, or
charity, for Christ. Increased equity deepens charity for Christ, which,
in turn, draws the soul still closer to Christ and his wisdom.

Origen now explains that equity, which is equivalent to love, or
charity, for Christ, is measured by obedience to God's commandments:

> And see if this saying of the Savior's in the Gospel does not come
> to the same thing: *If you love me, keep my commandments.* For if he who
> loves Christ keeps His commandments, and in him who keeps the
> commandments there is no iniquity, but equity abides in him, equity
> then is that which both keeps the commandments and loves Christ.
> And again, if the person who keeps the commandments is also the
> person who loves Christ, and it is by equity that the commandments
> are kept, and equity that loves Christ, then the person who does any-
> thing iniquitous neither keeps the commandments, nor loves Christ.[54]

Love for Christ, the Incarnate Word, is measured by obedience to
God. *Iniquitas* commonly means sin, vice, or blameworthy error,
which is the product of an uneven spirit. The person with an uneven
spirit cannot love Christ, because he does not keep God's commandments. Only if he keeps the commandments does he love Christ.

---

[54] *Comm. Cant.* 1.5 (quoting John 14:15; ACW 26:89); Et vide si non ob hoc videtur etiam illud in Evangelio a Salvatore dictum: *Si diligitis me, mandata mea servate.*
Si ergo qui *diligit* Christum, *mandata eius custodit,* et qui *mandata eius custodit,* nulla est
in eo iniquitas, sed aequitas in eo permanet, *aequitas* ergo est quae et *mandata custodit* et *diligit* Christum. Et rursum: si is qui *mandata custodit,* ipse *diligit Christum, mandata autem in aequitate* servantur et *aequitas* est quae *diligit* Christum, qui iniquum
aliquid gerit neque *mandata custodit neque* diligit *Christum* (SC [1.6.9–10] 375:254).

That is why a person cannot reach the fullness of the pneumatic sense—full intimacy with the mind or essence of Christ—as long as he clings to any amount of sin. He must shun iniquity and embrace equity so that his obedience to God is complete and, thus, his love for Christ is his sole preoccupation.

However, Origen does not suggest that this love for Christ can reach a point of completion, that is, satiation. Love, by its nature, is relational and dynamic. The potential for deeper intimacy always exists. Arguably, for Origen, love is never fully completed in the human person, because the pneumatic sense continues its edification into eternity.[55] The pneumatic truths about God's own wisdom and love are that very wisdom and love, and love for them (which is the same as love for Christ) is a dynamic, not static, activity within the devotee. Thus, Origen drives his audience of church leaders to greater diligence in working toward perfect equity through increased obedience to God, implicitly, by growth in virtues and the rooting out of sins. This perfection in virtue will be complete in eternity, when the soul will continue with single-mindedness to grow in love for Christ through an ever-increasing intimacy with pneumatic truths, which are Christ's wisdom.

After having lured his audience into considering, for fear of shame, their own levels of diligence in personal growth (given the fact that less advanced souls are always watching their example), Origen now feels free to address these church leaders directly. He explicitly exhorts them to become still more even of spirit through obedience to God's commandments and, thus, even truer lovers of Christ. As a church leader, Origen includes himself as one who also needs to heed this psychic call:

> It follows, therefore, that as far as there is any iniquity *in us*, to that extent precisely are we far from loving Christ, and to that extent also is there in us transgression of His commandments. Let us, therefore, make equity into a sort of straight-edge; so that if there be anything of iniquity in us, by using this ruler and adding thereto the rule of God's commandments, anything crooked or twisted that there may be in us may be put straight by this ruler's edge; so that it may be said *of us also*: "Equity has loved You."[56]

---

[55] See *Hom. Num.* 9, which is treated in chapter 3.

[56] *Comm. Cant.* 1.5 (quoting Cant. 1:4, emphasis added; ACW 26:89); Erit ergo, ut, quantum iniquitatis in nobis est, tantum longe simus a dilectione Christi et tantum mandatorum eius praevaricatio habetur in nobis. Et ideo regulam quandam

Each church leader, including Origen himself ("us"), is to measure himself by the "ruler" of *aequitas*, in order to expose any and all iniquity that still remains within his soul. He is to root it out and make his nature even by obeying more fully God's commands and thereby show that he is a true lover of Christ. Equity will love them, in that they have become truer imitators of Christ. This, indeed, will provide a fuller example to their less advanced, maiden congregations.

Origen now makes explicit what has been implicit in his prose so far: *aequitas* is the same as the virtues. To be even, through obedience to God and love for Christ, is to have taken on all the virtues:

> We can also take what it says here, "Equity has loved You," as being a similar statement to: "Justice has loved You," and Truth, and Wisdom, and Modesty, and all the virtues in turn. And do not be surprised that we speak of the virtues loving Christ, since in other cases we are wont to regard Christ as Himself the substance of those very virtues. You will find this often in the divine Scriptures, adapted to the context and conditions; we find Him, for example, called not only Justice, but also Peace and Truth. . . . All of which things are both said to *be* Himself, and to embrace Him. Moreover, He is both called Bridegroom and named Bride, as it is written in the prophet: *As a bridegroom has He decked me with a crown, and as a bride has He adorned me with jewels.*[57]

Each of the virtues not only loves Christ but *is* Christ. To love the virtues, then, is to love Christ. By cultivating the virtues, one transforms himself into the virtues and, thus, into an imitation of Christ. The result and reward of this imitation is entrance into the intimacies of Christ's own wisdom and an ever-deepening love for Christ. To arrive at union with Christ the Bridegroom (or Lover) is to find

---

directam ponamus esse *aequitatem*, ut, si quid in nobis iniquitatis est, hanc adhibentes et superducentes directoriam mandatorum Dei, si quid in nobis curvum, si quid tortuosum est, ad huius regulae lineam resecetur, ut possit et de nobis dici: *Aequitas dilexit te* (SC [1.6.10–11] 375:254, 256).

[57] *Comm. Cant.* 1.5 (quoting Cant. 1:4; referring to 1 Cor. 1:30, Eph. 2:14, John 14:6, Matt. 9:15; and quoting Isa. 61:10b; ACW 26:89–90); Possumus autem etiam sic accipere, ut videatur simile esse quod dixit: *Aequitas dilexit te*, ac si dixisset: iustitia dilexit te et veritas et sapientia et pudicitia et singulae quaeque virtutes. Nec mireris sane, si dicimus virtutes esse quae diligunt Christum, cum in aliis ipsarum virtutum substantiam Christum soleamus accipere. Quod et frequenter invenies in scripturis divinis pro locis et opportunitatibus aptari; invenimus namque ipsum et *iustitiam* dici et *pacem* et *veritatem*. . . . Quae utique omnia et ipse esse et rursum ipsum dicuntur amplecti. Sed et *sponsus* idem dicitur, idem etiam *sponsa* nominatur, ut in propheta scriptum est: *Sicut sponso imposuit mihi mitram, et sicut sponsam ornavit me ornamento* (SC [1.6.12–14] 375:256).

that Christ is also the Bride (or Beloved). It is the telos of every human soul, and, collectively, the church, to pursue the pursuer into eternity.

By this analysis, Origen informs his audience that even church leaders continue to grow in virtue, obedience and love for Christ during this life. Implicitly, then, they continue to need edification from the psychic sense as well as the pneumatic sense. Their continued growth toward perfection in virtue and fuller understanding of pneumatic truths are integral to their duty to teach and lead others toward these same goals.

This final passage demonstrates that the psychic call to virtue *is* the call to strive in this life to love and become like Christ, and, thus, its message is intrinsically *Christian*. It directs the soul toward union with Christ, which is an eternal abiding within the pneumatic truths themselves. Hence, we see how Origen understands the psychic sense to remain operative throughout the temporal life and then to cease in its usefulness, leaving only the pneumatic sense as relevant to the soul's continued, indeed, increasing enjoyment of God in eternity.

Recalling Origen's anthropology, we understand that the believer pursues the perfection necessary for salvation by making his three internal parts ordered, or even—*aequitas*. This right internal order is both an imitative reflection of Christ and a return of love to him. Yet, the believer can attain this internal order only communally. Within the church, each soul pursues intimate union with Christ, and, in turn, by the achievement of all believers, the church reaches this final state as well. The perfected soul's arrival at full union with Christ is also the Bride church's arrival at this same telos.

Origen's audience of church leaders, then, learns that their increase in love for, imitation of and advancement toward perfect union with Christ strengthens the church at both its leadership and congregational levels. The perfected soul's, or church leader's, shaping of himself into increasing perfection is the church's shaping, and it effects by example the same shaping in the less advanced believers who make up the heart of the church. In the final section of this book, the mingled pneumatic and psychic readings inform Origen's audience that their advances in virtue, which have brought them to their privileged grasp of pneumatic truths, must continue to increase further if they are to fulfill their duty to help every human soul, and, thus, the church, come to the fullness of Christ's wisdom and ever-deepening love for him in eternity.

VII. *Conclusion*

In this final section of *Comm. Cant.* 1 Origen brings together the
pneumatic and psychic senses into a deliberate, productive mingling
that emphasizes that salvation is not only an individual but also a
communal pursuit. These two readings are not fused, because, by
this fourth analysis, Origen's audience can easily recognize the different
senses at work.[58] Pneumatically, the biblical text informs his audience that the Bride church enjoys the presence of the Incarnate
Christ, who has entrusted her with the safeguarding of his direct
teachings in Scripture and the duty of dispensing them to young,
local churches throughout the world. Psychically, the text informs
Origen's audience that the perfected soul, while enjoying ever-increasing intimacy with God's own Word, has the temporal duty, as a
leader of the church, to instruct other individuals in the virtues and
the meanings of Scripture so that they too may be able to grasp the
pneumatic truths of Christ's mind. The Bride church is the place
for cultivating virtue and comprehending Scripture, and the perfected soul is, by definition and obligation, the instructor of Scripture's
truths within the Bride church.

Together, these readings inform Origen's audience that the telos
is the same for the Bride church and the perfected soul: to enjoy
intimate participation in the secret and mysterious truths of God's
wisdom eternally. The individual person can pursue this end only
within and through the church, both for himself by taking in Scripture
and growing in virtue *and* for others by teaching Scripture and the
virtues. When the perfected person fully plays out his role as teacher
to others, he becomes a fuller imitation of Christ, for he teaches by
direct instruction (running with the maidens) and by example (entering into Christ's chamber, or mind). Just as Christ's embodiment
through Scripture's three senses instructs hearers to become like

---

[58] De Lubac cites the *Commentary on the Canticle of Canticles* as an example of
Origen's use of a moral reading that has a Christian focus but is an extension of
the overall nonliteral (spiritual) sense of the biblical text (*Medieval Exegesis*, 142–150,
esp. 146–147; also, idem, *Histoire et Esprit*, 139–150). Also, see Hanson for his position that the moral and spiritual senses are "fused" or "absorbed" (*Allegory and Event*,
235–237, 243). Analysis of *Comm. Cant.* 1 in this chapter has shown that Origen
intends two separate psychic and pneumatic senses of the biblical text, Cant. 1:2–4,
and relies on this distinction in order to relate these two senses in a way that
enhances the spiritual edification of his audience.

him—by directly teaching and modeling the right order of body, soul and spirit—the perfected believer, as a leader in the church, teaches and models love for and imitation of Christ.

In relation, the two higher senses form a dialectic of eternal and temporal emphases. The attentive hearer learns from the pneumatic sense the following details: that the hope and telos of human existence is salvation as intimate union of love with God in eternity, that the path of ascent toward that end has been paved by the Word's own descent into the Incarnate Christ, and that this path is to be found within the church. These truths are inevitably mysterious to the time-laden person, because they are eternal truths, both in the sense that they point to things eternal and that they fully flower for the believer only in eternity. Heeding the psychic call to meditate on the Word of God in Scripture, and thereby grow in virtue and imitation of Christ, helps the soul understand how to access and begin to progress and persevere now in an upward ascent toward these eternally focused, pneumatic truths. The psychic sense, then, is the *temporal means* both of beginning to comprehend the pneumatic message and pursuing the *eternal goal* that it conveys.

Here we have the dialectic between contemplation and action that Greer articulated (as well as Torjesen's notion of the interacting effects of Scripture's moral and mystical pedagogies).[59] The psychic sense urges the temporal growth in virtue, as spurred on by engagement with Scripture, which, in turn, makes possible the initial comprehension and then advancement in understanding of Scripture's eternal, pneumatic truths. The two higher senses function together soteriologically, making it possible for Scripture's hearer to prepare himself both experientially and intellectually for salvation—both in action and in contemplation, by heeding the psychic call and thereby pursuing the pneumatic truths even now.

As the examples in chapter 4 and the text in this chapter underscore, for Origen, *Christ* is the way toward and goal of salvation, which means that the psychic and pneumatic senses each convey Christ. He paves the path of ascent by his descent to Incarnate form. He also is the goal, for salvation is union with Christ. For Origen, salvation is all in, through and for union with Christ. Christ offers the recipe for becoming like himself in the psychic message, as well

---

[59] See the discussions of these scholars' views in chapter 1.

as the vision of salvific union with him and God's loving ways of making it possible in the pneumatic sense.

The two higher senses, then, are, during this life, innately dependent upon each other. Each message is edifying in its own right, with separate figurative readings of text and distinct themes and, yet, achieves its full value only in relation to the other. Without the pneumatic sense, the psychic meaning has no anchor, no purpose, for Origen. Without the psychic sense, the pneumatic sense is a gnosis that refuses engagement. The seemingly various themes of the pneumatic sense, Christological, ecclesiastical and eschatological, all speak to God's plan of salvation for humankind, together reflecting the path of ascent toward God that Christ has paved by his descent. The psychic sense stands apart from these unified themes, because it makes it possible for the hearer temporally to enter upon the path of ascent outlined by them. Because of Scripture's psychic sense, the human person has a guidebook for directing his life toward salvation.

Origen's mingling of the two senses within this commentary shows that he understands the psychic sense to be a *Christian* sense. This Christian character is most apparent when viewing the relationship between the two higher senses. The psychic sense exhorts the hearer to open himself up to the Word of God in Scripture and cultivate the virtues within him and eventually teach them to others, *because* these are the temporal means of pursuing and achieving the eternal telos conveyed by the pneumatic sense. Taking on the virtues, which are Christ's own attributes, *and* condescending, like Christ, to assist others are both imitations of Christ.

The pneumatic sense also receives its force and effectiveness from relation with the psychic sense. As stated above, without the psychic sense, the eternal hope of the pneumatic message would be an inaccessible gnosis. Yet, Origen's pneumatic truths are not gnostic teachings intended only for a few. They are for everyone precisely because they are accessed by one and all alike through the temporal facilities of the psychic sense's Christ-filled direction.

The productive mingling of the separately functioning pneumatic and psychic senses, as shown in *Comm. Cant.* 1, reveals itself as the pinnacle or height of Origen's exegetical practice. While in his extant homilies and commentaries he does not always present both higher senses for every biblical passage, the full force of his exegetical purpose and method, as well as his fuller understanding of each higher sense, come forth on the occasions when he offers them both for the same passage.

While Origen sometimes mentions the psychic sense before the pneumatic when discussing theory, in practice he tends to place the psychic reading *after* the pneumatic reading of the text. This practical ordering of the senses creates the greatest effect of spiritual transformation on his most advanced audience members. For this commentary, Origen perceives that his audience members have grown enough to enjoy pneumatic meaning.[60] The psychic call to virtue and duty prepares them for deeper understandings of pneumatic truths, which, in turn, encourage further growth in virtue—or equity— that is, love for and imitation of Christ according to the psychic sense. The psychic call facilitates increased understandings of pneumatic truths, which, during this life, motivate increased submission to this psychic call. The relationship between the two higher, non-literal senses, then, and not the relationship between the literal and nonliteral interpretations of Scripture, is the centripetal force of Origen's exegesis. Revolving around Christ, the two higher senses work together to promote the spiritual transformation of the hearer, so that he grows in likeness to and, ultimately, full union with Christ. Thus, we find that Origen's exegetical method and spiritual theology of salvation are actually one and the same.

Correlatively, for Origen, even the psychic sense continues to edify the hearer of Scripture as long as he remains in this life. In this commentary, Origen directs the psychic readings especially toward the "perfected" soul, who already has made progress on the path of ascent and can grasp more than others the truths of Scripture's pneumatic sense. Having cleansed herself of sin and attained some advancement toward perfection in the virtues, the perfected soul has learned to love Christ. Yet, during this life, her struggle continues, as there is always more progress to be made. The psychic sense does not address only her need to continue growing in the virtues but also her need to use her own progress to help others within the church

---

[60] For the homilies treated in chapter 4, Origen perceived at least *some* of his audience members to be able at least to recognize pneumatic meanings. When such an advanced person first hears the pneumatic sense, he may not understand much. Yet, he likely hears, at the very least, that he was made for eternal union with God. He then benefits from the psychic sense again, being more aware of the promise and reward for persevering toward perfect imitation of Christ. This increase in moral preparation in turn allows him to understand even more fully the truths of the pneumatic sense. The interplay of the two senses will continue in this mutually reinforcing way throughout this life until the hearer comes to his goal of eternal union with God.

advance in virtue and the comprehension of Scripture. By teaching others, the perfected soul benefits herself, making herself more like Christ by imitating his condescension to help others. In addition, her continued progress is essential to being the best example to others that she can be. Success in the ascent toward God requires that one facilitate the same progress in others. The salvation of the one is tied to the salvation of the rest. Salvation is communal as well as individual, occurring in and through the church. Thus, Origen's exegetical method translates in practice into a spiritual theology of the individual person's—and, collectively, the entire church's—transformation into one who is worthy of and ready for eternal union with Christ, a transformation that continues throughout this life and into eternity.

During this life, then, *all* believers continue to grow in the virtues and deeper understandings of the pneumatic truths of God's salvation plan. The mutual reinforcement of the pneumatic and psychic senses continues for the attentive hearer throughout this life. The psychic sense, though, will disappear in eternity, when the pneumatic sense alone will continue to edify by perpetually feeding the saved soul's enjoyment of intimacy with Christ. As Origen suggests in *Comm. Cant.* 1, the content of the pneumatic sense is the very wisdom of God. It naturally will continue to edify in eternity, since love itself is a dynamic, continuous and ever-deepening process. The soul and the church will grow ever more in love with God's own wisdom, which in the end, is Himself. The fullness of the pneumatic sense *is* the experience of loving Christ eternally.

Also, in *Comm. Cant.* 1, we find Origen's anthropology at the core of his relationship between the two higher senses. To purge oneself of all iniquity and grow in equity, or virtue, is to make one's own nature "even," or rightly ordered. As the believer's spirit begins to take on and grow in leadership over the soul and body, the believer becomes more uniformly virtuous, more like Christ, and more in love with Christ. At the end of time, he will be perfect in the virtues and, thus, he will, as a lover, concentrate wholly on maintaining and deepening his intimacy with his Beloved. Of course, he will find that his love for Christ can never match Christ's love for him, since Christ is really the Lover of lovers. He is both Bridegroom and Bride.

The senses bring the believer to this telos not only through the direct instruction in their messages, but also by the way in which their messages interrelate as Scripture's own body, soul, and spirit.

The somatic and psychic senses, in urging this right ordering of the three human parts, actually *serve* the pneumatic sense, since the latter embodies the telos to which the somatic and psychic senses direct the hearer. The three senses are in relation to each other the way in which the three human parts are meant to be ordered within the person. The somatic and psychic senses urge the hearer on toward the pneumatic goal, and both will step out of the way at the end of time. Thus, both their messages and the interrelationship between their messages lead the attentive hearer to his perfection (that is, the perfect ordering of his three parts) and, thus, salvation.

For Origen, then, the three senses constitute Scripture's own internal interpretive structure. As he made explicit in *Princ.* 4 and developed in the homilies in chapter 3, Origen recognizes that the Holy Spirit conveys, through the three senses, the grace of Christ's own mind to humans. The right way to interpret Scripture, for Origen, is revealed in the make-up of Scripture itself, that is, its three senses. Scripture is self-directing. Because its three senses reflect the right order of the human person's body, soul and spirit, the person who models his own three parts after them will take on Christ and approach final entry into the chambers of Christ's own mind, the Word of God himself. In eternity, this person will find that Christ the Pursuer or Lover (Bridegroom) is also the Pursued or Beloved (Bride)—the perfection, completion and fulfillment of the human person. The believer will find that as Christ has been pursuing him, he has been pursuing Christ. In the end, Christ will have captured him, and he, indeed, will have captured Christ, and an eternally enriching relationship will abide in perpetuity. The believer will enjoy the ever-increasing abundance of God's love, as he finds himself increasingly exposed to and made one with the pneumatic sense, which is Christ's own mind.

AFTERWORD

This work has established that Origen defines three senses of scriptural meaning within his exegetical theory and applies them within his homilies and commentaries. Examination of his practical works shows that the two nonliteral—psychic and pneumatic—senses independently edify Scripture's hearer and also relate to complement the other's spiritually transformative effects. This work shows that the height of Origen's exegetical effort to transform his audience occurs through the interrelationship between psychic and pneumatic readings of the same biblical passage. Each is a pedagogy within Scripture, but together, they form a dialectic of mutual reinforcement, which adds meaning to Greer's observation that, for Origen, "virtue leads to vision, and vision empowers virtue."[1]

We have found a rich variety of ways in which to characterize this collaboration between the two higher senses. Fundamentally, the psychic sense is the temporal call to moral purification, and it makes the eternal focus of the pneumatic sense accessible presently. The pneumatic sense embodies the activity of heaven, and the psychic sense provides the means of rehearsing that eternal telos now. By beginning to heed the psychic call to virtue, Scripture's hearer becomes able to appreciate and, thus, grasp the pneumatic hope of salvation. In turn, this hope motivates him to continue purifying himself according to the psychic sense and, as a result, enjoy further insights from the pneumatic sense. In this way, each higher sense reinforces the other's spiritual benefit for the hearer, together spiraling him upward in an ascent toward eternal union with Christ.

This interrelationship reveals the essentially Christian character of each higher sense. In every text examined, the psychic sense calls the hearer to meditate upon Scripture, for which Christ is both instructor and content. This psychic sense reveals itself as a call to imitate Christ in virtue and wisdom. Such imitation makes the believer worthy of eternal union with Christ, which is the hope of the pneumatic message. Through the psychic and pneumatic senses, respectively, Christ emerges as both the way toward and goal of salvation.

---

[1] Greer, *Early Biblical Interpretation*, 191. See discussion of Greer's views in chapter 1.

Origen understands Scripture to transform its hearers into like-nesses of Christ and, thus, worthy companions of Christ for eternity. The human person suffers disorder when his soul chooses to allow fleshly tendencies to reign through the body and to ignore his spirit's godly guidance, but Scripture, as the Holy Spirit's construction of Christ's own instruction and content, unwaveringly reflects the right order of the human person's body, soul, and spirit. The pneumatic sense always directs and embodies Scripture's full story of salvation, and the somatic and psychic messages always point the hearer toward and prepare him for consumption of these deeper, eternal truths. The three senses, then, teach the hearer to submit his soul and body to his spirit, the divine imprint within him, by both teaching godly virtue and wisdom *and* by modeling, through the interrelationship of their messages, this right ordering.

Since Christ is the very content of Scripture, a logical implication of these findings—which merits further research and consideration—is that Origen may understand Scripture's somatic, psychic and pneu-matic senses to be equivalent to Christ's human body, soul and spirit. This view would explain why he understands that consistent medi-tation upon Scripture shapes the listener into a likeness of Christ. Perhaps, for Origen then, an encounter with Scripture is not only pedagogical but also sacramental: Christ sacrifices himself wholly—indeed, as a whole burnt offering—within the pages of Scripture, and the person who "consumes" Scripture's teachings through the three senses consumes Christ's body, soul and spirit.

To consider this additional insight more fully, one must join this work's findings with a study of Origen's Christology and sacramen-tal theology, especially his theology of the Eucharist (to the extent that his extant works make this possible). As a suggested starting point, in his *Dialogue with Heraclides*,[2] Origen states that Christ was born with and ascended to heaven with a human body, soul and spirit. Origen reasons that Christ had to assume and be resurrected in a "whole" human nature if he was going to save the "whole" human person.[3] Further study of Origen's Christology should shed light on how this view informs the interrelationship of the three senses within his exegesis. Also, study of Origen's views on the

---

[2] *Dial.* 5–8; ACW 54:61–64; (Greek) SC 67:66–72.
[3] This may reflect Origen's self-conscious reliance on Irenaeus' notion of reca-pitulation.

Eucharist may suggest to what extent he approaches Scripture as a sacramental consumption of Christ himself.

This work hopes to encourage students of Origen to employ its findings as a map for navigating through his works—both within and beyond the homilies and commentaries—to consider the variety of ways in which Origen applies psychic and pneumatic readings for the benefit of his audiences. The examples within this work have shown that, at the very least, Origen understands Scripture's soul and spirit to interact in a way that reforms the attentive believer into a likeness of God's own virtue and wisdom, or Christ himself.

SELECT BIBLIOGRAPHY

I. *Primary Sources*

A. *Critical Editions and Translations of* De Principiis

Origène: Traité des Principes. Edited and translated by Henri Crouzel and Manlio Simonetti. SC 252, 253, 268, 269. Paris: Cerf, 1978, 1980.
Origen: On First Principles: Being Koetschau's Text of the De Principiis. Translated by G. W. Butterworth. Torchbook edition. Gloucester, Mass.: Peter Smith, 1973.

B. *Critical Editions and Translations of Origen's Homilies*

Homilies on Genesis
Origène: Homélies sur La Genèse. Translated by Louis Doutreleau. SC 7. Paris: Cerf, 1985.
Origen: Homilies on Genesis and Exodus. Translated by Ronald E. Heine. FC 71. Washington, D.C.: Catholic University of America, 1982.

Homilies on Exodus
Origène: Homélies sur L'Exode. Translated by Marcel Borret. SC 321. Paris: Cerf, 1985.
Origen: Homilies on Genesis and Exodus. Translated by Ronald E. Heine. FC 71. Washington, D.C.: Catholic University of America, 1982.

Homilies on Leviticus
Origène: Homélies sur Le Lévitique. Edited and translated by Marcel Borret. 2 vols. SC 286, 287. Paris: Cerf, 1981.
Origen: Homilies on Leviticus 1–16. Translated by Gary Wayne Barkley. FC 83. Washington, D.C.: Catholic University of America, 1990.

Homilies on Numbers
Origène: Homélies sur Les Nombres. Translated by André Méhat. SC 29. Paris: Cerf, 1951.
W. A. Baehrens, ed. GCS 30 (1921) 3–285 [PG 12:583–804].

Homilies on Joshua
Origène: Homélies sur Josué. Edited and translated by Annie Jaubert. SC 71. Paris: Cerf, 1960.
W. A. Baehrens, ed. GCS 30 (1921) 286–463 [PG 12:825–948].
Origen: Homilies on Joshua. Translated by Barbara J. Bruce. Edited by Cynthia White. FC 105. Washington, D.C.: Catholic University of America, 2002.

Homilies on Judges
Origène: Homélies sur Les Juges. Edited and translated by Pierre Messié, Louis Neyrand, and Marcel Borret. SC 389. Paris: Cerf, 1993.
W. A. Baehrens, GCS 30 (1921) 464–522 [PG 12:951–990].

Homilies on (I Kings) 1 Samuel
Origène: Homélies sur Samuel. Edited and translated by Pierre Nautin and Marie-Thérèse Nautin. SC 328. Paris: Cerf, 1986.
Origen: Homilies on Jeremiah; Homily on I Kings 28. Translated by John Clark Smith. FC 97. Washington, D.C.: Catholic University of America, 1998.
W. A. Baehrens, ed. GCS 33 (1925) 1–25.
E. Klostermann, ed. GCS 6 (1901) 283–294 [PG 12:991–1030].

Homilies on Psalms
Origène: Homélies sur Les Psaumes 36 À 38. Edited and translated by Henri Crouzel and Luc Brésard. SC 411. Paris: Cerf, 1995 [PG 12:1320–1409].

Homilies on Song of Songs
Origène: Homélies sur Le Cantique des Cantiques. Edited and translated by Dom O. Rousseau. SC 37. Paris: Cerf, 1953.
Origen: The Song of Songs Commentary and Homilies. Translated by R. P. Lawson. ACW 26. New York: Newman, 1956.

Homilies on Isaiah
W. A. Baehrens, ed. GCS 33 (1925) 242–289 [PG 13:219–254; PL 25:937–972].

Homilies on Jeremiah
Origène: Homélies sur Jérémie. Edited and translated by Pierre Husson and Pierre Nautin. 2 vols. SC 232, 238. Paris: Cerf, 1976, 1977.
Origen: Homilies on Jeremiah; Homily on I Kings 28. Translated by John Clark Smith. FC 97. Washington, D.C.: Catholic University of America, 1998.

Homilies on Ezekiel
Origène: Homélies sur Ézéchiel. Edited and translated by Marcel Borret. SC 352. Paris: Cerf, 1989.
W. A. Baehrens, ed. GCS 33 (1925) 319–454 [PG 13:663–766].

Homilies on Luke
Origène: Homélies sur S. Luc. Edited and translated by Henri Crouzel, Francois Fournier and Pierre Périchon. SC 87. Paris: Cerf, 1962.
Origen: Homilies on Luke; Fragments on Luke. Translated by Joseph T. Lienhard. FC 94. Washington, D.C.: Catholic University of America, 1996.

C. *Critical Editions and Translations of Origen's Commentaries*

Commentary on Song of Songs
Origène: Commentaire sur Le Cantique des Cantiques. Edited and translated by Luc Brésard, Henri Crouzel, and Marcel Borret. 2 vols. SC 375, 376. Paris: Cerf, 1991 and 1992.
Origen: The Song of Songs Commentary and Homilies. Translated by R. P. Lawson. ACW 26. New York: Newman, 1956.

Commentary on Matthew
Origenes Matthäuserklärung. vol. 1 of *Origenes Werke* 10. Edited by Erich Klostermann and Ernst Benz. GCS 40. Leipzig: J. C. Hinrichs'sche, 1935.
Commentary on the Gospel of Matthew. Translated by John Patrick. In vol. 9 of *The Ante-Nicene Fathers.* Edited by Alexander Roberts and James Donaldson. 1885–1887. 14 vols. Repr. Edited by Allan Menzies. 4th Edition. Peabody, Mass.: Hendrickson, 1994.

Origène: Commentaires sur l'Évangile selon Matthieu. vol. 1. Edited and translated by Robert Girod. SC 162. Paris: Cerf, 1970.

Commentary on John
Origène: Commentaire sur Saint Jean. Edited and translated by Cécile Blanc. 5 vols. SC 120, 157, 222, 290, 385. Paris: Cerf, 1966, 1970, 1975, 1982, 1992.
Origène: Commentary on the Gospel According to John. Translated by Ronald E. Heine. FC 80, 89. Washington, D.C.: Catholic University of America, 1989, 1993.

Commentary on Romans
Der Römerbriefkommentar des Origenes. Edited and translated by Caroline P. Bammel and Charles P. Hammond VL 16, 33, 34. Freiburg: Herder, 1990 [PG 14:833–1292].
Commentary on the Epistle to the Romans. Translated by Thomas P. Scheck. FC 103, 104. Washington, D.C.: Catholic University of America, 2001, 2002.
"The Commentary of Origen on the Epistle to the Romans." Translated by A. Ramsbotham in *JTS* 13 (1911–1912) 209–224, 357–368; *JTS* 14 (1912–1913) 10–22.

D. *Other Sources for Texts of Homilies and Commentaries*

Selections
Oulton, J. E. L., and Henry Chadwick, trans. *Alexandrian Christianity: Selected Translations of Clement and Origen.* LCC 2. London: SCM, 1954.
Tollinton, R. B., ed. and trans. *Selections from the Commentaries and Homilies of Origen.* London: SPCK, 1929.
Trigg, Joseph W. *Origen.* The Early Christian Fathers. New York: Routledge, 1998.
Wiles, Maurice F., and Mark Santer, eds. and trans. *Documents in Early Christian Thought.* Cambridge: Cambridge University Press, 1975.

E. *Other Cited Works by Origen*

Dialogue with Heraclides. In *Origen: Treatise on the Passover and Dialogue of Origen with Heraclides and his Fellow Bishops on the Father, the Son and the Soul.* Translated by Robert J. Daly. ACW 54. New York: Paulist, 1992.
Entretien d'Origène avec Héraclide. Edited and translated by Jean Scherer. SC 67. Paris: Cerf, 1960.

F. *Other Ancient Sources*

Eusebius, *Ecclesiastical History.* Translated by H. J. Lawlor and J. E. L. Oulton. London, SPCK, 1928.

II. *Secondary Analyses Cited*

Balthasar, Hans Urs von. *Origen: Spirit and Fire: A Thematic Anthology of His Writings.* Translated by Robert J. Daly. Washington, D.C.: Catholic University of America, 1984.
Clark, Elizabeth A. *The Origenist Controversy: The Cultural Construction of an Early Christian Debate.* Princeton: Princeton University Press, 1992.
Crouzel, Henri. *Origen: The Life and Thought of the First Great Theologian.* Translated by A. S. Worrall. San Francisco: Harper & Row, 1989.

———. "L'anthropologie d'Origène dans la perspective du combat spirituel." *Revue d'ascétique et de mystique* 31 (1955) 364–385.

Daley, Brian E. "Origen's *De Principiis*: A Guide to the Principles of Christian Scriptural Interpretation." Pages 3–21 In *Nova et Vetera: Patristic Studies in Honor of Thomas Patrick Halton*. Edited by John Petruccione. Washington, D.C.: Catholic University of America, 1998.

Daniélou, Jean. *Gospel Message and Hellenistic Culture*. Translated by John Austin Baker. A History of Early Christine Doctrine before the Council of Nicaea 2. Philadelphia: Westminster, 1973.

———, *Origen*. Translated by Walter Mitchell. New York: Sheed and Ward, 1955.

Dawson, John David. *Christian Figural Reading and the Fashioning of Identity*. Berkeley and Los Angeles: University of California Press, 2002.

———. *Allegorical Readers and Cultural Revision in Ancient Alexandria*. Berkeley and Los Angeles: University of California Press, 1992.

Dillon, John. *The Middle Platonists: 80 B.C. to A.D. 220*. Ithaca, N.Y.: Cornell University Press, 1977.

Dupuis, J. *"L'esprit de l'homme." Étude sur l'anthropologie religieuse d'Origène*. Collection Museum Lessianum, section théologique 62. Bruges-Paris: Desclée de Brouwer, 1967.

Faye, Eugène de. *Origen and His Work*. Translated by Fred Rothwell. London: Allen & Unwin, 1926.

Gamble, Harry Y. *Books and Readers in the Early Church: A History of Early Christian Texts*. New Haven: Yale University Press, 1995.

Gorday, Peter. *Principles of Patristic Exegesis: Romans 9–11 in Origen, John Chrysostom, and Augustine*. Studies in the Bible and Early Christianity 4. New York: Edwin Mellen, 1983.

Greer, Rowan A., and James L. Kugel. *Early Biblical Interpretation*. LEC 3. Philadelphia: Westminster, 1986.

———, trans. *Origen: An Exhortation to Martyrdom, Prayer and Selected Works*. New York: Paulist, 1979.

Grant, Robert M. *The Letter and the Spirit*. London: SPCK, 1957.

———. *The Bible in the Church: A Short History of Interpretation*. New York: MacMillan, 1948.

Hanson, R. P. C., *Allegory and Event*. Richmond, Va.: John Knox, 1959.

Harl, Marguerite. *Origène et la fonction révélatrice du Verbe Incarné*. Patristica Sorbonensia 2. Paris: Éditions du Seuil, 1958.

Layton, Bentley. *The Gnostic Scriptures*. Garden City, New York: Doubleday, 1987.

Lebreton, J. "Les degrés de la connaissance religieuse d'après Origène." *RSR* 12 (1922) 265–296.

Lubac, Henri de. *Medieval Exegesis*. vol. 1, *The Four Senses of Scripture*. Translated by Mark Sebanc. Grand Rapids, Mich.: Eerdmans, 1998.

———. *Histoire et Esprit: L'intelligence de l'Écriture d'après Origène*. Théologie 16. Paris: Aubier, 1950.

———. "'Typologie' et 'Allégorisme.'" *RSR* 34 (1947) 180–226.

Margerie, Bertrand de. *An Introduction to the History of Exegesis*. vol. 1, *The Greek Fathers*. Translated by Leonard Maluf. Petersham, Mass.: Saint Bede's, 1993.

Nautin, Pierre. *Origène: Sa vie et son oeuvre*. Christianisme antique 1. Paris: Beauchesne, 1977.

Prat, Ferdinand. "Origène." Columns 1875–1876 in vol. 5 of *Dictionnaire de la Bible*. 2nd ed. Edited by F. Vigouroux. Paris: Letouzey et Ané [1907]–1912.

Sanlés, Ricardo. "Origène." Pages 933–962 in *Dictionnaire de Spiritualité*. Paris: Beauchesne, 1982.

Simonetti, Manlio. *Biblical Interpretation in the Early Church: An Historical Introduction to Patristic Exegesis*. Translated by John A. Hughes. Edinburgh: T&T Clark, 1994.

Torjesen, Karen Jo. *Hermeneutical Procedure and Theological Method in Origen's Exegesis.* Patristische Texte und Studien 28. Berlin: De Gruyter, 1986.

———. "'Body,' 'Soul,' and 'Spirit' in Origen's Theory of Exegesis." *ATR* 67:1 (1985) 17–30.

———. "Origen's Interpretation of the Psalms." Pages 944–958 in *International Conference on Patristic Studies (8th: 1979: Oxford, England)*, vol. 2. StPatr 17. Edited by Elizabeth A. Livingstone. Oxford: Pergamon, 1982).

Wiles, Maurice F. "Origen as Biblical Scholar." Pages 454–489 in *From the Beginnings to Jerome.* Edited by P. R. Ackroyd. vol. 1. of *The Cambridge History of the Bible.* Edited by P. R. Ackroyd and C. F. Evans. Cambridge: Cambridge University Press, 1970.

Young, Frances M. *Biblical Exegesis and the Formation of Christian Culture.* Peabody, Mass.: Hendrickson, 2002.

Zöllig, August. *Die Inspirationslehre des Origenes: Ein Beitrag zur Dogmengeschichte.* Strassburger theologische Studien 5.1. Freiburg im Breisgau: Herdersche Verlagshandlung, 1902.

INDEX OF ANCIENT SOURCES

Works by Origen

INDEX OF MODERN AUTHORS